The Nature of
Environmental Stewardship

The Nature of Environmental Stewardship

Understanding Creation Care Solutions to Environmental Problems

JOHNNY WEI-BING LIN

PICKWICK *Publications* · Eugene, Oregon

THE NATURE OF ENVIRONMENTAL STEWARDSHIP
Understanding Creation Care Solutions to Environmental Problems

Pickwick Publications
An Imprint of Wipf and Stock Publishers
199 W. 8th Ave., Suite 3
Eugene, OR 97401

www.wipfandstock.com

PAPERBACK ISBN 13: 978-1-61097-620-6
HARDCOVER ISBN 13: 978-1-4982-8704-3

Cataloguing-in-Publication Data

Lin, Johnny Wei-Bing

 The nature of environmental stewardship : understanding creation care solutions to environmental problems / Johnny Wei-Bing Lin

 xviii + 308 p. ; 23 cm. Includes bibliographical references.

 ISBN: 978-1-61097-620-6 (paperback) | ISBN: 978-1-4982-8704-3 (hardback)

 1. Ecotheology. 2. Ecology—Religious aspects—Christianity. I. Title.

BT695.5 L45 2016

Manufactured in the U.S.A.   02/05/2016

In memory of the K.E.N. Association
When Earth-keeping was child-keeping

He turned to Reason and spoke.

"You can tell me, lady. Is there such a place as the Island in the West or is it only a feeling of my own mind?"

"I cannot tell you," said she, "because you do not know."

"But you know."

"But I can tell you only what *you* know. I can bring things out of the dark part of your mind into the light part of it. But now you ask me what is not even in the dark of your mind."

"Even if it were only a feeling in my own mind, would it be a bad feeling?"

"I have nothing to tell you of good and bad."

— C. S. Lewis, *The Pilgrim's Regress,* 58 [emphasis in original]

Contents

Preface | ix
Abbreviations | xvii

1   Introduction | 1
2   If You Could See What I See: Worldviews | 19
3   The Bible Says It: The Christian Worldview and Creation Care | 46
4   The Good, the Bad, and the Ugly: Ethical Theories | 76
5   Science to the Rescue? | 103
6   Left, Right, and Center (or Not): Politics and Economics | 177
7   Not Just Hearers But Doers: The Practices of Stewardship | 222
8   It Isn't Easy Being Green: Putting It All Together and Finding a "Third Way" | 240

Glossary | 281
Bibliography | 287
Index | 297

Preface

WHY THIS BOOK? A PERSONAL REASON

Having spent years studying and working in the geosciences and teaching an environmental ethics course, I have been involved with environmental issues for decades. Through that time, as I have observed how we talk about and engage with environmental issues, I have become increasingly puzzled by three questions. First, why do people disagree so much with regards to the content of environmental stewardship? Even people who share the same worldview, such as Christians who agree that God created the world and commanded human beings to care for it, nonetheless disagree as to the content of "creation care." Second, why do people, when approaching environmental issues, tend to behave as if getting the science right (or, in the case of Christians, getting the Bible right too) automatically determines what course of action to take with regards to environmental problems? Is environmental stewardship really that simple? Are current environmental problems predominantly the result either of ignorance or willful sin? Finally, why in our disagreements over environmental issues do we seem to spend most of our time talking past each other instead of addressing the meat of our differences?

In my reading, I have witnessed too many discussions characterized by *ad hominem,* where one side accuses the other of ill will, whether with accusations of siding with a greedy, corporate cabal bent on destroying nature in pursuit of profit or with accusations of being misanthropic, tree-hugging, nature worshippers that see human beings as a virus ravaging the earth. In this book, we will see that there are schools of thought in the spectrum of environmental positions whose logical extremes lead to such conclusions but also that it is untrue that we must necessarily come to such conclusions. Even most people (though, admittedly, not all) who hold positions close to an extreme do not actually believe the extreme. To generally assume that someone is motivated by either soul-ravaging greed or life-ravaging misanthropy is unfair, does not lead to productive dialogue, and makes compromise nearly impossible. (*Mea culpa:* I have been guilty myself of such pigeon-holing of others.)

This book is an attempt to answer the questions I posed earlier by providing a taxonomy of what goes into determining the content of environmental stewardship. In doing so, I also hope to provide a structure we can use in our debates over how to care for the environment. Such a structure can help us identify what we really disagree over, hidden points of agreement, and possible avenues for dialogue and compromise. This, I hope, can lead to a more faithful, fruitful, and robust suite of environmental stewardship activities.

WHAT THIS BOOK IS AND IS NOT

The main purpose of this book is to propose an analytical structure or taxonomy to aid in describing and weighing the different factors that affect the content of environmental stewardship. There are many excellent works on environmental stewardship and theology, ethics, science and policy, politics, and economics, but this book is relatively unique in that it aims to comprehensively (though certainly not exhaustively) address all the above topics. Much of what is in this book has been said before by others; my contribution is in trying to bring those ideas together in a unified framework and to bring to the notice of one disciplinary community pertinent contributions from another that might have been missed. (Note, because this book is synthetic, the chapters do not always work in a linear order; later chapters may presume knowledge not presented in earlier chapters. I provide a list of abbreviations in the front portion of this book and a glossary and index in the back of the book as aids.)

I do not claim to have read anywhere near everything in every field (philosophy, theology, biblical studies, religion, ethics, politics, economics, epistemology, science-technology studies, etc.) touched in this book and I make liberal use of secondary sources.[1] Thus, I am sure experts in any of

---

1. When sources I quote use a parenthetical citation system (such as the American Psychological Association's style), I generally leave out the parenthetical citations, as my focus is what the source I am using is saying (even if they are presenting work by or ideas from another source). Another way to think of it is that I treat parenthetical citations as if they were footnotes; when quoting a work that has footnotes, we usually do not include the footnote markers within the quotation. In some instances, I will mention in a footnote that the text I quoted had a parenthetical citation(s) that I removed.

the fields touched on by this book can provide robust critiques of my arguments, and I welcome such critiques. The value of this work, however, is not in the depth of its detail but in the intertwining strength of its synthesis. I believe what the framework I have set out lacks in particulars it makes up in its breadth. For the task of fostering dialogue and convergence is necessarily a task of synthesis. Without such a synthesis, it is difficult for me to see how we can collectively discern what should be the content of environmental stewardship.

This book is also relatively unique in that it seeks to speak to two audiences simultaneously; I hope that each will benefit from hearing arguments they may be unaccustomed to. Readers who are evangelical Christians may find the discussion about the philosophy of science and science-policy connections to be new; I have seldom encountered those topics addressed in works of Christian environmental ethics or eco-theology. Readers who are not evangelical Christians, subscribing to another religion or, in particular, to no religion at all, may find the discussion about worldviews (and the Christian worldview in particular) to offer new ways of analyzing environmental problems and proposed solutions. In secular discussions of environmental ethics, I have rarely seen worldview considerations addressed, even though the secular worldview is itself a worldview.

Lastly, in this book I try to critique arguments, not people, and present the arguments of others fairly. When I mention a person in a critique, it is to provide credit to meet the requirements of intellectual honesty, not to critique the person being mentioned. If I use a source in favor of an argument I am making, I am not saying that that source agrees with me. I endeavor to use all sources fairly and accurately according to the plain sense of the source's argument, but I do not claim that source would make the conclusions I am making using their material and ideas. I also hope to present all arguments in a way that the proponents of those arguments would find to be fair presentations of their beliefs. In my mind, this is a minimum requirement of fairness and love towards those who hold those beliefs; it does not necessarily imply my agreement with those positions. I am sadly aware, however, of my own biases, temper, and weaknesses. To those who may feel my treatment of them or their arguments is unfair, I ask you for your forgiveness in advance.

WHO THIS BOOK IS WRITTEN FOR

As mentioned earlier, this book is written using the language of the cultures of two audiences: evangelical Christians and those who are not evangelical

Christians (both those from a different religion as well as those claiming no religion at all). I started this book from musings about how the Christian church can better care for creation. As I continued to explore the issue, I found many of the ideas I was exploring applied to both those holding the Christian worldview and those who hold other worldviews. Additionally, it seemed to me that while I wanted to address specific issues Christians are wrestling with regarding creation care, I saw that the taxonomy I was creating would be useful to a broad audience, irrespective of what worldviews one held. Given the history of this book, I have sought to both engage the Christian worldview in particular detail while at the same time make my argument accessible to all.

I also want to provide a few clarifying points to help explain some of the wording and content choices I made for this book. To those in the Christian church: I write as a brother in Christ—He of whom we say "Salvation is found in no one else, for there is no other name under heaven given to mankind by which we must be saved"[2]—and it is my fervent hope that this book will help the various parts of the Body of Christ communicate with one another and aid us in fulfilling God's creation care command. While I set out what I hope is a biblical way of understanding creation care, I also include non-Christian religious and non-religious worldviews. While Scripture is authoritative regarding all matters of life and faith, this does not mean that we cannot gain from comparing and contrasting other beliefs with our own creeds. That insight can help us better understand what Scripture teaches us about creation care, how to obey the creation care command, and how to communicate to those holding other worldviews the call given to us from Scripture.

To those who do not hold the Christian worldview: I hope you find that my argument respects and engages your perspectives and is useful to you as you seek to understand what excellent environmental stewardship looks like. I believe, however, that all readers, regardless of their religious (or secular) beliefs, will benefit from interaction with the Christian worldview. Despite the evangelical church being a relative newcomer to modern environmental discussions, Christianity has a rich philosophical and theological history that provides valuable tools to understanding environmental stewardship. In particular, Christian theological wrestling with the nature of paradox (found in the core of Christian faith in Jesus, who is both fully God and fully human), with the nature of the moral law, and with the nature of love offers help as we struggle with the complexities of environmental stewardship. (We will not be able to delve into these topics in any great detail in

2. Acts 4:12.

this book, but I encourage you to examine them. C. S. Lewis's *Mere Christianity* is a good place to start.) At the very least, Christianity asks us to consider the impact of worldviews—an understanding of what the world is—an impact secular thought often does not critically examine. One argument in this book is that *all* people have a worldview that influences their understanding of what environmental stewardship entails; by examining one worldview, Christianity, in depth, we may better understand how worldviews in general affect our understanding of environmental stewardship.

Because I am an evangelical Christian and am writing to multiple audiences, I will also refer to "environmental stewardship" using the term "creation care." The two terms are essentially interchangeable, for the purposes of this book. When Christians talk of creation care, the term "creation" refers to the doctrine that God created the world and that the world is not self-existing. "Creation" does not refer to a particular mechanism by which God created the world. Thus, when I speak of creation care, I am not saying anything about whether God used an evolutionary mechanism or not in creating the various forms of life, just that God made it. Finally, I frame the question of creation care in the language of a command. Christians believe God commanded human beings to care for the Earth and so it is natural for Christians to speak of creation care in terms of obedience to that command and the command-giver. From a secular perspective, while the concepts are slightly different, the idea of categorical or moral imperative works similarly well (though without the sense of relationship with a loving God that underlies the Christian notion of obedience). Thus, wherever I discuss "following God's command," those who have secular beliefs might substitute "doing what is moral" or something similar.

HOW TO USE THIS BOOK

Because this book sets out a taxonomy for understanding environmental stewardship, one way of using this book is as a list of questions to ask of different ways of thinking about environmental stewardship. It could, perhaps, be used as a diagnostic checklist to help us understand proposed solutions and compare those solutions against alternatives. Such diagnosis can be done individually, in private study, or in dialogue with a small or large group of people.

Because of the breadth of this book, it could be used as an introduction to the topic of environmental ethics in general and Christian environmental ethics in particular. This book, however, is not written with the pacing and pedagogical scaffolding of a textbook. If you are brand-new to the topic, you might want to start off with John Benson's *Environmental Ethics* or Steven Bouma-Prediger's *For the Beauty of the Earth*. Despite the wealth of good books on environmental ethics, both evangelical and non-evangelical, I am not aware of any single work that covers all the areas addressed in this book; the most prominent lacuna is epistemology of science and science-policy studies. Thus, this book may be a helpful companion to a textbook on environmental ethics.

This book might be fruitfully used as a reading in a small group or discussion group. Whenever considering a contentious topic, I find it often helpful to bounce ideas off of and engage in arguments with a group of friends. In particular, given the discussion in the last chapter on conflict resolution regarding creation care issues, the small discussion group format may provide a good venue in which to practice mutual listening and dialogue. I provide a few discussion questions suitable for individual and small group study at the end of each chapter.

As with nearly all books, I am sure I will need to make corrections and additions. I will post a list of *errata* and *addenda* at the book's website: see http://nature.johnny-lin.com. Other resources related to the book will also be available at that site.

ACKNOWLEDGMENTS

I am acutely aware of the debt I owe to family, friends, and colleagues who, over many years, generously nurtured many of the ideas I present in this book. We stand on the shoulders of giants, as Newton said, and my use of first person plural throughout the book reflects that debt. All shortcomings in this book, however, are my own, and the opinions expressed in this book should be considered solely those of the author.

Much of this book came from an environmental ethics course I co-taught at North Park University with Karl Clifton-Soderstrom and R. Boaz Johnson. I am grateful for their partnership and sharing of their knowledge and wisdom, as well as the contributions of all the students in our environmental ethics courses. Karl's outsized contribution to my thinking can be seen in the bibliography: no other single author has as many references. Additional faculty from the North Park Dialogue also taught me a great deal about ethics, philosophy, history, and theology: Ilsup Ahn, Greg Clark, David Koeller, and R. J. Snell.

The following people read portions of the manuscript: Susan Daniels, Daniel Kim, Han Li, Jung-Tai Lin, and Wesley Lindahl. Daniel, in particular, did yeoman's work for me. Their comments, suggestions, and unselfish hearts are greatly appreciated. I am grateful for editing help from Allan Lee, Vivian Lee, Karen Lin, Joann Oshima, Calvin Tsang, Christina Tsang, and Bradley Woodrum. And thanks to the staff at Pickwick Publications and Wipf and Stock, especially Robin Parry, Ian Creeger, and Amelia Reising, for all their contributions and assistance.

Discussions with Joseph Alulis, Jason Baird, David Barr, John Beckman, Alan Bjorkman, Steven Bouma-Prediger, David Buller, Keith Eng, Terry Gray, Michael Green, Alice Hague, Katharine Hayhoe, Alex Higgs, Heidi Ho, Jon Ho, Craig Ing, Paul Koptak, David Larrabee, James Lefeu, Steve Li, Kenneth Lundgren, Catherine Marsh, Linda McDonald, Donald Morton, John Mulholland, Rob Nash, Katherine Patterson, Kurt Peterson, Jay Phelan, Daniel Philpott, Cynthia Prescott, Christopher Rios, Richard Rood, Robert Rye, Lance Schaina, Dwight Schwartz, David Socha, Justin Topp, Mary Veeneman, and Linda Vick are greatly appreciated. I am grateful to Terry Morrison and Kaleb Nyquist for their kind and generous commendations.

Thanks to my supervisors at North Park University and the University of Washington Bothell—Linda McDonald and Munehiro Fukuda, respectively—for their support. Lawrence, Agnes, and I-Sha Liu and Jung-Tai and Anne Lin provided hospitable abodes where portions of the research and writing were done.

Portions of this book (in particular parts of chapters 7 and 8) were either previously published in or based upon work previously published in the *Covenant Quarterly*.[3] Parts of this book were presented at talks at Wheaton College, the University of Chicago, and at the 2009, 2010, and 2014 Annual Meetings of the American Scientific Affiliation (ASA). The ASA is a network of Christians in science and is one of the best (though imperfect) places I know of that supports dialogue between people of differing views regarding faith and science issues (including environmental issues). More information on the organization is available at http://www.asa3.org.

To my children Timothy, James, and Christianne, and my wife Karen, I owe everything. Without their love, support, understanding, and patience, this book would have remained my mumblings over the dinner table. In particular, words cannot adequately express Karen's selflessness, love, and partnership with me. She is the "wife of noble character."[4]

Writing this book has been one of the hardest things I have ever done, and the experience has made me more aware of God's strengthening grace than I have known before. Which is not to say this book bears

3. Lin, "Role of Science."

4. Prov 31:10.

His imprimatur or approval in any way, but merely that I am grateful and amazed that He who sends the rain on the righteous and unrighteous[5] and watches over every sparrow's fall[6] would also watch over a graying Chinese-American man muddling about on a computer and, most of all, condescend to call that man a friend.[7]

Johnny Wei-Bing Lin
May 2015
Bellevue, Washington and Chicago, Illinois

---

5. Matt 5:45.
6. Matt 10:29.
7. John 15:15.

Abbreviations

ASA	American Scientific Affiliation
ATOC	Acoustic Thermometry of Ocean Climate experiment
CBA	Cost-benefit analysis
CFC	Chlorofluorocarbons
DDT	The pesticide dichlorodiphenyltrichloroethane
EEN	Evangelical Environmental Network
EPA	U.S. Environmental Protection Agency
FDA	U.S. Food and Drug Administration
GMO	Genetically modified organisms
ICBEMP	Interior Columbia Basin Ecosystem Management Project
IPCC	Intergovernmental Panel on Climate Change
NRC	National Research Council
NSB	National Science Board
SAP	Scientific Advisory Panel
SR-Neutral	Supporting Role-Science Neutral
SR-NN	Supporting Role-Science May Not Be Neutral
USDA	U.S. Department of Agriculture
WG1	Working Group One of the IPCC
WG2	Working Group Two of the IPCC
WG3	Working Group Three of the IPCC

1

Introduction

A PARABLE

At the beginning of each chapter, we introduce each topic with the fictional story of a pastor, his church, and their engagement with the topic of creation care.[1] Stories convey ideas in ways direct argument or didactic writing cannot. Hopefully, our visits with Pastor Gabriel Lang and friends will give us additional grist for the mill as we consider the nature of environmental stewardship.

> *What's that saying, again,* Pastor Gabriel Lang thought to himself, *about where roads lead that are paved with good intentions?* When he decided to preach a few months ago on what the Bible had to say about creation care, he had thought it would be a way of helping his congregation wrestle with how to apply the Bible to their everyday lives regarding an issue of contemporary significance. What he didn't expect was the beehive of activity it would set off. To be sure, some of this activity was exactly what he had hoped for. People were engaging with one another, Scripture, and God in prayer and thinking about ways they could put their convictions into action. But in the mix, you would periodically hear mutterings of discord: remarks here about "those greedy businesses" or there about "those long-haired tree-huggers." Nothing usually came out of those *sotto voce* comments,

1. Daniel Taylor first gave us the idea of mixing fiction and non-fiction in this way (Taylor, *The Myth*).

but even worse, when a discussion actually did occur, Gabriel would see the two proverbial ships passing in the night. Instead of talking to one another, people seemed to talk past each other. It gave Gabriel a bad feeling; they reminded him of the minor earthquakes that come prior to the eruption of a volcano.

Which finally happened. It had started with Arnold Banks's suggestion at the monthly meeting of the church's creation care committee that the church leadership, on behalf of the church, sign a petition being circulated around town asking the Town Council to turn down the request of Acme Industries for a permit to expand its factory. "This expansion," Arnold explained, "would destroy the Franklin marshes, one of the last wetland areas that has remained unchanged since the pioneer days when the town was first settled." Clearly, Arnold continued, obedience to God's creation care command demanded the church align itself with the right side on this issue.

"But, Arnold," replied Ralph Lee, "that expansion will provide hundreds of jobs, and Acme has already set aside funds to purchase and restore a separate parcel of former wetland, nearly twice the size of the Franklin marshes. The environmental impact studies show that the ecological worth of the restored wetland area is much higher and will even provide increased flood protection for area businesses; their flood insurance rates may even decrease."

Ramona Anderson rolled her eyes. "Why is it always about money with you business owners, Ralph? Haven't you been listening to Pastor Gabriel's sermons? God cares about His creation, regardless of whether it makes us rich or not."

Ralph glared. "Ramona," he began, "yes, I have been listening to Pastor Gabriel." He paused. "I also want to take care of creation. But the problem with you tree-huggers is that business is always wrong and people are the cause of all our problems. Frankly," and here his brows furrowed, "I sometimes feel like you tree-huggers would be happier if human beings didn't exist at all."

The room grew quiet. People looked at their feet, shuffled papers, or checked their smartphones. Lourdes Garcia broke the silence. Like her geographical namesake, Lourdes had a heart for healing, and it didn't matter whether it was the healing of broken bones at her medical practice or the healing of frazzled relationships. "Ralph," she said, "I don't think Ramona meant that people have no legitimate needs, and Ramona, . . ."

"Lourdes," Ramona cut her off, "don't bother. It's high time people showed their true colors. The preponderance of the science is clear, that we are hurting the environment, so the real question is: are we going to obey God or not? That's what it comes down to. And I'm sick and tired of people pretending they're following God's commands to be green when they're really following mammon . . . ."

Ralph Lee pushed his chair from the table and walked out of the room. The people who remained heard his car door shut, engine start, and his car drive away. Everyone looked at Gabriel, but he didn't know what to say. Finally, he broke the silence: "Maybe we all need a little time to get our bearings. I'll email everyone to find a time for another meeting." People nodded and politely left. Gabriel locked up the building and started turning off the remaining lights. As he reached the last switch, his eyes glanced at the "Save energy, save God's world" sticker next to the switch. *I guess we'll have to add some relationships to the list of things that need saving,* he ruefully thought, as he turned out the last light.

WHY THIS BOOK?

Over the last several decades, the global environmental movement has grown in ways few could have imagined just a century ago. People from all kinds of backgrounds—different ethnicities, religious beliefs, socioeconomic classes, etc.—have begun to wrestle deeply with environmental issues. In parallel, a movement has grown within the evangelical church that seeks to renew her calling to live as a steward of creation. Theologians, philosophers, scientists, and other Christian leaders have faithfully reminded us of the Scriptural foundation for such a mandate and have prophetically exhorted us to consider ways we might live differently, both personally and as a society, in order to better fulfill this mandate. In response, whether in the form of policy declarations, lobbying efforts, youth rallies, Bible studies, or churches and individuals carefully and consciously changing their lifestyles to support environmentally-friendlier options, Christians from all walks of life, all political stripes, and all throughout the nation have begun a grassroots movement to obey God's call to us as stewards of creation. Yet for all the clear and compelling work that has been done regarding the importance of creation care to God and His church, comparatively little work has been done regarding how to translate those commands into obedience.

For many in the church, the idea of a difference between the two—that an understanding that God commands human stewardship of creation does not automatically tell us how we are to obey that command—seems exceedingly strange. After all, when confronted by a command in Scripture, we should not respond, "Let me think more about what obedience means," but, "Let's do it!" When God commands us not to steal, we do not reply, "How do I go about obeying this command?" We just stop stealing. And given the clarity of Scripture regarding our responsibility as stewards, as well as the lessons from science regarding environmental problems and solutions, the idea of needing to translate command into obedience seems more than odd: it seems evasive. Why do we need more clarity in order to properly obey the environmental stewardship command?

Consider the following thought experiment.[2] Pretend there are two Earths, identical to each other except in the following way:

1. In the first Earth, which we will call the "Fossil Fuel" world, human-caused greenhouse gas emissions are projected to result in a 2.8 degrees Celsius increase in global mean temperature by 2100, with attendant effects on climate, extreme weather, ice sheet melting, species population impacts, etc.

2. In the second Earth, which we will call the "Solar Variability" world, changes in solar luminosity are projected to result in a 2.8 degrees Celsius increase in global mean temperature by 2100, with attendant effects on climate, extreme weather, ice sheet melting, species population impacts, etc.—the same effects as in the "Fossil Fuel" world.

In both worlds, the certainty of the science describing the mechanisms involved are the same. Assuming a Scriptural creation care mandate, what should be our response in each of the two worlds? Are our responses the same or different between the two? Why or why not?

One possible response is that our actions in the "Fossil Fuel" and the "Solar Variability" worlds should be different: In the "Fossil Fuel" world, because the problem is due to human activity, we should act by stopping the emission of greenhouse gases to prevent the warming, but in the "Solar Variability" world, we should not (or cannot), do anything because the problem is natural. But why should the nature of the cause of the problem (human or natural) make a difference in our response? In both worlds, regardless of the cause of the warming, the same warming, with the exact same consequences to both human and non-human creation, will occur. If the translation of stewardship commands into obedience is straightforward, then does not "care" for the environment demand responses in both cases to prevent the effects of global warming?

---

2. This thought experiment comes from Roger A. Pielke, Jr., a professor of environmental studies and a science-policy researcher at the University of Colorado at Boulder.

Of course, other responses are possible; the point here is not which response is correct. Rather, the point is this: If we conclude in the "Fossil Fuel" world the correct response is to do something, while in the "Solar Variability" world the correct response is to do nothing, we have translated the biblical commands into obedience not directly, but rather through a number of mediating assumptions about the meaning of creation care. For instance, we may have decided that the goal of creation care is to keep the Earth "natural" (where we have defined this as meaning "unaffected by people"), and thus mitigating actions in the "Solar Variability" world are wrong, while the opposite is true in the "Fossil Fuel" world. The same is true if we believe we should act in both the "Fossil Fuel" and "Solar Variability" worlds: We also *have not directly translated biblical commands into obedience*. Rather, we have used a number of mediating assumptions about the meaning of creation care. Examining the question of how to translate biblical commands into obedience, with respect to creation care, requires more than getting our theology right.

If it takes more than faithful exegesis in order to determine how we are to obey God as stewards of creation, we might expect different groups of evangelical environmentalists, while agreeing on the imperative of creation care, to advocate very different prescriptions for that care. In fact, we see just such a dynamic in current evangelical approaches towards creation care, with various Christian environmental organizations emphasizing different practices of creation care: some emphasize the importance of living a life of simplicity, others focus on worship, others on social justice, while still others focus on the connection with mission work.

These differences, however, can encompass more than emphasis in a response. Consider two of the major evangelical declarations regarding creation care:[3] On the Care of Creation: An Evangelical Declaration on the Care of Creation[4] ("Evangelical Declaration") and The Cornwall Declaration on Environmental Stewardship[5] ("Cornwall Declaration"). Both declarations prominently proclaim a conviction of God as Creator and nature as His good handiwork: The Evangelical Declaration affirms, "The cosmos, in all its beauty, wildness, and life-giving bounty, is the work of our personal

---

3. By "evangelical," we mean declarations that have attracted support from notable evangelical leaders; the declarations themselves may or may not have been authored exclusively by evangelicals. The Cornwall Declaration, for instance, is an interfaith document, but includes prominent evangelical leaders such as James Dobson, Bill Bright, and Charles Colson, as signatories.

4. EEN, "Evangelical Declaration."

5. Cornwall Alliance, "Cornwall Declaration."

and loving Creator,"[6] while the Cornwall Declaration teaches, "The earth, and with it all the cosmos, reveals its Creator's wisdom and is sustained and governed by His power and lovingkindness."[7]

This similarity in core convictions regarding the relationship of nature to its Creator, as we might expect, is coupled with some similarity in the goals of the two declarations. And yet, we find their goals are far from identical, and that the two declarations even have substantial differences in their understandings of what constitutes environmental degradation. For instance, the Evangelical Declaration, on the one hand, claims:

> These degradations of creation can be summed up as 1) land degradation; 2) deforestation; 3) species extinction; 4) water degradation; 5) global toxification; 6) the alteration of atmosphere; 7) human and cultural degradation.[8]

while the Cornwall Declaration claims:

> While some environmental concerns are well founded and serious, others are without foundation or greatly exaggerated. . . . Some unfounded or undue concerns include fears of destructive man-made global warming, overpopulation, and rampant species loss.[9]

Agreement regarding the biblical understanding of the nature of creation, its connection to its Creator, and even the imperative of creation care, appears an insufficient condition for agreement regarding the nature of environmental problems or their solution.

Of course, there are many reasons why such differences exist, some creditable and others not. The absence of consensus regarding how to obey God's command to care for creation is also not necessarily undesirable; we should be grateful that the multi-faceted nature of God's gifts to the church would also find a multi-faceted expression in the fulfillment of creation care. The presence of such differences, however, provides an additional clue to us regarding the nature of the command to steward the environment. Through following this, and other clues like it, in this book we aim to unpack how the creation care command differs from other commands, explain how the process of translating command into obedience is more difficult than is usually appreciated, and make a modest contribution to understanding what it means to obey the command to be stewards of creation.

6. EEN, "Evangelical Declaration."
7. Cornwall Alliance, "Cornwall Declaration."
8. EEN, "Evangelical Declaration."
9. Cornwall Alliance, "Cornwall Declaration."

WHAT WE NEED TO KNOW TO TRANSLATE COMMAND
INTO OBEDIENCE

For any command or request, we can identify three issues or questions that need to be addressed in order for us to fully understand how to obey that command. These "criteria for obedience" are the importance, goals, and practice of the command. By "importance," we mean there has to be an understanding of the imperative of the command. The importance of a command tells us how to weigh it with respect to other commands and priorities. All commands require such an evaluation: even commands from God do not necessarily have equal weight in all circumstances. Jesus, after all, tells us there is a "greatest" commandment[10] and that the other of God's commands "hang on"[11] the first two commandments. And, in his criticism of the legalism of Israel's leaders, Jesus says, "Woe to you, teachers of the law and Pharisees, you hypocrites! You give a tenth of your spices—mint, dill and cumin. But you have neglected the more important matters of the law— justice, mercy and faithfulness. You should have practiced the latter, without neglecting the former."[12] In doing so, Jesus reinforces the obligation we have to obey everything God commands us while at the same time pointing out not all parts of the Law have the same importance.

Motivation for the command, the type and scope of the command, the value of the command, and the value of obeying the command are some of the issues to consider when evaluating a command's importance. In some cases—such as in Jesus's answer to the man who asked what was the greatest commandment—we are explicitly told the importance of a command. In other cases, understanding the importance of the command requires the appropriate use of wisdom, reason, love, intuition, and other means of judgment. As an example of such a means of judgment, consider a schema proposed by philosopher Charles Taylor. Taylor notes that there are two kinds of "evaluations" we make of desires, what he terms "strong" and "weak" evaluations.[13] In the latter, the depth of evaluation is superficial— we are interested merely in outcomes—while in the former, the worth of the desires is judged.[14] Strong evaluations thus are deeper, possess a richer language of articulation, and are of greater life import.[15] Commands requir-

10. Matt 22:37–38.
11. Matt 22:40.
12. Matt 23:23.
13. Taylor, "What Is Human Agency?" 16.
14. Ibid.
15. Ibid., 16–27.

ing strong evaluations to understand and obey would, in this schema, have greater worth and thus importance than commands requiring only weak evaluations to understand and obey.

The "goals" of the command describe what will result from following the command and in doing so clarifies the purpose of the practice. The goals represent what we are aiming to accomplish in following the command. Often, the range of possible goals for a command is broader than the range of rationales for the importance of a command. We can define multiple goals for a command, none of which are mutually exclusive. The goals of a command might be some sort of environmental state but could also be an outcome for a single individual (e.g., becoming a certain kind of person), group of individuals, or for a community or society as a whole. Goals also do not have to be material: emotional, ethical, and spiritual outcomes are also possible goals for following a command.

How do the goals of a command differ from the importance of a command? On one level, the two are certainly related: one reason a command may be important is that the goals of the command are compelling or important. Or, for some commands, the only goal of the command may merely be that the command is obeyed. But in many, if not most, situations, it is useful for us to separate the two criteria. As we will see later in this book, the range of determinants of the goals criterion is often broader than the range of determinants of the importance criterion. In addition, the kinds of concerns addressed by the determinants of each criterion often differs: the importance criterion is often mainly concerned with questions of meaning and purpose while the goals criterion is often more open to incorporating pragmatic concerns.

Finally, "practice" refers to the actual actions that implement the command. As in the case with the goals criterion, there is a wide range of possible practices. Practices may be individual or corporate. Practices can be physical or material activities, but practices can also be mental, emotional, or spiritual activities. While public policies (e.g., laws, regulations) are one form of practices, they are by no means the predominant form. Practices unrelated to policymaking—say, the everyday activity of an individual person or the combined activity of a club or group—are often the main practices through which we obey a command.

In sum, "importance" tells us why we should follow the command, "goals" tells us what that following the command will result in, and "practice" tells us how we will put that command into effect. Thus, the model of translating command into obedience is:

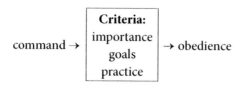

We can define two kinds of commands based on the kind of clarity a command has regarding the criteria for obedience of that command. When the criteria for obedience are clear, a command leads directly to obedience. By clarity, we mean either the answers for the criteria are clear or that it is clear that more detailed analysis, description, or understanding of the criteria is unneeded for obedience. When there is such clarity, we call such obedience "simple obedience." (Note that the adjective "simple" does not refer to whether the command is or is not easy to obey but rather that the connection between command and obedience is direct and clear.) When the command lacks this clarity, obedience requires thoughtful and detailed analysis of the three criteria for obedience. We call this kind of obedience "considered obedience."

The earlier example of "do not steal" is a simple obedience command. In terms of importance, the command is required and context independent. In terms of goals, there may be any number of goals—character development, social peace, love of neighbor, etc.—but because of the non-negotiable importance of the command, perfect clarity in goals is unneeded for obedience to be possible.[16] Finally, the practice of the command is also clear: do not take that which you do not own.

The creation care command lacks such simple clarity: The importance, goals, and practice are multi-faceted and complex, and understanding how to obey God's stewardship command requires detailed examination of the three criteria for obedience. Questions regarding the importance of creation care include: Is it central to the fabric of God's purposes, or peripheral, and in what way? If it is central, how does this command compare to other central commands? Questions addressing the goals of creation care include: What is the purpose of creation care? Is it to minimize human influence, or to shape nature in a certain way? Finally, in examining what creation care practices will accomplish those goals, questions we might ask include: what frameworks and tools can we use to ascertain which practices will best accomplish those goals? Are the practices primarily individual or cultural and societal too? What are the roles of economics and government, if any?

16. If the criterion of importance tells us the command is a non-negotiable duty, clarity in goals usually does not matter for obedience to be possible.

Again, because God has commanded us to care for creation, the question in addressing these criteria is not whether we should care for creation—that is non-negotiable—but what that care should look like.

While each of these three criteria are in some ways independent of each other—for instance, we can engage in a practice as part of obeying a command without necessarily believing in the command's importance (outside of it being commanded of us) or understanding the purposes of obeying the command—a healthy or proper response to the command, rather than a misguided, legalistic, etc., response, requires we rightly understand all three criteria collectively. Usually, we go through these three criteria in order, starting with understanding the importance of the command, then the goals, and finally deriving the practices that fit those goals. Sometimes, however, we may address these criteria out of order. For instance, when practice comes first, and our thinking changes in response to our actions, sociologists call this "praxis." Still, order is not as important as the fact that all three criteria are addressed.

In our discussion thus far, it may seem that understanding the three criteria for obedience is an entirely analytic or rational endeavor. While reason is important, it is not the only means to knowledge and understanding. Other ways of knowing exist (e.g., intuition) and those ways of knowing can also contribute to our understanding of the three criteria. Even subjective phenomena such as love, compassion, and aesthetic apprehension can be ways of knowing about a subject and have a place in our understanding of the three criteria. What kinds of knowing exist, how these different kinds of knowing interact with one another, and what are the strengths and weaknesses of each kind of knowing, will be (at least implicitly) addressed later in this book. For now, suffice it to say that as we make a detailed effort to understand the three criteria, we may use more than one way of knowing.

If importance, goals, and practice are the three criteria for obedience to a biblical command for creation care, what influences determine these three criteria? For the case of creation care, there are four such categories that determine the criteria for obedience: worldview, ethical theories, science, and society. We will call these four categories the "determinants" of the criteria for obedience:

Determinants:

worldview — nature of reality
ethical theories — value of nature and weighing values
science — knowledge about nature and connecting to policy
society — politics and economics

These determinants are not necessarily mutually exclusive and can affect one another. Combinations from these four determinants together address each of the three criteria, with some categories providing more or less to a given criteria. Schematically, this can be given as:

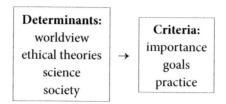

The term "worldview" commonly refers to a person's understanding of the ultimate nature of reality.[17] Many such worldviews are religious in nature (e.g., Christian, Buddhist, Muslim), but some are non-religious (e.g., nihilist, postmodern).[18] In this book, we use worldview in a narrower, more literal sense: what do we see when we view the world, especially the natural world? What is the world? Some worldviews would answer "something sacred," while other worldviews may see the natural world as primarily a source of raw materials. Still others see the world primarily in an aesthetic sense, perhaps as the canvas of a Master painter. Whatever our understanding, a worldview provides the foundation upon which our decisions of how to treat nature are based. This is not to say worldviews are completely determinant: We may act inconsistently with our worldview—for instance, we may say we believe God created the world but then treat His creation with disrespect—but the inconsistency highlights the foundational nature of worldviews, for eventually the cognitive dissonance will be resolved one way or the other, either by a change in practice or by a change in worldview.

Ethical theories provide the bridge between worldviews and practice. If worldviews tell us *what* nature is, ethical theories help us understand the *value* of nature: both what has value and how to weigh different values against one another. Put another way, worldviews specify the ontology of nature (i.e., the essence of the existence of nature) while ethical theories tell us the moral standing of that nature. Ontology and ethics are, of course, closely related. For instance, someone who considers nature to be created by God as an artist creates a work of art may be expected to feel a sense of responsibility to care for nature as a gift, in the same way we might care for

17. James Sire provides a definition of "worldview" in this sense: "a commitment, a fundamental orientation of the heart . . . [one holds] about the basic constitution of reality, and that provides the foundation on which we live and move and have our being." (Sire, *The Universe Next Door*, 17).

18. Ibid., Contents.

a portrait given to us by a painter. Such a valuing of nature, however, would differ from a valuing of nature as having intrinsic value or a good of its own.

Most of the work by evangelical Christians regarding creation care has focused on wrestling with worldviews and ethical theories. Comparatively little work has addressed the role of science in determining the content of creation care or the roles of political and economic systems in narrowing policy choice. Consideration of science often begins and ends with getting the science "right." For some, this results from a belief that once biblical exegesis has established the importance of creation care, science automatically prescribes the practice of creation care. Since science does so automatically, there is no need to analyze how science acts as a determinant for the criteria for obedience.

Science and society, however, play crucial roles as determinants for the criteria for obedience. In the case of science, proper creation care requires understanding the strengths and limits of scientific knowledge (e.g., its epistemology), as well as the ways science and policy can connect with each other. In the case of society, the way communities are organized and allocate power and responsibility (politics) and goods and money (economics) profoundly impact what creation care looks like. Creation care is conducted not only by individuals but also by communities: private and public, for profit and non-profit, free associations and state actors. As such, how the polity is organized affects which creation care practices work and which do not. And, because creation care logically affects creation, which in turn nearly always impacts the production and distribution of economic goods, an analysis of the proper system of economics is needed to help determine proper creation care practices.

What sources of knowledge can we bring to bear in fleshing out these four determinants? Scripture, as always, provides the authoritative understanding for all questions of faith and practice, including our worldview, ethical theories, and understanding of science and society; in chapter 3, we examine what Scripture says about these topics. But as we saw earlier in our thought experiment, Scripture provides only a partial answer to issues surrounding creation care, and so we expect other ways of accessing truth (e.g., reason, wisdom, tradition, love, etc.) may also help shape our worldview, ethical theories, science, and society. Thus, in this book we will look at the parts of the following picture of all the areas that make up considered obedience with respect to creation care:

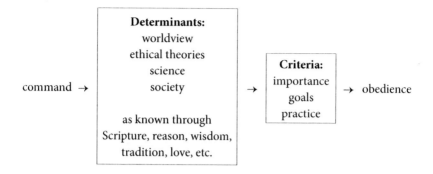

We can think of these determinants of the criteria for obedience in the following way: Our worldviews tell us, "what is nature," while ethical theories tell us, "what is the value of nature" and what ways are there to weigh those values against one another. Our understanding of science includes both the status of scientific knowledge and how science combines with ethics and other determinants to form policy. Our beliefs about the political and economic foundations for society further determine acceptable solutions. These determinants can each influence each of the criteria for obedience alone or in tandem with other determinants. In some cases, certain determinants tend to be related to specific criteria. For instance, worldviews and ethical theories, because of their foundational nature, usually address the importance of creation care commands more than science and society do. On the other hand, all four determinants contribute to the practice criteria. Ultimately, however, all four determinants are needed to evaluate the criteria for obedience.

A ROADMAP FOR THE REST OF THIS BOOK

In this final section of the chapter, we provide a preview or "roadmap" of the rest of the book. In this roadmap, we first list the topics and content of each subsequent chapter of the book and describe the approach we will take. Roadmaps, however, in addition to describing the path ahead can also describe pitfalls along the road. Thus, after our summary of the book, we address some possible concerns readers may have about our approach and method. We close with comments regarding our hopes for the reader.

In the subsequent chapters, we examine each of the determinants laid out in this introductory chapter. In chapter 2, we summarize some of the most prominent worldviews, their understanding of creation, and their relationship to environmental stewardship. Though other more comprehensive treatments exist, in chapter 3 we review the Scriptural understanding of creation care and summarize what Scripture can and cannot tell us about the importance criterion. In chapter 4, we examine different ethical theories used to understand environmental goods and how these assumptions relate to the imperatives from Scripture. Science—its meaning, authority, and relationships to policy—is considered in chapter 5. Chapter 6 broadly describes how various political and economic theories impact the content of environmental stewardship. Each of the chapters examining the determinants of the criteria for obedience (chapters 2–6) follows a similar outline, examining: what is the nature of the determinant, what does the determinant tell us and not tell us about the criteria for obedience, and how does our understanding of the determinant ultimately impact our understanding of the content of creation care. In chapter 7, we focus on the practice of environmental stewardship, examining the range of responses and some considerations when selecting amongst possible responses. In chapter 8, we outline the goals and process for synthesizing the determinants of the criteria for obedience.

Our approach in this book can be characterized as "synthesis through dialogue." This book is, first and foremost, a work of synthesis. This can be a synthesis of principle (that is, a synthesis regarding theories of environmental stewardship) as well as a synthesis regarding an issue (that is, a synthesis regarding a specific environmental problem). Regardless of the scope of the synthesis, we are convinced that one major difficulty in crafting excellent creation care solutions is the lack of synthesis through dialogue, both intellectually (since different disciplines are often siloed from one another) as well as personally (with people, instead, often talking past one another). When it comes to environmental issues, there is no lack of verbiage or polemic, but genuine dialogue, which is truly open to considering and possibly incorporating alternative viewpoints, is more lacking.

Synthesis through dialogue requires we consider multiple viewpoints. As a result, we consider a broad range of determinants and tap into a rich history of work in theology, ethics, epistemology, politics, economics, and science-policy studies. In addition, within each sub-topic, we examine a full range of positions possible for a given topic. Thus, for many of the determinants, we will describe a spectrum of positions that are reasonably consistent with the creation care command. As we do so, however, we will avoid claiming one view along the spectrum is "right" while others are wrong. Instead, we will focus on clarifying the assumptions that go into each position, the strengths and weaknesses of the position, enumerate the kinds of questions we might ask to judge which position (or positions) are better than others, and describe how these positions influence what we conclude about the three criteria for obedience.

The motivation for our study, as well as its analytical structure, may lead to a number of concerns. Before beginning the meat of our argument, we address three of those concerns. First, the argument that Scripture often does not fully dictate the content of creation care (or, in the secular context, that deontological categorical imperatives do not fully dictate the activities of environmental stewardship), may seem as if we are denigrating Scriptural authority, God's concern with His creation, or the duty to live responsibly. Many (if not most) treatments of environmental ethics begin with some sort of foundational theme or principle and from that theme directly derive personal and public policy responses. The approach we are advocating, it seems, overthrows this methodology for an academic version of "Stone Soup": a little bit from this discipline, a little bit from that discipline, throw it all into a pot, and *voilà,* we have the content of creation care. But, it starts with nothing more than a stone: there is no unifying theme or principle.

In reply, we argue that while the idea of directly deriving the content of creation care from a foundational belief is attractive, for many environmental problems, this is neither feasible nor advisable. As we examine each of the determinants, we will build upon the motivating arguments of this introductory chapter and find additional reasons why for many environmental problems, we need to exercise considered, not simple obedience. Additionally, in saying that we often cannot directly derive the content of creation care from a foundational belief, we are not saying foundational beliefs have no role in considered obedience. In the subsequent chapters, we will consider a variety of foundational beliefs and find they have much to say about environmental stewardship. Nonetheless, what foundational beliefs say and how they say it falls short of the enabling of simple obedience that many assume foundational beliefs make possible.

A second concern about our methodology is the suspicion that the model of human action we are using to understand environmental stewardship—with its large number of determinants of the criteria for obedience—is too complex to be successfully used. Is it possible to bring so many disciplines in fruitful dialogue with one another? Can we reach any kind of answer or synthesis of so many topics? Will this book merely ask a lot of questions without providing an answer? If so, is the real purpose of the book to argue that we cannot figure out one "right" understanding of the content of creation care, and thus environmental stewardship is ultimately a pragmatic endeavor?

In reply, we argue that because environmental stewardship involves so many facets of human endeavor, we cannot ascertain what excellent environmental stewardship entails without examining all the determinants of the criteria for obedience. Whether we can successfully synthesize these disparate fields, we admit, is an open question. While we believe our attempt in this book at synthesis does contribute something to our understanding of the nature of environmental stewardship, we concede that many questions remain unanswered. We see this work as a first step towards a broad synthesis, a work that proposes a taxonomy that can be used in further work in synthesis and one that prepares the ground for more fruitful dialogue. The entire endeavor of analyzing what environmental stewardship looks like in the modern world, we suggest, is itself quite young: much of the work done in the field has been done in the mid- to latter half of the twentieth century. While much scholarship has been done, much more remains to be done. To use an analogy with the history of mechanics, with regards to environmental stewardship, we have, perhaps, moved past an Aristotelian mechanics to a mechanics informed by Galileo and Kepler, but we have not yet arrived at a Newtonian mechanics, much less one that includes Maxwell's unified electromagnetic field theory, Einstein's general and special relativity, and quantum phenomena. Thus, if our attempts at synthesis fall short, this does not mean such a synthesis is not possible or that the only alternative is pragmatism. It is premature to make such definitive conclusions.

Third, our strategy of considering a range of options for each determinant, and our reluctance to claim one option in that range as "correct," may lead some readers to conclude the ultimate message of this book is that it does not really matter what we believe regarding creation care as any position is legitimate. In reply, we argue that the absence of a clear "position" in this book with regards to a number of the determinants does not mean that we believe all positions are equivalent nor that we do not have our own deeply held positions. However, because the goal of this book is to set out a taxonomy for understanding creation care, and to do so in a way that enables dialogue, the use of polemics would be fatal to the entire enterprise. Dialogue requires the views of all sides to be presented as accurately and winsomely as would be presented by those who hold those views.

That being said, implicit in our argument for a synthesis that covers all the determinants of the criteria for obedience is the contention (or, at least, the suggestion) that some aspects of the determinants and criteria for obedience regarding environmental stewardship are underdetermined. This does not mean everything is relative: there is truth and we can know at least some of that truth. But being underdetermined means that there are limits as to what of the truth we can know as well as limits as to the status of the truth we do know.[19] Being underdetermined also can mean that we may

19. In mathematics, an underdetermined system of equations is one where the number of equations is less than the number of unknowns. Being underdetermined does not mean the equations have no solution or that we can say nothing about a solution

understand some aspects of the truth about a determinant in some situations while in others it may be less clear. For instance, in chapter 5, regarding science, we will find different views of the epistemology of science lead to different views of its authority and, thus, different views of how science interacts with policymaking. This spectrum of views regarding the latter exists, partly, because the problem of demarcation (of determining what is and is not science) has not been convincingly solved,[20] and partly because for some kinds of environmental problems, science interacts with policy in one way while for other kinds of environmental problems, science interacts with policy in another way. In this book, we examine some of the reasons for this, but it is beyond the scope of this book to do so exhaustively. Our analysis, however, suggests that the role of science in environmental stewardship is more complex than is commonly appreciated.

Taken more broadly, we find that some aspects of environmental stewardship, in general, are also underdetermined. Rather than science (or Scripture, politics, etc.) automatically prescribing the practice of creation care, the contribution of the determinants is sometimes difficult to fully describe. This, however, neither denies truth nor the possibility of action. The philosopher and theologian Blaise Pascal has said:

> One must know when it is right to doubt, to affirm, to submit. Anyone who does otherwise does not understand the force of reason. Some men run counter to these three principles, either affirming that everything can be proved, because they know nothing about proof, or doubting everything, because they do not know when to submit, or always submitting, because they do not know when judgement [sic] is called for.[21]

The underdetermined nature of environmental stewardship does not mean that there are no moral absolutes regarding environmental stewardship. It does mean that the path from principles to practice is often incredibly complex and multi-faceted, not simple, and requires the highest levels of creativity to bring together many different fields of study—with different kinds of authority and expertise and different limitations in the kinds of knowledge provided—into an uneasy and unfamiliar dialogue with one another.

As far as we are aware, there are relatively few works that have sought to bring the breadth of topics considered by this book into dialogue with one another within a common framework.[22] By examining how each of

---

but merely that there is not enough information to determine a unique solution.

20. Hutchinson, "Warfare and Wedlock," 93.

21. Pascal, *Pensées*, 53–54 [Fragment 170].

22. Geographer Janel Curry's "social framework of analysis" regarding Christians

the determinants each inform each of the criteria for obedience, we hope to create such a taxonomy in the hopes that this kind of framework and the dialogue it supports can help us think more clearly and precisely about environmental stewardship. Along the way, we will find that the call to not only faithful stewardship but also excellent stewardship of creation is much more difficult than is commonly appreciated, and that the seeming simplicity behind the mandate to care for creation has within it pitfalls and snares that can harm creation and lead to a misguided conviction of biblical (or scientific, etc.) warrant for a given policy. We hope this book will help point the way towards some alternatives.

DISCUSSION QUESTIONS

1. The author argues that the Bible, while authoritative for all matters of faith and life, does not directly prescribe much of the *content* of creation care. What do you think of this argument? What are its strengths? Weaknesses? Why?

2. Is the distinction between the content of creation care and other aspects of creation care (e.g., motivation) a useful distinction to make? What pitfalls are possible for us to fall in if we make such a distinction? In what ways is that distinction helpful?

3. The author suggests proper obedience to God's commands requires clarity in three criteria: importance, goals, and practice. Can we obey without clarity in these criteria? Why or why not? Would you add or subtract any of these criteria? Why?

4. The author draws a distinction between determinants and criteria for obedience. Does such a distinction or taxonomy seem valid? Why or why not? In what ways might such a distinction be useful in trying to understand the nature of creation care?

5. What additional determinants would you subtract from the list the author provides? Why? Are there other determinants the author did not include that you would argue are vital if we are to understand the nature of creation care? Why?

---

and climate change, which integrates views on eschatology, how humans, nature, and God relate to one another, and models of responsibility of social change, is one attempt at a broad understanding of factors that affect one's understanding of climate change. (Curry, "Social Framework")

2

If You Could See What I See

Worldviews

A PARABLE, CONTINUED

Gabriel had been friends with Rob Lane since their under-graduate days in the aeronautical and astronautical engineering program at Titan University. While making wind tunnel measurements together, they found out they both loved engineering, shared three-quarters of their last name, and grew up playing tennis. For a few years after graduation, the two had drifted apart a little. Rob moved across the country to work at a defense contractor on the nation's next-generation fighter aircraft while Gabriel headed off to seminary to study Greek, Hebrew, and theology. But they had reconnected a decade later when both had moved to the same city, and their friendship became even deeper in the months following as Gabriel walked with Rob in his grief at the untimely death of Rob's mother. Rob was as good-hearted and loyal a friend as one could wish for, and Gabriel was grateful for the return of this friendship.

When Gabriel pulled up to the tennis court, Rob was already out hitting a few balls against the backboard. After joining him for a few minutes, Gabriel and Rob sat down on a bench together to adjust their rackets and wait for the pair who were finishing up a game on the court Rob had reserved.

"How're things going, Gabriel?" asked Rob. "Is your congregation treating you well?"

Gabriel paused. "Things are well overall," replied Gabriel, "but, well, we just had a big blow-up last week and I'm not sure what to do about it. I'm not even sure how I ought to think about it." And Gabriel explained his sermon series on creation care and the meeting of the church's creation care committee. Rob looked thoughtful.

"And what puzzles me the most," Gabriel finished, "is that I know both parties on the committee want to care for the environment and share the Christian worldview. Why, then, would their disagreement be so strong?"

"Well, Gabriel," replied Rob, "you know that I'm an atheist and don't have a worldview, and while I respect your faith, I don't share your beliefs." Gabriel nodded. Rob continued, "From my viewpoint, religious worldviews may be important when it comes to ethics and morals, but when it comes to environmental policy, what matters is what the science says."

"Thanks, Rob," replied Gabriel. "but at the risk of making our conversation end up like one of those late nights in the dorm philosophizing over pizza"—at this Gabriel's eyes glinted and Rob smiled back—"let me push you a bit. What do you mean that you don't have a worldview? Doesn't an atheistic materialism claim that matter in motion is all the universe is? Wouldn't that understanding of what is nature have an effect on your views on how to care for nature?"

Rob looked thoughtful again. "I suppose so, Gabriel," Rob said, "but if the universe is merely matter, to me that makes it all the clearer that science tells me how I should treat the environment. After all, science is the study of matter, and if the universe is matter, doesn't that make science the best way of discovering how that matter behaves and, by extension, should be cared for?" The players who had been on the court had just passed Gabriel and Rob on the bench, and Gabriel and Rob picked up their rackets and bags.

As they walked onto the court, Gabriel replied, "Yes, that makes sense, Rob, but if, hypothetically speaking, the world is more than mere matter in motion, then science wouldn't be enough to tell you how to care for the world, right?" Gabriel picked out a tennis ball and hit it over to Rob.

Rob chuckled as he returned the ball. "Hypothetically speaking, I suppose so," Rob said. "But if science isn't enough to tell us how to care for the environment," he continued, "what is?" The ball hit the pavement to Gabriel's backhand, just beyond his reach. "Nice return, hypothetically speaking," said Gabriel, and both of them laughed.

INTRODUCTION

As we noted in chapter 1, the term "worldview" commonly refers to "a commitment, a fundamental orientation of the heart . . . [one holds] about the basic constitution of reality, and that provides the foundation on which we live and move and have our being."[1] With regards to the environment, however, we can narrow our definition of a worldview to be the description of the part of reality we consider "the environment" or "nature." Put another way, in this more limited sense, a worldview—which may be religious or non-religious—literally means "what you see when you see the world." Do you see a universe of inanimate matter (quarks, electrons, etc.) in meaningless motion? Or a land inhabited by wood gods and water goddesses? Or an aesthetic paradise that draws human beings into awe and wonder? Or the handiwork of a loving and eternal God unconstrained by space and time? Or as something else? What *is* "nature" and the "natural"?[2]

Regardless of the kind of worldview one holds, we can use a common schema from the comparative study of religions to define five basic questions regarding the environment that worldviews address: reality, origin, condition, solution, destiny. In a lecture on world religions and the environment, theologian R. Boaz Johnson describes these five questions in the following way:[3]

1. Reality: What do we mean by reality and is there such a thing as an ultimate reality?

2. Origin: What is the origin of the universe and human beings?

3. Condition: What is the condition of the environment and humanity? Is the universe healthy or unhealthy?

4. Solution: What solutions exist for human and environmental problems?

5. Destiny: Where is humanity and the universe heading? Is there a destination or only the journey?

1. Sire, *The Universe Next Door*, 17.

2. In an essay on genetic engineering and the food industry, philosopher Mark Sagoff provides a concise summary of the different senses of the term "natural" (Sagoff, "Genetic Engineering," 5).

3. Johnson, "Crisis."

To that extent, we can define an environmental worldview as a foundational way of seeing the world that answers these five questions. Not all worldviews purposely address all of these questions, though the most comprehensive ones do. All five aspects of a worldview impact our view of creation care, for these five aspects tell us what we think nature *is*, in its most foundational sense.

In this chapter, we will explore how environmental worldviews affect the criteria for obedience. Some readers, however, may wonder about the value of considering this determinant. Christian readers may wonder how considering non-Christian worldviews will help them better understand the nature of a biblically-based creation care. Secular readers may feel that worldviews are matters of religion and wonder how examining such worldviews will help them understand excellent environmental stewardship. As the chapter progresses, we will find that understanding worldviews in general will help anyone—regardless of your worldview—in understanding the motivations behind different positions on environmental stewardship. Everyone, religious or not, has a worldview: we all understand the world as being *something*. As such, there are religious as well as secular worldviews, all of which can affect one's understanding of environmental stewardship. An analysis of worldviews not our own can also provide useful contrasts to help us better understand our own worldviews and their impact on questions of environmental stewardship. Finally, understanding worldviews different than our own can help us identify possible common ground on which to build agreement as well as clarify the true nature of disagreements.

In our discussion of worldviews, we will consider the range of worldviews, what worldviews cannot and can provide, and the impact of worldviews on each of the criteria (importance, goals, and practice). We will find worldviews to have an important though limited effect on the criteria, particularly on the importance of environmental stewardship. What we find in this chapter to be true of worldviews in general will set-up our more detailed discussion of the biblical worldview in chapter 3.

THE RANGE OF WORLDVIEWS

While the number of worldviews is probably uncountable, we describe six major environmental worldviews that span most of the range in worldviews and give a good sense of both what worldviews entail as well as what kind of influence worldviews provide with regards to environmental stewardship.[4] Of these six, four are religious and two are non-religious worldviews. Below,

---

4. Clifton-Soderstrom, "Summary."

we provide a description of these six worldviews. Our description will be a broad-brushed summary of the worldviews and will gloss over the spectrum of differences within each worldview. In our description, we do not provide a point-by-point answer to each of the five questions Johnson enumerates above. Nonetheless, the description shows what kinds of answers the worldview provides to Johnson's questions and how those answers are intertwined with the worldview's picture of reality.

The Christian Worldview

In the Christian worldview, nature is neither self-existing nor self-caused. Rather, all of reality, both physical and non-physical, is the result of the free creation of a good and loving God.[5] God is not far away from His creation but is instead immanent and sustains His creation. Yet, at the same time, God is entirely transcendent and "other" than what He has made. Because God creates and sustains creation, the creation is best understood through worshipping the Creator and the order, beauty, and fruitfulness that God has given it.

Although the creation is fallen from the perfection it once had, it still has a number of purposes and roles, and a destiny of redemption. It is a testimony of God's glory and providence. It provides resources for the use of human beings, but creation is also humanity's charge. We are to care for and steward creation; nature is a garden that humanity is to tend. That tenure will, one day, culminate in a joyous reunion of heaven and earth when God recreates and restores creation to what it was meant to be. (In the next chapter, we will provide a more detailed description of a biblical understanding of nature.)

The Buddhist Worldview

A Buddhist worldview understands existence as the primary constituent of reality. Existence is not atomic—individual identity between persons and objects has no ultimate ontological reality—but rather is holistic,

---

5. Writer Joe Carter notes that Christians have traditionally understood creation as being not merely physical and material but also non-physical and non-material (Carter, "Should Christians"). He argues that often when we use the term "supernatural," we seem to suggest all of creation is physical and material; angels, however, are created but non-physical, and there are natural entities such as ethics and aesthetics that are not reducible to physical manifestations (ibid.). This is also discussed in chapter 3.

interconnected, and relational.[6] Because of ego and the cravings of self, existence is full of suffering.[7] The destruction of desire, self-mastery, and increased sensitivity to the Buddha-nature frees us from suffering and enables us to achieve enlightenment, where we are fully one with the reality of existence because we are free from the deception of thinking our egos are substantial. Note that nature also inhabits the ontological reality of existence.[8] In addition to that ultimate reality, however, nature also provides a sacred context in which humanity moves towards enlightenment.[9]

The Confucian Worldview

The Confucian conception of reality is also holistic, with an understanding of the self that is connected with the cosmos.[10] This holism, however, is not as monistic as the Buddhist worldview: the operative metaphor relating humanity and nature in Confucian thought is the notion of humanity as an elder brother to the cosmos.[11] In that sense, right apprehension of reality involves recognizing we are kin with all that is part of the cosmos. Just as filial piety is the correct attitude in human families, this should also be our attitude to the cosmos.

As a result, humanity finds nature and the world to be its spiritual and physical home, rather than some other heavenly realm or some future perfected world. We find our place in the current world and we are to live in harmony with nature and tend and cultivate the harmony that is present within nature.[12]

The Taoist Worldview

The Taoist worldview, like Buddhism, sees reality in holistic terms, characterized by interrelatedness and continuity. This cosmos has no creator and there is nothing besides the universe. Like Buddhism, Taoism also sees humanity as best understanding reality when it destroys desires and

6. Gross, "Buddhist Environmental Ethic," 337–38; Swearer, "Principles and Poetry," 229–30.

7. Kinsley, *Ecology and Religion*, 84–85; Swearer, "Principles and Poetry," 226.

8. Swearer, "Principles and Poetry," 230.

9. Regarding the ideas in this paragraph, see also Kinsley, *Ecology and Religion*, 84–98.

10. Snyder, "Chinese Traditions," 108.

11. Kinsley, *Ecology and Religion*, 77–78.

12. Ibid., 78–79.

a self-centered view. The focus of human relationship with nature in this holism, however, is characterized by harmony with the rhythms of nature. Taoism sees nature as humanity's spiritual home whose patterns guide our development. Living in harmony with nature requires us to practice *wu-wei*, or "letting be": the operative metaphor for this practice is that of swimming with, rather than against, the flow of a river.[13] *Wu-wei* tells us to creatively cohere with nature, rather than resist nature.[14]

The Enlightenment Worldview

The Enlightenment worldview (a secular, non-religious worldview) sees reality as merely material, lacking any teleology or end, and operating impersonally by universal law.[15] (Note that here we use "Enlightenment" as a label for a popular, contemporary worldview that is descended from strands of thought held by some thinkers in the historical Enlightenment. In actuality, Enlightenment-era thinkers were not necessarily secular or materialist.) The best way to know reality is through the objectivity and rationality of mathematical and scientific inquiry. Nature is thus seen primarily as a resource for human use and to enable human progress, and the relationship of humanity with nature is that of a user or investigator of natural resources and phenomena.[16]

The Romantic Worldview

While the Romantic worldview, like the Enlightenment worldview, can also be secular and non-religious,[17] the Romantic worldview rejects the idea that the natural world can be reduced to "matter in motion." Instead, nature is seen as organic, shot through with beauty and sacredness; nature is an artistic masterpiece. As a result, reality is best apprehended through the fine arts (e.g., poetry, painting, etc.) and immediate experience. The relation of nature to humanity is that of a sublime garden through which we come to know both ourselves and any supernatural realm. Thus, our fundamental role with respect to nature is that of an appreciator.

13. Kinsley, *Ecology and Religion*, 79.

14. Snyder, "Chinese Traditions," 114.

15. Koeller, "Newton"; Kinsley, *Ecology and Religion*, 125–40.

16. Bouma-Prediger, *Beauty of the Earth*, 84; Kinsley, *Ecology and Religion*, 133–35.

17. While Romanticism is not necessarily religious, there are religious versions of Romanticism and religious worldviews that have incorporated major tenets of Romanticism.

From this summary of these six worldviews, we can identify a number of characteristics of worldviews. First, while environmental worldviews address issues that religions also address, worldviews do not have to be religious. Worldviews can be both religious and non-religious, and non-Christian worldviews can be both religious and non-religious. Second, amongst subsets of these six worldviews, we find both similarities and differences as to how the worldviews understand nature. These differences and similarities span the spectrum in importance. Some of these differences are fundamental—for instance, a created world versus an eternal world—but others appear more optional. In some cases, similarities and differences are interwoven together. For instance, Buddhism, Confucianism, and Taoism all exhibit some sense of holism. At the same time, the kinds of holism each exhibit are different from one another. In most cases, the similarities and differences between the worldviews encompass certain attributes of the worldviews; seldom are worldviews completely mutually exclusive in the ways they see nature.

WHAT WORLDVIEWS CANNOT AND CAN PROVIDE

This brief survey also suggests that while worldviews are foundational, there may be limits as to what worldviews can provide. For instance, while the above six worldviews address fundamental questions of ontology and cosmology, the answers the worldviews provide seem more abstract than concrete. How, then, do we translate a worldview into practice and ethics? In this section, we examine the limits of worldviews with regards to practice and ethics and find that, in general, worldviews alone cannot fully prescribe the practice of environmental stewardship nor fully determine the value of the environment. We will end the section with a brief description of what worldviews can provide: what it means for worldviews to be foundational.

Worldviews Generally Cannot Prescribe Actions

Because worldviews are foundational, some argue that they necessarily lead to a specific set of practices. For instance, some might argue that the Christian worldview, which sees the world as shot through with value from the hand of the loving God who created it, automatically leads to a specific set of personal and corporate actions. Proper creation care practice then merely requires getting one's theology correct. In chapter 1, we argued that in many situations, it is not possible to specify the content of creation care through the direct application of biblical command. Here we provide two more reasons for the more general argument that the "action prescriptive" way of understanding worldviews is unconvincing and that, as a result, adherents of a given worldview may find multiple ways of living out their convictions as to environmental stewardship while remaining within that worldview.

The first reason that worldviews are generally non-prescriptive of environmental practices can be seen from the structure of worldviews. Contrary to the stereotype that (particularly religious) worldviews are lists of "do's and don'ts," worldviews are structured to be non-prescriptive of many life practices. Worldviews provide all-encompassing frameworks in the sense that they cover all of reality, and many worldviews contain some specific rules or guidelines (e.g., dietary restrictions, codes of conduct, moral prohibitions, etc.). But worldviews do not provide specific, actionable information for every human action. For instance, while Taoism may suggest it is more harmonious with nature if we situate our house to match the landscape, Taoism does not specify the square-footage of the windows we should install. Similarly, the Enlightenment worldview that sees nature and humanity as fundamentally material and unified via the laws of nature may encourage a sense of interconnectivity between human beings and the natural world, but the Enlightenment worldview does not specify whether that interconnectivity implies we may have a pet or not. Indeed, because life is so complex and contains an uncountable number of possible actions, we would be surprised to find that any worldview could provide the near-robotic and deterministic direction necessary for worldviews to fully prescribe actions. We find that expectation expressed in the structure and content of worldviews themselves: a focus more on general principle and ontology and less on specific rules and strictures.

The second reason worldviews do not necessarily prescribe actions is a philosophical one: merely because something is "foundational" does not necessarily mean it is "prescriptive." Philosophical reductionism (the belief that all actions and thinking can be created from foundational elements) suggests that foundational principles are prescriptive. For a philosophical reductionist, all true arguments and beliefs can be derived from the correct set of first-principles. Thus, once we obtain those correct first-principles, any conclusions that are deduced from those first-principles are logically entailed. To the extent these conclusions are courses of action, we can say that those actions are *necessarily* prescribed by the foundational principles.

There are, however, strong reasons to doubt philosophical reductionism, in principle. While the laws of deduction might suggest the idea of unbroken continuity from first-principles to actions, in human thought, we actually observe that at each level of thinking and reasoning there are new levels of complexity and richness, levels that appear to be different in kind from the levels that came before. Ethics, for instance, adds something to ontology and cosmology beyond the mere deductions from ontology and cosmology. Put another way, ontology and cosmology may make an ethic possible, but the two more basic fields do not directly specify the ethic. We can see this difference in kind between different levels of thinking and reasoning in the relationships between the various natural sciences themselves. Chemistry, for instance, is not merely particle physics scaled-up to the molecular level and biology is not merely chemistry scaled-up to the organismic level; chemistry adds something to physics (structure and reactivity) while biology adds something to chemistry (life and living systems).[18] Thus, rather than exhibiting philosophical reductionism, science and philosophy are structured into different kinds and types, suggesting that it is not, in general, possible to derive logically required actions from a foundational worldview.

One might respond to these two arguments that while environmental worldviews may not be entirely prescriptive of actions, with regards to environmental issues, they are mostly prescriptive or at least prescriptive with regards to the stewardship issues that "matter." While this may be true, at least in principle, such an argument depends heavily on what the terms "mostly prescriptive" and "issues that matter" mean. How do we judge that a worldview is "mostly" prescriptive in the sense that those issues dealing with environmental stewardship practice are logically entailed by the worldview but other issues, in general, are not? How do we determine what are the issues that matter? These questions, which are questions of meaning that go beyond what worldviews directly specify, require a consideration of ethics and science. In later chapters in this book, we will find exactly that: our conceptions of ethics and the nature of science play critical roles in specifying the content of environmental stewardship. If so, worldviews, by themselves, do not fully prescribe the practice of environmental stewardship. Rather, worldviews require ethics, science, and other determinants to answer the questions of meaning that are implicit in the claim that worldviews prescribe stewardship practice in the issues that "matter."

Worldviews Generally Do Not Directly Determine Ethics

Similar to the idea that worldviews directly prescribe stewardship actions, many believe environmental worldviews directly determine environmental

---

18. For instance, physicist and philosopher James Cushing notes that the laws of geology and chemistry both have an empirical foundation, rather than being directly predicted or derived from physics (Cushing, *Philosophical Concepts in Physics*, 362–63).

ethics. That is, some argue that given what worldviews tell us of what nature "is," we can determine what nature "should be" and how human beings
should treat nature. For example, some Christians may argue that because
nature is God's good handiwork, this directly leads to an environmental ethic of care and value. Alternately, some Buddhists may argue that because existence is all there is and all of reality is interconnected, this directly leads to
an environmental ethic of sympathy and solidarity. In this line of reasoning,
what "is" automatically determines what "should be." In general, however,
there are strong reasons for doubting that worldviews determine ethics.[19]

Perhaps the most prominent argument against this position is known
in philosophy as the "is-ought dichotomy" or the "fact-value distinction."[20]
In short, this dichotomy argues that we cannot proceed from what is (ontology) to what should be (morality) without some mediating assumptions or
principles. Examples of this distinction are not difficult to find, particularly
with regards to environmental issues. For instance, a hydrologist may make
measurements of a wetland and find the wetland's acreage has decreased
over time: this is a statement of what "is." In order to turn that description
of what "is" into a statement of what "should be" (e.g., we should act to
increase the wetland's acreage), we need to provide a mediating assumption,
such as "wetland loss is undesirable."[21] Or, to give an example using world-

19. This disconnection between worldviews and ethics may strike some as strange,
particularly since various religions make strong ethical claims with regards to environmental care. Indeed, David Kinsley, at the conclusion of his survey of religions and
ecology, finds that:

> Perhaps the most consistent and pervasive theme in the materials we
> have covered is the assumption that there is an underlying moral or
> ethical unity that connects the human and the nonhuman world. In
> nearly all of the materials there is the idea that an ethical whole unites
> all aspects of reality in a shared moral system. . . . In all of these in-
> stances [of this theme], the assertion is made very clearly that ecologi-
> cal issues are moral and ethical issues first and foremost and that, to be
> dealt with effectively, environmental problems must be understood as
> such. (Kinsley, *Ecology and Religion*, 229–30)

What distinguishes Kinsley's argument from ours is two-fold. First, our definition of
"worldview" is not equivalent to "religion." By worldview, we are limiting ourselves to
questions of ontology and cosmology; religions often also address questions of ethics
and politics. Second, the purpose of our analysis is to understand *how* ontology and
cosmology (worldviews) affect the goals of environmental stewardship. It will not do
for our purposes to assume that ontology and cosmology dictate ethics merely because
some religions bundle the two together.

20. See, for instance, Benson, *Environmental Ethics*, 109–11.

21. See Lin, "Role of Science," 21–25 for further discussion of the difference between "what is" and "what should be," with respect to the knowledge science provides.

views, an adherent of the Enlightenment worldview may observe a meadow and see a collection of atoms and molecules in motion, but whether that justifies an ethic to treat the meadow carelessly depends on a mediating assumption such as "inert materials should not be treated with care." While facts do provide a substrate on which values act, and while there may be some circumstances where the is-ought dichotomy is not as strong—where ontology specifies some part of ethics—nonetheless, regarding phenomena in nature, a true distinction often exists between descriptions of what "is" and what "should be." The burden-of-proof in many cases rests on those who would elide from the former to the latter.[22]

22. The validity of the is-ought dichotomy (at least as presented in eighteenth-century philosopher David Hume's formulation) is certainly contested. Philosophers Matthew B. O'Brien and Robert C. Koons, for instance, summarize some arguments against the Humean version, in the context of modern work on the natural law tradition (O'Brien and Koons, "Who's Afraid"). Particularly with regards to environmental phenomena, some have argued that there is something about the "is" of life and living things that can tell us something of "goodness" or of our obligations (e.g., Clifton-Soderstrom, "Response," 36–37; Foot and Lewis, "Interview"; the discussion on biocentrism in chapter 4 in this book). These critiques have merit. There are cases where the connection between characteristics of some entity and our obligations towards that entity appear very tight. Without engaging in an extended examination of the reasons for and against the is-ought dichotomy, we merely make the following observations.

First, our argument is not that "is" has no relation to "ought" but rather that in environmental issues, "is" does not, in general, directly prescribe "ought." Our argument, thus, focuses on the need for additional input to translate worldviews into ethics, not on whether a given ontology is truth-telling, complete, adequate, etc. We question the claim that worldviews, regarding environmental issues, *fully prescribe* ethics, not that worldviews *affect* ethics.

Second, in many (if not most) cases dealing with environmental issues, where we hope to directly move from "is" to "ought," we implicitly assume that the "is" is, for all practical purposes, "material" in the sense of being disconnected from meaning and purpose (here we use "purpose" in the Aristotelian final cause sense as opposed to a teleology of function). Modern scientific descriptions, in particular, tend towards this naturalist sense of "material." But, since convincing ethical positions often need to connect with a sense of meaning and purpose, deriving an "ought" from an "is" requires adding back in such meaning and purpose. The derivation of the "ought," in such cases, comes not only from the "is" but also from the additional value propositions.

Third, in cases where "is" seems very closely connected to "ought," we suggest that it is a very special kind of "is." Nora Calhoun, for instance, speaks of how her experiences in attending births and spending time with the elderly taught her about the inviolable worth of all human life, no matter how apparently meaningless the life (Calhoun, "Learning from Bodies"). She argues that:

> There are things that can be learned—can be said—only in the language of bodies. There is a specific wisdom to be gained through the experience of being with actual people: their actual pregnancies, illnesses, births, and deaths. And many of the lessons that bodies teach can barely be translated into words. (ibid.)

If environmental worldviews do not directly determine environmental ethics, we would expect that any single worldview might lead to multiple understandings of the value of the environment. (Note that this paragraph relies on concepts we will not discuss in detail until chapter 4; we provide some orienting description in this paragraph, but some readers will benefit from skimming chapter 4 first and then returning to this section.) This, indeed, is what we find. For instance, an Enlightenment materialist worldview, which sees the universe, ultimately, as inert material with no end or purpose (i.e., no *telos*), may encourage the perspective that nature has only instrumental value (i.e., as a means to some other end). This can lead one to conclude that nature has no independent moral status, which in turn may lead one to adopt a strong anthropocentric view of environmental ethics, where the value of the environment is determined solely by the felt needs and desires of human beings. At the same time, a naturalistic assumption does not have to lead to strong anthropocentrism. There are philosophers who make the naturalistic assumption, but then justify weak anthropocentric perspectives without appealing to *telos* (purpose) in nature. Ronald Sandler does this for a virtue ethics perspective, which conceptualizes the ethical life as becoming a certain kind of person, fit for human flourishing.[23] Warwick Fox, while arguing for an ecocentric "deep green" environmentalism, proposes naturalistically-based forms of ontological and cosmological identification as a means of relating to nature; these forms of identification, however, can also be appropriated to support a weak anthropocentric ethic.[24] Thus, we see that worldviews—in this case the Enlightenment world-

---

We suggest, however, that human beings and the human body, as an "is," are special, at the very least, in the way Calhoun describes, and differ from the "is" that describes most environmental issues. The debate over the existence and nature of human exceptionalism is a long one, and we will not recap it here. We do claim, however, that the cases where an "is" seems very close to justifying an "ought" are rare, and those cases are rare because the kind of ontology that hints at bridging the is-ought divide is the kind of ontology associated with the "being" of human beings.

Fourth, we suggest that the way we obtain an "ought" is, in a fundamental way, distinct from the way we obtain an "is." C. S. Lewis has noted that there is a difference between looking "at" something and "along" something (Lewis, "Toolshed," 212). Obtaining an "ought," we argue, is something similar. It is not enough to look "at" something in order to arrive at an "ought"; we must also look "along." When we look "along" something, that is (at least one place) where meaning, purpose, and value come alongside to form our "ought."

23. Sandler, *Character and Environment*, 13–14, 21–26.

24. Fox, "Transpersonal Ecology," 259–60. The phrase "deep green" (along with the phrase "light green") comes from Benson, *Environmental Ethics*, 16–18, 25. See also Benson, *Environmental Ethics*, chapter 7, for additional discussion regarding "deep green" views of being a part of nature.

view—can support multiple forms of valuing, suggesting worldviews do not directly determine ethics.

What Worldviews Can Provide

If worldviews are neither necessarily prescriptive of actions nor directly determinant of ethics, what then does it mean for worldviews to be foundational? Worldviews are foundational in the sense that they provide the substrate on which further reflection and action are built. First, worldviews provide crucial context but not a determining context. Instead, worldviews provide a frame that defines bounds or limits of what should (or can) be considered and what is worth considering. For instance, a Buddhist worldview's monist conception of reality understands the nature of personhood very differently than a Trinitarian Christian worldview that considers personhood as integral to a conception of the Godhead. Second, worldviews provide a lens that enables us to ascribe, interpret, and understand the meaning of ourselves and the world around us. We can see this quite readily in a comparison of the narratives provided by the six worldviews we summarized earlier. The cosmological stories each tells differ dramatically from each other and thus the meaning of the world, according to each worldview, also differs dramatically. Finally, worldviews provide the foundational context through and in which we exercise our free will to choose and act. That is to say, worldviews are the first step in understanding the meaning of our intentions and actions. In the next section, we will consider in more detail how environmental worldviews behave in this foundational way as we examine how worldviews determine each of the three criteria for obedience.

WORLDVIEWS AND THE IMPORTANCE OF THE CREATION CARE COMMAND (WHY FOLLOW THE COMMAND)

As we might expect, even if worldviews do not directly prescribe actions or dictate ethics, worldviews still heavily influence the importance of the creation care command—why follow the command and how the command compares with other priorities. In this section, we detail how worldviews accomplish this. First, we examine how worldviews affect the importance of the creation care command through the influence of worldviews on ethical theories of moral status. Second, we examine how the ontology prescribed by a worldview impacts the importance criterion through affecting our understanding of value. Finally, we look at the reverse effect: how the importance criterion affects the worldviews determinant.

The first way environmental worldviews affect the importance criterion is through shaping one's ethical theory of moral considerability (i.e., our theory of what has moral status). This does not contradict what we argued earlier: worldviews do not, in general, determine ethics. Worldviews, however, tell us what the world is and thus provide the foundation or substrate on which we build an understanding of what in the world has moral status. This meaning then shapes the ethical theory of moral considerability we use for understanding nature's moral considerability (see chapter 4 for details as to those theories), which in turn informs the importance of the creation care command (though not necessarily to the specific moral conclusion of an activity). For instance, the ethical theory of biocentrism, as proposed by philosopher Paul Taylor, ascribes moral considerability to all living things on the basis that all living things, even those incapable of thought or feeling (such as plants), have a "good of their own" that we can understand as a purpose or *telos* of that being.[25] All else being equal, such an understanding of living things raises the importance of commands to protect life as compared to an understanding that sees living things as having no moral considerability.[26] However, not all worldviews provide equally fertile ground on which to build a theory of biocentrism. A philosophically monist worldview, such as Buddhism, that denies *any telos* in principle, does not provide much support for a biocentrism grounded on *telos,* as Taylor's does. Worldviews open to purpose (e.g., the Romantic, Christian, etc., worldviews) do provide at least a minimal level of support. Thus, while a worldview neither forces us to adopt a specific ethic nor fully determines the importance of the creation care command, the context or resources the worldview provides, in its influence on ethical theories of moral considerability, does affect the importance criterion. (In chapter 4, we will address in more detail both ethical theories and what leads to moral conclusions regarding a practice.)

Environmental worldviews not only influence the importance criterion through ethical theories of moral status but also through the effect of ontology (what we think nature is) on our understanding of value. This influence occurs because ontological forms come attached with values and

25. See Benson's review of Taylor's theory for a nice summary (Benson, *Environmental Ethics,* 88–93). The phrase "good of their own" can be found in Taylor, "Respect for Nature," 217.

26. We are not saying only ethical theories that grant moral considerability (i.e., independent moral status) motivate an adequate ethic of care. We are merely saying that moral considerability itself grants a level of importance to actions that aim to preserve entities that possess moral considerability.

ways of valuing. For instance, if we believe nature is merely material, then we will tend to value nature as material. If we believe nature is the handiwork of a Master Craftsman, then we will tend to value nature in the way we value such a handiwork. The value and ways of valuing we attach to an ontological form may be specific to an individual or may be shared with a community or culture. It may be related to a universal, objective moral principle but more frequently it will be a preference.

It is important to note when value and valuing leads to a moral demand. Moral demands are demands that a party can make on other parties. These demands are grounded in some theory of "should" or "ought." For instance, a view of humanity that understands human beings as possessing inalienable rights that should not be violated will produce a moral demand on others to respect those inalienable rights. In contrast, value preferences, though strongly felt, are not necessarily moral demands if it is illegitimate to require other parties honor the preference. Rather, value preferences become moral demands only if one provides some sort of grounding that elevates respect of the value until it becomes an obligation others should meet. A variety of ethical theories attempt to provide this grounding: Kantian deontology tries to accomplish this through reason, Natural Theology tries to ground this through natural law. Additionally, many religions provide such grounding through divine command.

Even if a value or valuing does not rise to the level of a moral demand, if we believe something is valuable, we will tend to want to protect it, in whatever state we perceive as being the most valuable. If we believe untrammeled wilderness is valuable (e.g., because of its beauty, the wonder it evokes, its testimony to the goodness of God, etc.), we will want to prevent that wilderness from being disrupted. This desire to protect we can call a "preference for preservation" of valuables. Through such a preference for preservation, derived from the ontological forms specified by our worldview, worldviews provide an additional influence on the importance and priority of environmental stewardship.

Lastly, not only can the worldviews determinant affect the importance criterion, but the reverse feedback can also occur, though to a weaker extent. One way this can happen is through strengthening our existing worldview. If our views of the importance of the creation care command dovetails with our professed worldview, we may find our belief in our worldview strengthened. Still, because worldviews are foundational, we will first choose our worldviews for reasons that are convincing and important in a foundational way: reasons may include truth, coherence, reasonableness, and/or revelatory importance.[27] Thus, the importance of the creation care command, in general, will not affect the content of our worldview.[28]

WORLDVIEWS AND THE GOALS OF FOLLOWING THE CREATION CARE COMMAND (WHAT FOLLOWING THE COMMAND WILL RESULT IN)

The goals of a command are what following the command will result in. Defining the goals of a command involves answering the question of "should": what do we want to have happen if we follow the command? Goals are often related to values (both what we value and how we compare values), because the desired results from our actions embody what we value. Thus, we would expect ethical theories to provide a substantial portion of the guidance of the goals of creation care. We will address the role of ethical theories on the goals criterion in chapter 4; in this section, we restrict ourselves to the role of worldviews. We begin by examining how much worldviews define the goals of creation care. Some may expect worldviews to contribute a great deal to the goals criterion, because of the foundational nature of worldviews. There are important limits, however, to the guidance the worldviews determinant can provide for the goals of environmental stewardship; we examine two reasons why.[29] Next, we consider the influence of worldviews on goals for worldviews with a substantial command component, in the form of direct and indirect commands. Finally, we examine four

---

27. As an example of this foundational way, consider one of C. S. Lewis's argument for Christianity (in particular *contra* the scientism worldview):

> The waking world is judged more real because it can thus contain the dreaming world; the dreaming world is judged less real because it cannot contain the waking one. For the same reason I am certain that in passing from the scientific points of view to the theological, I have passed from dream to waking. Christian theology can fit in science, art, morality, and the sub-Christian religions. The scientific point of view cannot fit in any of these things, not even science itself. I believe in Christianity as I believe that the Sun has risen, not only because I see it, but because by it I see everything else. (Lewis, "Is Theology," 92)

28. Though the importance criterion will not materially affect the *content* of one's worldview, it may affect the *profession* of that worldview.

29. In fact, as we discuss later on, goals can feedback on worldviews by encouraging us to emphasize elements of our worldview that support the goals we hold. For instance, if we believe that the goal of creation care is an untrammeled nature, we will focus on parts of our worldview that motivate or justify a hands-off or minimalist approach to interacting with the environment.

ways environmental worldviews affect the goals criterion outside of direct or indirect commands.

We can identify at least two reasons why worldviews provide only partial guidance for the goals criterion. The first reason is because of the "is-ought" distinction. As we saw earlier in this chapter, just as the is-ought distinction limits what worldviews can say about importance, it also limits what worldviews can say about goals. Recall that while worldviews are foundational, worldviews are about what "is"; worldviews are ontologies not ethics. As ontologies, because of the is-ought distinction, worldviews often cannot determine what "should be" (that is, the goals criterion) without a value assumption. For example, Enlightenment materialism does not automatically imply we should treat nature as raw materials unless we also include a value assumption that we should treat things based on their ontology. With such an assumption, the worldview does not determine the goals criterion by itself: ethics plus the worldview specifies goals.

A second reason worldviews provide limited guidance for the goals criterion is because the description worldviews provide are generally too non-specific to determine goals. A variety of goals (and practices) could, conceivably, fit within a single worldview. For example, the Enlightenment worldview of naturalistic materialism can be rationally paired with an ethic of "preserve all that exists as it exists" as well as an ethic of "use all that exists any way you see fit." The goals we would arrive at, however, with these two ethical pairings would be radically different from one another. Thus, because worldviews lack specificity, we often need the values defined by ethics to arrive at the goals (and practices) we understand as justified and motivated by the worldview.

Given these limitations, then, how do worldviews contribute to the goals of a command? For worldviews that have a substantial authoritative command component, such as the Christian worldview, goals may be explicitly prescribed in the worldview through a command.[30] This prescription may be direct or indirect. Direct commands set up a specific template for us to aim for; indirect commands enumerate principles that inform the goals of our obedience. (We address this in more detail in chapter 3 when we discuss how the Christian worldview influences the goals of environmental stewardship.) An example of a direct command would be the biblical

---

30. Note that while many of the commands described in this section seem ripe for "simple obedience," we do not need to assume that this is the case. In this section, we are merely describing the ways a worldview specifies goals; whether a command yields to simple or considered obedience is an issue of our *response* to a command, not an issue of what that command *describes*.

injunction to "be fruitful and increase in number."[31] This command specifies a practice that is itself a goal: nature should be a fecund place. An example of an indirect command would be the Old Testament injunction against taking a mother bird and her young:

> If you come across a bird's nest beside the road, either in a tree or on the ground, and the mother is sitting on the young or on the eggs, do not take the mother with the young. You may take the young, but be sure to let the mother go, so that it may go well with you and you may have a long life.[32]

The command regarding taking birds is direct but specifies a practice more than a general goal. The goal is specified indirectly: nature should have the ability to reproduce or replenish itself.[33]

Outside of direct or indirect commands, worldviews can influence goals in at least four additional ways: through the history and trajectory provided by worldviews, through the "intuitive consistency" of worldviews, by acting as a "substrate" upon which ethics can fill-in goals, and by providing motivation for the goals. Both worldviews that have a substantial command component, as well as worldviews that do not, can influence goals in these four ways. To understand the first way, through the history and trajectory that worldviews provide, recall that worldviews address five basic questions about the environment: reality, origin, condition, solution, and destiny. These questions not only provide an ontology for the universe, but they also paint a picture of the past, current, and future destiny of reality. That is to say, this past, present, and future history of reality defines a trajectory; presumably, an adherent of any given worldview wants to live in concordance with that trajectory.[34] To that end, the trajectory described by that worldview outlines goals of environmental stewardship. For example, in Buddhism, existence is all there is. Nirvana is reached when we are in complete union with this reality, and this is the endpoint of all (human)

---

31. In the creation account, this command is given both to aquatic creatures and birds (Gen 1:22a) and humanity (Gen 1:28a).

32. Deut 22:6–7.

33. In chapter 3, we specifically address the impact of hermeneutics in interpreting Scriptural commands and enumerate alternate ways of understanding the Deut 22:6–7 command.

34. Note that the imperative that "we should live in concordance with the trajectory of our worldview" is a value assumption that, generally, comes from outside the worldview. Again, we see the difficulty of obtaining an "ought" from an "is." Nonetheless, that value assumption flows out of the foundational nature of worldviews in general, and so it is not that much of a stretch to give the lion's share of the credit to the worldview in specifying the goals criterion, via the trajectory defined by the worldview.

existence. This trajectory, then, becomes a start of a goal of environmental stewardship. In the case of this Buddhism example, a goal that flows from this trajectory might be "to help facilitate human activity that helps lead one to Nirvana."

This example illustrates how a worldview's trajectory can specify the goals criteria. But this example also illustrates that the coherence and specificity of trajectories varies from worldview to worldview. In some worldviews, there is a strong and specific sense of destiny. In the Christian worldview, for instance, all of human and natural history culminates in Christ and the Kingdom of God; "history" is "His story" and "He is before all things, and in him all things hold together."[35] In other worldviews, the sense of destiny is diffuse or non-existent. In the Confucian worldview, for instance, there is no reality beyond our current reality—the universe is a fitting home for us; history is not progressing towards some goal. Thus, to the extent we believe goals of environmental stewardship include living in concordance with our worldview's trajectory, the coherence and specificity of the goals will likely follow the coherence and specificity of the trajectory of our worldview.

The second way worldviews lead to goals (and, to a lesser extent, the importance and practice criterion) is through "intuitive consistency" between the worldview and certain goals. Worldview descriptions utilize metaphors and command frameworks that, by themselves, create a picture of the goals of environmental stewardship.[36] For instance, agrarian metaphors and commands in the Bible can lead those who hold a Christian worldview to an intuitive understanding that the goal of creation care is a pastoral ideal. Similarly, the fluid flow analogy of "going with the flow" that characterizes the Taoist worldview's principle of *wu-wei*, or "letting be," can lead

35. Col 1:17.

36. We also find that language impacts our conceptualization of environmental issues via "intuitive consistency" even outside of the worldviews context. The prominent (or predominant) use of anthropomorphic and biological metaphors in discussions about environmental issues—such as talking about the "health" of the environment, Aldo Leopold's idea of treating the land as if it were a "fellow-member" of our "community" (Leopold, "The Land Ethic," 39), or Arne Naess's conceptualization of nature as an "ecological self" (Naess, "Identification," 246)—exerts an (often ignored) influence on how we conceptualize the goals of environmental stewardship; these kinds of terms can connote much more than they denote. For instance, the word "health" carries with it more than just the meaning of "well-functioning" but, because it is an anthropomorphic and biological metaphor, also a sense of moral import. When people are not healthy we do not treat them as if they were a machine that needs a new part but rather with empathy and even self-sacrifice to help them regain their health. Those connotations automatically become part of the discussion, regardless of the intentions of the parties involved.

to an intuitive sense that the goals of environmental stewardship mimic the behavior of a passive tracer (e.g., a float on the ocean, a leaf on the surface of a stream). In these examples, the connection between the worldview and the goal is implicit rather than explicit; the connection comes through the connotative meaning of the language and concepts of the worldview.

The appeal of intuitive consistency may seem strong: the implied goals appear to directly flow from the language of the worldview. There are, however, strong reasons to question whether intuitive consistency really provides an adequate justification for goals. First, the goal is not explicitly set out in the worldview but rather is implicit. As a result, we might wonder how derivative is the goal from the worldview. Does the goal really flow from the core of the worldview or is the goal peripheral? If the goal is peripheral to the worldview, to what extent can we say the worldview justifies the goal? It may be that the goal is mostly justified by another source with the worldview justification being incidental.

Second, if the worldview values a historical-critical approach to interpretation of its authoritative texts, there is the danger that our intuition concerning the language of the worldview is more conditioned by our culture today rather than the culture of the society in which the sacred documents were written. For instance, we have noted how the Bible often uses agrarian metaphors. But does this use imply the goal of creation care is a pastoral ideal or merely that the way we interpret agrarian metaphors *today* (partly influenced, as modern culture is, by Romanticism) is as if it represents a pastoral ideal? Would the biblical culture have understood agrarian metaphors as representing a pastoral ideal, or would that culture have given those metaphors a different meaning? Put another way, if the Bible were written today, would the language used incorporate agrarian concepts to the same extent or would the language use other concepts (e.g., industrial, technological, etc.) more characteristic of modern culture?

Both reasons suggest we have to be careful when we conclude our worldviews prescribe the goals of environmental stewardship via the intuitive consistency approach. It may be that those goals are actually justified by some other source and that the worldview only weakly, incidentally, or apparently justifies the goals. This concern is not problematic in principle: worldviews can be combined with other determinants (or other worldviews) to justify the goals of environmental stewardship. What is problematic is when the sources of goals are unrecognized. In such a case, we may believe that our worldview prescribes a certain set of goals when our worldview is not the source of the justification. In that case, because worldviews are foundational to who we are, challenges to our understanding of goals may appear as a threatening challenge to our worldview. But, if we realize that our worldview only provides incidental justification for our goals, challenges to those goals may be less threatening to us. For instance, if someone with a Christian worldview adopted a set of goals presumably because of their Christian beliefs, a challenge to those goals might be seen as a challenge to those core worldview beliefs. But, if the goals were justified more by a non-worldview determinant, rather than the Christian worldview, those goals might be more debatable.

Confusion over the justification of goals can also be problematic if our worldview commands a high degree of authority and we mistakenly appropriate that authority to the goals we see as derived from that worldview. For instance, because commands in the Christian worldview have unimpeachable authority, goals that appear to be derived from that worldview may also be seen as having unimpeachable authority. If, however, the source of the goals is actually something else, e.g., Romanticism, then the authority is misappropriated. This can lead to an intensity of advocacy for goals, or a resistance to goals, far greater than warranted by the actual source of justification for the goals.

The third way worldviews lead to the goals of environmental stewardship is by providing a substrate upon which ethical theories operate to fill-in and further define the goals of creation care.[37] This substrate can have an ontological nature to it: if, through our ethical theories, we conclude a goal of creation care is to live in concordance with reality, and worldviews define that reality, our worldview can then add detail and content to the goal of living in concordance with reality. The substrate provided by worldviews can also condition the goals of creation care by providing more fertile ground for certain ethical theories over others. Certain worldviews make certain kinds of moral valuing of nature more difficult to achieve. For instance, an Enlightenment worldview that sees all that exists as merely material, as compared to a Buddhist worldview, offers fewer openings to a Deep Ecology ethic that ascribes independent moral status to all of nature, including ecosystems. As a result, someone holding a Deep Ecology ethic would find it easier to define goals of environmental stewardship by drawing upon a Buddhist worldview versus an Enlightenment worldview.

Finally, and perhaps most frequently, worldviews affect the goals of creation care by providing motivation or impetus for a set of goals that are primarily justified from other sources. Rita Gross, in her work on formulating a Buddhist environmental ethic, gives an example of one such motivation. For Gross, an environmental ethic must decrease human impact

37. An example of this "substrate" role of worldviews, in the context of human ethics in general, is the role a Judeo-Christian account of human dignity plays in grounding a vision of human justice (Kraynak, "Justice Without Foundations," 120).

on the environment, and consumption and population are the drivers of that impact; she then looks for resources in her Buddhist faith tradition to decrease these drivers.[38] One resource she identifies is motivational: drawing from the Buddhist teaching of interdependence and critique of craving (*trishna*), she argues, "So long as limits, whether to consumption or fertility, are regarded as a dreary duty imposed from above and a personal loss, people will resent and try to evade them. But if one experiences such limits not as personal loss but as normal, natural, and pleasant in an interdependent matrix, then they are not a problem."[39] Thus, in this example, the motivation Buddhism provides supports the goal of decreased human impact, by framing the goal as something positive and making the goal more achievable; even if the motivation provided by worldviews is not the primary justification for a set of goals, the motivation can nonetheless be substantial. It is important, however, to remember that if a worldview only provides motivation for a set of goals, debates over those goals can only be resolved by addressing the original justification for the goals, not the worldview motivations for the goals.

WORLDVIEWS AND THE PRACTICE OF THE CREATION CARE COMMAND (HOW TO PUT THE COMMAND INTO ACTION)

While worldviews mainly influence the importance criterion (and, to a lesser extent, the goals criterion), there are a few ways environmental worldviews can yield actions. We can define two categories of ways worldviews affect practice: directly and indirectly.[40] For the direct ways, we can identify at least two such paths. First, worldviews can yield actions through a command component in the worldview. For example, in the Christian worldview, God creates nature and sustains His creation (Heb 1:3). But God is not far from His creation, some distant and remote Prime Mover or First Cause; He also communicates with and interacts with His creation. Through that interaction with His creation, He sometimes instructs us to do a specific action, which those who hold this worldview are compelled to

38. "That consumption and [human] reproduction need to be severely curtailed is rather obvious. But what will convince individuals and groups to make limiting their consumption and reproduction a top priority?" (Gross, "Buddhist Environmental Ethic," 336).

39. Gross, "Buddhist Environmental Ethic," 345.

40. Note that the direct and indirect ways worldviews affect practice is, in general, different from the ways direct and indirect commands in worldviews affect goals.

obey. In our discussion of worldviews and goals, earlier in this chapter, we saw specific examples of how worldviews with a command component can directly specify practice (God's injunction for fecundity, etc.).

While this mechanism is direct and mandatory, such an "action prescribing component" to the worldview might not yield many universal actions, that is, specific actions that everyone has to do. In the example of the Christian worldview, if the commands God gives are personal and individual (whether personal to someone in history or personal to us in the present), the actions prescribed by the worldview may only apply to the individual who receives the command. Those commands would, then, provide limited guidance to others.[41] With regards to environmental stewardship, this implies that while "do not steal" is a universal command to obey, "do not engage in mountain-top mining" may not be.

A second way worldviews can directly affect the practice of creation care is through opposing a negation of an expectation of the worldview. For instance, the Romantic worldview sees humans as appreciators of the aesthetic beauty of nature. This understanding tends to directly oppose actions that prevent such appreciation; examples of such actions include: development that destroys the raw beauty of wilderness, urbanization that hinders the appreciation of such beauty by creating cities where even the signs of nature are pushed out, etc. Thus, the Romantic worldview would directly prescribe opposition to those actions that prevent appreciation of the aesthetic beauty of nature. This does not mean that Romanticism *necessarily* prescribes actions against development, urbanization, etc. (as given in this example). Romanticism might permit some development and some urbanization while opposing other development and urbanization. Worldviews do, however, stand against the negation of the core expectations of the worldview, and thus the worldview would be expected to prescribe actions *of the class* of opposing the negation of the worldview's core expectations.

We can also identify two indirect ways environmental worldviews affect practice. First, worldviews can motivate ethical theories of value of the environment, which in turn yield actions. As we found earlier in our discussion of the importance criterion for environmental stewardship, what we think nature *is* influences our understanding of the value of nature. The value we ascribe to nature can in turn yield actions of care towards those aspects of nature we value. However, we again note that ontologically motivated values do not necessarily rise to the level of moral claims, and so

---

41. They might, for instance, provide a model or example, or they might suggest general principles to follow. Stories of men and women in the Bible are prime examples of both. Abraham models a life of faith for Christians while also suggesting general principles about faith.

even though those values, and the actions of care and preservation based on those values, may be strongly felt, neither the ontologically motivated values nor their concomitant actions of care are necessarily moral imperatives.

The second indirect way worldviews can yield actions is through motivating ethical theories of actions, not directly related to the value of the environment. Some worldviews support a given ethical theory of action better than other worldviews. For example, a reductive, materialist view of nature that tends to see nature as inert and ultimately random quantum mechanical fluctuations (including human beings) would have a more difficult time supporting a virtue ethic, because the idea of a virtue has no ontological meaning. Thus, a reductive, materialist view of nature would not offer much philosophical support for creation care practices that are intertwined with environmental virtues (e.g., wonder, awe, gratitude, humility, etc.). Rather, such a worldview is most supportive of a relativist theory of action;[42] thus, we would expect the materialist worldview to yield ethics that support actions of this nature. Thus, the worldview indirectly yields actions by supporting some ethical theories more than others.

Finally, we consider whether and how practices may feedback to worldviews. As worldviews are foundational, practices, in general, will not affect worldviews. However, it can happen, through what sociologists call "praxis." Normally, our actions follow our thoughts and feelings. We analyze, conceptualize, and elucidate concepts and ideas and then act on the mental understanding we have created. Or, we feel then act, based on those feelings. With praxis, our thoughts and feelings follow our actions. In a similar way, our values and actions can affect our understanding of reality, particularly through a habit built through repetition. For example, someone who purposely, wantonly, and repeatedly vivisects animals will tend to decrease their sense of animals as beings different from inanimate matter. This then can move one towards a worldview that sees all of nature, animate or not, as mere matter. Again, because worldviews are foundational, the effects of praxis are often limited. Nonetheless, because human beings are not linear calculating machines—where A leads to B then C, etc.—what we do affects how we think and feel, and what we do and the values we hold can affect our conceptions of reality.

---

42. A relativist theory of action is one that understands actions as being "justified" by a relativist framework for ethics, where morality is seen as completely context and culture dependent and thus with no objective, normative status. In that case, all actions are devoid of any absolute moral voice.

CONCLUSIONS

The first determinant—environmental worldviews—describes foundational understandings of what nature is, where it has come from, and where it is going. Worldviews describe, literally, what we see when we look at the world. And yet, though worldviews are foundational, their role in determining the criteria for obedience (importance, goals, and practice) are more attenuated than we might assume. Many times, particularly with regards to goals and practice, the effect of worldviews on the criteria for obedience goes through or is influenced by ethical theories. Additionally, we find that the foundational nature of worldviews often means that worldview understandings are broad-brushed and non-specific; worldviews often provide general understandings rather than particular guidance. As a result, when it comes to the influence of worldviews on the content of creation care, worldviews provide an important matrix in which we work out that content, using the other determinants, but worldviews often do not themselves prescribe what environmental stewardship should be.

In this chapter, we focused on a "big-picture" examination of what worldviews provide and what they do not. As a result, we provided only a cursory look at specific worldviews and what each of those worldviews can and cannot offer. In the next chapter, we focus on one particular worldview, the Christian worldview, and unpack what that specific worldview contributes to our understanding of the importance, goals, and practice of creation care. In particular, because the Christian worldview has a robust understanding of an active and sovereign God who reveals Himself personally to His followers and authoritatively through the Scriptures, believers in this worldview are ultimately not free to do whatever they want but are accountable to obey God's revealed will. Given the authority claimed by the Christian revelation, as we examine what the Christian worldview tells us about creation care, it will be doubly important for us to keep in mind the limits of what worldviews can and cannot tell us about the content of environmental stewardship.

DISCUSSION QUESTIONS

1. When you consider your own worldview, how do you see it affecting the importance, goals, and practice criteria? Why?

2. In this chapter, the author argues that worldviews are less prescriptive of the content of environmental stewardship than is acknowledged by conventional wisdom. Do you agree or disagree? Why? If the author

is correct, what are the implications for discussions regarding creation care?

3. The author, in this chapter, argues that many times goals of environmental stewardship are primarily justified by factors besides worldviews and that debates over goals need to recognize the true justifications behind the goals instead of assuming that the worldview provides the primary justification. What do you think of this argument? Agree? Disagree? Why? Have you encountered debates over goals where the argument was putatively over a worldview but seemed to ignore the actual justification for the goals? If so, how might the arguments in this chapter help clear up that kind of debate or make it more productive?

4. Some have pointed out many cultures show a marked disconnect between the presence of "environmentally-friendly" resources in the culture's dominant worldview and the state of the environment in that culture.[43] Does this confirm the present author's argument that worldviews are limited in their power to determine the content of environmental stewardship? Or, is there another reason for the disconnect between worldviews and environmental health? Why?

5. What additional ways, outside of those listed by the author, do worldviews affect the criteria for obedience: importance, goals, and practice? Which of the ways listed by the author would you remove from that list? Why?

43. Kinsley, *Ecology and Religion*, xx–xxi.

3

The Bible Says It

THE CHRISTIAN WORLDVIEW
AND CREATION CARE

A PARABLE, CONTINUED

Gabriel was filling up his glass at the water cooler when Rhonda Takata, the church secretary, told him that a Dr. Joseph Ridley had called yesterday and had made an appointment to see him before lunch. Gabriel looked at the clock and thanked Rhonda, just in time to see Joseph Ridley walk through the door and come over to give Gabriel a big bear hug. Joseph Ridley had been Gabriel's professor in seminary and was in town visiting for the day to give a talk at another school. Gabriel introduced Joseph to Rhonda and the two walked back to Gabriel's office.

"How're things going, Gabriel?" asked Joseph. "It's been years since you were in my theology course."

"Things are well overall, Joseph," Gabriel replied. "It really has been too long since we've last talked. But, actually, the timing of your visit couldn't have been better. There's a row in my church over the issue of creation care that I wanted to ask you about." Gabriel then described the recent events.

"And so," he concluded, "maybe one of the biggest things I don't quite understand is how different people in the church, even though they share a common relationship with God and

46

view of the Bible, can come up with such diametrically conflict-ing views of what creation care practice should look like."

Joseph Ridley looked thoughtful. After a long pause, he said, "I saw there's a nice park behind the church. Why don't we "take a turn in it," as Jane Austen might say, and continue our conversation there." Gabriel said, "Sure," and the two men went outside.

The evening before, there had been a short rain, and so the air was heavy with the crisp mustiness that follows. Birds flew overhead, darting around the tall oak trees that lined the path around the park. Gabriel and Joseph walked past a rose garden that had been recently pruned. Shoots had already started com-ing out, revealing thin, waxy leaves, half-unfurled. Across the field they could see the open plot of land set aside for the com-munity garden. Though most of the planting would not happen for a few weeks still, some of the soil had already been turned, and the smell of fresh earth blew past them with the breeze.

"You know I grew up on a farm," said Joseph. Gabriel nod-ded. "And while a suburban park isn't exactly "the fruited plains," one can feel a connection here with the land that is lost in the concrete jungle."

"Yes, I know what you mean," replied Gabriel. "And even though I never stepped foot on a farm until you took me to visit your family's farm while I was in seminary, I can see a glimpse of how much the land can live in a man's soul."

Gabriel and Joseph walked on. A car drove by on the road outside the park. "Yes," Joseph continued, "the land helps me understand who I am. What do you think the biblical writers would have said about the land?"

Gabriel thought a moment and replied, "I suspect they would talk about it in similar terms. After all, their society was primarily agricultural."

"Perhaps," said Joseph, "but perhaps not." He continued. "Yes, the biblical writers lived in an agrarian society, but it seems to me that this can result in the opposite conclusion. That is, the meaning of the terms they use may be *different* than how we would use those terms, because they lived in an agrarian society."

"What do you mean?" said Gabriel.

"Well, what I mean is that a society that daily, even hourly, enjoys the fruit God has provided through the land but also has to wrest that fruit out by sweat and tears, will find different meanings in words like "fruit," "land," "nature," and "wilderness."

And so, perhaps the way the Bible tells us about creation care is less straightforward than we think."

Gabriel furrowed his brow. "Are you saying that we can't understand what the Bible is saying about how to care for the environment?"

"No," replied Joseph, "that's not what I'm saying at all. God cares about His creation, and the Bible's story of redemption is intertwined with that care. However, to answer your original question, I am saying that how *we* understand that care and then translate that care into concrete actions for today may be less straightforward than we would hope. Perhaps, in the midst of that translation, there is some room for multiple views."

Gabriel was absorbed in thought. They had finished one circuit around the park. As they started a second turn, Gabriel wondered to himself whether Joseph's explanation made things easier and clearer or more difficult.

INTRODUCTION

In this chapter, we build upon the brief summary provided in chapter 2 by providing a more detailed description of the Christian environmental worldview and by exploring how that worldview affects the criteria for obedience (importance, goals, and practice).[1] Our summary and analysis of the Christian worldview will not be comprehensive. Indeed, given the vast number of works published in the last several decades exploring the theology of creation care, we would be surprised to find a comprehensive summary this brief.[2] Still, our summary will highlight the most important issues to consider as we move towards defining the content of creation care and will provide a basis for evaluating what the Christian worldview can and cannot prescribe.

1. In this chapter and throughout much of the book, the tenets of Christianity that we present are ones that would generally be shared by all major branches of Christianity: Protestant, Catholic, and Orthodox. Even in cases where we draw upon the work of a specific community (e.g., Catholic social teaching), the theological, ontological, and anthropological views are ones that would be shared by Christians from all the major traditions. Of course, each tradition has its own emphases and may make conclusions different than the ones we make in this book, but what we Christians share is of much greater import than what divides us.

2. Philosophy and religion scholars Wesley J. Wildman and Charles Demm have compiled a formidable bibliography of works on eco-theology and ecological ethics (Wildman and Demm, "Bibliography").

We begin by describing what the Bible teaches in these four areas: its view of reality, how reality is known, the role of nature for humanity, and what is the human vocation relative to nature.[3] Second, we describe two different emphases using this biblical description that are currently found in the evangelical church: the "stewardship" model and the "dominionism" model. In briefly comparing and contrasting these two models, we will find another example of how the Christian worldview, like worldviews in general, often lacks the ability of prescribing, by itself, the content of creation care. Third, because Christians are "people of the Word," in order to understand the possible ways of connecting a Christian worldview to the criteria for obedience, we need to examine different biblical hermeneutics for the creation care command. Finally, we will explore various ways the Christian worldview influences the criteria for obedience to the creation care command.

WHAT THE BIBLE TEACHES

Its View of Reality

The Christian worldview's view of natural reality can be summed up in one word: creation. But what does that mean? Contrary to what the public debate over origins suggests, creation is not primarily about the creating mechanism. Rather, the doctrine of creation means that reality is created, sustained, and redeemed by a transcendent and good God. We will consider each one of these attributes of creation in turn.

For creation to be created means, first, that there is a creator outside of nature who does the creating. All of reality (natural and supernatural) is one of two categories: created or non-created.[4] God is the only entity in the second category; He is the only entity that is not created. Everything else is in the first category. (As an aside, in the Christian worldview, to say something is created is not the same as saying it is material. There are entities that are created yet are non-material, such as angels, transcendentals like joy, ethics, etc.)[5] Nature being created, then, means nature came *from* something. *Where* nature came from is what is key to being created, not *how* nature was made. Historically, within Christianity, there has been a variety of views regarding the "how" question, including young-earth creationism,

---

3. Clifton-Soderstrom, "Summary."
4. Carter, "Should Christians."
5. Ibid.

old-earth creationism, and evolutionary creationism.[6] What all Christian views of origins—of the "how"—share is the idea that nature came from God.

God, however, is not merely responsible for bringing the world into being. He sustains and redeems His creation. God has not left the world to fend for and run itself, but God is intimately and continuously involved in the life of the world: "The Son is the radiance of God's glory and the exact representation of his being, sustaining all things by his powerful word."[7] Without God's work, the world would not run. This sustaining work, however, does not mean that all is right with the world, in its current condition. There is, instead, some sense that the creation is not right: creation is in a "bondage to decay."[8] Creation is, however, not doomed to stay imperfect; God's plan is to redeem her, just as it is His plan to redeem humanity.[9] In fact, creation's liberation will be to be "brought into the freedom and glory of the children of God."[10]

How Reality is Known

Because reality is the work—past, present, and future—of God, creation is understood best through worship of the Creator in light of creation's order, bounty, and beauty. Thus, the identity of creation is not found in creation itself but rather in her Creator. In talking about how reality is known, we can apply the opening lines from the Westminster Shorter Catechism, because what that Catechism says regarding people applies to creation too:

> Q1: What is the chief end of man?
> A1: Man's chief end is to glorify God, and to enjoy Him for ever.[11]

This idea, that the value of something finds its source in God, is known as "theocentrism."

When considering the question of how reality is best known, we should also note that in the Christian worldview the identity of knowledge itself, like the rest of creation, is also fundamentally from God rather than

---

6. Physicists Deborah and Loren Haarsma provide an excellent survey of Christian views regarding origins (Haarsma and Haarsma, *Origins*).

7. Heb 1:3a.

8. Rom 8:21.

9. Rom 8:18–25.

10. Rom 8:21.

11. "Westminster Shorter Catechism."

fundamentally independent of God. Unlike Enlightenment understandings of knowledge as "out there" and self-extant, the Christian view of knowledge is bound up intimately with God: Jesus, in fact, is the "Logos" or Word, and is "true light"[12] Thus, the Christian worldview sees creation, both as the object of knowing and as the knowing itself, as proceeding from God and known, ultimately, in terms of who God is.

The Role of Nature for Humanity

In the Christian worldview, the role of nature for humanity has at least two facets. First, nature serves as a witness to God's providence and goodness: His care, love, creativity, grace, and bounty.[13] Through nature and God's care for nature, we see His lovingkindness and mercy. The rain falls on the just and unjust and He sees the fall of even the sparrow.[14] Nature, however, also has an instrumental role, as a resource for sustaining God's people. As God says in His covenant with Noah, echoing but extending His covenant with Adam and Eve, "Everything that lives and moves about will be food for you. Just as I gave you the green plants, I now give you everything."[15] Thus, nature has a dual role: nature is not merely raw materials for people but neither is it *not* a source of raw materials. And these roles ultimately are contained neither in nature itself nor in humanity's view of nature; the identity of nature (and all of creation) is ultimately found in God and His valuing of her.[16]

What is the Human Vocation Relative to Nature

Relative to the environment, the vocation of humanity is as a steward of creation. A steward manages the property of the owner; a steward is a temporary caretaker. This management, however, is marked by care and

12. John 1:9. Krista Bontrager provides a concise summary of the argument that God is the author of knowledge (Bontrager, "God as the Source").

13. For instance, Rev 4:11. Richard Young describes the creativity of God, as shown in nature, in these terms: "The cosmos could also be considered as an artistic expression of a creative mind. We can see the hand of God in creation, just as we see the hand of Rembrandt in his paintings. By analogy, we know that God's creation is special to Him, because He poured Himself into what He created." (Young, *Healing the Earth*, 85)

14. Matt 5:45, 10:29.

15. Gen 9:3.

16. "God is the measure of all things, not humans. God is the ultimate good, not life. God is the beginning and end, not Earth. In such a vision, as portrayed in Dante's mystic rose at the end of his monumental classic *The Divine Comedy*, all things exist to praise God." [emphasis in original] (Bouma-Prediger, *Beauty of the Earth*, 120)

service. Stewards have a relationship not only to the owner but also with those for whom the resources are intended for as well as the personal needs of the steward.[17] Stewards also have an obligation to steward the things they have been given in accordance with the wishes of the owner,[18] and stewards are judged on whether they earn a return for the owner.[19] Stewards do, however, exercise some level of autonomy; they are creative and have real responsibility.

THE "STEWARDSHIP" AND "DOMINIONISM" MODELS

Within modern evangelicalism, there are a number of models or "flavors" of the Christian environmental worldview we outlined above. Two particular models, however, capture much of the range in the Christian environmental worldview: the "stewardship" model and the "dominionism" model, and so we will focus our discussion on these two models.[20] The two models are summarized in the two major evangelical declarations regarding creation care that we discussed in chapter 1, On the Care of Creation: An Evangelical Declaration on the Care of Creation[21] ("Evangelical Declaration") and The Cornwall Declaration on Environmental Stewardship[22] ("Cornwall Declaration"). In this section, we briefly compare and contrast the two models. The disagreement between the two models as how to implement the Christian worldview provides another example of the limits of worldviews to prescribe the content of creation care.

The earliest modern environmentalist critiques found Christianity wanting and guilty of contributing a great deal to environmental degradation.[23] Advocates of the stewardship model have led the rebuttal, arguing that this critique incorrectly links Christianity to the Enlightenment values that bear the lion's share of the responsibility for modern environmental

17. See theologian R. Scott Rodin's description of the general nature of a steward (Rodin, *Stewards*, 30).

18. At the same time, E. Calvin Beisner reminds us that the service is to be rendered to God, not nature *per se*, and argues further that, "Rather, man's cultivating the earth is designed, as Old Testament commentators C. F. Keil and Franz Delitzsch point out, to cause the earth to serve man . . ." (Beisner, *Garden Meets Wilderness*, 15).

19. Matt 25:14–30.

20. One alternate model, "reconciliation ecology," emphasizes the embeddedness of humanity in nature and argues the stewardship mentality creates too large of a gap between people and the environment (Warners et al., "Reconciliation Ecology," 227–28).

21. EEN, "Evangelical Declaration."

22. Cornwall Alliance, "Cornwall Declaration."

23. Bouma-Prediger, *Beauty of the Earth*, chapter 3.

degradation and that a truly biblical worldview is stewardship oriented, not abusive to the environment.[24] The focus of the stewardship model understands the Christian worldview as supportive—indeed, demanding—of an environmental ethic characterized by care. Steven Bouma-Prediger, for instance, notes that the rulership of human beings over creation is to be marked by service:

> For example, Genesis 2:5 speaks of humans serving the earth (*ādām* is to *ʿābad* the *ʾădāmâ*). And Genesis 2:15—the last part of which is painted on the door of every Chicago police car—defines the human calling in terms of service: We are to serve (*ʿābad*) and protect (*šāmar*). We are to serve and protect the garden that is creation—literally be a slave to the earth for its own good, as well as for our benefit.[25]

In the stewardship model, this emphasis of care and service is intertwined with a vision of nature as a place of blessing and goodness and humanity as interconnected with nature.[26] Such perspectives, argue stewardship model advocates, are integral to a life of "harmony" with nature and a wise, restrained, and gentle use of nature's resources.[27]

The dominionism model, in contrast to the stewardship model, places greater emphasis on the dominion or rule of human beings over nature. The label "dominionism" comes from the use of the term "dominion" given in the King James Version of Gen 1:26: "And God said, Let us make man in our image, after our likeness: and let them have dominion over the fish of the sea, and over the fowl of the air, and over the cattle, and over all the earth, and over every creeping thing that creepeth upon the earth."[28] In highlighting the rule of humankind over nature, dominionism places an emphasis on human exceptionalism—the view that human beings are special and unique in the created orders—as well as on the authority we have in exercising stewardship of the environment. This authority gives human beings the

24. See Bouma-Prediger, *Beauty of the Earth,* chapters 3–4; McGrath, *Reenchantment,* 28–31, 99; and Young, *Healing the Earth,* chapter 1.

25. Bouma-Prediger, *Beauty of the Earth,* 74.

26. Ibid., 95.

27. Larry Rasmussen, for instance, in laying out an ethic of Christian environmental responsibility, argues that, "Perspectives should be fostered that regard humanity as an integral part of nature and that promote stewardly harmony with nature rather than conquest. Furthermore, material resource use should reward conserving rather than spending, preserving rather than discarding" (Rasmussen, "Creation, Church," 129).

28. In the New International Version of Gen 1:26, the King James Version's phrase "have dominion over" is rendered "rule over."

duty to creatively transform the world to make it more productive.[29] In both of these emphases, dominionism offers a corrective to versions of the stewardship model whose understandings of being human shade towards too much commonality with the rest of creation. On the other hand, the focus on human exceptionalism may give license to human beings to do whatever they want with nature, including treating nature as a mere commodity. Critics of dominionism fear that focusing on the exercise of "dominion over" nature will lead to "domination over" nature.

Without wading too deeply into the debate between the stewardship and dominionism models, we can still use the contrast between the two models to help us better understand what the Christian worldview can and cannot do. On a number of levels, the difference between the stewardship and dominionism models is more a difference in emphasis—regarding the nature of humanity's rulership over nature— rather than a core difference. Both models agree that God created nature. Both models recognize human beings as exercising delegated rulership over the earth; though the stewardship model emphasizes human commonality with nature, the model recognizes human beings do have a special role. [30] Additionally, dominionism, though emphasizing human authority over nature, would not claim that human beings ultimately "own" nature, agreeing with those holding the stewardship model that only God is the true "owner" of nature.[31] Accordingly, dominionism would not claim that the ultimate value of nature (and human beings) lies in human valuing of nature; rather, both models believe the ultimate value of all creation lies in God's valuing of His handiwork. Granted, dominionism has such a strong sense of human vice-regency over

29. For instance, E. Calvin Beisner argues that in Genesis, there was a distinction between the Garden and the rest of the world; the Garden was to be tilled while the rest of the world was to be subdued so that it might become like the Garden:

> In short, it would have made little sense to tell Adam to subdue and rule the Garden. It was already in perfect order, and succeeding Biblical imagery indicates that it was a type of both the sanctuary and the New Jerusalem—through them of heaven itself. But the rest of the earth apparently lacked some of the fullness of the perfection of the Garden. It was Adam's task to transform all of the earth (to subdue and rule it) into a Garden while guarding the original Garden lest it lose some of its perfection and become like the unsubdued earth. (Beisner, *Garden Meets Wilderness,* 13)

See ibid., 167, for more on the creativity of human beings and creation care.

30. Bouma-Prediger, *Beauty of the Earth,* 94.

31. Dominionism would, however, be wary that an emphasis on God's ultimate ownership not be construed as denying the "subordinate ownership" human beings may exercise (Beisner, *Garden Meets Wilderness,* 166).

creation that at times it may seem that dominionism shades towards a view of God as an absentee landlord. Conversely, the stewardship model's view of human vice-regency may seem like it is a rulership without any ruling. Still, this level of disagreement between the two models, while substantial, is not fundamental. The two views can be bridged if dominionists add more emphasis to an immanent theocentrism and the contingent nature of humanity's dominion over nature and those holding a stewardship model give more emphasis on human exceptionalism. Both models are Christian worldviews.

But if both models are fundamentally Christian worldviews, what explains the conflict between these two visions of creation care? One answer is that the non-fundamental aspects of each worldview model provide "thick" enough ground on which to support divergent views. For instance, both may share a theocentric vision, but one's emphasis on tilling and the other's on subduing may be enough on which to build different "schools of thought" as to the content of creation care. But if so, what does it say about the prescriptive power of worldviews if the core parts of a worldview are not strong enough to bring agreement as to what creation care should look like?[32] If the non-fundamental aspects of a worldview are this important to determining our ideas as to the content of creation care, perhaps the worldview itself, *qua* worldview, plays a limited role in that determination, or, at least, a role that can be overcome or superseded by the non-fundamental aspects of the worldview.

A second answer is that the disagreement between the dominionism and stewardship models is actually over secondary, non-worldview issues. Areas of disagreement may include differing understandings of ethics (e.g., the value of nature), economics (e.g., the desirability of economic growth), and the role of government in solutions.[33] E. Calvin Beisner, recounting a

32. Perhaps this is a fundamental weakness of worldviews and is responsible for the inability, as noted by E. Calvin Beisner, of the "doctrine of dominion" to prescribe the content of creation care:

> One problem with the doctrine of dominion, however, is that it simply does not give direct, pat answers to lots of the specific questions that arise in environmental discussions. Should we drill for oil? Here? How? Should we mine coal? There? By boring (which is much more dangerous to the miners), or strip-mining (which can leave ugly scars on the land, although the scars can be restored to beauty)? (ibid., 17)

33. Robert H. Nelson argues that the modern era is host to a "war" between two "religions," one centered on environmentalism and one on economics:

> This book finds that the leading secular movements of our times are essentially religious in character, drawing on the various Christian

debate he had with Ronald Sider over what an evangelical environmental-ism should look like, makes just such a point: "There was indeed spirited debate, but not much over theological issues. On those, for the most part, Sider and I saw eye to eye."[34] Elsewhere, Beisner notes his critique engages in a broad range of topics outside of theology:

> The remainder of this book will interact with various theologi-cal, ethical, political, scientific, economic, and polemical aspects of some of the more important literature emanating from these and other evangelical environmental groups and individuals. While there is much to commend about evangelical environ-mental activities, our goal will be to identify some of its weak-nesses and to suggest ways to correct them.[35]

The list Beisner provides covers many of the determinants of the criteria for obedience we enumerated in chapter 1. Thus, if this second explanation for the debate between the stewardship and dominionism models is cor-rect, it suggests that, at least in this debate between competing visions of the content of creation care, worldview considerations only contribute so much; the other determinants of the criteria for obedience play a substantial role

---

traditions that produced Western civilization. The two most important secular movements of the late twentieth century were "economic re-ligion" and "environmental religion," both of them "religions" in the sense that they have comprehensive worldviews and myths that provide human beings with the deepest sense of meaning. The story of "eco-nomic religion" is that human beings can produce an ideal world, or heaven on earth, by ending material poverty through productivity, effi-ciency, and scientific management. The "religion of environmentalism" has emerged to protest economic religion, however, and has fought this counter-battle by presenting its own worldview and religious story. This message says that we once had an ideal world, or Eden, which was destroyed by progress, economic growth, and industry, and that we must repent and return to Eden. In other words, as I have argued in this book, the clash between "economic religion" and "environment [sic] religion" took place in the late twentieth century on the same scale as the clash of Roman Catholicism and Protestantism in the sixteenth and seventeenth centuries, minus the bloodshed, of course. Their con-flict has shaped our social debate on the place of human beings in the natural world and our hopes for material and spiritual well-being—the new holy wars of our time. (Nelson, *New Holy Wars*, 348–49)

34. Beisner, *Garden Meets Wilderness*, 10. While neither Beisner nor Sider should be pigeon-holed into one "camp" or another, it is fair to say that Beisner tends more towards the dominionism model than Sider and Sider tends more towards the steward-ship model than Beisner.

35. Ibid., 7.

and must be considered. And, if the Christian worldview, which has a substantial command component to it, is limited in this way as a prescriptive force for the content of environmental stewardship, other non-Christian worldviews may also exhibit the same limitation.

DIFFERENT BIBLICAL HERMENEUTICS FOR THE CREATION CARE COMMAND: GETTING FROM WORLDVIEW TO CRITERIA FOR OBEDIENCE

Christianity is a revealed religion: God reveals Himself corporately through the written Word and personally to individuals.[36] As a result, our principles of interpretation—hermeneutics—play a crucial role in understanding how to connect the Christian worldview to the criteria for obedience. In this section, we summarize different hermeneutical principles used in understanding the biblical commands regarding creation. This will complete our preparation for examining how the Christian worldview influences the criteria for obedience.

Christians are "people of the Word," but there is both the personal Word and the written Word, as God speaks to people both personally as well as through Scripture (though the status of the two Words, as we will see, are different). The Christian God is not the god of Deism, removed by both space and time and thus uninvolved in present life. God is present and is Himself the Present; He wants us to hear and follow His loving voice. Thus, in any analysis of the ways of understanding the biblical commands regarding creation, we need to first recognize that there are (at least) two sources for commands that Christians are given.

In describing the personal Word, we first recognize that by its very nature, it is difficult to codify a set of rules that govern it. Like in any relationship, what God says to someone is a word to that person: it is not merely a communication but a conversation and communion. The personal Word can come through to us in various ways, for instance, through prayer

---

36. Between the three major branches of Christianity—Roman Catholic, Protestant, and Eastern Orthodox—there are differences in the role of the church in how God reveals Himself. The approach we take in this book is generally Protestant Evangelical. Still, the differences between the three major branches play a relatively minor role in terms of understanding how the Christian worldview affects the criteria for obedience and, for the most part, are subsumed into our categories of different ways to connect revelation to the criteria. For instance, the Roman Catholic church treats papal encyclicals with much greater weight than Protestants would, but much of the hermeneutical work done in these encyclicals use one or more of the principles we describe in this section.

and meditation, in visions, via circumstances, through the counsel of the church, or by an audible voice. God also can speak His personal Word to us through His written Word. Still, despite the difficulty in codifying the personal Word, we can generalize two principles that apply to most circumstances and that are useful for creation care issues. First principle: The personal Word cannot contradict the written Word. If the Bible is "God-breathed"[37] and if God is self-consistent, then it is inconsistent for a Christian to claim a personal Word from God in direct contradiction to written revelation. Second principle: The written Word takes precedence over the personal Word. Throughout the history of the church, the written Word has been understood as authoritative in faith and life.[38] As C. S. Lewis has said, in talking about the authority of the imagery Scripture uses to picture heaven, "It [the imagery] comes to us from writers who were closer to God than we, and it has stood the test of Christian experience down the centuries."[39] We would be wise to assume Scripture tests our apprehension of God's words to us, rather than the reverse. Still, we recognize that while these two principles are robust, how they apply in a particular case can be complicated. Consider, for instance, the vision of Peter described in Acts 10 of ceremonially unclean animals that Peter was commanded by God to eat, despite their unclean status. "The voice spoke to him a second time, 'Do not call anything impure that God has made clean.'"[40] It is clear that God had altered an Old Testament-era understanding in a direct command to Peter; the way He did so, in light of the two principles we outlined above, may not yield to simple systemization.

In this brief description of the personal Word and the two principles comparing the personal Word to the written Word, we see that the personal Word is not something that should be considered in a vacuum, but that the written Word is not and should not be far away. Indeed, our understanding of the personal Word, regardless of whether it comes through prayer, meditation, etc., often comes to us intertwined in a dialogue with the written Word, and it is through that dialogue our understanding of the personal Word is formed. All this is to say that even though the personal Word is personal and individualized, the principles of hermeneutics we use for understanding the written Word still apply to the personal Word. It will not do for us to say that we have a personal Word from God, and thus, we do

---

37. 2 Tim 3:16.

38. The three major branches of Christianity would differ on the source of the authority of Scripture, but all three branches consider Scripture authoritative.

39. Lewis, "Weight of Glory," 9.

40. Acts 10:15.

not need to worry about how to interpret God's Word to us. Hermeneutics matter, even with regards to the personal Word.

With that in mind, we consider the range of possible hermeneutical principles for the creation care command. In chapter 2, we saw how in worldviews with a strong command component, commands can be direct or indirect. Here, we add more details to that categorization, as applied to the interpretation of Scripture. One way we can interpret biblical commands regarding creation care is literally as written, so that the commands as given to the original hearers/readers are exactly how they are given to all possible readers, regardless of location in time and space. Thus, in our chapter 2 example of the Deut 22:6–7 command about not taking a mother bird with her young, we would implement that command by doing exactly that: taking only the eggs or chicks of any nesting mother birds and leaving the mother bird alone. A second possible hermeneutical principle is to take the commands as applying literally in the context in which they were given but analogously in our own current context.[41] In the mother bird example, this might mean we understand that command as being a literal expectation for the ancient Israelites but that for ourselves, the bird is analogous to all forms of life and thus we are to follow the command with respect to all creatures. Third, we can take the biblical commands regarding creation care figuratively, literarily, or theologically, for instance, as expressions of God's love, as a warning to recognize limits, etc.[42] Thus, in our mother bird example, we might conclude this passage teaches us the importance of preserving the ability of nature to sustain itself without assuming there is any universal expectation to leave a mother bird (or any other particular species) undisturbed. Roughly, these three ways of interpreting Scripture with regards to creation care mirrors three of the categories in the typology given by ethicist James M. Gustafson: the Bible as a source of "moral law," "moral analogies," or "moral ideals."[43]

41. Gustafson, "The Place of Scripture," 442–44.

42. This is the strategy taken, for instance, by economist Donald Hay, utilizing systematic theology in his reading of Scripture to identify "theological themes" that inform his understanding of how to apply the Bible's commands about economics to modern economic life (Hay, *Economics Today*, 13). In a more directly environmental example, Dianne Bergant's interpretation of Hosea 2 finds the use of "creation theology" and the prophetic function and structure of the passage to offer a modern-day ecological critique of human arrogance, a call to return to a "primordial innocence" in how we treat nature, and a praise of "the intrinsic, not merely instrumental, value of nature" (Bergant, "Hosea 2," 13–14).

43. Gustafson, "The Place of Scripture," 439–45, 455. Gustafson's typology includes a fourth category, which we do not include.

Each of these principles have strengths and weaknesses, and we leave it as a task for more focused works on Christian ethics and eco-theology to provide the arguments for or against each of these hermeneutic principles, as well as to enumerate other possible principles.[44] For our purposes, it is enough to recognize that there is a spectrum of different ways of interpreting God's creation care commands and that these three principles are not necessarily mutually exclusive. Sometimes we may emphasize one principle more than another while other times we may use two or three of these principles together. In the next section, we will see how differences in hermeneutics can affect how the Christian worldview influences the criteria for obedience.

THE CHRISTIAN WORLDVIEW AND IMPORTANCE, GOALS, AND PRACTICE OF THE CREATION CARE COMMAND

Having summarized what the Bible teaches about reality and the relationship between human beings and nature, the stewardship and dominionism models, and different hermeneutics for interpreting the biblical commands regarding creation care, we can address the influence of the Christian environmental worldview on the criteria for obedience. In this section, we begin by examining four special ways the Christian worldview, as opposed to most other worldviews, affects the criteria for obedience. Then, we consider each of the criteria for obedience—importance, goals, and practice—in turn and discuss how the Christian worldview influences each criterion.

Special Ways the Christian Worldview Influences the Criteria for Obedience

We can identify at least four special ways the Christian worldview interacts with the criteria for obedience. First, and perhaps foremost, Christianity is a religion centered on a relationship with a Person. The God Christians worship is Someone we are in relationship with, not an impersonal force

---

44. Christian ethicist Charles H. Cosgrove, for instance, describes additional possible hermeneutical principles we can use in applying Scripture to ethical decisions (Cosgrove, *Appealing To Scripture*). One such principle he proposes argues against the "Scripture as law" mode we described above, instead contending that "The purpose (or justification) behind a biblical moral rule carries greater weight than the rule itself" (ibid., 3). This is not to say that moral rules have no role in Christian ethics but only that the justification is more important than the rule as a rule (ibid., 50).

for good, a divine principle, or even a distant deity. Thus, the creation care commands God gives are commands that come to us from Someone and are relationally embedded rather than disembodied principles. We are stewards working for a Master, not bureaucrats to a government or employees to an organization. As a result, our conclusions about importance, goals, and practice of creation care commands ultimately come out of dialogue and communion with God, though they are also informed by thought and reason. Communion involves supra-rational considerations, including trust and trustworthiness, knowledge through intimacy, and relational history. These aspects are not only personal but also depend, ultimately, on our actual relationship with God.

We can see this relational dependence in explorations of other commands God gives. Although the Bible and spiritual classics like Saint Augustine's *Confessions* or Saint Teresa of Avila's *The Life of Teresa of Jesus* can be fruitfully read for their historical, philosophical, theological, and psychological value, there is another kind of understanding accessible only to those who see with the "eyes of faith," who not only give their interest or their attention to God and His commands but give *themselves* to Him. Some knowledge is only accessible by being "inside"; mere spectating will not do.[45] We can only learn so much about prayer without praying; we can only learn so much about love without loving.

Because of the relational nature of Christianity, we need to be careful in generalizing what God has shown us personally and through our individual stories into normative principles for others to follow. Some aspects will generalize but others will not. In some cases, what God has shown us or asked us to do will be specific to our own lives and relationship with Him. Indeed, some of what God has shown us cannot be even *understood* (let alone practiced) by others, because what we have learned and experienced is unique to our own history and narrative. We are alone with God when it comes to being "inside" ourselves; everyone else is a spectator. None of this

---

45. In a memorable passage, C. S. Lewis describes this difference as looking "at" versus "along" something:

> A young man meets a girl. The whole world looks different when he sees her. Her voice reminds him of something he has been trying to remember all his life, and ten minutes casual chat with her is more precious than all the favours that all other women in the world could grant. He is, as they say, 'in love.' Now comes a scientist and describes this young man's experience from the outside. For him it is all an affair of the young man's genes and a recognized biological stimulus. That is the difference between looking *along* the sexual impulse and looking *at* it. [emphasis in original] (Lewis, "Toolshed," 212)

is to say that the creation care command is merely relative to individuals; it is, rather, to say we need to be humble in extracting categorical imperatives from what is "only" a personal Word to us.

The second special way the Christian worldview interacts with the criteria for obedience is due to the importance of hermeneutics. Because Christians are people who both read and are read by the Word, interpretational frameworks matter, in at least two ways. One way hermeneutics matter is by affecting which commands have Scriptural backing and authority. We saw earlier that there are multiple hermeneutical frameworks one can use to interpret what the Bible says about creation care. But, depending on which hermeneutic principle we use, some creation care commands or positions will have Scriptural justification and authority while others will not. For instance, if we only permit "literal-as-written" interpretations without any adjustments for context, we will obtain few commands that can be justified on the basis of Scripture because there are relatively few direct creation care commands. If we use a less restrictive figurative hermeneutic, we will obtain quite a few creation care commands from Scripture, because a figurative reading will produce a larger number of pertinent principles and ideas we can apply to creation care issues. Thus, in the first example, Scriptural authority is applied to relatively few areas of creation care while in the second example, Scriptural authority is applied to many more areas of creation care.

Another way hermeneutics matter is in helping set the level of standing or import of the creation care command. Different commands, as we have seen, may have different levels of standing/import. To some, the hermeneutical assumptions that were used in obtaining the commands may affect the level of standing/import of the command. For example, a direct command may be seen a different kind of command than an indirect one based on a principle of care, and direct commands may be understood as carrying more import than indirect commands. This may be true because indirect commands require more interpretation and can, as we noted earlier, lead to a larger range of possible goals and practices. As a result, indirect commands may seem less focused and more diffuse: "Do this" makes us sit up and take notice; "do this or this or this or this or this or this" may merely make us cock our heads. (Whether we *should* understand direct and indirect commands differently from one another is another matter.) Thus, if we use a literal hermeneutic to obtain direct commands versus a figurative hermeneutic that leads more to indirect commands, we may obtain commands with very different levels of standing.

The third special way the Christian worldview influences the criteria for obedience is due to the "hybrid" way it understands the ontology of nature. By seeing the universe as being both material and non-material, the Christian worldview has a "both/and" rather than "either/or" ontology, and the importance, goals, and practice of the creation care command have to make sense of both attributes of reality. Under the Christian worldview, we cannot reduce everything to mere matter, as in Enlightenment materialism, nor reduce everything to mere existence, as in pantheistic religions like Buddhism. This hybrid ontology has a particularly pronounced effect with regards to the goals criterion, and we will examine the effect in more detail when we address goals.

Finally, the fourth special way the Christian worldview affects the criteria for obedience is through the contingency that comes from considering God's transcendence and immanence. Because God is the center of reality, and He is both not of and in the world, what we see or can know must be a subset of ultimate reality. Thus, we have to be careful that our justifications for creation care and the goals of creation care are contingent and provisional; creation is dependent on something not of it and so our knowledge of creation must be partial. This contingency is reflected in personal humility. This contingency is also reflected in a recognition that our solutions cannot fully encompass all that creation means. Eschatologically, the re-creation of creation is the joining of heaven and earth.[46] Our creation care, however, falls short of this, even as we desire to partner with God in that work, because this is the work of God.

The Christian Worldview and the Importance of the Creation Care Command

Using the worldview taxonomy we derived in chapter 2, the elaboration of the Christian worldview we provided earlier in the present chapter, and keeping in mind the special ways the Christian worldview affects the criteria for obedience, we can make further comments as to what the Christian worldview tells us about the importance of the creation care command. As we have already seen, regardless of whether one chooses the stewardship or dominionism model, under the Christian worldview creation care is a command from God and an integral part of what God means for us to be human. Creation care is part of our worship of God, our relationship of love with God, and is part of our responsibilities as image-bearers of God and servants of God. The value preferences attached to the ontology of the

---

46. Bouma-Prediger, *Beauty of the Earth*, 125–26; Johnson, "Biblical Theology of the Environment," 14–16.

Christian worldview is a core preference that can rise to a moral demand through Natural Theology (as we described in chapter 2).[47]

However, while a core command, creation care is a derivative command because the universe centers on God and not on itself. Creation care, in the Christian worldview, is not a "self-justified" or "self-evident" command. The command comes from and is justified by God. On the one hand, this lends the command a high degree of authority. On the other hand, creation care is a command whose priority competes with all other derivative commands, i.e. all the other commands given by God. We expect in some cases the creation command would take priority over other commands but in other cases the importance of the non-creation care commands may be higher. Thus, while the creation care command is important, we should not expect it to automatically have priority over God's other commands. If so, other determinants will likely have something additional to say about the importance of the creation care command; we explore this in later chapters.

The Christian Worldview and the Goals of the Creation Care Command

In chapter 2 we created a taxonomy of ways that worldviews affect the goals of environmental stewardship. In this section, we apply that taxonomy to the Christian worldview and enumerate five claims the Christian worldview makes about the goals criterion. The first three claims are ways the Christian worldview suggests creation care goals. These first three claims will not follow the order of the taxonomy we gave in chapter 2. Instead, we start with the 30,000 feet view and examine the core, overall goal of creation care, based on the trajectory of history provided by the Christian worldview. Next, we examine the kinds of goals given by direct and indirect commands in Scripture. Finally, we explore the goals that arise from "intuitive consistency" with the metaphors used in the Bible. After examining these three ways of obtaining creation care goals, we round out our five claims by describing two general considerations that need to be taken into account when examining what creation care goals arise from the Christian worldview.

First, the core creation care goal described by the Christian worldview comes from the trajectory of the creation-Eden-Fall-redemption-re-creation storyline that the history of the universe is threaded around.[48] As

47. Like all worldviews, the ontology of the Christian worldview does not, in and of itself, transmit the value preferences associated with the ontology.

48. This storyline, and its connection to the creation care command, is ably summarized by theologian R. Boaz Johnson:

we saw earlier in our analysis of worldviews, when a worldview prescribes a trajectory for history, it may be reasonable to assume that our core goal for creation care is to participate in and further that storyline.[49] This is particularly the case when the worldview has a normative authority component to it. If the trajectory of history is uncaused and purposeless, there is no moral imperative to participate in furthering that trajectory; if the trajectory does have a purpose, there may be a moral imperative to further that trajectory. In the Christian worldview, then, the core creation care goal is to participate in and support the redemptive history trajectory that God is authoring.

However, while this goal is robust—God's authority undergirds the goal—the specifics of the goal are somewhat ill-defined. First, what does it mean that creation is fallen and is thus "bent" and how does that affect the goals of creation care? For instance, one evangelical understanding of the Fall is that it introduced physical and/or spiritual death into the world. If that understanding is primary, then an important goal of creation care would be to work against the presence and/or effects of death, in anticipation of the full redemption and re-creation to come. But given that any sustainable ecosystem requires a symbiotic predator-prey relationship, what

---

The creation narrative sets out the importance of the environment as God's creation. The universe is God's first fruits offering to humanity. The human fall into sin sadly results in the complete disjuncture of the relationship between God, humanity, and creation. It leads to environmental and societal de-creation. The laws of the Pentateuch and the worship pattern of the Hebrew Bible were designed to point towards the complexity of this de-creation and desecration of the environment. They also gave God's people the tools to minimize environmental degradation and maximize the enrichment and the renewal of creation. However, it becomes clear these were a provisional solution to the problem of the environment. They pointed to a completely radical act of re-creation in Jesus Christ. The new creation will be fully realized when the Messiah, "the seed of the woman," will come a second time to recreate a new heaven and a new earth. God, humanity, and the creation will then be in complete harmony, a return to the Garden of Eden. It is the resurrection of creation. Until then there will be relative degrees of disharmony and disequilibrium. The mission of the church is to minimize the de-creation and disequilibrium and to maximize the re-creation and equilibrium. This can only happen through a proclamation and living of the holistic gospel—the good news for all humanity and all of creation. (Johnson, "Biblical Theology of the Environment," 16)

49. We recall that neither trajectory nor ontology, by themselves, fully define the goals of creation care (due to the is-ought dichotomy, for instance), but by assuming that we should preserve (or at least respect) the trajectory and ontology of the Christian worldview, both trajectory and ontology tell us something about the goals of creation care.

would it mean to care for creation by working against physical death? This example is, admittedly, something of a straw man. At the same time, it illustrates the difficulty in reading goals from the fact that creation is fallen.

In addition to the difficulty in understanding what the fallenness of creation means for creation care goals, it is also difficult to obtain goals from the fact that creation is to be redeemed and re-created. The eschatological language, describing a creation made new and perfect, while lyrical and beautiful, is non-specific and nearly unintelligible in terms of specifics for the goals of creation care. This is the case whether we interpret the eschatological texts literally or metaphorically. For instance, in the new heavens and earth God dwells with us, but what does that mean for the goals of creation care? Perhaps it means we should strive to return to Him the "best" possible earth for Him to dwell on. If so, what would such a "best" entail? Lush tropical rainforests? A desert environment of desolation that inspires awe? Again, obtaining creation care goals based on the principle of participating in God's re-creating of the universe appears to be a non-trivial task.

While the trajectory of history provides the core creation care goal, because the Christian worldview has a strong command component, some goals are also specified by direct and indirect commands. Eco-theologians have identified a variety of goals that Scripture appears to command. (We note, but do not explore, that the relative importance of these command-derived goals will at least partly depend on the hermeneutical considerations we mentioned earlier in this chapter.) Some creation care goals, as we might expect, are attributes of an ecologically well-functioning world.[50] For example, as we saw in chapter 2, one such goal may be fecundity. Another goal, as environmental studies scholar Calvin B. DeWitt describes, is a "sabbath principle" that specifies the goal of rest for nature after use of its resources by human beings.[51]

Other creation care goals are relational goals, that is, goals related to the relationship between human beings and God and between people and the earth. One such goal is the deepening of our worship of God. Fred Van Dyke, David Mahan, Joseph Sheldon, and Raymond Brand point out how often Christian worship is inward and sadly shallow, "But the Hebrew mind understood that the great power of God is displayed in his *works,* and in the beauty, enjoyment and understanding of them" [emphasis in original].[52]

---

50. We note that the term "well-functioning" has many meanings. We use the term "ecologically" to narrow down the scope of meanings but acknowledge the incompleteness of our discussion here of the goals of a well-functioning ecosystem.

51. DeWitt, "Ecology and Ethics," quoted in McGrath, *Reenchantment,* 29.

52. Van Dyke et al., *Redeeming Creation,* 37.

Scripture is shot through with praise of God for His mighty works shown through nature,[53] and all of life is about the worship of God:

> Blessed be your glorious name, and may it be exalted above all blessing and praise. You alone are the Lord. You made the heavens, even the highest heavens, and all their starry host, the earth and all that is on it, the seas and all that is in them. You give life to everything, and the multitudes of heaven worship you.[54]

Van Dyke et al. argue that if our worship remembers that work, our worship will grow in joy.[55] Thus, one goal of creation care is more vibrant worship of God.

Another relational goal of creation care is the fostering of *shalom* between all parts and aspects of creation, as part of obedience to God's purposes.[56] The term *shalom* is often translated "peace" in English. Unfortunately, the English term often does not capture the breadth of the state of *shalom*. *Shalom* is not merely the absence of conflict, and *shalom* is not ushered in merely by enacting the right political, economic, or environmental regulations. The peace the Christian worldview reveals as a goal of creation care is a "global" and all-encompassing peace.[57] For instance, William Dyrness, in examining instructions in the Hebrew Bible to care for the land and for people, notes that the two are often connected and difficult to separate, "But this is to be expected if all alike reflect God's single blessing, a state that is identified with *shalom* (peace) in the Old Testament (cf. Isa. 55:12; Mal. 2:5)."[58] Thus, that peace is not reducible to biological or ecological functions, but is the state of right relationship between God and all.[59] As Dyrness summarizes:

> We have found that we cannot abstract principles of ecology and stewardship from the theological complex in which they are found. God has created the world as a place where righteousness and beauty will be established. But this involves a system of relationships—among God, his people, and the land—which are all included in the covenant God has established with the earth.

53. Van Dyke et al., *Redeeming Creation*, 35–37.

54. Neh 9:5b–6.

55. Van Dyke et al., *Redeeming Creation*, 35–37.

56. Clifton-Soderstrom, "Response," 17; Dyrness, "Old Testament," 64.

57. Philosopher Nicholas Wolterstorff further notes that the meaning of *shalom* even includes "delight;" the lack thereof renders *shalom* incomplete (Wolterstorff, "Teaching," 23).

58. Dyrness, "Old Testament," 56.

59. Ibid., 64.

There is every encouragement to use wise methods of stewardship, though this is more often assumed than debated. But these
are a part of a larger response to God's covenanting love. When
we respond in obedience, we will enjoy the fruit of the earth,
and the poor will be cared for. When we turn from God, we
can expect ecological disaster and social oppression. And this is
precisely what history and our own experience attest.[60]

Besides through the trajectory of history and direct and indirect commands, the Christian worldview specifies creation care goals through the
intuitive consistency between the worldview's metaphors and description
and certain goals. As we noted in chapter 2, the Bible utilizes metaphors and
command frameworks that themselves create a picture of the goals of the
creation care command. Agrarian metaphors and commands in the Bible,
for instance, can lead to an intuitive sense or understanding that the goals of
creation care involve a pastoral ideal. However, if we use a historical-critical
hermeneutic, it is not clear that such an intuition reflects the worldview per
se rather than the culture of the society in which the Bible was written. If
the Bible were written today, would it contain mainly appeals to agrarian
concepts or also to industrial concepts? Nor, is it necessary that the connotations of the biblical terminology regarding the environment map neatly
into our modern understandings. For instance, the way we understand the
term "wilderness" today is very different from how it was understood in the
past. Environmental historian William Cronon notes that while today many
conceive of wilderness as a positive term, this was not the understanding
of those in biblical times or even of the Western world in the eighteenth
century:

> Go back 250 years in American and European history, and you
> do not find nearly so many people wandering around remote
> corners of the planet looking for what today we would call "the
> wilderness experience." As late as the eighteenth century, the
> most common usage of the word "wilderness" in the English

---

60. Dyrness, "Old Testament," 63–64. Pope John Paul II expresses the centrality of
a right relationship between human beings and God and His purposes as a condition
for proper creation care:

> Man thinks that he can make arbitrary use of the earth, subjecting it
> without restraint to his will, as though it did not have its own requisites
> and a prior God-given purpose, which man can indeed develop but
> must not betray. Instead of carrying out his role as a co-operator with
> God in the work of creation, man sets himself up in place of God and
> thus ends up provoking a rebellion on the part of nature, which is more
> tyrannized than governed by him. (John Paul II, *Centesimus Annus*, 37)

language referred to landscapes that generally carried adjectives far different from the ones they attract today. To be a wilderness then was to be "deserted," "savage," "desolate," "barren"—in short, a "waste," the word's nearest synonym.

Many of the word's strongest associations then were biblical, for it is used over and over again in the King James Version to refer to places on the margins of civilization where it is all too easy to lose oneself in moral confusion and despair. The wilderness was where Moses had wandered with his people for forty years, and where they had nearly abandoned their God to worship a golden idol.[61]

Thus, while the Bible uses agrarian metaphors that paint a rich image of harmony and fecundity, it is not necessarily clear how that image (or parts of that image) is to be normative. An appeal to the intuitive consistency between the worldview's metaphors and description and the goals of creation care may take us only so far.

Having enumerated three ways the Christian worldview provides goals, we finish our discussion of goals by noting two general claims the worldview makes regarding goals of creation care. First, the dual material-spiritual nature of reality the Christian worldview presents means preservation of nature is not only about goals for matter.[62] Because the Christian worldview does not understand nature as merely material, preservation of nature, or God's designs for nature, has an element that is non-materialistic in nature. Thus, we cannot define creation care goals merely in terms of restoring or guiding the environment into some particular material state (though creation care goals also involve the manipulation of matter). We saw earlier that one non-materialistic goal is to give worship to God for His creative work. Another goal may be the inculcating of ecological virtues (or a culture of these virtues), such as wonder or awe.[63] A third example of a non-material goal may be the cultivation and propagation of certain attitudes or rhythms of interacting with nature. Farmer and writer Wendell Berry, for instance, describes the idea of a "beloved country":[64] a way of knowing about and living with the land that understands the land holistically and not merely analytically and that realizes discovering the "*best* use

61. Cronon, "The Trouble." Parenthetical citations/footnotes removed.

62. Note that here we are not assuming reality is dualistic, in the sense that matter and spirit are somehow antithetical to each other, but merely that reality is neither entirely material nor entirely spiritual.

63. See Bouma-Prediger, *Beauty of the Earth*, 137–60 for a rich discussion of Christian environmental virtues.

64. Berry, "Argument for Diversity," 115.

of people, places, and things" [emphasis in original]⁶⁵ will require considering the affection of a specific, situated place.⁶⁶ How does this work? Berry
explains:

> The question of what a beloved country is to be used for quickly
> becomes inseparable from the questions of who is to use it or
> who is to prescribe its uses, and what will be the ways of using
> it. If we speak simply of the use of "a country," then only the first
> question is asked, and it is asked only by its would-be users. It
> is not until we speak of "a beloved country"—a particular coun-
> try, particularly loved—that the question about ways of use will
> arise. It arises because, loving our country, we see where we are,
> and we see that present ways of use are not adequate. They are
> not adequate because such local cultures and economies as we
> once had have been stunted or destroyed. As a nation, we have
> attempted to substitute the *concepts* of "land use," "agribusiness,"
> "development," and the like for the *culture* of stewardship and
> husbandry. [emphases in original]⁶⁷

For Berry, the proper use of nature is inextricably linked to the users of (and
their love for) the land. One non-material goal of creation care, thus, may be
the cultivation of this situated affection for the land.

Second, we note that the ontology of the Fall itself (as opposed to the
Fall as a component of the trajectory of history) affects the goals of creation.
Because all of creation has been affected by the Fall, nature, in and of itself,
cannot fully specify what the goal of creation care should be. This reality is
both constraining and freeing. It is constraining because it means that we
cannot take any "snapshot" we currently have of nature (e.g., through observation, scientific study) and conclude only on the basis of that snapshot that
the goal of creation care is to alter nature to conform to that snapshot. That
is to say, preserving nature exactly "as is," post-Fall, cannot be *the* goal under
a Christian worldview because nature is meant, ultimately, to be redeemed,
not returned to a post-Fall state. This is true whether we are talking about a
specific material state (e.g., a specific realm of climate, population of species,
a particular ecosystem dynamic) or about a particular principle derived
from environmental science (e.g., maximal diversity, maximal resiliency to
habitat disturbances). Principles like these may be worthwhile goals for the
command of creation care, but the state of nature *by itself* cannot lead us to a
justification of such goals; something besides the ontological state of nature

---

65. Ibid., 113.
66. Ibid., 113–15.
67. Ibid., 115.

has to provide the justification. Other determinants—ethical theories, politics, economics, science epistemology, etc.—may provide that grounding.

On the other hand, the inability of the post-Fall ontology to specify the goals of creation care can also be freeing, for it implies that there can be a range of goals that are commensurate with the Christian worldview. Instead of a single picture of what creation care activity should achieve (at least in some aspects of creation care), a variety of pictures may be appropriate. If so, this provides greater flexibility as to the content of creation care and also provides greater ground on which to build compromise and understanding between differing viewpoints in the Christian church.

The Christian Worldview and the Practice of the Creation Care Command

We saw in chapter 2 that environmental worldviews can interact with practice of the creation care command either directly or indirectly. In our chapter 2 discussion of how a worldview with a command component directly impacts practice, we detailed the primary way the Christian worldview affects practice: Because God communicates with us and we must obey what He tells us, the Christian worldview impacts practice through God's words to us. These may be universally applicable actions that everyone must do or commands that only apply to someone individually. They may be very specific commands (e.g., the Deut 22:6–7 command regarding not taking a mother bird with her young) or general principles (e.g., that of sustainability). They may be absolute or categorical imperatives or rules we apply prudentially. Whatever the specific context, the Christian worldview's command component directly impacts creation care practice. In this section, rather than revisit the chapter 2 discussion about the direct interactions, we focus on the indirect ways the Christian worldview informs practice. The Christian worldview indirectly impacts practice by motivating various theories of value of the environment which in turn motivate certain kinds of practices. We can identify three aspects of the Christian worldview that motivate certain kinds of valuing: theocentrism, non-materialism, and plurality of value-sources.

First, in the Christian worldview, God is the center of everything and all of creation finds its ultimate meaning, purpose, joy, life, and expression in Him. This theocentrism provides a number of motivations for practices. First, it motivates practices that augment humility. The mindset that the ultimate value of everything in the universe comes from God, rather than ourselves, encourages us to choose and evaluate practices using not only metrics based on human viewpoints but also metrics based on non-human viewpoints. This does not necessarily denigrate human-based metrics but motivates a broader consideration of views when justifying practices. Second, theocentrism motivates practices that eschew the worshipping of nature, since nature's value is derivative rather than ultimate. Finally, theocentrism motivates and encourages practices that are motivated by worship of God and are themselves acts of worship of God. Theocentrism does not prescribe much of the form or nature of this worship: it can be individual or corporate, formal or informal, liturgical or non-liturgical, artistic and aesthetic or practical and pragmatic, embedded in everyday work or a separate event. Whatever the form, however, the practice is tied in with worshipping God.

Besides theocentrism, the Christian worldview also possesses a non-materialist view of nature, and that view can affect motivations for practices. By non-materialist, we are only saying that the Christian worldview sees the universe as being more than "matter in motion." As we described earlier in this chapter, the Christian worldview understands that nature has both a material aspect to it (atoms, molecules, radiation, etc.) as well as a non-material aspect (spirit, intelligence, love, etc.). The non-materialist aspect of the Christian worldview motivates practices that honor and respect nature (and human existence) as having more than instrumental value. Practices that are consistent with such a view of nature (and human beings) give room for moral and spiritual value and purpose. Of course, "spirit-benefiting" practices are difficult to describe and define. Modern categories of knowledge tend to break down when addressing spiritual questions because the spiritual realm is more than ethics and psychology. Nonetheless, such practices are possible and supported under a Christian worldview.

Finally, while in the Christian worldview the value of creation is ultimately theocentric, the Christian worldview also has room for secondary sources of value besides God: people and the environment can be sources of value. The kinds of value generated by people and the environment may be moral or not and will have different statuses; because of human exceptionalism in Christian thought, human-based value will tend to be of higher priority than environment-based value. The fact, however, that the worldview leaves room for and genuinely welcomes alternate sources of value—human valuing, for instance, is genuine and not merely overridden by God's sovereignty—motivates practices that honor multiple sources of value. Put another way, for the vast majority of issues, "value-source pluralism" pushes for practices that recognize multiple stakeholders rather than merely one. The notion of multiple value-sources means the Christian worldview does not advocate policies that only recognize human value as overriding or only the value of nature as overriding. Indeed, though God is the ultimate source of all value, the Christian worldview even would not advocate policies that deny legitimate interests of people and the environment because all other value is derivative from God. The Christian worldview recognizes those other secondary value sources as truly real, despite their dependence.[68]

For example, consider the case of food. Because Scripture does not contain a direct command post-Fall that we must adopt only one kind of eating (i.e., carnivorous, vegetarian, vegan, omnivorous, etc.), we are free to choose what form of eating we practice.[69] But because the Christian worldview is value-source pluralist, it would eschew justifications for forms of eating that negate or deny plural sources of value. For instance, misanthropic justifications for strict vegetarianism would be contrary to the value-source pluralist aspect of the Christian worldview. This is not to say those who hold the Christian worldview cannot practice strict vegetarianism but rather that the worldview suggests other justifications besides misanthropy are required to motivate the practice.[70] Likewise, those who advocate carnivorous or omnivorous eating practices by assuming nature has no value outside of human will (and thus people can use nature however they wish) would seem to deny the idea of value-source pluralism. Such a mindset denies both the value of nature as God's creation as well as the value of nature that comes

---

68. E. Calvin Beisner notes a similar pluralistic dynamic with respect to God's ownership and humanity's stewardship and argues that neglect of that pluralism results in poor creation care practice:

> Emphasizing only that the earth is the Lord's, while neglecting or denying that He has given it to men [sic] tends to lead toward making decisions at broad, societal levels, often encroaching on people's legitimate rights to determine the use of their own property. The disastrous record of socialist countries on environmental protection is grim testimony to how poorly such a policy works. But emphasizing only that God has given the earth to men while neglecting or denying that it still ultimately belongs to God tends to lead toward asserting human autonomy in the use of the earth and exalting individual prerogative over the needs of the community. The sad environmental record of late-nineteenth-century Social Darwinist capitalism should warn us away from that policy. (Beisner, *Garden Meets Wilderness*, 11–12)

69. Of course, the Old Testament does specify dietary laws to the Israelites, and some argue that Adam and Eve were herbivores (Gen 1:29) in Eden. Those special cases, however, are not pertinent to our discussion here, as we are considering the impact value-source pluralism has on practices. Put another way, we are considering the issue of food insofar as the question of eating intersects with questions of value.

70. These justifications may be part of the Christian worldview (e.g., the Christian virtue of simplicity) or part of philosophies outside that worldview (e.g., physical health).

from it being "good" in God's eyes (as originally created).[71] Again, this is not to say those who hold the Christian worldview cannot practice strict meat or mixed diets but rather that the worldview suggests other justifications besides assuming nature has no value outside human will are required to motivate the practice. Again, in recognizing multiple sources of value, this does not mean all kinds of value have the same status. The value inherent to nature might not be a moral value, that is, a value that places demands on others. The value that nature has may also be dependent not only on God but also on human beings (we will discuss different kinds of value in more detail in chapter 4). Nonetheless, the key point is that the Christian worldview honors multiple sources of value and thus prefers motivations for practices that honor that kind of pluralism.

CONCLUSIONS

We have seen that knowing that nature is the handiwork of God motivates an attitude and priority of care. While such a motivation is non-trivial, at the same time it gives a limited understanding of what that care entails. For instance, the ways the Christian worldview determines the practices of creation care, as we outlined above, are quite general. While they provide some guidance regarding practices, they have little to say about even broad categories of policies, such as regulation, taxing structures, etc. In addition, merely because God has made something does not necessarily tell us the value that something has nor necessarily prescribe how we should treat it. Consider the following list of things in the created realm: human beings, hummingbirds, bacteria, oak trees, avalanches, nebulae, quarks, love, fallen angels. God created all of these entities; none of them independently exist. Yet, the kinds of value intrinsic to each, and our obligations to each in light of that value, wildly differ.

In general, we find that the Christian worldview, by itself, seldom prescribes policy. In certain cases—such as in the cases of explicit, literal creation care commands—the Bible can be understood as policy-prescriptive.[72] Yet, even a completely literal reading of creation care commands still results in a limited degree of policy-prescription because most contemporary environmental issues are unmentioned in the Bible. Since biblical and contemporary technology are so divergent, there is little a literal reading of

71. Gen 1.

72. Using an entirely personal hermeneutic, where we believe God specifically reveals to each of us exactly what creation care commands we should carry out, the Christian worldview will also directly yield practices. Few, however, make such a claim.

the Bible can say about chlorofluorocarbons, anthropogenic greenhouse gas emissions, and nuclear power.

Thus, to put it another way, while God is the creator and sustainer—the owner—of the universe, and we are His stewards, it is not entirely clear how we are to understand the owner's wishes. This is not to say that God has made none of His wishes clear to us; the analysis of this chapter enumerates what wishes are clear. It does, however, appear that if we are looking for the Christian worldview to provide dogma that dictates what environmental policies we are to support and what personal environmental practices we are to engage in, we will be disappointed. We need to punt some hard questions down the field to where we consider ethical theories and the other determinants, as biblical justifications can only take us so far in determining the content of creation care. Thus, while the Christian worldview provides a vital context for understanding the nature of creation care—particularly in the importance and goals criteria—that context only serves as a foundation; the structure requires something more.

DISCUSSION QUESTIONS

1. What does being a steward mean for you? How do you think your stewardship will be judged? What will be the criteria of that judgment?

2. Would you consider yourself more sympathetic to the "dominionism" or the "stewardship" model? What about each model do you find attractive or unattractive? Why? How do your sympathies affect your understanding of how the Christian worldview sees the nature of creation care?

3. How important do you believe a Christian should consider the creation care command? What in the Christian worldview leads you to that conclusion? How does that compare with other commands or imperatives for human beings to obey?

4. The author sets out a series of paths by which the Christian worldview influences the goals of creation care. Do you find the goals that result to be clear and robust? If so, why? If not, why not? What additional paths would you suggest by which the Christian worldview influences the goals of creation care?

5. In this chapter's conclusion, the author argues that the Christian worldview has limited amounts to say about creation care practice. Is this conclusion warranted? Does it even matter whether this conclusion is true or not? Why or why not?

4

The Good, the Bad, and the Ugly

Ethical Theories

A PARABLE, CONTINUED

Mondays are the day of Sabbath rest for pastors, but as few other professions take Mondays off, who can a pastor share his Sabbath rest with? Gabriel spent many of his Mondays with his cousin, Kimberly Okeke, who worked as a server in a classy French bistro that closed on Mondays. Gabriel and Kimberly were nearly the same age—their mothers were sisters and lived just two blocks apart—and so, for much of their childhoods, Gabriel and Kimberly tromped together through the creeks and greenbelts that dotted the area where they lived. They built dams out of rocks and sticks and forts out of tarps and branches. They grabbed flashlights and went out on snipe hunts during summer evenings. They caught fireflies in jars and watched the flashes of light prick the dark. During middle school, Kimberly's family moved to another state, and Gabriel and Kimberly only saw each other at family reunions, but as Gabriel's current church was located in the town next to where Kimberly had recently moved to, the two picked up their friendship and wilderness explorations where they had left off.

Their favorite hike was along a winding trail in Placid National Forest that was only an hour's drive away from the city. Besides possessing an encyclopedic knowledge of wine and entrée pairings, Kimberly had worked for years staffing a Forest Service fire lookout during summers and could tell Gabriel more practical facts about the animals, plants, and trees in the forest than he could think of asking.

This Monday, they took a different spur off their normal path, which led them to the crest of a hill that overlooked much of the northern half of Placid National Forest. In many ways, the panorama resembled what Kimberly saw out of the lookout she used to live in. A seemingly endless carpet of trees spread out in front of them, punctuated only by empty areas that had been cleared as part of a timber harvest.

"It's a shame," said Gabriel, "that the logging companies have clear-cut these large swathes of trees. The patchiness looks a little like the edge of my receding hairline," he grimaced.

Kimberly laughed. "Yes, it is unsightly—the clear-cut patches, that is, not your hair." Gabriel laughed. "But," continued Kimberly, "at the same time, timber harvesting is important too. It looks bad, but those trees will grow back."

"I'm a little surprised," replied Gabriel. "I would have thought that you would be more disturbed by the trees being cut down. After all, you worked so hard to prevent those trees from being destroyed by fire; isn't it a little shocking to see them removed, wholesale, by people?"

"I hear what you're saying, Gabriel," said Kimberly, "but as much as I love the outdoors, I've always believed that the value of nature—of those trees—is in its value as a resource as well as the value of its beauty and its value as a part of creation. The forest is an amalgam of all these and other kinds of values. Sometimes, the trees will be used in ways that seem inconsistent with other ways of valuing them, but in my mind, the inconsistency is more apparent than real. The inconsistency comes from insisting only *one* kind of value—as lumber, as a source of wonder, as part of the ecosystem, etc.—really matters."

Gabriel was silent as he thought about what Kimberly said. "But surely, there are ways of harvesting timber that avoid the blight?"

"Yes, there are alternatives to clear-cutting, and clear-cutting can be overused. But if we say that blight is the most important factor to consider when harvesting timber, it isn't too far from saying that the aesthetic value of a forest is the most important value to consider when harvesting trees."

Gabriel and Kimberly walked on. The Sun was nearing its highest point and the shadows were growing shorter. They neared a small stream and paused to rest and enjoy the cool of the water and the trees growing around the stream.

"I see what you mean," said Gabriel, "about nature having multiple kinds of value. But if so, how do you go about weighing those different values? It seems like a hopeless exercise. The task of comparing the value of lumber for building a house with the beauty of a forest makes comparing apples and oranges seem like child's play."

"Yes," replied Kimberly, "it sure isn't easy. But, hard doesn't necessarily mean hopeless. Maybe I can use waiting on tables as an analogy. When I'm serving a table, there are innumerable things I have to consider: what kind of tastes do my guests have, what mood are they in, how fresh were today's vegetables, what has chef really done well this evening, what is the vibe of the dining room tonight, and so on. I consider all of these things and adjust my service accordingly, but I can't break it down into an algorithm."

"Of course, there are rules I follow, and there is the wisdom that has been passed down from older servers, but those cannot tell me exactly what matters most as I figure out how to serve this table. Perhaps," continued Kimberly, "weighing competing values is a juggling act. If I remember to keep all the balls up in the air, and act nimbly, I'll have a better chance of getting things to work out."

Gabriel nodded. "Maybe you're right," he said, and smiled. "And, after seeing you carrying the order for a party of four, if anyone can successfully juggle anything, I'd bet my money on you." Kimberly laughed and smiled back. "C'mon," she said, "I'll race you to the next trail marker!" And the two sped off together.

INTRODUCTION

Ethics is the field of philosophy concerned with actions: what we do and why. Ethical theories, then are ways of figuring out what we should or should not do; they are systems of critiquing actions and behavior. As philosopher Karl Clifton-Soderstrom describes it, "A goal of ethics is to provide us with a language, a set of concepts, effective arguments, and a comprehensive vision whereby we can claim that some kinds of action are right or wrong, or some forms of living are better or worse, perhaps independently of one's cultural or legal context."[1] Often times we talk about different kinds of ethics based

---

1. Clifton-Soderstrom, "Environmental Ethics." See also Clifton-Soderstrom, *The*

upon different areas of application. The field of business ethics seeks to understand what business practices and behaviors are right and wrong. The field of medical ethics seeks to identify right and wrong medical practices. Environmental ethics, then, seeks a system to figure out what is right and wrong with respect to our treatment of the environment.

Historically, environmental ethics has focused on asking and answering questions of value: what has value in the environment and how to weigh different values. Questions about what has value include asking what kind of value does the environment have: Is the value of nature moral—where nature can make demands on others—or non-moral? Does nature have merely instrumental value—as a means to some end—or does it also have non-instrumental value? Given certain kinds of values that nature has, what is the source of the value of the environment? Does the value come from outside or from within nature? If outside of nature, does the value of nature come from human beings (anthropocentrism), God (theocentrism), or something else? If from within nature, is the source of value life (biocentric), the ecosystem (ecocentric), or some other part or aspect of nature? Finally, once we understand the kinds of value nature does or does not have, environmental ethics asks how do we weigh the value of nature against other goods. What values of nature are priorities? When are they priorities: always or only under certain circumstances? Ethical theories that address the question of how to weigh values include deontology (i.e., thinking of actions in terms of duties), virtue ethics, and utilitarianism or consequentialism.

As this brief description of both ethics in general and environmental ethics in particular shows, the field of ethics is rich and storied. Yet, in most of our everyday decisions, we seldom make conscious use of the elaborate infrastructure of the discipline. When is it important for us to explicitly consider ethical theories when asking what obedience to a command looks like? For simple obedience, where importance, goals, and practice are clear (or do not need to be clear), the need for explicit consideration of ethical theories is not that important. We do not need a "system" for critiquing our actions because the correct conclusions are considered obvious.

On the other hand, for issues of considered obedience, explicit consideration of ethical theories is vital, for ethical theories act as a "translator," "mediator," or "substrate" on which to build our thinking of how to understand and connect the various determinants and criteria. First, an ethical system helps give our thoughts coherence when we are thinking about how we should act; conclusions are more likely to be logically consistent with one another when we use a system to define what is right and wrong, rather

---

Cardinal, 3.

than relying on intuition. Second, an ethical system gives us a means to compare and integrate various goods. In most cases, decisions are not arithmetic in nature—in general, we cannot add up rights and wrongs to obtain an answer (unless you are a strict utilitarian). We need an ethical system to help us do that comparison. Third, an ethical system enables us to predict and extrapolate what possible actions are probably right or wrong given some starting assumptions. This ability becomes particularly important if our starting assumptions do not directly address the practices at hand. For instance, the Christian worldview, being a pre-modern worldview, says little directly about modern technologies or environmental problems. Finally, ethical theories are vital for considered obedience because ethical theories impact all three criteria for obedience: importance, goals, and practice.

In this chapter, we address three topics regarding ethical theories and environmental stewardship. First, we examine what is the value of the environment, i.e., what "goods" come from the environment. With a sense of the kinds of value possessed by the environment, we then consider how to weigh the values of different goods. Finally, we analyze what ethical theories tell us about the three criteria for obedience. As in chapter 2, we summarize the spectrum of thought regarding ethics and the environment, while at the same time giving a sense of what the ethical theories determinant can and cannot say about the importance, goals, and practice of environmental stewardship. Rather than arguing for the validity of only one set of ways of understanding ethical theories and creation, we focus on building our taxonomy of how to apply ethical reasoning to analyze the content of environmental stewardship.

THE VALUE OF NATURE

Perhaps as a hallmark of her fecundity, nature is shot through with value; we all agree that nature is "worth something." What we disagree about is what that "worth" is: Is nature's value mainly as raw materials? As untrammeled wilderness? As a teleological center of life? In this section, we examine the range of answers to the question of what is nature "worth" by examining the kinds of value nature has and the sources of that value. Using that examination, we sketch an analytical process or "flow chart" with which we can think about the worth nature has.

Before considering the kinds of value nature has, we note that, in general, there are two kinds of values: moral value and non-moral value. Moral value is the kind of value that can make demands on another. If an entity possesses moral value, that entity has the ability or right to restrict what another entity can do. Even if someone violates another's moral value, moral value cannot be ignored. For instance, a person has a moral value of life that restricts what others can do to the person: others are not permitted to take the life of the person. A car owned by someone has the moral value of property that restricts the use others can make of the car: taking the car without the owner's permission is theft. These examples of moral values illustrate that there are different kinds of moral values and different sources of moral values. However, in both examples, the value is moral precisely because the entity that possesses that value restricts or places demands on others with respect to how they can treat the entity.

While moral value can make demands on others, the kind and scope of demands that a value can make has limits. That is to say, merely because an entity possesses moral value does not mean that someone must treat that entity in any way it desires. For instance, a human being has the moral value of life others are required to respect, but this does not mean that that person has the right to demand something else—say all their neighbor's money— from others. The kind of respect and consideration we need to give to an entity with moral value is a function of many factors, including the nature of the entity, the nature of what grants the entity moral value, the kind and scope of moral value the entity possess, etc. For example, Karl Clifton-Soderstrom notes that, "A piece of lettuce may be a teleological center of life,"— that is, have a purpose inherent to it as a living entity—"which demands respect, but the nature of that teleology informs what respect means (with also perhaps some consideration of our own teleology)."[2] The teleology of a piece of lettuce is not the same as that of a dog, which in turn is not the same as that of a human being. Thus, even if we ascribe moral value to entities that have "teleological centers of life," the type of moral value will differ, in general, from entity to entity.[3]

The second kind of value is non-moral value. As the name suggests, non-moral value is value that cannot make demands on another. For example, someone may have a preference that their home be painted a certain color, but this preference does not make a demand on others. There is no "right to have your home painted a certain color" that others need to honor

2. Clifton-Soderstrom, "Discussion." See also Clifton-Soderstrom, "Response," 37.

3. James A. Nash, in a defense of biocentrism, makes a similar argument: "Rights cannot be assigned arbitrarily; they must have some reasonable basis. However, the basis of biotic rights need not be the same—indeed, cannot be the same—as the grounding of human rights in universal human equality. There can be more than one basis for moral rights. One need only establish a moral status that is sufficient to warrant appropriate moral treatment from the human community." (Nash, "In Flagrant Dissent," 109–10)

or respect. In this example, the value preference seems unimportant, but non-moral values do not have to be of little worth; being non-moral only means that the value has no standing to dictate the actions of others. Sentimental value of an object is an example of a non-moral value that nonetheless has great import to the one who values the object. Likewise, prudential value—a value derived from and in accordance with practical wisdom—also often has great import. That being said, because something with moral value can make demands on others, moral value is generally considered as having priority over non-moral value.

The environment has both moral and non-moral value. Environmental ethics, however, mostly concerns itself with questions of moral value rather than non-moral value, because, historically, we assume that positive environmental policies are achievable only if backed by a set of values that can compel people to act contrary to their natural self-interest. Garrett Hardin, perhaps, provides the clearest example of this impulse in his influential essay "The Tragedy of the Commons," in which he argues that the inability of rational actors to sustainably manage commonly held goods might sometimes justify coercive measures to alter the behavior of those actors.[4] But we can see this desire—to define a set of moral values in order to ground environmental policies on something that can counter human

4. Hardin, "Tragedy." In making this defense of coercion, Hardin argues that, "The social arrangements that produce responsibility are arrangements that create coercion, of some sort" (ibid., 194). These arrangements, Hardin argues, while limiting of individual liberty, can be necessary:

> Every new enclosure of the commons involves the infringement of somebody's personal liberty. . . . But what does 'freedom' mean? When men mutually agreed to pass laws against robbing, mankind became more free, not less so. Individuals locked into the logic of the commons are free only to bring on universal ruin; once they see the necessity of mutual coercion, they become free to pursue other goals. (ibid., 196)

In particular, he continues, the Tragedy of the Commons means:

> The most important aspect of necessity that we must now recognize, [sic] is the necessity of abandoning the commons in breeding. No technical solution can rescue us from the misery of overpopulation. Freedom to breed will bring ruin to all. At the moment, to avoid hard decisions many of us are tempted to propagandize for conscience and responsible parenthood. The temptation must be resisted, because an appeal to independently acting consciences selects for the disappearance of all conscience in the long run, and an increase in anxiety in the short. (ibid., 196)

Hardin, thus, not only argues in favor of population control but also against the use of moral suasion to secure such control.

selfishness—latent in other classic works in environmental ethics, for instance, in Richard and Val Routley's "Last Man" argument in which they argue human-based ethics cannot adequately condemn the full spectrum of possible environmental degradations and thus that environmental ethics needs a totally different foundation.[5] This focus on defining values that can sustain a robust environmental ethic thus favors discussion of moral over non-moral values. In this book, we will follow that lead and also focus on moral values, because comparatively little work has been done on the role non-moral value plays in environmental ethics. Additionally, if we determine nature has moral value, whatever that may be, we can use the fruits of millennia of philosophical thinking on ethics to help translate that value into moral ways of treating nature.

What are the sources of the environment's moral and non-moral value? Earlier, we noted that we would focus on moral value because non-moral values play a relatively minor role in the literature on environmental ethics. That being said, the sources of non-moral value are as myriad as the kinds of possible non-moral values and the kinds of unique valuers. Non-moral value is a much less constraining category than moral value, and so we expect it is relatively more difficult to categorize the sources of non-moral values. In contrast, we can usefully categorize the sources of moral value into two kinds of sources: those "within" (or internal to) the environment and those "without" (or external to) the environment.

If moral value comes from "within" the environment, the environment has "independent moral status."[6] Moral status is the status an entity has if it possesses moral value. If that status is independent, it means that the moral status does not depend on something else but only on the entity itself. Human beings, for instance, have independent moral status because many of the moral values human beings possess adhere to human beings solely on the basis of their identity as human beings. That is, it is a moral value intrinsic to being human. The moral value of life for human beings is an example of an intrinsic value. It does not matter whether the person is healthy, deserving, rich, intelligent, a citizen, etc. All human beings have the moral value of life, and as a moral value, it places demands on others (in this case, the demand is that others may not take that person's life). In the case of human beings, there are a number of moral values people possess solely because they are human. A number of these values ground different justifications for independent moral status for human beings. We often call

5. Benson, *Environmental Ethics*, 18–23.

6. Ibid., 13–18 and ibid., chapter 5 summarize and explore the concept of "independent moral status."

these moral values "human rights" because they are rights (or values that confer obligations others must honor) that human beings possess just by being human. Another such right is the right to be protected from inhumane treatment; again, people possess this right solely on the basis of their humanity, not any extrinsic factor.

In the case of non-human entities in the environment, it is debated whether or not any (or which) entities in the environment possess a moral value that comes from within the entity itself, i.e., whether and what entities have independent moral status. Some argue that entities in nature only have dependent moral status (which we discuss later). For those who argue that entities in nature do have independent moral status, there is debate over what entities in nature have that status and what entities do not. Does a pile of sand have independent moral status? A tree? A frog? An elephant? An ecosystem? To answer that question, we can define a "status-conferring characteristic" that delineates between what entities have independent moral status and what entities do not: possession of the status-conferring characteristic grants the entity independent moral status.[7] Thus, if sentience (the ability to feel pain) is the status-conferring characteristic, all beings that can feel pain (e.g., dogs, pigs) have independent moral status while those that cannot feel pain (e.g., bacteria, plants) do not have independent moral status. In ascribing independent moral status to sentient beings, we are not saying that those beings necessarily have a set of rights identical to human beings; which moral values adhere to independent moral status is a separate question. Nonetheless, by claiming sentience is a status-conferring characteristic, we are saying that any sentient being has a moral worth that comes from within the being itself; the worth does not come from outside the being. Other status-conferring characteristics that have been proposed include existence, life, and being.[8]

If moral value of the environment comes from "without" (external) the environment, the environment has "dependent moral status."[9] That is to say, the source of the moral status comes from outside the environmental entity in question. That source may, in turn have moral value that also depends on something outside of itself, and so on, until we reach a source that has independent moral status and thus depends on nothing outside of itself for moral value. Note that an entity may have dependent moral status with respect to one moral value yet have independent moral status with respect

7. Ibid., 15. Much of the discussion in this and related paragraphs comes from ibid., chapters 1 and 5.

8. Ibid., 15 and chapter 5.

9. Ibid., 13–16.

to another moral value. As an illustration, consider the value of a wetland. The wetland has moral value to its landowner as property; that value is moral because as a property right, it makes demands on others (for instance, through an injunction against trespass). Thus, we can say that the wetland has a dependent moral status with respect to this moral value. The source of that dependent moral status, the landowner, has independent moral status, and so the "dependency chain" stops with the landowner. At the same time, for someone who believes wetlands have independent moral status with respect to certain aspects of its existence (for instance, some Deep Ecologists might hold that the wetland as an ecosystem has an existential right to realization, similar to how human beings have a right to self-realization), the wetland has both independent and dependent moral status.[10]

Because dependent moral value and status requires an external valuer to confer that value or status, we can gain a better sense of the nature of dependent moral status by analyzing valuing itself. First, a valuer, by definition, must be an entity (e.g., a person, organization, God) that can value. Thus, inanimate entities (e.g., a pile of sand) cannot be sources of value. Second, there are two ways a valuer can value something: instrumentally and non-instrumentally.[11] When we value something instrumentally, we are valuing it as a means to an end; when we value something non-instrumentally, we are valuing it for something intrinsic to what it is, that is, as an end in and of itself. Finally, something can have both instrumental and non-instrumental value. For example, a forest has instrumental value to people as a source of raw material for paper, housing, furniture, etc., while at the same time it also has non-instrumental value to people through its aesthetic qualities, such as beauty, peaceableness, majesty, etc. Note that in this example, the value of a forest not only may be instrumental or non-instrumental but it may also be moral or non-moral. Thus, merely because an entity is valued does not mean it has moral value, and dependent moral status can be due to instrumental and/or non-instrumental valuing.[12]

Using these categories of kinds of value—moral versus non-moral and instrumental versus non-instrumental—we can define and describe four schools of thought regarding the sources of value in the environment. The first school of thought, theocentrism, is closely related to the Christian worldview we described in chapter 3. In it, God is the valuer of nature and nature's moral value depends on that valuing. Theocentrism understands

10. Ibid., 123–27 discusses some different understandings of "self-realization."

11. Howarth, "Neither Use," 161–62.

12. Non-moral valuing is often understood as merely a preference, in which case it has limited impact on prescribing or proscribing the actions of others.

the value of nature (as well as the value of human beings) ultimately as dependent on God, and thus, nature ultimately has only dependent moral status. Being rooted in God, however, this moral value is one to which human beings are answerable, because human beings are subordinate to God.

In contrast, the second school of thought, anthropocentrism, sees people as the valuers of nature, and thus, all moral value is dependent on human valuing.[13] When the standard of that valuing is solely human will and desire, this form of anthropocentrism is called "strong" anthropocentrism.[14] When the valuing can itself be judged by cultural and religious norms and codes, that form of anthropocentrism is called "weak" anthropocentrism. Weak anthropocentrism is generally seen as more environmentally friendly because it offers constraints on what kinds of human valuing are legitimate.[15] Strong and weak anthropocentric valuing may value nature instrumentally and/or non-instrumentally. In general, however, strong anthropocentric valuing is instrumental while weak anthropocentric valuing is non-instrumental.

In the third school of thought, biocentrism, life is the status-conferring characteristic that gives living things an independent moral status human beings must respect even if no one values that aspect of nature.[16] How human beings must respect living creatures is a separate question, but if all living things have independent moral status, the creatures themselves make some kind of claim human beings must honor. As a corollary to life as the status-conferring characteristic, under a biocentric perspective, aspects of nature that are not living have, at best, dependent moral status. Thus, for a biocentrist, plants have independent moral status but a pile of sand does not.

In the fourth school of thought, Deep Ecology, the status-conferring characteristic is the existence or reality of nature itself: Nature in both its parts and in its entirety has independent moral status and is a Self whom we identify with and treat accordingly with care.[17] Thus, according to Deep Ecology, not only animate and inanimate entities in nature have independent moral status but so too do abstract entities or characteristics of nature

---

13. See Benson, *Environmental Ethics*, 16–18 for an introduction to anthropocentrism. Much of this paragraph comes from Benson, *Environmental Ethics*, chapter 2.

14. Norton, "Environmental Ethics," 165.

15. Ibid., 165.

16. Much of this paragraph comes from Benson, *Environmental Ethics*, 87–101. The core of Benson's discussion comes from philosopher Paul W. Taylor's form of biocentrism.

17. Much of this paragraph comes from Benson, *Environmental Ethics*, 18 and chapter 7.

such as ecosystems, food webs, etc. As philosopher Arne Naess, one of the authors of Deep Ecology, puts it:

> The well-being and flourishing of human and non-human life on Earth have value in themselves (synonyms: intrinsic value, inherent worth). These values are independent of the usefulness of the non-human world for human purposes. . . . The term "life" is used here in a more comprehensive non-technical way also to refer to what biologists classify as "non-living": rivers (watersheds), landscapes, ecosystems. For supporters of deep ecology, slogans such as "let the river live" illustrate this broader usage so common in many cultures.[18]

While this list of four schools of thought regarding the source of value in the environment is by no means exhaustive, they illustrate some general features regarding sources of value in the environment. First, if the value of nature is found outside nature, that source may be either human-based (anthropocentric) or non-human based (e.g., theocentric). While both anthropocentrism and theocentrism are sources of value external to nature, the kind of guidance each provides differs markedly. Second, instead of grouping these schools of thought regarding the sources of value in the environment by whether they are internal or external to nature, we can group these schools by whether they are supernatural or natural. The former includes theocentrism while the latter includes anthropocentrism (strong and weak), biocentrism, and Deep Ecology.

If we consider that last grouping, natural sources of value, we note that strong anthropocentrism and Deep Ecology define two paradigmatic extremes. At one pole, nature's value is entirely determined by the felt needs of human beings; critics of strong anthropocentrism claim that such a grounding of value reduces nature to merely the supplier of raw materials for human consumption. At the other pole, the most important aspects of the value of nature are found within nature itself, and those values can take priority over human goals. Critics of Deep Ecology claim this grounding of value reduces human beings to the same status as bacteria. These two poles define a spectrum that philosopher John Benson sees as running from a "light green" to "dark green" environmentalism.[19]

The presence of such a spectrum of thought regarding sources of value of the environment has three implications. First, the spectrum suggests that there are choices besides these poles. Indeed, weak anthropocentrism and biocentrism are such alternatives. Second, the presence of a spectrum

18. Naess, "Deep Ecological," 264–65.
19. Benson, *Environmental Ethics,* 25.

suggests that we can define theories of the value of the environment that are themselves made up of other theories of value. Biocentrism, for instance, is such a hybrid in the sense that it understands parts of nature as having independent moral status while other parts as having only dependent moral status. Steven Bouma-Prediger proposes another hybrid combination: one between a Leopoldian "land ethic" that sees the land (in some ways) as an organism together with an ethic that includes some kind of human exceptionalism.[20] Finally, the presence of a spectrum, rather than a binary either/or choice, suggests one possible ground for compromise may be in creating hybrid groundings of the value of nature that enable us to move from the two poles towards something in the middle.

With this analysis of the kinds and sources of value in the environment, we can sketch a "flow chart" of questions to ask to determine the value of nature. First, we ask, "does nature have moral status (through at least one moral value)?" If nature does not have *any* moral status, we can, presumably, treat nature however we want. If nature does have moral status, we ask a second question, "where does that moral status come from?" Is it dependent on something external to nature or does it come from within nature? If the latter, i.e., if nature has independent moral status, what grounds that status? If the former, i.e., if nature has dependent moral status, what kind of moral value is associated with that status? Is it an instrumental moral value or a non-instrumental moral value? In general, non-instrumental moral value is more successful at motivating a deeply caring form of environmentalism than instrumental moral value, and does so even though it only grounds a dependent moral status.[21]

This analytical framework provides clarity to our understanding of the value of nature, which in turn informs the criteria for obedience. Different kinds and sources of value for nature support different ways of motivating and caring for creation, and later on in this chapter we enumerate what those different ways look like when we examine the impact of ethical theories on the criteria for obedience. But in order for values to create motivations and actions, those values must first be weighed against other goods and values. We may find that while we value nature, other goods and values have higher priority to us. Only the "net" results of our hierarchy of values create motivations and actions for creation care. We address how to weigh differing values in the next section.

---

20. Bouma-Prediger, *Beauty of the Earth*, 133–34. "Leopoldian 'land ethic'" here refers the ecological philosophy of Aldo Leopold (Leopold, "The Land Ethic").

21. Norton, "Cultural Approach," 146.

HOW TO WEIGH DIFFERING VALUES

Once we have determined what kind of value the environment has, we need to consider how to weigh those values with other values. After all, most creation care decisions are seldom between one option that has no value and another option that has infinite value, but rather over partial and competing values or goods. The field of ethics has a host of different schema for weighing values with each other. In this section we consider three of the primary ways we weigh competing values—consequentialism (either as utilitarianism or cost-benefit analysis), deontology, virtue ethics—and examine each paradigm's strengths and weaknesses. These three schools of thought are not necessarily mutually exclusive, though for any given issue in a given context, we tend to use one or the other of these ways of weighing values. In addition, there are other important ways of weighing values we will not cover in detail (most prominently natural law).[22] However, these three

22. Natural law argues that we can obtain some guidance regarding how we should act or live from the physical and social realities of who we are, as human beings and as a part of a cosmological order. As James A. Nash describes, "The natural law, as Aquinas claims, is those norms necessary to promote the good associated at least with our instincts for self-preservation, our animal needs, and our rational (including our social) nature. For example, prima facie prohibitions against killing and theft follow from this [first] mandate [of natural law] to do good" (Nash, "Moral Norms in Nature," 242). As applied to environmental ethics, this might take the form of a kind of "following nature," not in the sense of drawing moral norms directly from how nature behaves but in the sense of "ecosystemic compatibility." Again, quoting Nash, "Rather, it [ecosystemic compatibility] is following nature, first, in a 'homeostatic sense' of fitting into the stability of ecosystems and the ecosphere, and, second, in an 'axiological sense' of respecting and being guided by the values we encounter in nature" (ibid., 244).

While we do not address natural law in any detail in the present work, we can apply some, if not much, of our discussion of virtue ethics to the application of natural law as a means of weighing values in questions of environmental ethics. Both natural law and virtue ethics are ends-focused and interested (at least in Christian virtue ethics), not merely in a socially constructed ethic but one grounded in a true apprehension of the good. Theologian Cristina L. H. Traina further argues that natural law offers a way of completing virtues:

> The particular advantage of the natural law tradition is its ability to unite character and consequences. According to the natural law theological tradition, a person's temporal goals include physical well-being, on the one hand, and natural or acquired virtue (disciplined habits of rational thought and action), on the other. Yet, because virtue is telic—it conduces to well-being, even perfection—these two temporal ends are interdependent. Infused or theological virtue in turn is the keystone between an individual's transcendent end in God and her efforts toward temporal well-being for herself and others. Grace, through charity, lifts, transforms, and perfects natural virtue rather than eradicating it. So the

dominate discussions regarding environmental ethics and illustrate general principles when considering how to weigh differing values with regards to environmental issues; those principles provide a foundation on which we can analyze other weighing paradigms. After covering consequentialism, deontology, and virtue ethics, we end this section with a discussion of the use of these ways of weighing values in environmental ethics.

Consequentialism

The first paradigm for weighing values, consequentialism, weighs values based upon the consequences of the actions and non-actions that result from those values. Two forms of consequentialism that figure prominently in environmental ethics discussions are utilitarianism and cost-benefit analysis.[23] In both utilitarianism and cost-benefit analysis, one evaluates all possible environmental actions on the basis of a criteria or quantity to maximize. In classical (or act) utilitarianism, the criterion to maximize is pleasure versus pain. The right action is the one that maximizes the total amount of pleasure in the universe over pain. In cost-benefit analysis, the criterion to maximize is monetary benefit versus monetary cost. Thus, the way we weigh competing environmental goods using a utilitarian or cost-benefit analysis framework is to choose the combination of actions that leads to the highest amount of total pleasure over pain or monetary benefit over cost, respectively.

We can enumerate at least three benefits of using these two forms of consequentialism to weigh values. First, utilitarianism and cost-benefit analysis are universal and non-egoist. That is to say, these frameworks are objective and treat all parties involved equally. In utilitarianism, it is the total amount of pleasure over pain in the universe, not in the amount in any particular person or part of the environment, that matters. Similarly, in cost-benefit analysis, it is the total amount of monetary gain or cost that matters. Second, utilitarianism and cost-benefit analysis provides a framework that reduces difficult ethical questions to a mathematical optimization exercise.

---

individual's graced journey toward God, her temporal ends, and her advancement of the common good are not merely coherent but entail each other. (Traina, "Response," 254–55)

In that completion, natural law, like virtue ethics, also offers a way out of a merely utilitarian or consequentialist understanding of environmental and other goods (Ibid., 254).

23. Snell, "Utilitarianism"; Benson, *Environmental Ethics*, 40–47. The discussion in this and following paragraphs also reference these sources.

This enables us to apply the tools from the mathematical, economic, and social sciences to bear on otherwise nearly insoluble philosophical, political, and social problems. Finally, policymaking is understood by many, if not most, as a predominantly consequentialist enterprise. As a result, cost-benefit analysis is the entrenched, default position in policy debates. This creates potentially common ground where disputing sides on a policy issue can meet. This also provides a tool for those disputing sides to use to communicate with the general public.

Utilitarianism and cost-benefit analysis, however, also suffer from severe, and possibly fatal, weaknesses. We enumerate three of these weaknesses.[24] First and foremost, critics of these two forms of consequentialism argue that the value of most kinds of goods are not reducible to a single, universal, quantifiable metric, whether it be pleasure or money.[25] For instance, while love can lead to pleasure (e.g., companionship) and bear economic fruits (e.g., gifts), love cannot be reduced to pleasure or money, nor can many of the goods of love be converted into pleasure or money "equivalents." Indeed, many of the goods of love can only be apprehended and appreciated on their own terms.[26] As another example, with regards to environmental goods, dif-

---

24. Snell, "Utilitarianism." See Benson, *Environmental Ethics,* 40–47 for a discussion of the strengths and weaknesses of cost-benefit analysis.

25. While, in a strict sense, the value of all goods is not reducible to money, and thus cost-benefit analysis is fatally flawed, at the same time neo-Scholastic economics might offer a way to monetarily value even non-instrumental environmental goods because it provides a theory of final distribution, a theory that explains the end "for whom" economic activity occurs (Muller, *Redeeming Economics,* 20). We describe neo-Scholastic economics in more detail in chapter 6.

26. This is somewhat related to the "particularity" of things that philosopher Jane Howarth notes is so critical to a Heideggerian notion of Care:

> Appreciation of the irreplaceability, the particularity, of things is, I believe, part of what Heidegger means by Care, part of what is largely covered up by modern life. He recommends that we should 'let things show themselves.' One thing which would be revealed would be that all things that 'show' themselves are in fact particular things: that is the character of the world and of our ways of encountering it. This is part of what Heidegger meant when he bemoaned our loss of Being behind meaning. We have lost sight of the particularity of things, we concentrate on the *kinds* of things they are and not on the particular things they are. [emphasis in original] (Howarth, "Neither Use," 165)

Charles Taylor also notes that even if the utilitarian project of doing away "with qualitative distinctions of worth on the grounds that they represent confused perceptions of the real bases of our preferences which are quantitative" were successful, this would not in itself guarantee that all choices—even those involving mere preferences—are calculable (Taylor, "What Is Human Agency?" 17).

ferent people value different aspects of the environment differently, and in few areas is there any convergence. What to one person is a grand and majestic desert is desolate and lifeless to another. Given such subjectivity, it is difficult to reduce the value of those goods into a common "currency." Second, critics of utilitarianism and cost-benefit analysis question whether pleasure and money are universal in their value. Both appear heavily subjective and personal; what one person finds a trivial sum of money another sees as a king's ransom. If the "metrics" of utilitarianism and cost-benefit analysis are themselves unstable in value, how can one solve the optimization problem? Finally, critics of utilitarianism and cost-benefit analysis find the justifications for the metrics of pleasure and money to be wanting. Why should pleasure or money be the metric? Is there an implicit teleology, or purpose, that grounds those metrics? If so, the framework of consequentialism is not fully determined by the consequences of actions, which suggests something else needs to be added into this method of weighing values. Questions that need to be answered may include: What is the purpose of being human? What is the purpose of nature? To the extent consequentialism, in order to be well-grounded, has to address these questions, consequentialism begins to look more and more like virtue ethics.[27]

Deontology

In the second paradigm for weighing values, deontology, the nature of ethics is one of duty: what commands should be obeyed, categorical imperatives to be fulfilled, laws to follow, and universal rights to honor.[28] These duties may be grounded on the basis of supernatural authority. For instance, Christianity and Judaism justify commandments for us to follow on the authority of God. Secular versions of deontology aim to justify categorical imperatives without recourse to a deity. For instance, Immanuel Kant's deontology strives to justify duties on the basis of reason alone. Regardless of the source of the duties, under the deontological paradigm, to be ethical *means* to do your duty; intention means everything when judging the morality of an action and consequences have no moral bearing. Thus, to weigh values in a deontological way, we produce a hierarchy of duties and laws that tells us the relative priority of our duties, and the weighing of values involves finding where various goods fit in this hierarchy. For example, if we believe both preservation of biodiversity and economic growth are goods, the task of weighing these goods using deontology is accomplished by determining

27. Snell, "Utilitarianism."
28. Ahn, "Immanuel Kant."

which of these goods are duties and if both are duties, which duty has the higher priority (and when).

With regards to environmental ethics in Western societies, one particularly prevalent form that deontology takes is the idea of "rights." In Western human ethics, we often talk about rights an individual or group has—human rights, civil rights, property rights, and, in the language of the Declaration of Independence, "unalienable Rights." When applied to environmental ethics, this takes the form of animal rights, ecosystem rights, etc. In a way similar to how we determine what entities in the environment have independent moral status, we can define a "rights conferring characteristic," where any entity that has that characteristic is considered to have some suite of rights associated with and proper to that characteristic. For example, the ability to feel pain (sentience) is often considered a characteristic that imbues animals with rights such as humane treatment in slaughterhouses and a right to be protected from cruelty. At least partly in consideration of these rights, we have passed laws to protect these rights, such as laws prescribing the means by which animals are slaughtered for meat, penalties for the practice of cruelty to animals, etc.[29]

As a means of weighing values, deontology has two major positive traits. First, deontological duties are understood as universal, absolute in their proper scope, and independent of culture, time in history, and geographical location. As a result, properly grounded deontological structures possess a high degree of moral force and can act as a strong motivation for people to change their behavior. Second, the language of duties, as we saw with consequentialism, is also deeply engrained in Western culture. Nearly all Western value debates use rights language in some way (e.g., right to choose, right to life, etc.). Thus, the use of deontology to weigh values is familiar and readily understood.

At the same time, we can identify some negative traits of deontology as a means of weighing values. First, we may ask if every perceived right or duty is truly a right or duty. One suspects, with the proliferation of rights and duties in our age, that some perceived rights are not rights that have the moral force of Mount Sinai but rather are more suggestions cloaked in the language of duty. In some cases, some proposed rights are not rights at all, but are suggested to be rights in order to appropriate the moral force of the categorical imperative; deontology can easily degenerate into an excuse to make others do what we want rather than defining a true universal duty that applies to all. A second possible weakness of deontology is whether the authority that establishes the duty truly has the authority to do so. In

29. Wise, "Animal Rights."

the modern world, our collective understanding of the nature, dynamics, and grounding of authority is weaker than in ages past. In a individualistic culture where the self is often the locus of authority, and preferences thus become moral claims merely because they are *personal* preferences, it is difficult to recognize what authorities are legitimate. Finally, taken to its logical extreme, a life lived solely through the lens of deontology seems a bit empty. Ethics becomes merely "following the rules" and devoid of love and passion, or it becomes one continuous protest march against those who would infringe upon our rights.[30] Is that truly the end all and be all for life?[31]

Virtue Ethics

The third paradigm for weighing values, virtue ethics, understands living the "good life" not as following a checklist of "dos and don'ts," nor as success in maximizing pleasure, but rather as becoming a certain kind of person, one whose life is marked by virtues.[32] Virtue ethics has been applied in both religious and non-religious value systems, and depending on what the system considers as the "good life"—such as Aristotle's life of philosophy or Christianity's Kingdom of God—the kinds of virtues exhibited by a virtuous person may differ.[33] These virtues are, in general, grown through repetition and practice and the following of exemplars. However, these actions and practices themselves are not the focus of virtue ethics. The "good life" does not consist of merely doing those actions. Rather, one's actions are a means to becoming the kind of person who is characterized by the virtues as well as the natural fruit of being a virtuous person. Thus, in a sense, in responding to the question, "how do you weigh values," virtue ethics says that this is ultimately not the important question to ask, but rather the question to ask is what and how do we become that certain kind of person, the virtuous person.

Additionally, nearly all virtues are neither "good" nor "bad" in the deontological sense of categorical imperatives. Virtues are not duties we *must* practice. As Aristotle pointed out, nearly all virtues in excess or in defect become vices.[34] With virtues, we can have not only too little of a good thing, but unlike rights or duties, we can also have too much of a good thing. As an

---

30. Clark, "What Is the Good."

31. Ibid.

32. Clifton-Soderstrom, "Virtues." Many of the ideas in this paragraph have come through discussions with and lectures by Karl Clifton-Soderstrom.

33. Clark, "What Is the Good" and Clifton-Soderstrom, "Virtues."

34. Bouma-Prediger, *Beauty of the Earth*, 139.

example, consider the ecological virtue of respect. Steven Bouma-Prediger defines this virtue in the following way: "*Respect* is an understanding of and proper regard for the integrity and well-being of other creatures" [emphasis in original].[35] Such a virtue is praiseworthy; who would not want to cultivate respect? Yet, exercised the wrong way, respect can become a vice. Bouma-Prediger notes that, "Two vices correspond to the virtue of respect. The vice of deficiency is *conceit,* for conceit is ignorance of and disdain for other creatures. . . . The vice of excess is *reverence,* or inflated regard for the other" [emphases in original].[36] It is difficult, then, for a person to be successfully virtuous without wisdom and virtues like temperance and prudence. Unlike categorical imperatives that one merely need to *intend* to carry out, virtues are embedded in a matrix of character and personhood.

When applied to environmental issues, virtue ethics argues that human beings should live in accordance with certain types of environmental virtues, e.g., love, generosity, patience, simplicity, etc.[37] For instance, a person may practice the virtue of simplicity by carefully evaluating how they use goods and services and looking for ways to "do more with less." The practice of these virtues both creates and marks the person who is virtuous towards the environment. In virtue ethics, the weighing of values, then, is not act-based, but rather is "life-" or "character-based." Specific environmental actions are not necessarily right or wrong; instead the focus is on becoming a certain kind of person that will in turn treat the environment in accordance with environmental virtues.

Virtue ethics has two main strengths as a paradigm with which to weigh values. First, in comparison with consequentialism and deontology, virtue ethics seems more in tune with a richer and fuller sense of being human, particularly those aspects which are non-quantifiable and non-instrumental. Life consists of more than legalistic duty or maximizing universal pleasure or money; virtues such as honesty, love, and honor are more than mere rules to follow or tools to achieve the optimal outcome. Virtue ethics seems more in tune with this reality than consequentialism and deontology.

Second, virtue ethics seems to provide the implicit *telos* or purpose that justifies many of our duties towards the environment or the metrics of consequentialism that are applied to the environment. That is to say, the purposes of environmental duties or environmental policy consequences are the purposes that virtues and virtuous living focus on. Consider the

35. Ibid., 143.

36. Ibid.

37. Many of the ideas in this paragraph have come through discussions with and lectures by Karl Clifton-Soderstrom.

following example of a possible environmental duty that, in some sense, actually stems from virtue ethics: the duty to keep wilderness areas in their current state. Using deontology to ground such a duty is somewhat problematic because it is not clear how such a specific duty is a categorical imperative. Some may ground this duty on a duty to protect the rights of future generations. That is to say, if we assume future generations have a right to experience wilderness in the exact state that we experience it, then we have an obligation to honor that right by preserving wilderness areas. But how do we define a right for a generation that does not exist? What if future generations do not want wilderness to be in the state we experience it but rather want to experience it as it evolves with geological forces? Are we not actually grounding the right to wilderness in its current state on an implicit *telos* that values stasis? Considering further the idea of a duty with respect to wilderness areas, some argue for this duty because it enables us to have places where we can disinterestedly contemplate nature in its majesty and respond with awe. Yet, here too, we end up appealing to the value of environmental virtues. Is not the *telos* of such contemplation to become a certain kind of virtuous person? Thus, much of our reasoning about environmental duties and environmental policy consequences are, perhaps, really grounded on a virtues framework. In some way, then, weighing values in environmental issues should include the virtue ethics approach.

We can, however, identify at least four areas of weakness in environmental virtue ethics. First, virtue ethics is imprecise. Virtue ethics is qualitative both with regards to describing the content and weight of a virtue as well as how to compare virtues to one another. For instance, virtue ethics offers no schema for quantifying wonder and awe: how then do we evaluate how much wonder or awe there is and how to weigh the two (or other virtues) against one another? Second, virtue ethics, with its emphasis on becoming a certain kind of person, seems a bit "slow" to use as a means of weighing values. Since the very means of the weighing requires "fully-formed" and virtuous people, and such people, some would argue, are not abundant, it is unclear how useful virtue ethics is as a means of weighing competing values. Additionally, by the time people have developed the character we need for them to live out the good life as defined in virtue ethics, perhaps the environment will already have been destroyed. A third weakness of virtue ethics is that it is not entirely clear how to translate virtues into laws, one of the major ways of implementing environmental policy. To the extent creation care requires state (versus individual or private) action, this may be problematic. Fourth, the moral force of virtue ethics seems somewhat limited. If we need ethics to provide a prophetic voice of urgency in order to overcome the shortcomings of human nature, virtue ethics seems somewhat wanting. In virtue ethics, we seem to have the words of a wise sage rather than injunctions with the thunderous voice of the Ten Commandments.

The Use of These Paradigms to Weigh Values

With such a range of ways to weigh values, what principles can we give to guide our choice and use of these paradigms in weighing different values related to environmental problems and resources? In this section, we reflect on the range of paradigms and their use. First, the mere presence of a spectrum of ways to weigh values does not necessarily imply all paradigms are equal. Rather, in certain cases, one ethical theory of weighing values may be more applicable than others, because the strengths (versus weaknesses) of one ethical theory may better connect with certain contexts than other ethical theories of weighing. For instance, when the costs and benefits are relatively well-known and accurately quantifiable in monetary terms, and there are no clear and compelling moral duties at stake, consequentialism may be a preferred paradigm to use in weighing values. In contrast, a virtue ethics focus may be more helpful in addressing environmental issues that are broader (in possible causes, scope of effects, range of possible solutions, etc.) rather than narrow and focused. Climate change is an example of a broader environmental issue while local dumping of a pollutant is an example of a more focused issue. And, when weighing the values of non-instrumental goods, a virtue ethics approach tends to work better than a consequentialist approach, because of the inherently apples-to-oranges nature of many non-instrumental goods.

Second, while sometimes it is better to go with one ethical theory of weighing values (e.g., one outperforms all the others), other times the opposite is true. The spectrum of methods to weigh values may be non-exclusive rather than exclusive. For instance, when making decisions in contexts with a high risk of "groupthink"—where uniformity of opinions amongst decision-makers leads to overconfidence, unrecognized threats, and missed opportunities—multiple ways of weighing values may help decision-makers improve the quality of their analysis and decisions.[38] Additionally, in any given context, there may be aspects of the context that link better to the strengths of one ethical theory of weighing while other aspects of the context link better to the strengths of another ethical theory of weighing. In considering food production and consumption, for instance, some values may be better weighed consequentially (e.g., those with monetary aspects), some deontologically (e.g., those involving interactions between people),

38. See Janis, *Groupthink* for a classic analysis of the groupthink phenomena.

and others using virtue ethics (e.g., those related to interactions between people and nature). In such contexts, applying multiple paradigms to the environmental issue may lead to a better weighing of values.

Third, whether or not we use more than one ethical theory to weigh values (but particularly when we do), we need to remember that the different kinds of theories to weigh values are different from one another; we confuse them at our peril. In particular, with environmental problems, there is often a temptation to turn environmental virtues or consequentialist conclusions into a duty in order to tap into the persuasive power of the deontological moral voice. Many virtues, both environmental and non-environmental (e.g., simplicity, patience, beauty, awe), however, lack adequate grounding to be given the moral voice of a duty. Consequentialist conclusions also often lack such a grounding; there is no duty to maximize universal pleasure, utility, or monetary return. Thus, to treat nurturing of awe, for instance, as if it were a categorical imperative (or as having deontological biblical warrant) is a category error and can lead to unjustifiably hasty action as well as to a rigidity in policymaking that does a disservice to creation care. It behooves us to apply ethical theories of weighing carefully and conservatively.

ETHICAL THEORIES AND IMPORTANCE, GOALS, AND PRACTICE

By describing what has value in nature and how to weigh values, ethical theories give a language and a method we can use to think through the nature of all goods (both those related to the environment as well as strictly human goods that are the traditional domain of ethics) and how those goods relate to one another. As we might expect, ethical theories, then, have much to contribute to the criteria for obedience. The value of nature and the goods of nature affect each of the criteria. In this section, we take each of the criteria—importance, goals, and practice—in turn and describe how ethical theories affect them.

First, with regards to the importance of the creation care command, ethical theories, when paired with worldviews, tell us both *what* the command is trying to care for and *the value* of what the command is trying to care for. Thus, ethical theories plus worldviews tell us why we should follow the command; we have a complete picture of "fact" and "value" that we can evaluate against other commands. In chapters 2 and 3, we saw that worldviews give us an ontology of nature and the rest of reality. Ontology, we found, gives us some sense of the importance of the creation care command, but only a limited sense. Because of the fact-value distinction, worldviews cannot fully specify the value of the ontology worldviews provide. When worldviews are paired with ethics—when a description of what "is" is connected to a description of the value of what "is" and how to weigh those values—we obtain a description of the comparative importance of what is being cared for in the creation care command. This comparative importance extends both to the "is" of ontology proper as well as to the "is" of any environmental goods that result from caring for the ontological "is." Ethical theories, then, have a crucial role in enabling ontologies derived from worldviews (including, as we will see in more detail in chapter 5, in ontologies derived from science) to provide a description of the importance of the creation care command; without ethics, the "importance" described by worldviews tells us little, because it cannot tell us the importance of the command *compared to* other responsibilities.

Second, the influence of ethical theories on the goals of the creation care—what following the command will result in—also comes from the complete description of ontology and value that comes from joining worldviews with ethical theories. To the extent that we have already addressed the importance criterion and have concluded a particular set of environmental goods has a comparative value justifying a particular kind of care, the goal, then, of creation care would be to achieve that particular set of environmental goods. For example, if the set of environmental goods includes beauty, then one goal of environmental stewardship actions would be to attain or preserve that environmental beauty. This may mean the realization of a particular material state (e.g., protect specific species or even a specific tree, animal, etc.) that exhibits beauty or the realization of an environment that, on the whole, exhibits beauty. The specifics of the kind and source of beauty being preserved are given in the analysis guided by worldviews and ethical theories.

Finally, ethical theories can affect the practice of the creation care command (how to put the command into action) both directly and indirectly, and practice can also have a reverse effect on ethical theories. The directness of the effect of ethical theories on practice depends on the moral force associated with the ethical theory. If the value that is the goal of environmental stewardship has substantial moral force (e.g., the value is considered a right or categorical imperative), we can consider the ethical theory involved as directly leading to a practice, namely, honoring the right or executing the imperative. That is to say, the practice that results from the value prescribed by the ethical theory naturally follows from that value and requires no further consideration of other factors. In the contrary case, when the value that is the goal of environmental stewardship has lesser moral force (e.g., as is often the case when considering virtues), the value can still act to remove some practices from consideration and give preference to other practices. We consider this role of ethical theories on practices in chapter 7.

In addition to directly leading to creation care practices, ethical theories can also indirectly motivate practices. This happens through the motivation provided by the kind of value nature has. We saw earlier that the kind of moral status nature has—both the source of that status (e.g., anthropocentric, theocentric, etc.) as well as the nature of that status (e.g., instrumental versus non-instrumental for non-moral status)—may motivate different ways of caring for the environment. For example, if we believe the living part of the environment has some form of independent moral status (i.e., biocentrism), it may prompt us to, in some way, identify with that part of the environment. That, in turn, may motivate a particular type of caring for living things that would be different if we felt more distant and unrelated to the living part of nature. In saying so, we are not necessarily claiming that connectedness and identification necessarily leads to *more* caring creation care practice; in some cases, as we have noted, it may, while in others it might not.[39] We are saying, however, that different motivations tend to result in different practices. To the extent this is true, ethical theories that provide one kind of motivation for environmental stewardship practice versus another kind of motivation will lead to different kinds of practices.

While what and how we value usually influence what we do, the reverse can happen. That is to say, as we saw in chapter 2 with regards to environmental worldviews, what we do can affect how we think; we call this "praxis." In considering worldviews, we saw how praxis can affect how we view all of nature. Likewise, with respect to ethical theories, praxis can affect what we find valuable and how we value nature. For instance, if we treat animals kindly and with respect, this may predispose us to consider them as having the moral status (possibly independent moral status) to demand that respect from people in general. Or, if every time we consider questions of creation care we engage in monetary cost-benefit analysis (e.g., asking, "If I drive this bag of cans to the recycling bin, this will result in X dollars of cost and Y dollars of benefit"), this will tend to reinforce our belief that cost-benefit analysis provides a good way of weighing values. Thus, while, in general, the dominant effect of ethical theories is to influence our actions, in considering our actions, we should be aware that the actions we engage in may in turn influence what we value in nature and how we value nature.

39. For a similar idea, applied to religious teaching versus actual practice, see Kinsley, *Ecology and Religion*, xx–xxi.

CONCLUSIONS

Ethical theories give us meaning: they take what exists—an ontology—and tell us what it means, both in and of itself and relative to others. With that meaning, we can begin to deeply think through the criteria for obedience to the creation care command. Without that meaning, we can say relatively little about what kind of environmental stewardship we *should* practice. That is to say, ethical theories enable us to move past what is to what ought to be.

However, the range of ways of understanding the value of nature and how to weigh that value against other values is incredibly broad. This breadth must result in highly divergent views regarding the very meaning of nature. Therein lies both risk and opportunity. On the one hand, because ethical theories provide such a divergent set of understandings of the value of nature, we can easily find ourselves in disagreement because of our differing ethical presuppositions. When we leave unstated those core understandings of what kind of value nature has and how to weigh that value against other goods, dialogue breaks down and we do not know why. One person sees nature's value as primarily connected with human flourishing while another considers nature's value as intrinsic to itself. One person conceives of nature as having rights that must be honored while another believes our treatment of nature must be examined through the lens of costs versus benefits. Each person believes nature is "valuable" and takes offense when others accuse them of lacking "care." If we are to understand one another with regards to discussions and debates over the content of creation care, we need to explicitly dialogue with one another regarding the ethical theories we use. While some of this dialogue has occurred, in evangelical circles, we are at the beginnings of communicating these presuppositions with one another.

At the same time, the breadth of ethical theories also presents opportunity. Environmental issues are seldom simple and reducible to elementary morality plays. There are a myriad number of competing (and sometimes mutually exclusive) stakeholders involved, confounding factors, positive and negative feedback loops, and uncertainties. By admitting a range of ways of understanding the kinds of value nature has and how to weigh those values, we can tailor our analysis of environmental issues in creative ways. Such creativity may ultimately result in solutions with greater flexibility, nuance, and political acceptability and stability.

DISCUSSION QUESTIONS

1. The author argues that ethical theories play a critical role in augmenting what we can learn from environmental worldviews. In particular, the author suggests that worldviews, in general, can only tell you what nature is, not what nature's value is. What do you think of the author's argument? Are worldviews limited in that way? Do ethical theories add as much to what worldviews provide as the author suggests? Why or why not?

2. What kind of value do you believe nature has? What is the source of that value? What are your reasons for this belief, and why do you find other answers to these questions not as convincing?

3. Of the different ways the author describes of weighing values, which one do you find most convincing? Most useful? Why? Does it matter if the paradigm you find most convincing is (or is not) also the most useful? What impact might that have with regards to practicing environmental stewardship?

4. Pick an environmental problem and a proposed solution. Examine how proponents of different ways of weighing values might analyze this problem and solution. What is similar or different in these analyses of the problem and solution? Do you find those similarities and differences acceptable and why?

5. For an environmental problem, analyze whether the problem permits the application of multiple ways of understanding the value of nature and how to weigh that value with other goods. What enables us to apply more than one ethical theory? Does this affect the range of possible solutions we can consider?

5

Science to the Rescue?

A PARABLE, CONTINUED

Gabriel had known Peter and Anne Haas since their days in their church's high school youth group. Peter had raven black hair and was reserved almost to the point of melancholy, while Anne had blonde hair and was happy as a cricket. Yet, both loved surfing, physics, and Jesus. After high school, all of them had gone their separate ways, and both Peter and Anne had walked down difficult personal paths and away from the faith of their youths, before returning again to the church. Years later, in one of those random twists of fate (or twists of divine intervention, mused Gabriel), Peter and Anne met again at, of all things, a surfing-for-Jesus exhibition. Both were in graduate school by then—Peter studying quantum mechanics and Anne studying astrophysics ("I'm into really big, and he's into really small," Anne would like to joke)—and between being pummeled by waves and walking along the beach, renewed a friendship that blossomed into love. After getting married, both found faculty positions (another near miracle) at the same physics department, and near the Pacific Ocean, no less. Gabriel had to take a trip to California, and they all decided to meet up at the beach Saturday morning.

"So, how are things going at your church, Pastor?" asked Peter. Peter loved teasing Gabriel with his title.

"Things are well, though I'm dealing with a dust-up that I'm not quite sure I understand," replied Gabriel.

"What's the issue?" asked Anne.

"Well," said Gabriel, "it's actually about something you two might be able to help me with professionally. At my church, we've been trying to figure out what we should do as a congregation and individually to help care for the environment. Recently, there's been disagreement over what that should look like, and people on different sides have been saying science agrees with their position and disproves the other side. And each side cites scientists and studies to make their point. I'm not quite sure what to make of it."

The three of them looked out towards the ocean. "Well," began Anne, "what do you think, Gabriel?" Anne always did love the Socratic method. "Why do you think people would rely on science to make their argument?"

Gabriel and Peter chuckled at Anne's questioning. "Well," replied Gabriel, "I suppose because they believe science has something authoritative to say about the environment. Otherwise, why bother with the science?" Gabriel smiled and then said, "I have a hard enough time understanding how to tie my shoelaces."

Peter and Anne laughed. "Yes, science is hard," Peter said, "but I shudder to think what I'd do if I had to learn biblical Hebrew or Greek." Gabriel laughed in return.

"But back to my question," said Anne, "why should science be the authoritative word when it comes to the environment?

"I would think," said Gabriel, "that because science studies nature, it tells us what nature is and how nature behaves."

"Yes," said Anne, "science does do this. But, that only explains part of the story. We all study many different things, but it doesn't mean that people consider our opinions on those topics to have authority. For instance, all of Peter and my surfing friends are intense students of ocean waves. I would bet that few oceanographers in the world have as detailed an intuition regarding coastal wave dynamics than an expert surfer. Yet, no one would think of asking a surfer for advice regarding fluid dynamics."

As if to underscore her point, Gabriel saw a surfer in the ocean in front of them cruise so elegantly and effortlessly through the curl formed by a breaking wave that he felt his heart palpitate with excitement. Gabriel turned back to Anne and asked, "So, if it isn't subject matter expertise alone that gives authority, what gives science its authority regarding environmental problems?"

"Because it's science," Anne answered. She smiled at her cryptic reply, as Gabriel rolled his eyes in bemusement.

Peter decided to jump into the conversation. "It's like this, Gabriel. Science is a way of knowing, but like any way of knowing, it has its strengths and weaknesses. Not only that, there are different kinds of science, each of which is not only differentiated by different areas of expertise but also by different ways of thinking. Biologists do not think the same way as physicists who do not think the same way as chemists, and so on. Sometimes, one way of thinking is better, sometimes another; it depends on what question you're asking. But, because of the Enlightenment, our culture thinks of science as both monolithic and omnicompetent."

"So," continued Anne, where Peter had left off, "the most difficult problems will attract the attention of different kinds of science and result in different understandings of the problem. But since our culture thinks of science as monolithic and omnicompetent, few try to understand the nuances between these different understandings or put in the hard work to integrate them all, opting instead to conclude that the differences are due to some science being 'good' and some science being 'bad.'"

Gabriel thought silently. It all seemed rather confusing. The science Peter and Anne were describing seemed foreign and odd. Doesn't science automatically produce the right answers to environmental problems? What was he to make of this nuance Peter and Anne were describing? And, how should it affect the role science should have in environmental debates?

Peter and Anne looked at their friend and saw his uneasiness. "I realize this all sounds strange," said Peter. "We've been taught since elementary school that science has all the answers." Gabriel cracked a smile. Anne smiled back and said, "Let's all go grab some brunch. Difficult questions seldom have easy answers, but the wrestling is always easier with a Mamma Saunders's omelet in front of you."

"Sounds good," said Gabriel, as the three started walking back to their cars. Trying to think through the role of science didn't look like it would be easy, Gabriel thought, but the omelet would go a long way in making up for the effort.

INTRODUCTION

It is a common belief that science tells us whether we have a problem because it tells us what the state of nature is. Both those who argue, "The state of our home planet is not good. The earth is groaning"[1] as well as those who contend, "The world is not without problems, but on almost all accounts, things are going better and they are likely to continue to do so into the future"[2] use science to reach their conclusions. The view that scientific advice provides the foundation on which to build environmental policy has motivated or been the justification for environmentally related governmental agencies and initiatives starting at least as far back as the founding of the U.S. Fish Commission in 1871.[3] As Naomi Oreskes observes, "Nowadays a common political response to an environmental problem is to establish a scientific agency, program, or initiative to investigate it."[4] Regarding environmental issues, science often appears to provide both the first and last word.

In investing science with such authority, however, we often neglect to ask at least two prior questions: what is nature and what is science? And yet, what science can tell us of nature is fundamentally determined by our answers to both questions. As a thought experiment, consider the understandings of "what is nature" provided by two different worldviews, Buddhism and the Enlightenment, and the question "what can a model of ecosystem dynamics say about nature" in light of those understandings. In the Buddhist worldview, nature is sacred/divine while in the Enlightenment worldview, nature is a machine. A model of ecosystem dynamics is a mathematical model that uses statistical relationships and algorithms to simulate the change of an ecosystem over time. Some of the variables in an ecosystem model may be directly measured while others are composite or abstract quantities. Given the very different understandings between the Buddhist and Enlightenment worldviews of what nature is, and this description of what an ecosystem model describes (there are other ways of describing such models), what science (in the form of the model) can say about nature will differ dramatically depending on the worldview.

In chapters 2 and 3, we addressed the question of what is nature by examining a variety of worldviews. In this chapter, we begin by answering the second question—what is science—with a particular focus on understanding how we know there are environmental problems. Next, we

---

1. Bouma-Prediger, *Beauty of the Earth*, 65.

2. Lomborg, *Skeptical Environmentalist*, xxiii.

3. Oreskes, "Proof," 370.

4. Ibid.

examine the connection between science and policy. In a way reminiscent to what we saw in worldviews, we often assume that the translation from science to policy is direct and automatic. In that section, we examine that assumption and create a taxonomy of different ways of connecting science and policy. Finally, we analyze how science influences the criteria for obedience—importance, goals, and practice of the creation care command—and draw some conclusions.

A few final introductory comments regarding this chapter: because the questions of what is science and how do we connect science to policy are not frequently addressed when it comes to analyzing the content of creation care, this chapter is longer than the others. Additionally, we will spend most of our time describing alternatives to the conventional wisdom regarding science and science-policy connections. Since the conventional wisdom regarding these particular topics is widely (if not nearly universally) held, detailed description and analysis of those understandings is not the best use of our time; nearly anyone who has been to middle school can give a description of the hypothesis-testing model of science and policy prescriptive model of science-policy connections.

WHAT IS SCIENCE AND HOW WE KNOW THERE IS A PROBLEM

In general, human beings come to know something one of two ways: someone tells us or we figure it out ourselves. The former, when applied to God, is termed revelation, but revelatory knowledge or knowledge by authority can also be had from human authorities (e.g., experts, parents, etc.). As to "figuring something out," we accomplish this by using our intuition, feelings, or reason. These three methods, along with authority, can be used singly or with one another, and each has its own strengths and weaknesses as an avenue to gaining knowledge. Authority works well if the authority is reliable and competent, but if not, authority can lead us astray. Feelings are very powerful and immediate, but they are easily misled and are ephemeral. Various disciplines use different combinations of authority, intuition, feelings, and reason as part of their characteristic epistemology.

The way science studies the world is popularly understood as having two major characteristics. One, of the four general ways we know—authority, intuition, feeling, and reason—science eschews the first three and is instead based on reason alone.[5] Thus, to say that science studies the world

5. This is related to a myth of the "scientist as computer" (Castel and Sismondo, *Art of Science*, 13–17).

is tantamount to saying science reasons about the world. Two, science reasons about the world using a special methodology (that sets science apart from other non-scientific disciplines that also heavily utilize reason, such as philosophy), often called "the Scientific Method" or the "hypothesis-testing model," that follows this process. First, we start with a tentative hypothesis about the material world. For instance, in an investigation of electricity, we might hypothesize that electrical force varies with distance between charges. Second, we create a test that demonstrates whether the hypothesis is true or not. In our electrical force example, this might be an experiment where we suspend on wires charged balls that are separated by a given distance and then vary the distance between the balls and measure the force between them. Third, we carry out the test, and the results of the test demonstrate whether the hypothesis is true or not true. Fourth, we repeat this process by formulating a new (or revised) hypothesis or a new (or revised) test and testing the hypothesis by conducting the experiment we have devised. Through repeated cycles of testing, we arrive closer to the truth. In this popular understanding, the emphasis on reason, plus the Scientific Method, enables science to provide objective, logical, certain, and authoritative knowledge about nature.[6] We see the fruits of this knowledge everyday—in new and more wondrous technologies, in more detailed and predictive theories, and in new dimensions of awe revealed about the world we live in—and conventional wisdom tells us the credit for this success lies with science's use of reason and the hypothesis-testing methodology.

As another example of hypothesis-testing, consider an investigation into the properties of a force acting on an object. One might make a hypothesis that a force acts in such a way so that the product of mass and acceleration is constant, i.e., $F = ma$. Thus, if we increase the mass of an object, and the force is unchanged, the acceleration of the object will decrease. An experiment to test this hypothesis might be to pull objects with different masses across a surface and calculate the acceleration. If the pulling force is the same each time, and the acceleration decreases by the same factor the mass increases, then we keep the hypothesis. If the acceleration does not change in that way, we discard or revise the hypothesis. After enough time, and enough experiments, an accurate description of the phenomena in question arises, in this case codified as Newton's Second Law.

In this section, we first describe and evaluate the nature of reason and its role in science. Second, we examine critiques of the hypothesis-testing methodology, particularly those that have come during the last half of the

6. Surveys suggest that for many, what makes science scientific is the process by which science progresses, for instance, whether the investigation is impartial or whether other scientists can replicate the result (NSB, *Science Indicators*, 7-31–7-32).

twentieth century from the work of philosophers and historians of science. Third, we consider implications of this critique as to how we understand what is science. Finally, we ask what science can and cannot tell us about nature.

Reason and Science

When we say science uses reason and not the other three types of knowing, what kind of "reason" do we have in mind? The picture many have is of a machine-like calculation process, where conclusions are logically entailed from data. Science thus avoids problems of human bias and error because results in science are in some sense "automatic"; theories naturally flow from data without the need for human mediation. Scientists are still talented, but their role is to faithfully apply the rules of logic to the data they have collected, not to exercise uniquely human judgment, at least insofar as the reasoning process goes.[7]

When one examines the history of science and what scientists actually do, however, a different picture emerges. Instead of exercising the machine-like logic of the calculator, the kind of reason scientists practice uses informed judgment, honed through practice, creativity, and developed intuition. In many ways, scientific reasoning resembles the creative process of the fine arts. Consider even, for instance, how scientists are trained.[8] In science classes, unlike the humanities or arts, doing homework problems (often many of them) is a vital part of class pedagogy. Why? Because it is through doing problems that a person learns not only the laws and principles in the field and ways to apply them, but even what it means to reason using those ideas and principles. Physicist Boris Castel and philosopher Sergio Sismondo compare this process to the way all of us learn languages:

> Most often we learn the meaning of words by hearing them, reading them, using and abusing them and being understood or corrected, until we know their ranges. In the same way we learn the meanings and ranges of ideas. Thus, the student of physics understands that the watchspring and the rocking horse both are harmonic oscillators and learns to see harmonic motion in a variety of objects. Skill in recognition must be learned, because a definition alone cannot allow one to recognize harmonic oscillators in all their variety. Once a person has learned to perceive

7. The discussion in this and the following paragraph is derived from Castel and Sismondo, *Art of Science*, especially chapters 1 and 3.

8. This example comes from Castel and Sismondo, *Art of Science*, 57.

in terms of theoretical concepts, he or she has learned much of
what it means to reason with those concepts.[9]

Two conclusions flow from the fact that scientific reasoning requires
human judgment. First, there is, at its base, a level of under-determinedness
to the scientific endeavor. Human skill, creativity, and judgment is really
required in the reasoning process, and a lack thereof may mean one scientist may understand the results of an experiment in an entirely different
way than another. Second, because scientific reasoning requires more than
just pure reason, other ways of knowing are vital for learning and applying
the human skill, creativity, and judgment needed to complete the reasoning process. For instance, with regards to Castel and Sismondo's problem-
solving training example, we need to ask how students even come to know
what ideas in science are worth studying. Obviously, for those students and
today's practicing scientists, the understanding that force is proportional to
mass times acceleration (F = ma, or Newton's Second Law) did not come
from intuition, feeling, or self-reason. Rather, this knowledge was learned
from and accepted on the authority of credible teachers who in turn learned
it from their teachers, and so on, until one reaches Newton and his precur-
sors.[10] We also see that the use of feeling and other non-rational judgment
can play a role in obtaining scientific knowledge. Kekulé was famously inspired by a dream of a coiled snake biting its own tail to discover the ring
structure of the organic molecule benzene.[11] And in the seventeenth century, mathematician and philosopher René Descartes paired intuition and
reason together, arguing that certain knowledge could be obtained if one
started starting from first-principles apprehended by intuition, and then
deductively reasoned from those first-principles to conclusions.[12]

9. Castel and Sismondo, *Art of Science,* 57.

10. Theologian Edward T. Oakes describes how sociological epistemologist Peter
Berger has shown how science (and other knowledge systems) create certain "social
structures" to convey authority and thus believability of the findings being reported:

> All these factors [of penalizing skeptics] and more (such as peer pres-
> sure, rhetorical bullying, loaded words like *Flat-Earther,* and the like)
> are absorbed by the individual in the process of socialization, during
> which he internalizes what Berger calls "plausibility structures." By that
> term he means those social structures—schools, degrees, peer-refereed
> journals, reputable reference works, credentials, even white lab coats—
> that signal to the individual mind that all this reported knowledge
> he has been learning is *plausible* knowledge. [emphases in original]
> (Oakes, "Epistemic Pathologies")

11. McKim, *Experiences,* 11.

12. Cushing, *Philosophical Concepts in Physics,* 7–9.

The idea that science uses reason plus other forms of knowing, and thus is a human activity using human judgment, does detract from the notion of science as pure and "unsullied" by human characteristics. It also means, however, that science can access truth it otherwise could not if scientific rationality did not involve human judgment, for reason is not omnicompetent in obtaining knowledge. To Christians, who are marked by an intimate awareness of human sinfulness and finitude, this is unsurprising, for we know that no one but God can know everything. We also know that God is much more than reason, and that His characteristics and attributes go beyond even the grandest conceptions of rationality bequeathed to us from Plato, Aristotle, and the rest of ancient Greek philosophy. That reason is a limited means to knowing, however, is not only a revealed truth. Interestingly, mathematics demonstrates that even on its own terms, reason is not omnicompetent. This demonstration uses one of the great achievements of modern mathematics known as Gödel's Theorem, proved in 1931 by the mathematician Kurt Gödel. The details of the theorem and proof are beyond the scope of this book, but we can summarize the main point of what he demonstrated.[13]

Consider some system of mathematics that contains basic arithmetic (e.g., +, ×) and logic (e.g., equal, not). Using such a system, we can create statements that may be true or false. For instance, $1 + 1 = 2$ is a statement that uses the arithmetic operation "+" and the logical operator "=," which stand for addition and equality, respectively. This is an example of a true statement in the system of mathematics we commonly call "arithmetic." An example of a false statement would be $1 + 1 = 3$. In this and any system of mathematics, given a set of rules and postulates, we use those rules and postulates to prove theorems, which in turn can be used in different combinations to prove yet more theorems. In that way, a system of mathematics can be thought of like the trunk and branches of a tree:

13. More precisely, Gödel's Theorem shows that "in any consistent formal mathematical system in which one can do at least arithmetic and simple logic there are arithmetical statements which can neither be proved nor disproved *using the rules of that system* (i.e., using its axioms and rules of inference), but which nevertheless are in fact true statements" [emphasis in original] (Barr, *Modern Physics*, 212). For a well-written and accessible sketch of Gödel's Theorem, see ibid., appendix C. The tree description presented in the figure below comes from mathematician Lance Schaina (personal communication).

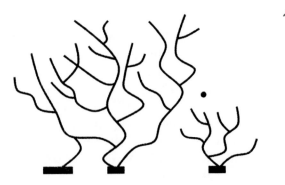

In this figure, the bases of the trunks (the thick, horizontal lines) are the axioms we start with, and the branches are connected chains or sequences of true statements we can prove. The dot in the middle of open space (its location, otherwise, is unimportant) represents a statement we know is true even though we cannot prove it is true *using the rules of the system.* Statements we cannot prove or disprove are represented by the open space between the branches. Regardless of which tree or branch we pick, there is no way to reach those open spaces. Note that while we cannot ever reach the open spaces on these trees, this does not mean that the statements represented by the open spaces are false. They may be true, or they may be false, but given the axioms and rules of the mathematical system, we cannot determine whether they are true or false.

The amazing thing Gödel showed was that amongst "undecidable" statements (shown in our figure by open spaces), there exists a statement that is nonetheless true (shown in our figure by the dot).[14] Using our tree analogy, this means there is a place in an open space that *we can show is true,* even though we can never reach it along a branch. Gödel showed this to be true for not just one arithmetic system, but for all arithmetic systems that are consistent (i.e., systems where we cannot prove two statements true that are also contradictory to one another). Put another way, Gödel's Theorem shows that it is impossible to choose arithmetic axioms and rules that will enable us to prove *all* true statements; there will always be true statements our axioms and rules cannot reach. Because logical reasoning is, at least in its basic form, similar to the mathematical systems Gödel's Theorem applies to, this theorem shows that logic has limits, that there are truths out there that human logic can never, no matter how cleverly postulates are chosen, discover on its own. Reason, then, instead of being sufficient in and of itself to access truth, requires other ways of knowing to assist it. That scientific reasoning utilizes human judgment and creativity in addition to logic high-

14. Barr, *Modern Physics*, 212.

lights both how reason is not omnicompetent as well as the need for other ways of knowing to enable science to properly function. This hints that the role science should play in determining the content of creation care should be one that is more flexible than the one the "myth of scientists as computers" argues for.[15]

In response to this picture of reason in science, some might say that while it may be true that logic alone cannot discover all truth, and science requires some input from forms of knowledge besides reason, still, an augmented reason, when applied in the hypothesis-testing model, will produce certain and authoritative knowledge, and thus, science has an authoritative role in determining the content of environmental stewardship. In other words, one might argue that the source of scientific authority comes from a special methodology, the hypothesis-testing method, not from a perfect form of reason. We now consider that method in detail.

Critique of the Hypothesis-Testing Model of Science

As mentioned earlier, to many, the hypothesis-testing model is a special methodology. It differentiates science from other fields that utilize reason. The hypothesis-testing model also provides a methodology where personal, cultural, and methodological biases play no role in inquiry. By abstracting evaluation of a hypothesis to the comparison of an objective and repeatable test to observed reality, we presumably remove human judgment (and thus bias) from consideration. The data entirely determines the result. And, the method is also inherently self-correcting; successive testing cycles eliminate errors, given enough time.

As we saw in describing and evaluating the use of reason in science, however, the history and philosophy of science paints a more nuanced understanding of the nature of scientific methodology. In this section, we examine a number of the critiques of the hypothesis-testing model, and in the following two sections, we enumerate implications of these critiques. Questions we hope to address include: What kind of knowledge results from hypothesis-testing and its combination with reason? Is this knowledge objective, logical, and certain? If not, to what extent is scientific knowledge about nature authoritative? And what kind of authority does science have?

The first critique raised against the hypothesis-testing definition of science is that it does not provide much guidance as to what constitutes an appropriate test. Unanswered questions include: What kind of control is required for an appropriate test? Must tests be physical experiments or

15. Castel and Sismondo, *Art of Science*, 13–17.

can we conduct a test with a mathematical model? How about a computer model? These questions are not merely academic. If, for instance, we find that tests using computer models have limited epistemological value and say little about whether a hypothesis is true or not, then nearly every branch of science has major subareas that are not scientific; computer modeling is ubiquitous in science.

To give a concrete example, consider the field of global climate dynamics. In global climate research, it is impossible to conduct a controlled experiment because we have only one earth and thus one climate to study.[16] As a result, global climate research must make extensive use of computer models. Computer models, however, by necessity, can only approximate nature. The entire Earth, in those models, is divided up into boxes, and the physical parameters of climate (e.g., temperature, humidity, wind) are calculated assuming there is no variation in climate conditions inside each box. Because the Earth is so large, each box is also very large, typically 1–100 km along a side. Our own experience with weather tells us that there are many phenomena that occur at scales smaller than 1–100 km (for instance, how temperature changes dramatically between being in the sun and under shade), and indeed, climate also varies with scale.[17] But this variability is not explicitly calculated in climate models, being instead approximated by simplifications called "parameterizations." So, when an experiment using a climate model produces a given result, there is always uncertainty whether or not that result reflects the actual behavior of the climate system or rather is a previously unknown consequence of the model's approximations.

This uncertainty, however, is not eliminated even when we can conduct a physical experiment, but instead it only takes a different form.[18] Instead of uncertainty due to computer model approximations, the uncertainty and ambiguity now arises in the mental model we use to interpret the results of the physical experiment. Consider again the hypothesis-testing model

16. Some may argue that extraterrestrial planets can act as controls, since the same physical laws that describe our climate also operate on other planets. But since there are no planets *identical* to Earth, this only moves the question to what are the standards by which we can judge whether another planet is a proper control.

17. Which is why scientists talk about global climate, regional climate, and even microclimates.

18. In a related but slightly tangential note, philosopher Margaret Morrison has argued that the difference between computer and theoretical models and mechanical or physical models is not as large as might be expected (Morrison, "Models, Measurement"). She argues, instead, that the way computer and theoretical models are used in some ways resembles the use of experiment, and thus the "materiality" of experiments may not give experiments much epistemic privilege over simulations (Morrison, "Models, Measurement," 40, 55–56).

example we saw earlier, that of investigating the relationship between force, mass, and acceleration. If we use everyday objects (which tend to be a few inches large and a pound or so in weight) moving at everyday speeds, and a surface that is relatively frictionless (such as ice or an air hockey table), the results of our experiments will closely approximate the predictions of the hypothesis. However, if we use certain less common objects, such as a feather, the experimental results will not fit the hypothesis. It will appear that we have shown the hypothesis (and Newton) was wrong. Of course, we know why the feather gives such different results: air resistance acts against the motion of the object. But what if we did not realize air could provide such resistance? All we have is an unexpected result and whatever mental model we have for viewing those results: Should we assume that the test proves the hypothesis false or conjure up some *ad hoc* explanation, perhaps an unknown force we'll call the "atmospheric medium impulse," to save our hypothesis in spite of our experimental result?[19] By what standard shall we use to choose between the two options? We cannot really know, *a priori*; only with hindsight will the choice be obvious. If so, on what basis do we have to believe the experiment actually falsifies the hypothesis? This, then, is one way in which the standards for an acceptable test are ambiguous under the hypothesis-testing methodology.

Second, the hypothesis-testing model of science suggests that any field with untestable hypotheses is not science. And, yet, throughout history there have been fields of inquiry, commonly recognized as scientific, but containing important untestable hypotheses. For instance, superstring theory, the current front-runner in theoretical physics for a "theory of everything," for decades was considered untestable, a theory that "cannot be falsified by any conceivable experimental result."[20] While the current picture may be less bleak,[21] does this imply that superstring theory was not science until it became testable? Or does a field only have to be theoretically testable in order to be considered science? But if the latter, what then does a test actually do, as far as the hypothesis-testing model is concerned, if the test

19. Aristotle, in fact, used something similar to the latter approach for explaining projectile motion. Lacking the notion of inertia, and convinced motion can only occur with the application of some external agent that gave the projectile a "natural tendency," Aristotle asserted that the curved path of projectiles results from air closing around the projectile and pressing it along (Cushing, *Philosophical Concepts in Physics*, 21–22).

20. Wolt, "String Theory." To be precise, superstring theory is a version of M-theory, the latter of which is considered the best bet for a grand unified theory. However, the term M-theory is less well known, and when we say superstring or string theory in popular discourse, we often mean M-theory; thus, we use the term superstring in the present work.

21. Grossman, "Something Useful."

never has to be run in the real world in order for it to "count?" What would that test, test?[22]

Third, the hypothesis-testing definition of science does not tell us how much evidence we need to amass in order to demonstrate whether a hypothesis is true or false. That is to say, when do we know we have reached the truth? According to the hypothesis-testing model, as we conduct more and more tests, we arrive closer to the truth. Thus, we might assume that if a theory has been tested and found stable and accepted for a long time (e.g., a century), we can have confidence the theory is correct. The history of science, however, is replete with examples of theories that have withstood the test of time for centuries, or even millennia, only to crumble at last. Geocentrism and Newtonian mechanics are two prominent examples from physics. With the former, heliocentrism supplanted geocentrism, and in the latter, Newtonian mechanics was superseded by relativistic or Einsteinian mechanics and quantum mechanics. What then gives us confidence in the correctness of current scientific theories?

One answer to this question comes from an epistemology formulated by the philosopher Karl Popper. In this epistemology, we acknowledge that while we cannot know positively that a hypothesis is true, we can evaluate its truth negatively. That is to say, we cannot know whether a hypothesis is correct but we can demonstrate that it has not yet been shown to be false. Under this kind of epistemology, the only acceptable tests are those that aim to falsify a hypothesis, not those that aim to prove the hypothesis true.[23] "Popperian falsification," while it gives science a dose of epistemic humility and prescribes limits on how science arrives at truth, nonetheless provides a straightforward process by which we can answer how much evidence is needed for us to demonstrate whether a hypothesis is true or not. For, while hypotheses cannot be proved true, Popperian falsification implies that only one failed test is enough to overthrow a hypothesis. As author Michael Crichton has argued:

> Let's be clear: the work of science has nothing whatever to do with consensus. Consensus is the business of politics. Science, on the contrary, requires only one investigator who happens to be right, which means that he or she has results that are

22. Even if we conclude, on the basis of these first two critiques of the hypothesis-testing definition of science, that climate science, superstring theory, etc. do not qualify as science, we still have to decide what they actually are and what kind of knowledge they provide. Are they examples of pre-science? Science in a "hypothesis generating" stage? Theology or philosophy? The hypothesis-testing definition does not appear to help us much with these questions.

23. Cushing, *Philosophical Concepts in Physics*, 32–33.

verifiable by reference to the real world. In science consensus is irrelevant. What is relevant is reproducible results. The greatest scientists in history are great precisely because they broke with the consensus.

There is no such thing as consensus science. If it's consensus, it isn't science. If it's science, it isn't consensus. Period.[24]

Thus, just as in the popular version of the hypothesis-testing model, hypotheses that have survived falsification for an extended period of time appear to be well-founded. The end result is that Popperian falsification provides a means by which science can claim a substantial amount of epistemic authority.

Yet, here again, the history of science again suggests that science does not clearly follow Popperian falsification's straightforward methodology. Consider, for instance, the history of the theory of heliocentrism. Contrary to popular belief, heliocentrism was not first proposed by Copernicus in 1543 but was proposed over 1700 years earlier by Aristarchus of Samos (c. 310–230 B.C.).[25] Aristarchus's model, however, was discounted because heliocentrism predicts that we should observe stellar parallax, the shift in apparent position of the stars that results from the movement of the Earth.[26] Because of the vast distances between the Earth and the stars, this shift is too small to be detected with the naked eye, and thus, for ancient astronomers who lacked telescopes or any other observational aid and who had no sense of the enormous distance separating the Earth from the stars, the absence of observations of stellar parallax appeared to falsify the heliocentric model. So far, this sounds like a textbook case of the use of Popperian falsification in science. However, by the time Copernicus wrote *De Revolutionibus,* stellar parallax was still unobservable. In fact, the first direct observation of stellar parallax was not made until 1837–1839, nearly 300 years after Copernicus proposed his heliocentric model and long after the Copernican model was accepted by the scientific community.[27] That is, one could in some sense say that observations prior to 1839 continued to falsify the heliocentric hypoth-

24. Crichton, "Aliens."

25. Cushing, *Philosophical Concepts in Physics,* 48, 59–60.

26. Ibid., 48–49. We can easily observe parallax by extending out an arm, holding up a thumb, and looking at the thumb while alternately closing one eye and then the other. Because of the separation distance between our eyes, the apparent position of our thumb relative to the background shifts depending on which eye we use to view our thumb. With stellar parallax, the separation distance is the distance between different positions of the Earth as it travels along its orbit around the Sun.

27. Cushing, *Philosophical Concepts in Physics,* 48–49.

esis, and yet no one by that date would even question the idea that the Earth went around the Sun.[28] On what basis, then, did the scientific community have to accept the heliocentric model? Popperian falsification does not appear to provide the full story; the methods of science, as practiced, appear to be more complex than is captured by the popular version of the hypothesis-testing model or Popperian falsification.

A fourth critique of the popular version of the hypothesis-testing model is that it does not give much guidance regarding how to understand uncertainty. There are no perfect measurements. Thus, how do we know when we are seeing a real signal or not? Each discipline, of course, has standards for deciding what qualifies as a discovery and what does not. In some cases in sub-atomic particle physics, a finding is not considered a discovery unless it reaches the "5-sigma" uncertainty level.[29] In climate science, we often consider a 2-sigma result to be noteworthy; geophysical data, compared to particle physics data, is generally much less precise, more difficult to obtain in quantity, and has a weaker signal-to-noise ratio. The point, however, is that these standards are not specified by the hypothesis-testing methodology. They are instead the result of a mix of philosophy, history, and decision-making by the scientific community.

Fifth and finally, the popular version of the hypothesis-testing model does not appear to do an adequate job of explaining how science actually functions, both in the past and the present, while other theories appear to do better. We have seen, in examples such as heliocentrism and stellar parallax, that the history of science suggests the hypothesis-testing model is incomplete. Indeed, the concerted work by historians and philosophers of science over the past half century to study how science has actually functioned, as opposed to how we think it should function, has led to insights regarding the nature of science and the status of the knowledge it provides and alternative models to describe the methodology of science. While the field is rich, here we describe one of the best known and groundbreaking alternatives, Thomas Kuhn's theory of paradigm shifts, as a contrast to the hypothesis-testing model and to illuminate what alternate ways of thinking about science entails.

The Kuhnian theory of paradigm shifts was articulated in *The Structure of Scientific Revolutions*, first published in 1962. Kuhn starts by arguing that scientists all work under a "paradigm," or way of looking at the world.

28. Scholars Dennis Danielson and Christopher M. Graney provide a nice summary of the observational evidence against the Copernican model prior to the nineteenth century (Danielson and Graney, "The Case").

29. That is to say, the level of confidence that the signal is real extends plus or minus five standard deviations (i.e., sigma). See Bialik, "How to Be Sure."

A paradigm is complete in that it provides unity to an inquiry but is incomplete enough that it provides unanswered questions to investigate.[30] A paradigm does not have to explain all observations, or even be true, but in order to be adopted, it does have to be better than its competitors. Scientists conduct what Kuhn calls "normal science" in a paradigm, and normal science is characterized by "puzzle-solving."[31] A crisis comes when the paradigm no longer "works": anomalies occur repeatedly making it difficult to continue the "normal technical puzzle-solving activity" characterized by normal-science.[32] If, at the time of crisis, an acceptable competitor paradigm also exists that better deals with the anomalies of the current paradigm, a wholesale "paradigm shift" occurs. In a paradigm shift, it is important to note that the change is not accretive. The change accompanying a paradigm shift is revolutionary—the world literally changes—with data and results from old experiments reinterpreted in light of the new paradigm and even the meaning of familiar terms changing.[33] For instance, when Einsteinian relativistic mechanics supplanted Newtonian mechanics, the nature of the term "mass" changed. Under Newtonian mechanics, mass refers to the amount of "stuff" in an object; a 1 kg mass has 1 kg worth of stuff. Under Einsteinian mechanics, mass is interchangeable with energy: thus, the famous equation $E = mc^2$.

30. Kuhn, *Scientific Revolutions*, chapter 2.

31. Ibid., chapters 3–4.

32. Ibid., 69.

33. Ibid., 149–50. Others would not go as far as Kuhn. Physicist Stephen Barr, for instance, argues that all theories are built on approximations, and what distinguishes a post-revolution theory from a pre-revolution theory is that the post-revolution theory can explain the pre-revolution theory as a limiting condition in the newer theory (Barr, *Student's Guide*, 58–62). Thus, he argues:

> The word revolution is misleading when applied to scientific theories. In a revolution, the old order is swept away. However, in most of the so-called revolutions in physics, the old ideas are not simply thrown overboard, and there is a not a radical rupture with the past. A better word than *revolutions* to describe these dramatic advances in science would be *breakthroughs*. [emphases in original] (Barr, *Student's Guide*, 59)

While Barr is correct that older theories are not completely ignored during a revolution, the *meaning* of the very words used in those old theories are completely different after a revolution. If it seems there is no radical rupture between Newtonian and Einsteinian dynamics, it is because the practical, everyday utility of Newtonian dynamics more than compensates for whatever loss in status it has suffered from being supplanted by Einsteinian dynamics. In the case of the Copernican revolution, since the level of practical utility for the Ptolemaic model is minimal, even the categories of thought used in the Ptolemaic system (e.g., heavenly perfection requiring geometric analogues) have been discarded.

Physicists often treat Newtonian mechanics as the "low velocity limit" of relativistic mechanics, whose relationships are accurate if speeds are much less than the speed of light. This treatment, however, ignores the fact that the meaning of the quantities in those relationships are not really the same because the two paradigms—Newtonian versus Einsteinian—are ultimately incommensurate.[34] In the change from Newtonian to Einsteinian dynamics, the physical world has literally been redefined.[35] It is as if a man leaving for work in the morning in a Newtonian universe kissed his wife and hugged his kids goodbye, then returned in the evening in an Einsteinian universe to find his wife and kids replaced by an anchovy and a pile of LEGO® blocks. The difference between a Newtonian universe and an Einsteinian universe is not a difference of degree but of kind. Finally, when a paradigm shift or scientific revolution is completed, science operates under the new paradigm and returns to its puzzle-solving focus.

When we contrast Kuhn's alternative model of science against the popular hypothesis-testing model, we find a number of rather substantial differences. First, under the Kuhnian model, science is not accretive, where every advance adds to what came before. New paradigms do not merely add on new findings but rather change even the meaning of old findings. Second, science is not necessarily progressing towards truth, which is what the idea of an accretion of knowledge and the hypothesis-testing methodology suggests; that is to say, the *telos* of the hypothesis-testing methodology is truth through successive refinement. Instead, science is "merely" moving from one paradigm to another (though the new paradigm is considered more "useful" by the community). Truth is no longer the ultimate aim of science but rather community acceptance, and at any given moment in time, the methodology does not guarantee that we have the most "truthful" description possible. Third, while both models have room to understand science as a social endeavor, under Kuhn's model, the social and philosophical aspects determine what paradigms ultimately survive and thus, in contrast to the hypothesis-testing model, play a more prominent role in the evolution of science.

This last point deserves additional explanation. What does it mean that "social constructionist" models of science, of which Kuhn's is an example, reveals a greater social and philosophical aspect to science than is commonly appreciated? First, the social constructionist description of science argues that the rules of science, rather than being objective and

---

34. Kuhn, *Scientific Revolutions*, 101–2. In the cited pages, Kuhn argues that Newtonian mechanics cannot be derived from Einsteinian mechanics.

35. Ibid., 102.

detached, are themselves determined by scientific communities, for their disciplines. As described by the physicist Boris Castel and the philosopher Sergio Sismondo:

> Communities build up canons of rationality that apply to specific domains, learning appropriate ways to think clearly about certain problems, even defining what constitutes clear thinking about those problems. . . . The things that scientists find most useful, and pass on to their students and colleagues, survive in the scientific canon.[36]

Even lone investigators use work done by others and release their work to the acceptance or dismissal of others in their community. Thus, to the extent we invest science with authority because of the belief that its methodology is impersonal and self-validating, social constructionism argues such reasons for confidence in science is misplaced; the rules of science are a human creation. If that authorship delegitimizes scientific findings, something else must give science authority.

Second, social constructionists argue not only that the scientific community authors the rules of science, but also that the community itself plays a critical role in the practice and methods of science using those rules. The hypothesis-testing model views the epistemic methodology of science as primary and the community as merely the venue in which those methods are practiced. Social constructionism views the community dynamics as part of the epistemic methodology of science itself, in particular functioning as *the* critical component during a scientific revolution. For instance, the hypothesis-testing model, because it understands science as objective and impersonal, argues that the testing of hypotheses solely consists of comparing theory with observations of nature. Certainly, scientists compare experimental and theoretical results with observations all the time. The Kuhnian model, however, contends that scientific development during scientific revolutions does not consist solely in comparing results with nature, but also one paradigm with another paradigm. As Thomas Kuhn describes:

> No process yet disclosed by the historical study of scientific development at all resembles the methodological stereotype of falsification by direct comparison with nature. . . . The decision to reject one paradigm is always simultaneously the decision to accept another, and the judgment leading to that decision

36. Castel and Sismondo, *Art of Science*, 79.

involves the comparison of both paradigms with nature *and* with each other. [emphasis in original][37]

Paradigms are human constructs. Thus, the development of science inevitably involves and incorporates evaluation of subjective and human frames of reference; science is not merely an enterprise trafficking in impersonal facts and data.[38]

Indeed, social constructionism ultimately shows that not only is science a social endeavor but that science is fundamentally a *human* endeavor. Scientific knowledge is not "pure" thought but human thought, governed by and in dialogue with philosophy. For example, it is not commonly known that the heliocentric model, as proposed by Nicolaus Copernicus, did a *poorer* job of making astronomical predictions than did the geocentric Ptolemaic model.[39] In order to match the quantitative accuracy of the Ptolemaic model, Copernicus needed to include more than thirty circles (minor epicycles and eccentrics) to his heliocentric model, an addition similar to the additional circles that made the Ptolemaic model cumbersome.[40] That is to say, based on a *quantitative* match to the astronomical data, it was not clear that Copernicus's model outperformed the Ptolemaic model. Rather, it was the *qualitative* strengths of Copernicus's heliocentric model (e.g., providing a natural explanation why the separation angle between Venus and Mercury is so small) that gave it its appeal.[41] But this appeal is fundamentally an appeal based on philosophical reasons (e.g., simplicity, elegance, etc.); it is not an appeal based on numerical accuracy. This example illustrates what Matthew Rees describes as Kuhn's legacy:

> The lasting value of Kuhn's thesis in *The Structure of Scientific Revolutions* is that it reminds us that any science, however apparently purified of the taint of philosophical speculation, is

37. Kuhn, *Scientific Revolutions*, 77.

38. As physicist W. Jim Neidhardt, in summarizing and applying Michael Polyani's work, describes:

> All knowing, whether the subject area be science, philosophy, art, religion, or everyday experience, shares a common structure; acts of discovery are embedded in matrices of personal commitments which the person *indwells* in order to explore reality [sic] thereby bringing about new knowledge. Augustine's insight is still sound: "Unless you believe you shall not understand." [emphasis in original] (Neidhardt, "Personal Knowledge")

39. Cushing, *Philosophical Concepts in Physics*, 65.

40. Ibid.

41. Ibid., 64–65.

nevertheless embedded in a philosophical framework—and that the great success of physics and biology is due not to their actual independence from philosophy but rather to physicists' and biologists' dismissal of it. Those who are inclined to take this dismissal as meaning that philosophy is dead altogether, or has been replaced by science, will do well to recognize the force by which Kuhn's thesis opposes this stance: History has repeatedly demonstrated that periods of progress in normal science—when philosophy seems to be moot—may be long and steady, but they lead to a time when non-scientific, philosophical questions again become paramount.[42]

To the extent the natural sciences seem to progress without recourse to philosophical considerations, and to the extent that the natural sciences seem objective and free from the subjectivity that accompanies any human endeavor, it is not because the natural sciences are free from philosophy; rather, during periods of normal science the natural sciences ignore philosophy, while reengaging philosophy during scientific revolutions.[43] To some, this recognition "delegitimizes" science, stripping it of its Olympian authority, while others find that this reinfusion of humanity makes scientific knowledge humbler but richer. In the next section, we examine these and other possible implications of the critique of hypothesis-testing.

Implications of the Critique of Hypothesis-Testing on How We Understand What is Science

In this section, we examine three implications of the critique of hypothesis-testing on how we understand the nature of science. First, we ask, in light of the critique, how objective is science. Second, we ask how logical is science. Finally, we examine what the critique says of the level of privilege accorded

---

42. Rees, "*Scientific Revolutions at Fifty*," 85.

43. Some have argued that even during normal science, philosophy—in the form of value judgments—still plays an important role in the activity of science. Scholars Erich W. Schienke, Seth D. Baum, Nancy Tuana, Kenneth J. Davis, and Klaus Keller, for instance, argue that three kinds of ethics are present in scientific research: procedural, extrinsic, and intrinsic (Schienke et al., "Intrinsic Ethics," 505–6). Procedural ethics deals with norms of the profession regarding how scientists do their work (e.g., not falsifying results, etc.) and extrinsic ethics deals with the impacts of scientific work (e.g., connection with policy); intrinsic ethics, however, deals with the value judgments scientists make as part of their research, e.g., the choice of variables, how to handle error, etc. (Schienke et al., "Intrinsic Ethics," 505–6). The judgments that are part of intrinsic ethics are, at least to some degree, human judgments, being neither necessarily objective nor necessarily determined by the hypothesis-testing method.

to scientific knowledge. Is scientific knowledge special? In exploring these implications, we find that the different ways of understanding the nature of science that comes from the critique of hypothesis-testing offers cautions about how we use science in determining the content of environmental stewardship as well as opportunities for incorporating science in ways the popular model of hypothesis-testing does not as easily support.

Perhaps the most obvious implication of the critique of the hypothesis-testing model is to question how objective is science. The hypothesis-testing model presents science as a method of inquiry that "automatically" results in truth: the human role is limited and truth is logically entailed. And, because of the accretive view of knowledge, while human imagination plays a role in creating insightful leaps, nonetheless truth will still result (albeit more slowly) without such imaginative genius through the incremental accumulation of knowledge. Thus, the hypothesis-testing model implies science is objective and its knowledge claims are ultimately free from human error (or creativity). But, the critique of hypothesis-testing suggests that human involvement is crucial to science. For instance, we still need to make decisions of what constitutes an adequate test and how much evidence is required for a hypothesis to be confirmed or falsified. Additionally, history shows, particularly outside the periods of normal science, that philosophical concerns can be fundamental. Science, then, does not appear to be an escape hatch through which human knowledge can entirely leave subjectivity.[44]

Second, the critique of the hypothesis-testing model also questions how logical is science. While science uses logic, it is more than logic.[45] Science uses reasoning that is a skill that develops over time.[46] We have seen that this reasoning skill also addresses non-quantitative factors such as simplicity, elegance, fit, etc. and thus is not confined to logic alone. This does not mean that science is subjective in the sense that an individual's opinion has fiat power; it does mean that science is not objective in the sense of being logically entailed.[47] These limits on the logical nature of science, however,

44. As W. Jim Neidhardt summarizes:

> Positivistic philosophers have portrayed scientific research as completely impersonal, yielding knowledge that is truly "true" [sic] devoid of all personal involvement and metaphysical assumptions. What [Michael] Polanyi has done is to show that scientific knowledge is not completely objective, free of all personal involvement; rather scientific knowledge has its personal component whose structure it shares in common with other human activities. (Neidhardt, "Personal Knowledge")

45. Castel and Sismondo, *Art of Science*, 71–75.

46. Ibid.

47. Ibid., 97.

are in some sense required if science is to produce useful knowledge of the real world. As Boris Castel and Sergio Sismondo suggest:

> Logic, while very pretty, is by itself quite useless. Logic is self-contained, and doesn't by itself hook onto the material world. It is the science of statements, describing which statements follow strictly from others. Most of the time very little follows logically from what we know, and when we think that it does we learn that most of our knowledge consists of generalizations that don't hold 100 per cent of the time.[48]

Thus, while the critique of the hypothesis-testing model suggests science is not merely logic and thus is, in some sense, not "pure" reasoning, at the same time these supra-logical considerations enable science to say more about nature than mere logic can.[49]

Third and finally, if science is not as objective or logical as commonly thought, then science is not necessarily absolute or privileged in certainty, authority, or applicability in the way that is popularly understood. In the popular conception of science, the certainty of science is founded on its putative objectivity and rationality. The authority of science, in turn, is based on that certainty (along with its objectivity and rationality), and the applicability of science—that through science we properly understand the workings of the environment—in turn is based on that authority. Thus, to the extent science has authority in our society because of its objectivity and rationality, social constructionism questions that authority. In the place of privileged authority, social constructionism portrays science as a discipline as messy as any other, one where it may be difficult to demarcate what is and is not science[50] and one where rigid tests of what is "true" are not necessarily obvious.

---

48. Ibid., 71–72.

49. The limitations of logic go beyond its inability to provide much useful knowledge about the natural world. Both deductive and inductive reasoning have difficulties: with the former, it often is difficult to satisfactorily justify first-principles while with the latter, the standard justification for the reliability of induction is guilty of begging the question (Cushing, *Philosophical Concepts in Physics*, 11, 31–32). T. J. Logan notes philosopher Johann Georg Hamann goes further by contending the Enlightenment view of reason is the result of a self-deification of reason by reason, an ultimately groundless exercise absent the transcendent call of God (Logan, "Radical Enlightener"). Finally, pragmatically speaking, as C. S. Lewis describes in the epigraph given at the beginning of the present work, reason only reveals what you already know (Lewis, *The Pilgrim's Regress*, 58). We need something more than logic—imagination and revelation—to suggest to us what we do not yet know.

50. For instance, ancient science can contain mystic elements, something not characterized by modern science. Yet, it is not clear that pre-modern science and scientists

This critique of the level of privileged authority afforded science, taken to the extreme, implies science has no more value as a source of knowledge than a personal hunch. However, while the social constructionist critique of science does suggest science lacks privileged authority, this is not the same as saying that science lacks any capabilities whatsoever or that science has no role in understanding environmental issues.[51] Under most definitions of science, including social constructionist models, science is marked by rationality. A high value and role for reasoning helps science produce knowledge that can be less subjective and less driven by emotional considerations than other sources of knowledge. Science can minimize personal bias, provide "neutral" ground where contending sides can meet, and provide a kind of knowledge that is more transparent than emotional and intuitive knowledge. But science is not the only source of knowledge utilizing reasoning (philosophy, for instance, is another) nor is rational knowledge the most useful or applicable form of knowledge in all contexts. For environmental issues, science can provide much: a limited material description of "what is" (though, similar to what we saw with worldviews, "what is" does not necessarily tell us the *meaning* of "what is"),[52] monitoring, and "informed opinions about the plausible consequences of our actions . . . ."[53] But this does not mean the knowledge provided by science trumps all other kinds of knowledge.

Put another way, a science without pretensions to epistemic privilege is not necessarily a science that is lame but rather one that is humble. Applied

---

can be so easily written off as non-scientific merely on this basis. Isaac Newton wrote possibly more on alchemy and biblical studies than on physics (Cushing, *Philosophical Concepts in Physics,* 91–92). All attempts at solving the problem of demarcation are now generally understood as having failed (Hutchinson, "Warfare and Wedlock," 93).

51. A similar critique is that social constructionism leads to a view of scientific knowledge that is "relativistic," i.e., that science does not lead to truth. In response, Thomas Kuhn argues that there is progress in science in the sense that "Later scientific theories are better than earlier ones for solving puzzles in the often quite different environments to which they are applied." (Kuhn, *Scientific Revolutions,* 206) However, in his reading, science does not lead to truth in an ontological sense (i.e., that a scientific theory matches what "really is"):

> I do not doubt, for example, that Newton's mechanics improves on Aristotle's and that Einstein's improves on Newton's as instruments of puzzle-solving. But I can see in their succession no coherent direction of ontological development. On the contrary, in some important respects, though by no means in all, Einstein's general theory of relativity is closer to Aristotle's than either of them is to Newton's. (Kuhn, *Scientific Revolutions,* 206–7)

52. Lin, "Role of Science," 22–25.

53. Oreskes, "Proof," 381.

to people, humility, contrary to conventional wisdom, does not mean "pretty women trying to believe they are ugly and clever men trying to believe they are fools."[54] Rather, as C. S. Lewis points out, humility is a kind of "self-forgetfulness" that results in someone being "so free from any bias in his own favour that he can rejoice in his own talents as frankly and gratefully as in his neighbour's talents—or in a sunrise, an elephant, or a waterfall."[55] As applied to science, humility does not mean thinking *poorly of* scientific knowledge—it does not mean turning the Enlightenment engines of radical skepticism back onto science—but perhaps thinking *less about* scientific knowledge.[56] That is to say, a self-forgetful science sees itself also as similar to other human endeavors rather than a peculiar genius "other."[57]

Such an epistemic humility may have the salutary effect of opening up the consideration of multiple sources of knowledge to complement the knowledge provided by science.[58] We all have an intuitive sense that much of the knowledge used in everyday life is different from scientific knowledge but is important and critical. The sacrificial love of a mother for her child, the joy and sense of belonging that comes from curling up with an old, familiar, classic novel, or the determined practice of the virtue of perseverance: while some effects of each may be understood by scientific inquiry, yet a scientific

54. Lewis, *Screwtape Letters*, 64.

55. Ibid., 63, 64.

56. See Harvey, "Democratization" for an analysis of how Enlightenment skepticism dissolved religious authority structures in the past and are working to dissolve scientific authority structures in the present.

57. For a discussion on the "myth" of scientists as geniuses, see Castel and Sismondo, *Art of Science*, 17–25.

58. Similar to (though different from) our argument regarding a more humble science, Boris Castel and Sergio Sismondo argue for a more "human" understanding of science that they believe will ultimately lead to a better understanding of and respect for science:

> The myths of the computer and the genius make science an otherworldly activity, by making scientists appear inhuman. Because they are so clearly myths, they lend little legitimacy to science. In contrast, we have emphasized the humanity of science, its continuity and comparability with other activities. Thus we have tried to portray science not as an object of veneration from afar, but as an art for appreciation from next door.... None of this provides any reason to doubt the knowledge produced by the sciences. Instead, it provides a better understanding of the solidity of scientific knowledge, which is based in the efforts of many brilliant and hard-working people. Revoking public myths regarding science should allow science to gain, not lose, authority. (Castel and Sismondo, *Art of Science*, 175)

understanding of each will "fail to go to the heart of the matter."[59] We know the knowledge is real even if the knowledge cannot be proven scientifically. Non-scientific knowledge can also have a role in helping us understand and address environmental issues.

A taxonomy of the different kinds of knowledge that can complement scientific knowledge is beyond the scope of the present work. Yet, even without attempting to be complete, we can say something about the kind of complementary knowledge that is important with respect to questions of environmental stewardship. Scientific knowledge, it almost goes without saying, is highly intellectual. It often is analytical and sometimes may be synthetic, and it utilizes both logic and imagination, but science is almost predominantly an activity of the mind and the will. Scientists may love their work and the part of nature they are studying, but the methodology of the work itself is seldom an activity of the heart. In that limitation, science ignores what philosopher Jean Bethke Elshtain calls "local knowledge and lived experience"[60] and (as we briefly saw in chapter 3) what farmer and writer Wendell Berry calls the knowledge that comes with use of "a beloved country,"[61] where expertise is not merely "scientific" in this intellectual sense but lived. It is a knowledge and understanding that comes not only from thinking but doing with love and care.[62] An example Berry gives—of the way a farmer named Mr. Yeary built water breaks on his farm—illustrates this kind of knowledge:

> The way to make a farm road that will not rob the land cannot be learned from books, then, because the long use of such a road is a part of the proper way of making it, and because the use and improvement of the road are intimately involved with the use and improvement of the place. It is of the utmost importance that the rocks to make the water breaks were hauled from the fields. Mr. Yeary's solution did not, like the typical industrial solution, involve the making of a problem, or a series of problems, elsewhere. It involved the making of a solution elsewhere: the same work that improved the road improved the fields. Such work requires not only correct principles, skill, and industry, but a knowledge of local particulars and many years; it involves slow, small adjustments in response to questions asked by a particular place.[63]

59. Hutchinson, "Warfare and Wedlock," 94.
60. Elshtain, "My Mother."
61. Berry, "Argument for Diversity," 115.
62. Ibid., 117, 122.
63. Ibid., 121. See also Karl Clifton-Soderstrom's exploration of the use of

How we incorporate this kind of lived, affectionate knowledge with scientific knowledge is non-trivial (science is not the only form of knowledge in need of humility). While some are sanguine about the possibility of communion between these different kinds of knowledge, rightly finding shared affection for a place to be powerfully unifying,[64] love and care are themselves often too diverse to support such a unification. Even love that is rooted in a place may not be monolithic. As we have seen in our consideration of worldviews and ethical theories, we passionately disagree with one another precisely because our loves compete amongst themselves. The bringing together of scientific and lived knowledge, as well as the knowledge in worldviews, ethics, and the other determinants of the criteria for obedience, requires the bridging of the diversity of affections that characterize these forms of knowledge. The initial thoughts we provide in chapter 8 regarding synthesizing the determinants may also help in bringing scientific and lived knowledge together in conversation.

Implications of the Critique of Hypothesis-Testing Regarding How Monolithic Science Is

Besides the three implications described earlier, the critique of the hypothesis-testing model also suggests science may not be monolithic—that there are limits to which we can talk coherently about a single "science"—but rather that there may be multiple, valid ways of understanding the nature of science. Different disciplines and sub-disciplines have different strengths and weaknesses, and different knowledge domains and applications of knowledge have varying types and levels of certainty and authority. These nuances are non-trivial and can have a substantial impact upon the dynamics of environmental policy, yet they are not often discussed when considering the role of science in environmental issues; thus, we consider this implication of the critique of hypothesis-testing separately from the other three. Based on our brief presentation of the popular hypothesis-testing understanding of science and some of its critiques, we can sketch a suite of spectra of various proposed definitions of science, and in this section we enumerate three such ranges of understanding regarding science.

---

particularity and locality in formulating personal (and community) responses to environmental issues (Clifton-Soderstrom, "Becoming Native").

64. Wendell Berry, for instance, suggests, "'That a scientist and an artist can speak and work together in response to such questions [as to the best use of a place] I know from my own experience. All that is necessary is a mutuality of concern and a mutual willingness to speak common English" (Berry, "Argument for Diversity," 118).

First, different definitions of science will differ on understandings of science's epistemic status: its level of certainty, authority, and applicability. On one end of the spectrum, a logical positivist understanding of science (much in line with the popular hypothesis-testing model) considers science, because of its objectivity and empiricism, the only source of true knowledge. On the other end of the spectrum, some social constructionists may consider science as having the same epistemic status (though different epistemic strengths and weaknesses) as any other form of knowledge, whether philosophical, historical, literary, or artistic.[65]

A second way science may not be monolithic is seen in how definitions of science will differ with respect to whether they describe science in terms of how it works or whether they describe science in terms of the tools it uses. The popular hypothesis-testing model and Popperian falsification, as well as Kuhn's paradigm shift model, all describe science in terms of the method science follows ("how it works"). That is, science is defined in terms of the way it conducts scientific inquiry. In the "tools" definition, we define science based on what tools science uses to conduct that inquiry. An example of the "tools" definition of science is the mathematical-logical definition of science that understands any field utilizing inductive and deductive logical reasoning and mathematics as scientific. Thus, even branches of philosophy that utilize mathematics would be considered scientific, based on the mathematical-logical definition.

A third way we see science may not be monolithic is in the existence of a spectrum of comprehensiveness with regards to the definition of science. Some definitions seek to identify rules or methodologies that describe all aspects of "true" science, regardless of the discipline. The popular hypothesis-testing model, Popperian falsificationism, and some versions of social constructionism, are examples of such comprehensive definitions. Others define science on the basis of identifying a few key traits of science without attempting to be comprehensive. For instance, physicist Ian Hutchinson provides one such "non-comprehensive" definition, arguing only that science is characterized by two criteria: reproducibility (that experiments can be replicated given the same conditions) and clarity (that scientific results must be universally understandable by scientists).[66] Hutchinson does not attempt to go beyond identifying these two criteria in his definition and freely acknowledges that some disciplines that may be considered scientific

---

65. Social constructionist views of the authority of science can sometimes reinforce the radical skepticism that comes from the didactic Enlightenment. Regarding the democratization of scientific knowledge, see Harvey, "Democratization."

66. Hutchinson, "Warfare and Wedlock," 93.

may not meet these criteria.[67] Yet, while the definition may not be comprehensive, Hutchinson's definition permits dialogue to occur regarding how science works in certain contexts.

When we find there is a diversity of definitions of something, it often suggests whatever is being defined is not as monolithic as commonly believed.[68] That is to say, instead of speaking of one simple entity called "science," perhaps it is more accurate and useful to speak of different kinds of "sciences."[69] Each of these different kinds of sciences has different levels of certainty, different attributes (e.g., some will be characterized by a certain way of thinking while others will be characterized by certain tools), and different levels of clarity as to whether it constitutes a "science" (as popularly understood). Given these differences, we have to be careful that we treat the science we are using in a way that is proper for that kind of science in that specific context. The lack of care in this area can result in confused analysis and hampered dialogue.

Sometimes, diversity between different kinds of sciences is due to different levels of complexity of phenomena, different levels of theoretical

67. Hutchinson, "Warfare and Wedlock," 94. Hutchinson restricts his definition in order to better address debates over faith and science, which is the focus of his work.

68. Of course, the lack of convergence of a definition of science does not have to mean that science is diverse and that all of the definitions, in some sense, are correct. It could mean that one (or a few) of the definitions is correct and all others are false or that none of the definitions are correct. Still, as all attempts at solving the problem of demarcation are now generally understood as having failed, this provides *prima facie* evidence that science is not monolithic (see Hutchinson, "Warfare and Wedlock," 93 for a discussion of demarcation).

69. This is in contrast to the claim of reductionism, which contends that all sciences (or at least all natural sciences) can be described in terms of the dynamics of simpler phenomena. Thus, all chemistry can be described in terms of physics, all biology in terms of chemistry, all psychology in terms of biology, and all social and political sciences in terms of psychology. Reductionism thus claims there is ultimately only one science, physics. Physicist and philosopher James Cushing, however, notes that the broader claims of reductionism are questionable and probably unable ever to be tested. He considers geology as an example and argues that:

> Geology would appear to be an example of a natural science that is explicable in terms of the laws of classical physics. Given certain initial conditions of the earth's crust, the system developed according to basic mechanical laws under the influence of the stresses generated by heating and cooling. However, the system is so large and complex that a mathematical calculation based on Newton's laws alone would be hopeless. (Cushing, *Philosophical Concepts in Physics*, 362)

When extended to living systems, the situation becomes more intractable. The claim reductionism makes regarding the monism of the sciences, we suggest, is improbable.

understanding, and differences in availability and quality of data. This diversity, we might say, is due to common differences in the level of advancement between different scientific disciplines and sub-disciplines. In the study of global warming, there are some aspects we understand well (e.g., the greenhouse effect) as well as others we do not understand as well (e.g., feedbacks within the climate system). The Intergovernmental Panel on Climate Change (IPCC) reports have attempted to convey these differing levels of certainty; the Fourth Assessment Report, for instance, assigns a "level of scientific understanding," "confidence," or "likelihood" to various findings or conclusions.[70] Yet, seldom in debates over global warming do we discuss the implications of differing levels of certainty regarding different aspects of the issue.[71] Concomitantly, there is a danger in appropriating the certainty of things we understand well and applying it to those we do not.[72]

The differences between the sciences may also relate to the different *kinds* of sciences involved. As we noted in the previous section, the level of statistical significance that a potential discovery has to clear to be considered a discovery in climate science is much different than in sub-atomic particle physics. This reflects, in part, the differences in kinds of datasets and investigative methodologies available to each field, as well as the field's investigative philosophy. Experimental particle physics can, in general, achieve higher precision, but the phenomena climate science studies has a clearer and more direct connection to human-scale experience. Whether we consider one science "better" than the other depends on the kinds of questions we are interested in. To consider them the same, however, in certainty or applicability (even with their similarities), is incorrect.

70. Solomon, "Technical Summary," 22–23.

71. When we do describe uncertainties, it is usually to claim the science on the issue *as a whole* is reliable or not.

72. In the issue of global warming, the radiative forcing properties of carbon dioxide are well-understood, but the water vapor-related feedback processes, for instance, are not. It is easy, however, to group together all questions related to global warming and talk about our scientific understanding regarding the issue monolithically. Atmospheric scientist Richard Lindzen describes a similar "lumping" process with regards to how we understand "what the science says" regarding global warming:

> The IPCC [Intergovernmental Panel on Climate Change]'s Scientific Assessments generally consist of about 1,000 pages of text. The Summary for Policymakers is 20 pages. It is, of course, impossible to accurately summarize the 1,000-page assessment in just 20 pages; at the very least, nuances and caveats have to be omitted. However, it has been my experience that even the summary is hardly ever looked at. Rather, the whole report tends to be characterized by a single iconic claim. (Lindzen, "Climate Science")

We also see different kinds of sciences in the assessment work done on global warming. The IPCC Assessment Reports include the work of three main Working Groups, numbered 1–3 (which we abbreviate WG1, WG2, and WG3). WG1 addresses the physical science regarding climate science, WG2 the impacts, vulnerabilities, and adaptation to climate change, and WG3 the mitigation of climate change.[73] The topics of each working group naturally draw on the expertise of different disciplines. WG1, for instance, focuses on the natural sciences. WG2 incorporates the natural sciences but focuses on the social sciences and economics. Likewise, WG3 uses the natural sciences but focuses on environmental science, policy studies, and economics. Just as particle physics is a different kind of science compared to climate science, so too are the different disciplines that study global warming. The natural and social sciences are not the same. Accordingly, conclusions by WG1 have a different status from those by WG2 and WG3: there are different levels of certainty, different levels of applicability, and the levels of consensus present in each discipline regarding global warming are different (as is the value of consensus as a metric of certainty or believability). Again, this does not mean one discipline or Working Group is "better" than another; that evaluation depends what topics we are interested in. However, to claim that the work products of WG1, WG2, and WG3 can be, in general, treated interchangeably in terms of the status of the knowledge they provide, because they all represent "science," is incorrect.

Historian Naomi Oreskes describes one particularly dramatic example of two different sciences studying one interrelated environmental system but whose differing approaches and investigative foci led to sharp and very public disagreement.[74] The Acoustic Thermometry of Ocean Climate (ATOC) experiment was conceived by physical oceanographers in the late 1970s as a means of directly measuring the long-term temperature of the Earth without the noise and other difficulties that bedevil atmospheric temperature datasets.[75] The project would take advantage of the direct dependency on temperature of the speed of sound in water by measuring how long sound waves generated from sonar sources took to traverse known distances; those measurements of sound velocity would yield a measure of oceanic temperature and repeated measurements over time would reveal how the Earth's temperature changed with time.[76] Feasibility tests for the experiment in the early 1990s demonstrated the probability of success, but in 1994 a

73. IPCC, "Working Groups / Task Force."
74. Oreskes, "Proof."
75. Ibid., 377.
76. Ibid.

consortium of environmental groups filed suit to stop the ATOC project, citing concerns raised by some biologists over the possible effect the ATOC sonar signal would have on marine mammals, whales in particular; that potential impact fueled an intense and passionate opposition.[77] Throughout the 1990s, a battle played out in the media and permitting process, pitting physical oceanographers against cetacean biologists and conservationists, ending in 1999 when the permits for the project were not renewed.[78]

What does the ATOC controversy illustrate? We could chalk up the different views between the oceanographers and biologists involved in the ATOC debate to mistrust, ignorance, or error on one side or the other, and certainly, Oreskes describes various participants accusing the other side of such views.[79] But the ATOC controversy also illustrates that between different natural sciences—indeed, even between different scientists within a single discipline—there are different yet legitimate ways of approaching and understanding what is being studied.[80] As Oreskes notes:

> Even when there is no transparent political, social, or religious dimension to a debate, honest and intelligent people may come to different conclusions in the face of the "same" evidence, because they have focused their sights on different dimensions of that evidence, emphasizing different elements of the evidentiary landscape. Even when a scientific community reaches consensus on a previously contested issue—as earth scientists did in the 1960s over moving continents—there are always dimensions that remain unexplained.[81]

The ATOC controversy suggests a monolithic conception of science is mistaken and that science, by its very nature, often speaks with more than one voice.[82]

77. Ibid., 378–79.

78. Ibid., 378.

79. Ibid., 378–79.

80. As Daniel Sarewitz notes regarding the ATOC controversy, "Oceanographers were primarily concerned about conducting an oceanographic experiment that would document global warming. Biologists were primarily concerned about the effects of acoustic transmissions on the well-being of marine mammals already under assault from human activities. These positions are not reconcilable because there is nothing to reconcile—they recognize and respond to different problems." (Sarewitz, "Environmental Controversies," 390)

81. Oreskes, "Proof," 380.

82. Sarewitz, "Environmental Controversies," 390–92. This multiplicity of voices, Daniel Sarewitz points out, is inherent to the cultural and value differences encoded within scientific disciplines, and thus, "Even the most apparently apolitical, disinterested scientist may, by virtue of disciplinary orientation, view the world in a way that

But the issue of whether or not science is monolithic is not merely an academic exercise. In environmental controversies, the idea that science is monolithic may hamper efforts at dialogue by hiding the root causes of the controversy. To understand how this works, we first need to examine how environmental controversies become "scientized."[83] Scientization refers to how debates over environmental issues often become debates over the science concerning those issues—is there a problem, how bad is it, what we should do in response, etc. Once an environmental issue is scientized, different sides of the controversy align themselves with one set of scientists versus another; often, each side accuses the other of "manipulating" or "politicizing" the science by distorting the evidence or the scientific process.[84] Conventional wisdom tells us the scientization of environmental debates occurs because science tells us "the truth": what the environmental problem is and what to do about it. Thus, disagreements regarding an environmental issue *must be* disagreements over what the science says. Only through clearing away errors (and manipulations) regarding the science to obtain the correct scientific result can we properly understand the environmental problem and its possible solutions; debate over the science of the controversial topic is the way we discover what is true about the topic.[85]

---

is more amenable to some value systems than others. That is, disciplinary perspective itself can be viewed as a sort of conflict of interest that can never be evaded" (ibid., 392). This, however, brings up the question of how we go about evaluating the claims of scientists when scientists do not agree with one another. Naomi Oreskes suggests one approach is to listen to the "relevant experts," where relevance is not only a function of the field of study but also the nature of the questions we want answered, based upon the value priorities we hold:

> In the case of DDT, food scientists were qualified to speak to the agricultural benefits of DDT, and wildlife biologists were better placed to speak to the ecological harms. In this sense both sides were right in what they affirmed but wrong in what they denied, and ultimately the question was not so much who was "right," but which set of concerns—an enhanced food supply for humans or greater protection of wildlife—would be viewed as more pressing. (Oreskes, "Proof," 380)

83. Sarewitz, "Environmental Controversies."

84. Ibid., 388.

85. Ibid., 386. Conventional wisdom also suggests other reasons for the scientization of environmental controversies. For instance, because science has such prominent authority, all sides in an environmental controversy will be interested in securing that authority to bolster their respective positions. While this political use certainly can be a motive for scientization, it is somewhat tangential to our primary question: How does the nature of science influence dialogue regarding environmental issues? Thus, for our purposes, we focus on arguments stemming from the nature of science itself rather than political, psychological, or social uses of science.

While science, of course, does have much to say about the state of nature and plays an important role in understanding environmental issues, the conventional wisdom explanation does not adequately explain why environmental controversies become scientized. For implicit in its narrative is the assumption that there is a single, monolithic science that remains at the end of the scientific debate. We have already seen that such an assumption is questionable in the organization of science: different scientific disciplines show marked diversity in tools, culture, and values. With most environmental controversies, to the diversity of disciplinary viewpoints is added the complexity of nature itself; environmental controversies tend to occur with problems—such as global warming—where the complexity of nature (and our limits in understanding) create an "excess of objectivity" where a large pool of facts permit multiple, divergent, but legitimate interpretations.[86] Science-policy scholar Daniel Sarewitz explains:

> This condition may be termed an "excess of objectivity," because the obstacle to achieving any type of shared scientific understanding of what climate change (or any other complex environmental problem) "means," and thus what it may imply for human action, is not a lack of scientific knowledge so much as the contrary—a huge body of knowledge whose components can be legitimately assembled and interpreted in different ways to yield competing views of the "problem" and of how society should respond. Put simply, for a given value-based position in an environmental controversy, it is often possible to compile a supporting set of scientifically legitimated facts.[87]

Thus, the very nature of science provides the ammunition that *all* sides of an environmental debate can fire with the guns of science. This is not, as Sarewitz points out, merely the case of cherry-picking the facts one prefers. Rather:

> The point is that, when cause-and-effect relations are not simple or well-established, *all* uses of facts are selective. Since there is no way to "add up" all the facts relevant to a complex problem like global change to yield a "complete" picture of "the problem," choices must be made. Particular sets of facts may stand out as particularly compelling, coherent, and useful in the context of one set of values and interests, yet in another appear irrelevant to the point of triviality. [emphasis in original][88]

86. Ibid., 389.
87. Ibid.
88. Ibid., 390.

When an environmental controversy is scientized, all sides argue that theirs provides the correct scientific understanding of the problem and, at the same time, that opposing views are held because of unscientific reasons (e.g., political, religious, error, etc.). Sarewitz's argument suggests that the nature of science feeds this scientization, by providing multiple, reasonable interpretations. A monolithic understanding of science, by hiding the diversity of science and the underdetermined nature of nearly all complex environmental problems, helps prevent the "de-scientization" of environmental controversies. That is to say, by hewing to a monolithic understanding of science, we will tend to believe science (and our interpretation of the science) will provide the correct answer to the environmental problem. Under that belief, it becomes more difficult for us to consider our opponents as "reasonable"; the possibility of dialogue suffers. Additionally, to the extent we consider the environmental controversy as mainly a scientific problem, it becomes more difficult for us to recognize the degree to which our position and our opponents' is a value proposition.[89]

What Science Can Tell Us about Nature and Environmental Problems

Because there are multiple ways of understanding what is nature (i.e., worldviews) as well as multiple ways of understanding what is science and what kind of knowledge science provides, there are multiple answers to the question "what can science tell us about nature." Indeed, because there are two "variables" that contribute to answering the question, the total number of possible answers will be substantially larger than the number of possible worldviews. A Buddhist can subscribe to a hypothesis-testing

89. Daniel Sarewitz argues that environmental controversies are fundamentally value conflicts and that the successful resolution of the controversy requires explicit attention to those conflicts. Thus, environmental controversies do not have to be "scientized" and:

> Even if science brings such a controversy into focus (for example, by documenting a rise in atmospheric greenhouse gases), the controversy itself exists only because conflict over values and interests also exists. Bringing the value disputes concealed by—and embodied in—science into the foreground of political process is likely to be a crucial factor in turning such controversies into successful democratic action, and perhaps as well for stimulating the evolution of new values that reflect the global environmental context in which humanity now finds itself. [parenthetical citation removed] (Sarewitz, "Environmental Controversies," 399)

understanding of science, a Popperian falsificationist view, a social constructionist understanding, etc. Likewise, an Enlightenment materialist, a Taoist, a Christian, etc., can make the same or different choice. In this section, we illustrate the process of thinking through what science can tell us about nature and environmental problems by examining one possible pairing in detail: a theocentric Christian worldview coupled with a Kuhnian notion of science and an understanding that science is limited to the material realm. We do not claim this particular pairing to be representative of any other pairing. It is, however, given the arguments we have advanced thus far, reasonable and educational. Regarding its reasonability: while our primary goal in this chapter has been to describe the spectrum of views regarding the epistemology of science rather than to advance one particular view as the one correct view, we trust that our discussion of the Kuhnian understanding has established it as an option worth considering. Regarding its educational value: because the Kuhnian model is less generally well-known compared to the hypothesis-testing model, we believe further examination of the Kuhnian model will pay greater dividends in terms of understanding. Other reasons certainly exist for this and any other possible pairing. For our current purposes, we believe this is a good place to start.

Given this pairing, we can enumerate some attributes about nature and science:

1. Nature is a witness to Christ and brings glory to God.

2. Nature is God's handiwork.

3. Nature is material but not merely material. Nature exhibits regularity but is not a machine, as it has purpose and is sustained by God Himself. Thus, nature is not empty material.

4. God's activity in nature is both mediated (natural laws) and unmediated (miracles).

5. Science focuses on explaining material regularities.

6. Science does not necessarily provide the complete truth regarding characteristics of these material regularities, because of the paradigm-shifting nature of science.

7. Even if tentative, science provides some knowledge about the world. This knowledge may not be privileged or complete but it is still real knowledge.

8. The demarcation between science and non-science is fuzzy.

Given these attributes of nature and science, what can science tell us about nature? We can identify three aspects. First, science can describe the material state of nature, where "state" is in terms of material and conceivably measurable quantities.[90] Second, science can describe the mathematical dynamics of the material state nature: its history, how it changes, grows, and adapts, and the interactions between parts of nature and human beings. While this provides substantial knowledge about the natural world, at the same time the range of phenomena adequately describable or solvable by mathematical tools is limited.[91] Third, science can give us only hints of God's glory as witnessed to in nature, since the material world is a fallen, limited, and non-exhaustive reflection of God's glory (who is beyond space-time) and science is a fundamentally human (and thus limited) endeavor. Yet even these hints glimpse a testimony of uncontainable power to the glory of God:

> The heavens declare the glory of God;
> > the skies proclaim the work of his hands.
> Day after day they pour forth speech;
> > night after night they reveal knowledge.
> They have no speech, they use no words;
> > no sound is heard from them.
> Yet their voice goes out into all the earth,
> > their words to the ends of the world.[92]

Conversely, given the attributes of nature and science we enumerated, what can science *not* tell us about nature? We can identify five aspects. First, while science can tell us much about how nature is functioning (within the limits of the tools of science), science cannot tell us what that means. Second, science cannot describe everything regarding what it means for nature to flourish, because nature is not merely material and the knowledge science provides has limits. Third, science does not provide an exhaustive description of God's activity in nature, even with regards to the material parts of nature. Fourth, while in principle science could describe all humanly accessible regularities in the material world, the lack of ontological

---

90. In this example, we consider fields of science that traffic in theoretically measurable quantities, such as superstring theory, as "science," even if it is doubtful whether the technology will ever exist to directly measure the tiny quantities superstring theory studies.

91. A classic example, partly mentioned earlier in this chapter, from the field of climate dynamics is the parameterization or representation of convective cloud systems. While it has long been recognized that precipitation heavily influences atmospheric circulation, the scales at which precipitation occurs is unresolvable by climate models. Thus, climate models need to represent convective phenomena as functions of large-scale phenomena which, almost by definition, is an approximation. For a description of aspects of this problem, written for a non-specialist audience, see Lin, "Little Things."

92. Ps 19:1–4a.

correspondence between scientific claims and "truth" prevents science from actually doing so (or, at least, from us realizing it). Fifth, science describes regularities, but those regularities in and of themselves, except in rare cases, do not create logically entailed moral obligations, because science can tell us what the world is in its material sense but not what that means.

From this example, we make two observations. First, under the pairing of one possible but reasonable Christian worldview and a more limited understanding of the nature of science, science will have a more limited role in determining the content of creation care than many people recognize. Under those assumptions, science is unable to provide more than a partial understanding of nature and we have to look elsewhere for additional guidance. Second, this example illustrates the controlling importance of our assumptions about the nature of nature and the nature of science for determining what science can tell us about nature. If the above description of what science can and cannot say about nature seems odd to us, it probably means that we hold a different view of the nature of nature and/or the nature of science than was presumed in the example. Depending on what we believe is the nature of nature and science, we will answer the question "what does science tell us about nature" differently.

In our examination of the nature of science, we have seen that while science is predominantly characterized by reason, this reason may not be some "pure" form of logic but makes use of the other forms of knowing. This cooperation between forms of knowing, while at odds with an understanding of science as authoritative because of its pure rationality, provides a way for science to access truth pure reason alone cannot. This suggests that when it comes to the role of science in determining the content of creation care, it may be better to use science in partnership with other methods of knowing. With respect to the hypothesis-testing model, a study of the history of science suggests a similar story as in the case of reason: science, though powerful, may not provide as conclusive an understanding of the state of nature as commonly believed. This also suggests it is important for science to act in partnership with other methods of knowing. Finally, we have found that depending on our pairing of worldviews and scientific epistemologies, the answer "science determines the content of environmental stewardship" may ask too much of science. In the next section, we delineate a range of ways that science can connect to policy.

CONNECTING SCIENCE TO POLICY[93]

In the previous section we saw that the idea of science having a single fixed nature is questionable. Science may follow the popular conception of being based on reason and hypothesis-testing, but science and scientific reasoning may be more complex than the popular conception suggests, and the knowledge we gain from science may in turn be more complex than we often realize. Not only is there a range of possible understandings of what is nature, there is also a range of possible understandings of what science can tell us about nature. Even for those who adhere to the Christian worldview (as we saw in the example in the previous section), it is not necessarily true that science can tell us everything about nature. Thus, given the diversity of views of worldviews, ethics, and what is science, we might expect that there is a range of views of the authority and role of science in policymaking. (Note that throughout this section, "policymaking" refers not only to governmental and legal decisions and courses of action but also to personal and community ones.)

What might this range look like? Consider two possible "extremes" in a spectrum of answers on the authority and role of science in policymaking.[94] We may hold the Enlightenment worldview that nature is material and that science is the only true knowledge because it is empirical.[95] Given these assumptions, we may conclude that science has absolute authority in terms of environmental policy because it gives knowledge about all there is to know. At the other extreme, we may take a monist view of nature, where nature's material aspect is unimportant relative to its existential status (e.g., a Buddhist worldview), and couple that to an understanding of science as completely socially constructed. Given these assumptions, science has limited authority over environmental policy.

Of course, between these two "extreme" views are a variety of intermediate positions. One such position, that many may find more reasonable, views nature and science in the following way: that nature has a

93. Most of the key ideas (and diagrams) in this section come from a collaboration with philosopher Karl Clifton-Soderstrom. Any deficiencies, however, are my own.

94. This spectrum is not one-dimensional (e.g., left-right, top-bottom, etc.), as the term "extremes" implies, but we still use the phrase because at least one factor in the answer occupies an extreme on another range.

95. In this understanding, sometimes termed "logical positivism," the only true knowledge concerns empirically accessible phenomena (i.e., phenomena that you can measure and sense), and thus science provides the only true way of knowing because it has an empirical foundation. All non-testable knowing is seen as meaningless (Uebel, "Vienna Circle"). For a summary of the philosophical principles and reasoning underlying logical positivism, see Uebel, "Vienna Circle."

material component (though may not be exclusively material) and that science's mathematical knowledge of the material world is authoritatively true in some aspects but is incomplete. What would be some implications of this more "moderate view" regarding the authority of science for policy? First, scientific description may be necessary for some policymaking, if the policymaking requires us to describe material parts of nature. Second, scientific description, while necessary, might not be sufficient for policymaking. The degree to which science is sufficient for policymaking depends on the degree of "incompleteness" of scientific knowledge. (Incompleteness, in this sense, is not merely epistemic incompleteness but also sociological and political. That is to say, it is not only whether science gives complete knowledge about nature but also whether this knowledge is "enough" to translate into policy.) This opens multiple alternatives for science-policy connection. Third, science may not be able to answer certain questions that impinge upon policy. These questions include: quantifying some non-instrumental values of nature, weighing different values and understandings of risk, especially between people, and justifying a particular ethical theory or worldview.

In the rest of this section, we describe a taxonomy of five ways science may connect with policy: policy prescriptive, fact-value dualism, supporting role (science is neutral), supporting role (science may not be neutral), and the "Honest Broker of Policy Alternatives."[96] These ways are not necessarily mutually exclusive (hybrids and simultaneous combinations are quite possible), but they do represent different ways of connecting science to policy. The categories in the taxonomy are, to some extent, functions of different understandings of nature, ethics, and science; they are not exhaustive and other worldviews, ethical understandings, and views of science can lead to a different taxonomy.[97] Nonetheless, these five ways are a broad and representative sampling of ways to connect science with policy. After describing each model in the taxonomy, and the strengths and weaknesses associated with each model, we consider one final topic with regards to the connection between science and policy—handling uncertainty—and describe a range of strategies used to deal with the uncertainty inherent in nearly every environmental policy issue.

---

96. The last item in the taxonomy is from Pielke, *Honest Broker*, 11.

97. Roger A. Pielke, Jr., for instance, describes a taxonomy of four "roles for scientists in decision-making" that is a function of one's view of "the role of science in society" (linear vs. stakeholder model) and view of "the role of the expert in a democracy" (Schattschneiderian vs. Madisonian). (Pielke, *Honest Broker*, 11, 14) The four roles that arise from these two variables are the "Pure Scientist," "Issue Advocate," "Science Arbiter," and "Honest Broker of Policy Alternatives." (Pielke, *Honest Broker*, 11)

Policy Prescriptive Model

In the policy prescriptive model, science directly leads to policy.[98] "Science proves it, now do it" might be the motto. As might be expected, the policy prescriptive model arises naturally from a view of science as providing privileged and authoritative knowledge about environmental problems. It also fits in with an understanding of nature as having substantial material attributes that are amenable to study and description by the tools of science. As a corollary to the policy prescriptive model, the best policymakers are scientists, because they have the deepest understanding of the scientific knowledge needed to make optimal decisions. Schematically, we can diagram the policy prescriptive model as saying:

$$science \rightarrow policy$$

$$values$$

In the diagram, science directly leads to policy, as shown by the arrow. Additional perspectives, ethics, priorities, and forms of knowledge are denoted by the word "values." These values co-exist with the science but do not play a role in determining policy.

The policy prescriptive model has a number of strengths. First, it is a simple and straightforward model that closely describes the general public understanding of science and its relationship to policy. Surveys repeatedly show public confidence that science provides benefits that outweigh costs and trust that scientists offer impartial and knowledgeable leadership regarding policy issues (e.g., global warming, stem cell research) that relate to science,[99] this despite a reluctance in American democracy to wholly leave policymaking to a technocratic elite.[100] Perhaps the presence of public support for a pol-

98. The policy prescriptive model is similar to what Roger A. Pielke, Jr. describes as the "linear model" of the role of science in policymaking (Pielke, *Honest Broker*, 13).

99. For instance, see NSB, *Science Indicators*, 7-3-7-4. Beyond opinion surveys, the public appears also to have put its money where its mouth is: Global spending on research and development was US$1.1457 trillion in 2007 (The Royal Society, *Global Scientific Collaboration*, 16).

100. Science-policy scholar Sheila Jasanoff summarizes this tension in the following way:

> Like Yaron Ezrahi's "pragmatic rationalist," many Americans are persuaded that even the most technical policy decisions require a judicious mixture of scientific and nonscientific judgment, and there is a concomitant fear of letting experts usurp that part of decisionmaking which should be truly political. Yet an alternative view—that components of decisionmaking requiring specialized knowledge should be

icy prescriptive approach is unsurprising. As the hypothesis-testing model of science, with its high understanding of the authority of science, is the model many, if not most, elementary and high school students are exposed to in their science classes, we would expect an understanding of the role of science for policy in line with the authority implications of that model.

Of course, earlier in this chapter we described the critique of the hypothesis-testing model of science. Yet, even if that critique is justified and science is not entirely objective, science may still be the knowledge system closest to the objective ideal. To that extent, we may argue that science should still be the basis of policymaking for technical issues. In this sense, the policy prescriptive approach is the best of imperfect options for the role of science in policy. The alternative to a policy prescriptive role for science—for policymaking controlled at least by partly rational and objective input—appears to be either subjective, human judgment or the exercise of raw power. Thus, a second strength of the policy prescriptive model is that there may not be a better alternative.

What are the weaknesses of the policy prescriptive model for science? Here we examine three possible weaknesses. First, there are solid philosophical reasons why we should doubt science alone without ethics can justify policy.[101] The "is-ought" dichotomy, as we saw in chapter 2, suggests that it is generally not possible to directly conclude an "ought" from an "is." As science describes (at least partially) what "is," when it comes to the material aspect of the environment, and policies in some way describe how we believe the world "ought" to be (e.g., cleaner, healthier, wealthier, etc.), the "is-ought" dichotomy suggests that when science is used to help formulate policy, something besides science must also involved. There are many candidates for that "something"—worldviews, ethics, etc.—but what is provided is the "meaning" of the "is" science describes. A scientific description of what is, when coupled with the meaning of what is, can help lead to knowing what should be (and thus to policy). Schematically, we can summarize this argument as saying:

science → what is
what is + meaning of what is → what should be.[102]

Of course, the degree to which science can tell us what is depends on both our philosophy of science as well as our worldview. That caveat aside, the

---

depoliticized and left to experts—continues to reassert itself in American politics. (Jasanoff, *The Fifth Branch,* 9)

101. For instance, see Lin, "Role of Science."

102. Lin, "Role of Science," 22.

is-ought dichotomy suggests that even if we believe science tells us the state of the environment, it may not be possible to directly translate that scientific description into policy.

A second weakness of the policy prescriptive model for connecting science to policy is the inability of the model to accurately describe science-policy connections in (at least some) environmental issues. Consider, for example, the issue of stratospheric ozone depletion and the attendant international ban on chlorofluorocarbons (CFCs). The conventional wisdom regarding ozone depletion fits the policy prescriptive view of science and policy: Scientists discovered the depletion of stratospheric ozone and found that the cause of this depletion was the use of CFCs. Once the science was settled, policymakers listened to the findings of the scientists and banned CFCs through the adoption of the Montreal Protocol, and as a result, the ozone hole was closed. While certain elements of this conventional wisdom are true—for instance, research indicating CFCs might damage the ozone layer did put the chemical on the radar of policymakers[103]—other elements of the story do not so neatly fit the policy prescriptive model. Political action, for example, occurred even while the science was uncertain,[104] tiered policies (instead of an immediate, all-out ban) helped stimulate research into alternatives,[105] and those alternatives, in turn, defused probable conflicts between stakeholders.[106] As Daniel Sarewitz describes it, "The ozone story is less one of controversy resolved by science than of positive feedback among convergent scientific, political, diplomatic, and technological trends."[107]

The inadequacy of the policy prescriptive model to fully describe how science enters into policymaking is symptomatic of a deeper problem: scientific knowledge or consensus often is insufficient to drive policy decisions. Science-policy researchers have identified a number of limitations of

103. Pielke, *Honest Broker*, 97.

104. Sarewitz, "Environmental Controversies," 397; Grundmann, "Ozone and Climate," 89–90, 92–93; Benedick, "Avoiding Gridlock."

105. Pielke, *Honest Broker*, 140.

106. Ibid., 97–98; Sarewitz, "Environmental Controversies," 397. A detailed account of the interactions between science and policy regarding stratospheric ozone depletion is given in Pielke and Betsill, "Policy for Science."

107. Sarewitz, "Environmental Controversies," 397. Something similar can be seen in the history of regulatory policy regarding formaldehyde and the risk of cancer, as Sheila Jasanoff notes: "Skeptics could well ask, therefore, whether the cessation of scientific controversy in the United States was a product of new knowledge, certified by improved review procedures, or a reflection of the formaldehyde industry's gradual admission that lower standards were technically achievable" (Jasanoff, *The Fifth Branch*, 207).

scientific knowledge in settling policy controversies. Sometimes, scientific knowledge is unneeded to settle a policy debate, as the debate is settled on other terms.[108] In other cases, science encounters a debate between entrenched positions, and science, rather than providing authoritative and neutral knowledge to end the debate, becomes itself a battleground between those competing positions.[109] As Sheila Jasanoff concludes from examining the history of formaldehyde regulation, "when the stakes are high enough, no committee of experts, however credentialed, can muster enough authority to end the dispute on scientific grounds."[110] Instead, as Roger A. Pielke, Jr. notes, science can only compel action when in situations of "shared values and low uncertainties about the relationship of alternative courses of action and those valued outcomes."[111]

The weaknesses of the policy prescriptive model, however, may not be only descriptive; the policy prescriptive model may inadvertently work to cause harm to both science and policymaking. In the policy prescriptive model, because science directly translates into policy, the natural inclination is to settle the science first and then enact policy using the science. This "linear model" of science policy, however, as Roger A. Pielke, Jr. points out, can create a "mutually reinforcing iron triangle of shared interests [that] serves to replace explicit political debate about policy issues with implicit political debate shrouded in the language and practice of science."[112] In one corner of the triangle we have politicians who wish to avoid unpopular decisions; the linear model enables the politician to delegate hard decisions to science. In another corner of the triangle, we have scientists who want research funding. The linear model provides justification for such funding while freeing scientists from having to ascertain how that research may or may not help policymakers.[113] In the last corner of the triangle, we have special interest advocates who are looking for science to give authority to their policy preferences. Earlier in this chapter, we saw how science provides

108. Ibid., 8.

109. Ibid.; Sarewitz, "Environmental Controversies," 386.

110. Jasanoff, *The Fifth Branch*, 234.

111. Pielke, *Honest Broker*, 36.

112. Ibid., 145. The description of this "iron triangle" in the rest of this paragraph is from Pielke, *Honest Broker*, 143–45.

113. Under the linear model, because science is understood as policy neutral and scientific findings automatically flow into policymaking, the scientist has no role in ascertaining whether the knowledge from science is useful to policymakers (Pielke, *Honest Broker*, 144). For a review of the science-policy research regarding the kinds of information policymakers need from scientists, see McNie, "Reconciling the Supply."

an "excess of objectivity"[114] that provides multiple lines of valid, scientific reasoning regarding environmental controversies; special interest advocates thus have "a vast pool of knowledge from which information and data can be carefully cherry-picked to support a predetermined view."[115] The linear model, then, provides the conditions for the use of science for policy to be determined by special interest advocates. The result is the scientization of value debates that results in greater gridlock[116] and, because of the use of science primarily by advocates, an increased risk that science will be seen as merely a political tool.

Fact-Value Dualism Model

We have seen that in at least some cases, rather than being a straightforward exercise in the application of information, policymaking has an intrinsic value component.[117] The fact-value dualism model acknowledges that value component and separates science and policymaking into two completely separate realms. In this model, science provides objective facts about nature that are then interpreted into policies using subjective values.[118] Schematically, we can diagram this model as:

$$\text{science} \rightarrow \text{values} \rightarrow \text{policy}$$

114. Sarewitz, "Environmental Controversies," 388.

115. Pielke, *Honest Broker*, 144–45.

116. Disagreement over values can be settled only by a dialogue over values; value debates are not, in general, amenable to direct, technical solutions (Sarewitz, "Environmental Controversies"; NRC, *Using Science*, 42).

117. For instance, in his analysis of the hydraulic fracturing (a.k.a., fracking) debate, philosopher Adam Briggle argues that politics, not science, should decide policy because policymaking is an exercise in weighing values:

> But I actually think politics, not science, should dictate outcomes, because the larger questions at stake with fracking are about values: How much risk is acceptable? How do we weigh competing goods? What is the proper place of humans in nature? In short, what kind of world do we want to live in and pass down to our children? These questions are not reducible to science. There is no scientific way to determine an optimal distance between fracking sites and playgrounds. That decision depends on how we want to balance the goals of safety, community character, and access to mineral rights. (Briggle, "Let Politics")

118. Roger A. Pielke, Jr. calls a scientist following the fact-value dualism model a "science arbiter" (Pielke, *Honest Broker*, 2).

Another way of stating this model is that the role of policymakers is solely to take the facts provided by science and interpret and apply (non-scientific) value understandings to arrive at policies. Because the two realms, science and values, are entirely separate from each other, if scientists wish to be policymakers, they can only do so by leaving the world of science (with the attendant risk that such a switch may injure one's credibility as a scientist). Alan Leshner, the chief executive officer of the American Association for the Advancement of Science, describes this view of science-policy connections in the following way:

> Credible scientists never contradict or go beyond the available data. We should never insert our personal values into discussions with the public about scientific issues. On the other hand, it is important to recognize that the rest of society is not constrained in that way and can mix facts and values at will. That is another principle scientists find hard to accept, as they often have strong moral values. When a scientist brings personal views on, say, the beginning of life into a supposedly scientific discussion on the use of embryonic stem cells in research, his or her credibility as a source of neutral facts is automatically diminished. No matter what a scientist believes about moral issues, if an opponent in a debate introduces values or beliefs, the scientist should disclaim any ability to comment on those issues as outside the scientific realm.[119]

Note that under this model, we do not necessarily have to believe that science has biases or epistemological limitations within its domain. We could, for instance, consider science to be authoritative and reliable regarding scientific matters while holding the fact-value dualism model for understanding science-policy connection. However, the model does, in some sense, require an understanding of science as domain-limited regarding value judgments, i.e., that while science may be authoritative about scientific matters, it is not authoritative about non-scientific matters such as issues of ethics, values, or religion.

The fact-value dualism model has a number of strengths. First, it neatly separates science from ethics and values, minimizing confusion between the two and enabling us to evaluate each area independently, on their own terms. As the methods of inquiry and scope of competence differ between worldviews, ethics, and science (at least under most understandings of these three areas),[120] this permits the most accurate and appropriate

119. Leshner, "Science and Public Engagement."
120. One exception would be a completely materialist and reductionist view of

analysis to be conducted in the creation of policy. Second, the fact-value dualism model also restrains us from presenting values as science (and vice versa). To the extent that the scientization of environmental controversies requires the idea that science has the ability to say something about value propositions, the fact-value dualism model may work against the tendency to convert value debates into scientific ones. Lastly, by establishing a wall of separation between science and values, the fact-value dualism model builds up the reputation of science as objective. The desirability of such a reputation depends on the epistemology of science we hold, but as the majority of people in the United States subscribe to an epistemology that considers science as objective and authoritative, the fact-value dualism model may help maintain the objectivity of science valued by this majority.

We can identify at least three weaknesses in the fact-value dualism model. First, is it possible to separate moral views from scientific judgment? Is there such a thing as a truly disinterested scientist? The Leshner quote suggests there is, but in the admission of the difficulty of separating science from values, we find a caution that human beings in general, including scientists, may tend to mix facts with values. Indeed, part of the critique of science that we saw earlier was the claim that it is not possible to escape the biases individual scientists bring to science;[121] it may not even be desirable to separate a scientist from their biases, as a scientist's "human" side may sometimes be the wellspring from which comes imagination, creativity, and perseverance. To the extent these critiques of the conventional wisdom understanding of the epistemology of science are accurate, they suggest that the fact-value dualism model cannot explain many, if not most, instances where science and policy connect.

Apart from more philosophical considerations, when it comes to common situations where science is used to inform policies (such as in expert panels that are part of the regulatory process),[122] we often have to combine both science and policy judgment. While a strict separation between science and values, as specified in the fact-value dualism model, may be possible in theory, in practice, the inclusion of science into policy may require

---

nature, ethics, and science, where all nature is material, ethics is completely determined by the chemical composition of the brain and brain states, and science authoritatively understands nature. In this view, values, as much as nature, are fully described by science and scientific tools.

121. See, for instance, Sarewitz, "Environmental Controversies," 398 and Oreskes, "Proof," 375–76.

122. In the science-policy literature, expert panels are an example of "boundary institutions," which operate at the boundary of science and policy and where questions as to the "boundary" between what is science and what is policy are often addressed (e.g., Jasanoff, *The Fifth Branch*, 14).

a mixing of the two. Consider, for instance, the task of determining how much risk (such as from the use or non-use of a pesticide) is acceptable for society to bear: while such a judgment is fundamentally value driven, and thus is a non-scientific question, nonetheless in practice it is often answered by scientific advisory committees.[123] Indeed, as Sheila Jasanoff describes, a 1983 National Research Council (NRC) study of federal risk management practices concluded that:

> First, ... risk regulation should be conceived as two distinct ana-lytical processes—"risk assessment" and "risk management"—the former comprising primarily scientific decisionmaking, and the latter integrating scientific determinations with legal, economic, and political concerns. Second, the study concluded that risk assessment can never be completely separated from risk management, since bridging uncertainty in risk assessment always involves some elements of policy choice.[124]

The fact-value dualism model has an elegant clarity, but the process of regulatory policymaking does not appear to offer such a strict demarcation between science and values.

Finally, in a number of cases from regulatory case history where the fact-value dualism model has been used, more conflict—not less—can oc-cur in the negotiations between scientific advisory boards and the regula-tory agencies they advise.[125] Put another way, the siloing of science from policy results in a regulation-development process marked by dysfunction-ality. Of course, there is more than one meaning to this dysfunctionality. It may suggest the fact-value dualism model is incorrect, inadequate, or that human weaknesses are unable to adapt to the boundaries imposed by the model. Perhaps human beings, when required to confine their input to policy questions to "merely" the scientific (or "merely" the political) chafe at the restriction, resulting in an adversarial relationship with their counterparts at the other end of the science-policy divide. Regardless, that regulation-development processes encounter such dysfunctionality when science and values are strictly separated is a "fact" we have to contend with. The fact-value dualism model for connecting science and policy may be true, but it may be a truth with limited usefulness. As Sheila Jasanoff con-

---

123. Ibid., 232. See ibid., 141–49 for a description of the 1989 furor over the use of the chemical Alar on apples and the role of the Environmental Protection Agency's (EPA) Scientific Advisory Panel (SAP) in adjudicating between different understand-ings of what the data showed and different understandings of acceptable risk.

124. Ibid., 185.

125. Ibid., 231.

cludes, "Studies of scientific advising leave in tatters the notion that it is possible, in practice, to restrict the advisory process to technical issues or that the subjective values of scientists are irrelevant to decisionmaking."[126] If so, other ways of connecting science to values may need to be used, if only to permit the work of government to occur in an effective manner.[127]

Supporting Role (Science Is Neutral) Model

In the "Supporting Role-Science Neutral" (SR-Neutral) model of connecting science with policy, science is not generally considered to be policy-prescriptive but rather plays a more supporting role. In the model, science still has some "epistemically neutral" characteristics associated with it, though the model does not require the neutrality to be grounded in the nature of science. That is to say, as far as the SR-Neutral model is concerned, what is important is not that science is intrinsically neutral but that it is instrumentally neutral: the stakeholders for an environmental policy issue believe science has enough neutrality, authority, or respect to play a lubricating and stabilizing role in the negotiation process between stakeholders. It is in this sense that science has a "supporting role" in policymaking.

One example of science playing a role in supporting dialogue between various stakeholders—while taking a "neutral" role—is the Interior Columbia Basin Ecosystem Management Project (ICBEMP), an approximately ten year federal interagency effort (begun in 1993) to create a scientifically-based ecosystem management plan for the Interior Columbia River basin (about the region comprising Eastern Washington State and Eastern Oregon, most of Idaho, and part of Western Montana).[128] Needless to say,

126. Ibid., 230.

127. Science-policy researchers Lisa Dilling and Maria Carmen Lemos, for instance, in a study of the use of climate science in policymaking, finds that usable climate science requires iteration between users and scientists. Such "iterativity" needs to be intentional:

> It [this study] finds, first, that climate science usability is a function both of the context of potential use and of the process of scientific knowledge production itself. Second, nearly every case of successful use of climate knowledge involved some kind of iteration between knowledge producers and users. The paper argues that, rather than an automatic outcome of the call for the production of usable science, iterativity is the result of the action of specific actors and organizations who 'own' [sic] the task of building the conditions and mechanisms fostering its creation. (Dilling and Lemos, "Creating Usable Science," 680)

128. USDA Forest Service PNW, "ICBEMP"; Quigley et al., *Integrated Scientific*, 18.

such a comprehensive effort would involve numerous stakeholders with sometimes divergent goals.[129] As described by Thomas J. Mills, a forest economist, and Roger N. Clark, a social scientist (both of the U.S. Department of Agriculture (USDA) Forest Service), the ICBEMP incorporated scientific expertise through assessments and consistency evaluations (of the science as well as the draft preferred policy alternative) as well as extensive dissemination of this work through publications and numerous public and stakeholder forums.[130] In this role, science, without prescribing policy or remaining entirely detached from policy considerations, helped produce a better policy product. For instance, Mills and Clark note that in ICBEMP, "The projection of effects of the alternatives by the science team lead [sic] to higher quality estimates than might otherwise have been developed, avoided unproductive debate about the likely outcomes, and helped focus public dialogue on the values being traded off among the alternatives."[131] In the end, based on the ICBEMP experience as well as other efforts, Mills and Clark conclude that:

> *Scientific information, when properly generated and presented, is neutral to differing values and can help facilitate productive discussion among different and competing interests.* Discussion of the science underlying decisions can help create a forum within which otherwise polarized interests may engage in productive dialogue and analysis of options. [emphases in original][132]

Sheila Jasanoff describes another case where a scientific advisory panel played a stabilizing role in a regulatory controversy, though in this case the role was less of creating a forum for stakeholder dialogue than to facilitate a "quasi-legislative"[133] process that helped defuse potential animosity between stakeholders. In the 1980s, the U.S. Food and Drug Administration (FDA) was petitioned to limit the use of sulfites, which are commonly used in food preparation and preservation.[134] As part of the process of crafting sulfite regulations, the FDA requested a third-party scientific advisory panel conduct a review of the current literature regarding sulfite sensitivity. The scientific advisory panel, however, did not confine itself to merely review-

129. The draft environmental impact statement, released in 1997, generated over 83,000 public comments (USDA Forest Service PNW, "ICBEMP").

130. Mills and Clark, "Roles," 195–96.

131. Ibid., 196.

132. Ibid.

133. Jasanoff, *The Fifth Branch*, 168.

134. The description in this paragraph of the FDA and the sulfite controversy is taken from ibid., 165–72.

ing the literature, nor did the panel sit in judgment of the FDA's work on sulfites, but rather behaved more "legislatively."[135] For instance, the panel held a public hearing to receive comments on its work, and a broad range of views were represented.[136] At the public hearing, the panel was not confined to reporting only on the science; instead, as Jasanoff notes, "the bulk of the discussion at the public meeting focused not on the medical data but on designing an appropriate policy response to the threat posed by sulfites."[137] This quasi-legislative use of an expert panel by the FDA helped head-off controversy and encouraged compromise.[138] Again, quoting Jasanoff:

> Finally, the panel's most important contribution to the dynamics of decisionmaking had little or nothing to do with its specialized expertise. The public hearing conducted by a seemingly neutral party had the salutary effect of defusing what could otherwise have developed into a showdown between FDA and consumer or food manufacturing interests. All parties were afforded an opportunity to influence the panel's determinations, thus gaining a sense of having participated meaningfully in the decisionmaking process.[139]

Yet, at the same time, it was crucial that the panel was a *scientific* advisory panel; the authority of science was important to enabling the creation of a stable regulation. As Jasanoff states:

> Yet it would be misleading to suggest that the panel's scientific credentials were irrelevant to the legitimacy of the regulatory outcome. In the first place, the panel's expertise bolstered the credibility of the conclusion that sulfites posed a health threat deserving of attention, especially since the evidence on this issue was not conclusive. FDA's decision to limit the sulfite ban to raw fruits and vegetables also drew support from the panel's finding that these were the most problematic uses of the compounds. Although relatively little of the panel's public work was scientific in form or substance, it is unclear whether FDA could successfully have reached the same results without invoking the authority of impartial science. In any event, the absence of serious criticism or litigation following the partial ban suggests that

135. Ibid., 168.
136. Ibid.
137. Ibid.
138. Ibid., 171.
139. Ibid.

the panel's hybrid review process assisted FDA in arriving at a stable policy consensus.[140]

Thus, in the FDA sulfites case, we see both the supporting role played by science as well as the importance of a perception of the neutrality of science in successfully fulfilling its role.

The SR-Neutral model fits well with a view of science as mostly objective but not necessarily authoritative. That is to say, science may be mostly unbiased, but the lack of bias does not necessarily imply science should have the last word on every question. This view of science recognizes other, non-scientific ways of knowing that may be equally or more valid, or, at the very least, suggests that regarding political questions, other forms of knowing should have a significant say. As we saw in the ICBEMP and sulfites examples, however, science needs to take a neutral role (actual or perceived) in the policymaking process, as its credibility and contribution to the process depends on this neutrality.

Schematically, we can describe the SR-Neutral model as:

values (1)
values (2) + science → policy
values (3)

On the left-hand side, the values of multiple stakeholders and points of view are represented by differently numbered values (the numbers do not indicate any hierarchy). These values are combined with science to obtain policy. Science and these values, however, have different roles and status in the process, and the combination is not confined to a single direction nor embedded in a hierarchy. We indicate these characteristics by putting science and values in different columns and connecting them by a plus sign rather than arrows or other lines.

We can enumerate three strengths of the SR-Neutral model of science-policy connection. First, the SR-Neutral model can enable science to function as a stabilizing force in the policymaking process. This stabilization, as we have seen, actually seems to occur more easily if there is some flexibility on behalf of both the scientific advisory boards and the regulatory agencies in defining the boundary between science and policy.[141] Nonetheless, when science advisory boards are able to play a role in negotiating both scientific and political conflicts, without becoming so political as to lose the mantle of neutrality, the resulting policies are less likely to be contested.[142] A

---

140. Ibid., 171–72.

141. Ibid., 236.

142. Ibid., 236–37, 244. An extended quotation from Sheila Jasanoff is worth noting,

second strength of the SR-Neutral model is that it assigns science a "humbler" role, which avoids investing an impossible-to-meet expectation of omnicompetence to science and gives more room for different kinds of uses of science in the policymaking process. Third, the SR-Neutral model may give a role to science that works against the scientization of environmental controversies. Daniel Sarewitz notes that scientization can be prevented if "value positions are well articulated from the beginning of the controversy" and "effective mechanisms for eliciting and adjudicating value disputes are already in place and well-accepted. . . ."[143] While science itself cannot adjudicate between values, science acting according to the SR-Neutral model may be able to create a venue in which value adjudication occurs.

With the SR-Neutral model, we can also identify three weaknesses. First, though science is ostensibly neutral in this model, its active role in boundary work (i.e., in determining what is science and what is policy) may lead to accusations of capture. Recall the concerns Alan Leshner expressed about the negative impact on credibility when scientists become swept up into value debates.[144] Second, we may ask whether the SR-Neutral model is truly honest about the nature of science. Science (and different kinds of science), we saw earlier, may have its own epistemic biases,[145] and it seems like the SR-Neutral model papers over that. If science is not really neutral in the way the model suggests, the SR-Neutral model rests only on the perception of neutrality. If so, the use of science in policymaking becomes, in some

---

as it nicely summarizes the mechanisms by which policy stabilization can occur:

> The picture presented above of the advisory process is markedly at odds with the simple technocratic paradigm of "speaking truth to power," although, paradoxically, not inconsistent with it. According to this account, the committees attached to EPA and FDA do indeed help the agencies define good science—and this consensus view of science in turn influences policy—but they perform this function in part through skilled boundary work and in part through flexible role-playing. Protected by the umbrella of expertise, advisory committee members in fact are free to serve in widely divergent professional capacities: as technical consultants, as educators, as peer reviewers, as policy advocates, as mediators, and even as judges. Though their purpose is to address only technical issues, committee meetings therefore serve as forums where scientific as well as political conflicts can be simultaneously negotiated. When the process works, few incentives remain for political adversaries to deconstruct the results or to attack them as bad science. (Ibid., 236–37)

143. Sarewitz, "Environmental Controversies," 398.

144. Leshner, "Science and Public Engagement."

145. Oreskes, "Proof," 375–76.

sense, a function of optics rather than reality. Third, we may ask whether the SR-Neutral model is really that much different from the fact-value dualism model. Because science retains the reputation of neutrality, the SR-Neutral model resembles the fact-value dualism model, though with a slightly porous boundary between science and values and with science acting as an organizing medium for discussions between stakeholders. If the SR-Neutral model is not substantially different from the fact-value dualism model, the criticisms we enumerated earlier of the latter model may also apply to the former.

Supporting Role (Science May Not Be Neutral) Model

In the "Supporting Role-Science May Not Be Neutral" (SR-NN) model, we begin with the argument that science is not epistemically special or privileged but has its own epistemic biases.[146] In a few cases, science may be policy-prescriptive, but for most controversial issues, the role of science, while important, is relatively limited compared to the previous models we have described. The SR-NN model fits well with an understanding of science as being one way of knowing amongst many.

There are a number of ways science can play a "supporting" role under the SR-NN model. Science may provide policymakers "informed opinions" about consequences and "monitoring" as to how we are doing[147] (in contrast to being a "predictive oracle"[148]). The "scientization" of environmental controversies, as suggested by Daniel Sarewitz and that we described earlier in this chapter, is another example of the role of science under the SR-NN model (albeit a somewhat pathological role). The role of a scientist as an "issue advocate,"[149] who works to convince policymakers of a preferred policy option, can also be an example of science acting in an SR-NN way, if that advocacy is not based on science as epistemically privileged.

146. Ibid.

147. Ibid., 381.

148. Sarewitz, "Environmental Controversies," 400.

149. Pielke, *Honest Broker*, 2.

Schematically, we can describe the SR-NN model as:

$$\left.\begin{array}{l} \text{values (1)} \\ \text{values (2)} \\ \text{science} \\ \text{values (3)} \end{array}\right\} \text{policy}$$

To indicate that science is one source of knowledge—without pretensions to privilege—and that science does not "stand apart" (as in the SR-Neutral model), science is listed (and interspersed) in the same column along with different values (the order in the column has no meaning). These various forms of knowledge are synthesized into a policy response (as shown by the curly brace), but in that synthesis, one form of knowledge does not necessarily come before the other (as in the fact-value dualism model).

The key strength of the SR-NN model of connecting science with policy is that it elevates the relative importance of values—philosophy, ethics, politics, etc.—in the policymaking process, which in theory enables value debates more likely to be conducted and resolved.[150] In that way, the SR-NN model may help work against the scientization of environmental debates. (This mechanism differs from the SR-Neutral model. Science under the SR-NN model does not readily produce a venue wherein stakeholders can engage in productive dialogue, as the SR-Neutral model does through the neutrality of science.)

We can describe two weaknesses of the SR-NN model of science-policy connection. First, under the SR-NN model, policymaking occurs on an epistemically level playing field; no knowledge system or perspective has greater validity than another. As a result, policymaking may be reduced to a completely adversarial process, with differing value systems and science contesting for the high ground of public opinion and political power. This adversarial nature also applies to the process of determining which interpretations have the right to be called "science." As we saw earlier in our discussion of the ATOC experiment, different disciplines within science can have different interpretive frameworks that lead to divergent conclusions, but nonetheless all are reasonably considered "science." The presence of these multiple perspectives and a level epistemic playing field under the

---

150. Again, see Adam Briggle's argument that we should depend on politics instead of science for environmental policymaking because the questions we are answering are fundamentally value questions (Briggle, "Let Politics"). Nancy Tuana argues that philosophy has an important role to play in climate science policymaking, for instance, in helping evaluate what policy options are fair and equitable (Tuana, "Leading With Ethics," 488–90).

SR-NN model will tend to make the policymaking process involve science as an adversary against various values as well as against other kinds of science.

This "doubly adversarial" policymaking approach can produce noticeable dysfunctionalities in policymaking. Daniel Kemmis, Director of the University of Montana's Center for the Rocky Mountain West, describes some of these dysfunctionalities with regards to natural resource planning.[151] While describing an alternative policymaking process he calls "collaboration," he notes that:

> Collaboration has arisen and spread because it offers an alternative to the highly adversarial form of public involvement that now dominates almost all public decision processes. An integral part of that approach has been adversarial science. Each side in any contentious resource issue hires as many scientists as it needs or can afford and puts their conclusions in the record. The resulting image of science for sale creates deep public cynicism about scientists, of course, but it also corrodes confidence in the decisionmaking process itself. How can lay people, either citizens or officials, possibly hope to know what is right for their ecosystems when scientists cannot even agree about it? This leads either to alienation from public life altogether or to one more spurious invocation of good science to save democracy from this quandary.[152]

Even when the adversarial nature of the process is confined to the science itself, the result is often greater difficulty in coming to agreement as to what the science says. As Sheila Jasanoff describes, in the context of scientific advisory panels:

> . . . submitting science policy disputes to adversarial processes promotes an unproductive deconstruction of science and fosters the appearance of capture. It follows from this analysis that the format least likely to bring about a durable consensus on contested technical issues is one that leads to confrontation between alternative constructions of uncertain scientific data.[153]

Thus, following the SR-NN model might, in these ways, lead to less policy stability.[154]

151. Kemmis, "Science's Role."

152. Ibid.

153. Jasanoff, *The Fifth Branch*, 246.

154. Interestingly, the "collaboration" alternative Daniel Kemmis describes is something of a hybrid of the SR-Neutral and SR-NN models. In the collaboration natural resource planning model, the starting point for policymaking is not what science says but

Finally, we can challenge the SR-NN model in its fundamental assumption that science is epistemically "just the same" as any other form of
knowledge. Does science truly offer nothing objective and is every form of
knowledge irredeemably subjective? While we can critique science as having epistemic biases, this is not the same as saying the biases are wrong.
Some epistemic biases may be constructive; for instance, skepticism with
an emphasis on falsification can inject humility and provisionality to any
claims science makes. Even if these biases have no firmer foundation than
the culture of science, we can still argue that knowledge systems that value

---

what local knowledge—the lived knowledge from long-time residents of the area under
discussion—tells us. The reliance on local knowledge plays a critical role in bringing
together disparate stakeholders to create a shared resource management plan. This
knowledge, as Kemmis describes, "provides a way of knowing the ecosystem that an appeal to objective, external, expert science simply cannot supply. . . . It would be difficult
to exaggerate the central role that such ingrained knowledge plays, time and again, in
enabling longtime adversaries to discover a common base of factual understanding on
which they can then develop innovative and sustainable management decisions" (Kemmis, "Science's Role"). So, whither science? As Kemmis describes, under collaboration,
science has a different role:

> Rejecting the adversarial approach to decisionmaking, it [collaborative
> efforts at resource management] necessarily rejects the use of adver-
> sarial science as well. Collaborators begin by determining what they
> already know about their ecosystem on the basis of their local knowl-
> edge. They then agree on what they don't know but need to know in
> order to make wise and sustainable decisions about their ecosystem.
> The need to know is the crucial element here. What they don't know
> about their ecosystem is infinite, and therefore in a sense irrelevant.
> Collaboration works when diverse interests can agree on what portion
> of that infinity they need to explore. Even more important, collabora-
> tion works when opposing interests can agree on the specific scientists
> or scientific procedures that can give them reliable information to fill in
> the relevant gaps in local knowledge. This move rescues science from
> its adversarial perversion while enabling it to play a role that is actu-
> ally within its grasp: providing reasonably reliable information about
> a reasonably determined set of ecosystem parameters. Without that
> consensual determination of the questions science is expected to an-
> swer, we continually set science up by expecting it to give us the answers
> without having done the civic work of first deciding what the questions
> are. (Kemmis, "Science's Role")

Collaboration is a hybrid of the SR-Neutral and SR-NN models in this way: Similar
to the SR-NN model, science (in its external form) no longer has epistemic privilege
and authority, in and of itself; its authority is framed by local knowledge. However,
similar to the SR-Neutral model, *local knowledge* has the role of a "neutral," respected
party that provides common ground for the various stakeholders to engage in dialogue.

these biases will yield knowledge that is, at the very least, worth taking seriously, if not with a dose of privilege.

Honest Broker of Policy Alternatives Model

Under the Honest Broker of Policy Alternatives model—coined by Roger A. Pielke, Jr.—science is neither a "pure" creator of objective knowledge nor is it a policy advocate. Instead, while science informs policymaking by "help[ing] us to understand the associations between different choices and their outcomes,"[155] when science acts as an honest broker of policy alternatives, science acts to expand the range of options rather than constricting them.[156] Thus, in the honest broker model, science is policy "neutral," not in the sense of being necessarily objective but in the sense of how it *acts*—namely, to expand alternatives. It is also in this sense that the honest broker model is the mirror image of science as a policy advocate (operating, for instance, under the policy prescriptive or SR-NN models), where policy advocacy is defined as an exercise in narrowing options.[157] The honest broker model fits well with understandings of science as not necessarily authoritative and omnicompetent.

What would it look like for science to act as an honest broker? Pielke suggests consumers of science—policymakers, regulators, voters, etc.—ask scientists who provide policy recommendations two questions regarding their contributions that might encourage those scientists to act as honest brokers:

- If your policy recommendation is indeed based on scientific results, what scientific information would be necessary to change your policy position? (If the answer is "no information" then why depend on science at all?)

- A range of policies is consistent with particular scientific results. What is the full range of options that you see as consistent with the state of science in order to achieve particular desired ends? Within such a range, what factors other than science do you use to settle on one policy, or group of policy options, over others?[158]

155. Pielke, *Honest Broker,* 139. Much of the description and analysis in this section comes from ibid.

156. Ibid., 140–41.

157. Ibid.

158. Ibid., 141–42.

Both questions encourage the scientist to consider perspectives and alternatives apart from their own preferred policy recommendation. Additionally, both questions highlight the limitations of science—absent values—to prescribe policy and encourage the scientist to help delineate where those limitations are. As an example of an institution that has played the role of honest broker, Pielke points to the U.S. Office of Technology Assessment, whose reports included a broad range of options and took one to two years to produce.[159]

Schematically, we can describe the honest broker model as:

$$
\left.\begin{array}{l} \text{values (1)} \\ \text{values (2)} \\ \text{science} \end{array}\right\}
\left.\begin{array}{l} \text{policy (1)} \\ \text{policy (2)} \\ \text{policy (3)} \\ \text{policy (4)} \end{array}\right\}
\left.\begin{array}{l} \text{values (1)} \\ \text{values (3)} \end{array}\right\} \text{policy}
$$

In the left-hand column, different values and science are listed together in no particular order or hierarchy of dependence, indicating that science is not necessarily neutral or privileged (or if neutral or privileged, we consider those characteristics as having no bearing in policymaking).[160] Collectively, these values and science lead to multiple policy choices. Those multiple policy choices are then evaluated using (same or different) values and other criteria, resulting in a single policy.

We can describe two strengths of the honest broker model. First, integrating science into policymaking according to the honest broker model can increase the probability of policy success when dealing with difficult environmental controversies. As Pielke notes, "One way beyond the apparent limitations on the role of science in decision-making presented by conflicts over values and inherent uncertainties is to recognize that in situations of gridlock, policy-makers frequently need new options, and not more science."[161] As we saw with the case of chlorofluorocarbons (CFCs) and stratospheric ozone, one way to defuse controversies is by enacting policies that create alternatives to render moot the conflict between stakeholders; for ozone, this was done through policies that encouraged the development of alternative chemicals to CFCs.[162] As many environmental debates are cast as "win-lose" conflicts, the ability to transform that debate into a "win-win"

159. Ibid., 17, 156.

160. In this first step, science behaves in a way similar to how it behaves in the SR-NN model.

161. Ibid., 140.

162. Ibid., 140.

(or at least a "tie-tie") situation offers the opportunity to remove the conflict altogether. The honest broker model provides a way for science to play such a role.

A second strength of the honest broker model is that it may help to reduce the relative influence of "stealth issue advocates"[163] in environmental controversies and the negative repercussions such advocacy can have on both science and the role of science in policy. Issue advocates, who seek to narrow policy choice to their preferred alternative, have a necessary role in a democracy.[164] In stealth issue advocacy, however, scientists act as issue advocates while portraying themselves as merely "focus[ing] only on science."[165] That is to say, stealth issue advocates argue they are not engaging in advocacy or politics but just following the science. This kind of advocacy plays an integral role in the scientization of environmental debates, as scientization is about taking a debate over values and transforming it into a debate over science. Stealth issue advocacy thus can have a number of negative consequences, as Pielke explains:

> If the public or policy-makers begin to believe that scientific findings are simply an extension of a scientist's political beliefs, then scientific information will play an increasingly diminishing role in policy-making, and a correspondingly larger role in the marketing of particular political agendas. This will be tragic because not all politics are Abortion Politics—society has a wide range of issues on which there are widely shared values and an opportunity for science to contribute knowledge to helping to realize those values—scientific information often matters a great deal.[166]

When science functions using the honest broker model, science takes on a role to increase the scope of policy options. In that way, scientists operating as honest brokers provide a counterbalance to stealth issue advocacy.[167]

We can also describe two weaknesses of the honest broker model. First, how realistic is the honest broker model? Pielke acknowledges the honest broker model is an "ideal type" and that it is impossible to produce a completely comprehensive set of options.[168] Following the reasoning behind the SR-NN model, we can also argue that even the honest broker model

163. Ibid., 94, 142.
164. Ibid., 135.
165. Ibid., 7.
166. Ibid., 95–96.
167. Ibid., 142.
168. Ibid., 142.

oversells the epistemic uniqueness of science. Why should we give special credence to any scientific description and analysis, over and above other sources of knowledge, merely because the analysis considers more than one policy response?

A second possible weakness of the honest broker model deals with how often should the model be applied: Is the model appropriate for most instances of connecting science to policy or only in rare cases? Perhaps most science-policy interactions should be through other models besides the honest broker model. For instance, Pielke notes that most scientists involved in policy issues are involved as issue advocates or science arbiters (the latter merely provides facts to policymakers, as in the fact-value dualism model);[169] while we should be careful to argue from an "is" to an "ought," the preference scientists have in terms of their involvement in science-policy issues may be an important clue pointing us towards how science and policy should be connected.

When to Use Different Models of Connecting Science to Policy

Our list of five ways that science connects with policy, while not exhaustive, nonetheless illustrates the broad range of ways that science and policy can mix. We note that under different models, science plays very different roles in the policymaking process. Additionally, for any given context, not all models are equally useful or constructive, depending on the goals we have for bringing science into the policymaking conversation. Our choice of models matters. In this section, we provide a few guidelines to help us decide which models are more applicable for any given environmental issue.

First, the policy prescriptive and fact-value dualism models, as Roger A. Pielke, Jr. suggests, appear to apply only when environmental issues are characterized by value agreement and low uncertainty.[170] Sheila Jasanoff, in reviewing the FDA's incorporation of expert advice in the sulfite controversy, similarly found that expert advice is best utilized when dealing with situations characterized by "highly focused" scientific issues, "well-defined risk to health," relatively few policy options to evaluate, and the lack of public controversy.[171] Expert advice is also more productively utilized when the governmental agency and expert organization involved have a track record of working together.[172] While some environmental issues exhibit these

169. Ibid., 140–41.
170. Ibid., 136.
171. Jasanoff, *The Fifth Branch*, 167.
172. Ibid.

characteristics, few of the controversial ones do. From climate change to genetically modified organisms, environmental issues that are controversial are also the ones that are complex and wide-ranging, marked by multiple modes of uncertainty, and deeply infused with value conflict. For these issues, the policy prescriptive and fact-value dualism approaches do not seem promising.

Second, as we mentioned earlier, we can create hybrids and simultaneous combinations using the five models. For instance, we could argue for a place for both the policy prescriptive and honest broker models by arguing that policy prescriptive issue advocates have a critical role of making sure no debate becomes one-sided—that all sides of an issue are heard—while scientists acting as honest brokers have a critical role in helping policymakers envision and create policy alternatives. Depending on what criteria we use to justify the hybrid or combination, any number of permutations are possible. However, one characteristic that distinguishes each of the five science-policy models is their understanding of the epistemic authority of science, and this characteristic can affect the stability of combinations of these five science-policy models. Using the criteria of epistemic authority, we can categorize the five models into three groups. The first group—the policy prescriptive and fact-value dualism models—fit well with an understanding of science as privileged and unique. The second group—the SR-Neutral and honest broker models—fit well with a humbler understanding of the epistemic status of science: unique, in certain ways, but with less epistemic authority than commonly believed. The third group—of which the SR-NN model is an example—understands science as merely one source of knowledge amongst many, without any more or less epistemic authority. To the extent that the criteria we use for creating hybrids and combinations requires consistency on the epistemic authority of science, it will be easier to create combinations within groups than between groups.

Third, if the goal of including science in the policymaking process is to obtain the "correct" policy, we have to consider the possibility that such a goal may be asking too much from science. Certainly, public opinion and the most widely held understandings of scientific methodology believe science can make such a contribution to policymaking. Still, as we have seen in this chapter, the number of cases where scientific knowledge has been decisive, particularly concerning controversial environmental issues, does not make one sanguine about the ability of science to contribute in this way to policymaking. In the context of scientific advice for policymakers, Sheila Jasanoff concludes that we can only expect "serviceable truth":

The regulatory experiences of EPA [Environmental Protection
Agency] and FDA [Food and Drug Administration] indicate
that it is almost inconceivable for a marginal scientific school
to dominate the entire spectrum of decisions about the environment or public health and safety. The primary concern for
regulators, then, is not how to guard against capture by science
but how to harness the collective expertise of the scientific
community so as to advance the public interest. In this effort,
agencies and experts alike should renounce the naive vision of
neutral advisory bodies "speaking truth to power," for in regulatory science, more even than in research science, there can be
no perfect, objectively verifiable truth. The most one can hope
for is a serviceable truth: a state of knowledge that satisfies tests
of scientific acceptability and supports reasoned decisionmaking, but also assures those exposed to risk that their interests
have not been sacrificed on the altar of an impossible scientific
certainty.[173]

Fourth, if policy stability—particularly in cases marked by strong
value conflict—is one of our goals in including science in the policymaking process, models that conform to a humbler view of science, such as the
SR-Neutral and honest broker models, may offer a better alternative. Both
models provide ways for science to facilitate dialogue between divergent
stakeholders or to clarify the value positions that drive policy disagreements.
In so doing, they offer avenues of communication that may lead to compromise and acceptance of whatever policy is adopted. Models that conform
to a view of science as having essentially *no* special epistemic status, such
as the SR-NN model, may not necessarily lead to policy instability—where
environmental policies change with each election—but nonetheless may
exhibit the same level of fragmentation that exists with non-environmental
political issues, since in that model, science plays a role similar to other
political players in environmental policymaking.

Finally, while in this section we have focused on the role of the epistemology of science in influencing the way we understand how science
and policy connect with each other, other factors also play a role. Roger
A. Pielke, Jr., for instance, highlights the importance of our conception of
democracy on our understanding of science-policy connections. Those
who hold a "Madisonian" view of democracy—where a wide spectrum
of interest groups propose policies and compete with one another in the
public square—may be more apt to favor the policy prescriptive, fact-value

173. Ibid., 250.

dualism, or SR-NN models.[174] Those who hold a "Schattschneiderian" view of democracy—where decision-makers, instead of acting on policies created at the grassroots level, act on recommendations distilled by experts—may be more apt to favor the SR-Neutral or honest broker models.[175] It probably does not come as a surprise that our political conceptions, such as of the nature of democracy, will influence our views on the connection between science and policy. In chapter 6, we expand on the role of politics and economics on the content of creation care. Before doing so, in the next section, we discuss how different determinants interact with science, both through the epistemology of science as well as how we connect science to policy.

SCIENCE AND IMPORTANCE, GOALS, AND PRACTICE

We have seen there are multiple views of what science is and what kind of authority it has. In a different but related way, we have also seen there are multiple views of how science connects with policy. In this section, we examine how these two aspects of science (what it is and how it connects with policy) determine the criteria for obedience. After considering each of the criteria in turn (importance, goals, and practice), we conclude with examining the implications for effectively connecting science with policy.

Science and the Importance of the Creation Care Command (Why Follow the Command)

In previous chapters, we have seen that worldviews and ethics are significant determinants of the importance of creation care. (Though, as we will find in chapter 6 when we address politics and economics, there are additional sources of values still to be considered.) In the current chapter, we have seen that while conventional wisdom considers science as having the authority and ability to establish and describe the importance of environmental stewardship, there are substantial arguments against the conventional wisdom. For many worldviews and under most definitions of science and models of science-policy interaction, the importance of the creation care command

---

174. Pielke, *Honest Broker*, 11–14. "Madisonian" is named after James Madison. What this present work calls the policy prescriptive and fact-value dualism models share some similarities to what Pielke calls the "Issue Advocate" and "Pure Scientist" roles, respectively (ibid., 14).

175. Ibid., 11–14. "Schattschneiderian" is named after E. E. Schattschneider. What this present work calls the SR-Neutral model shares some similarities to what Pielke calls the "Science Arbiter" role (ibid., 14).

is one question that science does not answer. Even if we consider science as having very high authority and hold an ethic that is interested mainly in those entities that science studies, science does not tell us why to care for the environment.

For example, consider the case where we believe cost-benefit analysis properly weighs all pertinent values and that science is the primary and proper tool of cost-benefit analysis. Given these beliefs, we might conclude that science determines the importance criterion; after all, science generates the cost-benefit analysis. Yet, even in this example, the science, per se, does not tell us how important it is to care for the environment. Rather, it is the value claim that something is important to preserve if doing so maximizes benefits over cost—namely, a cost-benefit analysis consequentialism—that leads us to conclude whether it is important or not to care for nature. Science, in this example, only provides a description of the state of nature that is then translated (using other value assumptions) into costs and benefits. Only under a small set of understandings of worldviews and science—for instance, a strictly materialist worldview coupled with a logical positivist epistemology of science—will science have a substantial role in determining the importance criterion.

Science and the Goals of Following the Creation Care Command (What Following the Command Will Result In)

With regards to the goals criterion, we find that science can describe some of the goals of creation care, but not all the goals. Material goals are one category of goals science can help describe. Under most worldviews and epistemologies of science, science (at a minimum), describes the material state of the world. Science, thus, describes the goals of following the creation care command that are given by the material state of the world; that is to say, science describes the material state of what environmental stewardship is aiming for: number of acres of wilderness, rate of species decline, kinds and diversity of biomes, concentration levels of pollutants, etc. However, while nearly all worldviews and epistemologies of science understand science as describing the material state of the world (and thus the material description of the goals of creation care), the level of authority accorded to the scientific description varies. Some epistemologies of science consider the description of science of the material state as authoritative (e.g., logical positivism). Other epistemologies, however, give more consideration or prominence to other ways of knowing besides science that address material creation care goals. Philosophical reasoning—natural law, for instance—can describe additional material creation care goals. Whether non-scientific reasoning can do a better job than science in describing the material nature of creation care goals is an open question, but non-scientific reasoning such as philosophy is likely better than science at describing non-material creation care goals, since most views of science confine science to material description.

In contrast to material goals, non-material creation care goals are not, in general, described by science. Non-material goals may include the inculcating or growing of virtue and the preservation or nurturing of transcendental qualities (e.g., beauty, truth, justice). For instance, simplicity is a virtue associated with creation care and is sometimes mentioned as a desired result of creation care, i.e., that our society would be characterized by greater simplicity. (Simplicity is mentioned as both a way of caring for creation as well as a result of creation care, and thus may be both a means and a goal.) Science has little to say about non-material goals, except insofar as those goals have a material manifestation that is measurable in scientific terms. Again considering simplicity as a goal, to the extent simplicity is understood as a character trait of individuals or societies, science is unable to provide much of a description of the goal. However, to the extent simplicity is understood in empirical or material terms, such as the tons of waste a person generates or the number of miles a workforce commutes, simplicity as a goal of environmental stewardship is at least partly described by science.

However, whether the goals of creation care are material or non-material, science does not describe the *relative* values of the goals of creation care. That is to say, science does not, by itself, prescribe that one of these goals is preferable over and above other possible goals for creation care. For example, consider a creation care practice to reduce air pollution (e.g., the Clean Air Act). Science describes the kinds of pollutants to be regulated, the levels of the pollutants consistent with certain public health goals, the dynamics of the pollutants in the atmosphere and in human respiratory systems, etc., but science cannot say whether certain creation care goals are more or less valuable than other creation care goals (e.g., ozone versus particulate concentrations) or other goals in general (e.g., public health versus business and consumer expense), without input from ethics and other determinants.

As another example, consider the question of whether plastic shopping bags harm the environment.[176] Proponents of plastic shopping bag bans may argue that shopping bags harm the environment through filling landfills with trash that does not (easily) degrade, producing unsightly litter that

---

176. See Agresti, "Bans on Plastic Bags" for an argument against plastic bag bans that also describes some of the reasons in favor of such bans. Some of the reasons given later in this paragraph also come from this article.

mars the landscape, and fostering a "throw away" or "disposable society" mentality that itself is the seed for environmental degradation. Opponents of plastic shopping bag bans may argue that even organic matter does not degrade in landfills and that plastic bags are more environmentally friendly than alternatives such as canvas totes because it takes so little energy and material to manufacture plastic shopping bags.[177] These arguments may be founded on and strengthened by scientific studies, but the relative value of the goals behind these arguments—the weighing of "good" and "bad" for the environment—does not come from those studies. How do we weigh the aesthetics of plastic bag litter versus the energy used to manufacture them? How do we weigh the importance of working against a "throw away" society versus the use of raw material to manufacture plastic bags or their alternatives? Science comes to such questions mostly with silence. Thus, regarding the goals of creation care, science describes material goals and may describe the aspects of non-material goals that have a material manifestation, but in both cases, science cannot tell us the comparative importance of these goals.

Science and the Practice of the Creation Care Command (How to Put the Command Into Action)

As we described earlier, there are a number of ways to connect science and policy and thus a number of ways science impacts the practice of environmental stewardship. As a result, the "direct" versus "indirect" categorization we used in considering the effect of other determinants on the practice criterion is not as helpful in the case of science. Instead, in this section we first address the question of how science determines the practice of creation care by asking how science epistemology and other determinants interact to affect our choice of a model of science-policy interaction. We focus on the role of worldviews and science epistemology and also examine the limits of these determinants in influencing which model of science-policy interaction we adopt. After examining how we choose a science-policy model, we consider how to critique our science-policy model on the basis of whether the model can provide an effective connection between science and policy. This two-step process yields an appraisal of how science affects the practice criterion.[178]

As we have seen, worldviews describe our ontology of nature—what we believe nature *is*. How does this affect our choice of model of science-policy

177. Ibid.

178. In this section, we will not address the reverse feedback the practice criterion exerts on science, asserting that this feedback is not all that significant.

interaction? Certain models, as we noted earlier, fit more naturally with elements of particular worldviews. Worldviews that have a substantial material component to them (e.g., Enlightenment, Christian) may be more open to giving science more of a role in policymaking, because science studies the material world that is part of the worldview. Worldviews with a substantial non-material component to them (e.g., Buddhism, Romanticism) may tend to give science less of a role in policymaking: since science cannot speak on the non-material component of nature, science would seem to not have much to say about environmental stewardship under such a worldview. Other forms of knowing (e.g., philosophical, mystical, spiritual, artistic, etc.) may be more preferred ways of learning about the (non-material) world and thus may play a more important role than science in policymaking.[179] Thus, if we hold a non-material worldview such as Romanticism, we might expect to choose one of the science-policy models that gives science a more supporting role in policymaking.

In addition to worldviews, our epistemology of science also plays a role in our choice of science-policy model. If we accord science substantial authority with respect to its understanding of nature, we will tend to choose a model that gives science a more privileged place in policymaking. We see this most prominently in the conventional wisdom justifications for the most common science-policy model, the policy prescriptive model. From our earlier discussion, we know that science has historically been understood as having a privileged epistemic status and afforded substantial authority in policy discussions and that public opinion surveys reveal widespread support and trust of science and scientists in policymaking. It should not surprise us then that these epistemic justifications result in the adoption of the policy prescriptive view of connecting science with policy as a default position. In contrast, if we consider science as having its own epistemic biases, we may be more disposed to choose a science-policy model where science has less of a prescriptive role. Combining worldviews and science epistemology together, a material worldview combined with a sense of science as epistemically privileged would encourage a policy prescriptive view of science while a non-material worldview combined with a sense of science as having epistemic limits would encourage adoption of a science-policy model where science had limits.

While worldviews and science epistemology greatly influence our choice of science-policy models, the two determinants do not necessarily dictate our choice of model. This is because there can be more than one

---

179. Again, we are using "policymaking" in a more general sense than "lawmaking"; the policy may be political, cultural, or individual in nature.

science-policy model that is consistent with any given worldview and nature of science pairing. For instance, we might believe in a worldview with a substantial material component and believe that science provides some (though incomplete) knowledge, and because of these beliefs, choose the Supporting Role-Science May Not Be Neutral (SR-NN) model connecting science and policy. Someone else, however, might hold the same worldview and nature of science positions and yet choose the fact-value dualism science-policy model. Nothing in the formulation of either model conflicts with this worldview/nature of science pairing. Still someone else might choose a modified form of the policy prescriptive model, arguing that while science may be an incomplete way of knowing, where it does have knowledge, science translates directly into policy. Such a model is also consistent with this worldview/nature of science pairing. As a result, while worldview and science epistemology plays a crucial role in our understanding of which science-policy model makes the most sense, plenty of room exists for different people, holding the same worldview and understanding of the nature of science, to understand the science-policy connection in very different ways.

Having examined how the determinants influence our choice of science-policy model, we consider how to critique our chosen model on the basis of whether it effectively connects science and policy. In our description of a spectrum of ways of connecting science to policy, we already presented some of the work from the science-policy studies literature regarding what mechanisms enable science to positively impact policy. In this section, we make three points summarizing the implications of that work regarding models of science-policy interaction and the role of science in affecting the practice criterion.

First, we have seen that non-policy-prescriptive ways of connecting science to policy may provide a number of benefits with regards to decision-making. Such ways of connecting science to policy can provide more stable policies, that is, policies that have a broader base of support among stakeholders and are not as sensitive to the winds of political change. With such stability, trust between disparate stakeholders increases and decisions have greater hope of being implemented. The example of ICBEMP illustrates how a process that uses science in a humbler fashion can result in greater policy stability.

The humbler understanding of and use of science can also provide greater recognition of the importance of the interpretation of facts and help prevent the premature shutting-down of debate. Conventional wisdom holds facts to be self-interpreting. We have seen, however, reasons to conclude the contrary: facts cannot be atomized and even the nature of the collection of facts we consider can affect our interpretation of those facts. The widespread use of facts in environmental debates as if they were self-interpreting, however, shuts down debate. Facts cannot be questioned, only denied, which eliminates nuanced dialogue as a category of discussion, leaving only a winner-take-all debate. Furthermore, if facts are not self-interpreting, but we use assume they are, it makes it very difficult for a reasoned critique to convince us to use them in a humbler way: After all, we *know* facts are self-interpreting. Nuanced dialogue becomes a further impossibility. We do not have to look very far to find environmental controversies that exhibit this pathology. The use of science by both skeptics and non-skeptics of the climate science community's findings regarding anthropogenic global warming, as if scientific facts were bullets fired by gunslingers rather than common ground for dialogue or as only one component in a larger discussion, exemplifies how environmental controversies become scientized and impoverish debate.[180]

In addition to nurturing policy stability and dialogue, humbler, non-policy-prescriptive ways of connecting science to policy may also nurture more effective policy responses to environmental problems. When science is seen as dictating policy, solutions may tend to be limited to those conceived by scientists studying the environmental problem. Effective solutions, however, may require creative and alternative ways of conceptualizing solutions that draw upon wisdom and expertise from less- and non-scientific fields, such as politics and management. (Chapter 7 provides a more detailed discussion of the range of policy options available for any environmental problem and the ways we artificially limit that range.) We saw this in the case of CFCs and stratospheric ozone depletion in how a tiered set of policies, rather than an all-out ban, enabled the creation of effective and economic solutions (including the removing of costs associated with misaligned stakeholders). A humbler role for science may also result in more effective policy responses by fostering policies that are more adaptable to new knowledge and changing context. A policy prescriptive view of science-policy interactions can foster a tendency towards comprehensive and expansive solutions. In contrast, a humbler role for science leaves more room for incremental, reversible, and "no-regrets" strategies.[181] To the extent that this enables action in the face of scientific uncertainty, results in policies that are more nimble and adaptable in the face of new knowledge, and fosters policies that the public can more easily adopt and adjust to in

---

180. See Sarewitz, "Environmental Controversies."

181. See Sarewitz, "Environmental Controversies," 400 for similar points regarding the kinds of low-stakes solutions that become more possible when environmental controversies are de-scientized.

their everyday lives, and these policy traits are desirable, a humbler role for science may produce more effective policy responses to environmental problems.

Second, while adopting or considering non-policy-prescriptive ways of connecting science to policy has potential benefits with regards to policymaking, the use of non-policy-prescriptive models has its own challenges. As the policy prescriptive model is the default model for many in the public, it may be difficult to introduce alternative ways of connecting science to policy. Such ways may even be *prima facie* unacceptable to those who accord science a high level of authority, and attempts to use science in non-policy-prescriptive ways may result in opposition from those who feel science is being ignored, abused, or politicized. Indeed, if a given environmental issue really is a technical problem best solved by science, those in the policy prescriptive camp would be right; does adopting a non-policy-prescriptive model then run the risk of ignoring science when science really is the answer? In addition, and perhaps most difficult, the adoption of non-policy-prescriptive ways of connecting science to policy requires all advocates in an environmental controversy to avoid using their most naturally persuasive line of reasoning. In nearly any policy dispute, the words "scientists say" and "studies show" carry formidable weight, not least with the public whose support is vital to the adoption of policies in a democracy. Admitting models of science-policy connection that diminish the authority of such statements may seem to advocates on all sides as a form of tying your hands behind your back. Given the social and political systems we have, perhaps we default to the policy prescriptive view of science-policy connection because we *cannot* (except in rare occasions) establish another.

Third, regardless of whether we hold a policy-prescriptive or non-policy-prescriptive view of science, the existence of a spectrum of models has some important implications. Perhaps the most obvious is that the existence of a spectrum suggests that whatever model of science-policy interaction we hold, that model needs to be justified. We cannot assume one model is necessarily true or appropriate for all circumstances. Different models can produce different results in policy quality, stability, and comity. As we will see in chapter 8, however, the need to justify our choice of science-policy models (or our understanding of the nature of science) is not very commonly acknowledged or practiced, so perhaps this implication is not quite so obvious.

Another implication of the spectrum is that the range of possible policies that even *exist* for us to consider may be heavily affected by our understanding of the nature of science and our model of science-policy connection. If we hold a strong policy prescriptive view, solutions proposed by fields outside of science (e.g., politics, philosophy, religion, etc.) are automatically excluded. If we hold an honest broker view, we may end up giving some solutions less weight than may be warranted by the level of scientific certainty, political ripeness, etc., because of our goal of expanding the range of policy options. Thus, the question of the nature of science and science-policy connections is not some kind of "neutral" choice or an academic exercise. How we answer that question profoundly affects our understanding of the content of creation care.

CONCLUSIONS

In the modern, Western world, few disciplines have exerted as much influence as science. Certainly, for environmental issues, we often see science as *the* discipline to consider: science reveals to us the existence of the problem, the effects of inaction, and the solution to enact. In this chapter, however, we have seen that the role of science in determining the criteria for obedience may not be as simple and direct as conventional wisdom suggests. The work of philosophers of science and researchers in science-policy studies has revealed a spectrum of reasoned views regarding how we know using science, the level of authority scientific knowledge has, and how that knowledge can and should be connected with policymaking.

Given the influence science has on environmental issues, we might expect that different understandings of the nature of science and science-policy connections will lead to very different understandings of how science affects the importance, goals, and practice of environmental stewardship. Indeed, we find precisely such an effect and a non-trivial one at that: the assumptions and beliefs we hold about how science can encourage dialogue or deadlock, policymaking creativity or conflict, and policy stability or sojourning. One person understands science through a Popperian falsification framework and cannot understand how another, who sees science as more of a social construction, places so much stock in scientific consensus and is apparently unable to see how much current scientific thinking is undermined by contradictory results. The social constructionist, in turn, cannot understand how the falsificationist can apparently ignore the testimony of the majority of the scientific community. A third person believes science possesses high authority and that scientific findings compel particular policy responses and cannot understand a fourth person who is more skeptical that science automatically leads to specific courses of action. We are left with both mutual misunderstanding of the worst sort—that which is based upon hidden disagreement—as well as a raft of missed opportunities to improve the content of creation care. Because we are unaware of why we disagree, we may be tempted to assume we disagree due to ignorance or ill-motives. Because we default to a policy prescriptive understanding of the role of science in policymaking, we miss alternative ways of incorporating science into the policymaking process that might yield more effective policies.

In conclusion, we might say that the effects of our understanding of science are eclipsed only by the magnitude of our lack of consideration of its importance. Even though we routinely appeal to science in debates over environmental problems, seldom do we ask what we mean by "science" or what implications flow from those meanings; few works on environmental ethics, eco-theology, or environmental activism have examined the nature of science and its implications for environmental stewardship. Sadly, because of our lack of examination of these questions, unnecessary conflicts result, and science is sometimes used in ways that hinder rather than help our efforts at creation care. At the very least, if we are to strive for excellence in creation care, we need to expand our dialogue to address not merely the findings of science but science itself.

DISCUSSION QUESTIONS

1. The author presents arguments that science may not be as strictly logical and authoritative as commonly believed. What do you think of these arguments? What parts of these arguments are convincing and what parts are not?

2. Do you believe that the choice is between a science that is completely authoritative versus one that has an epistemic value exactly the same as all other forms of knowing? Why or why not? What reasons might someone give for seeing the choice as either/or, and what reasons might someone who disagrees with this dichotomy give in reply?

3. Does it matter whether science is an authoritative way of knowing or not? Is it not enough that science produces good knowledge without demanding that it be perfect? What might someone who believes science is authoritative say about why that status is important? What might someone who believes science is not authoritative say in reply?

4. Of the five ways the author described as to how science may connect with policy—policy prescriptive, fact-value dualism, supporting role (science is neutral), supporting role (science may not be neutral), and

honest broker—which of these models seem the most reasonable to you? Why?

5. Of the various ways the author discussed as to how science connects with policy, which do you think is the most problematic? In what way is that model(s) problematic? Why?

6

Left, Right, and Center (or Not)

Politics and Economics

A PARABLE, CONTINUED

Gabriel was out in his front yard, working in his garden, when a friendly, middle-aged woman walked up to his home. She looked familiar, but Gabriel couldn't remember where he had seen her face.

"Hi! My name is Brenda Campbell, and I serve as your representative to the Town Council." *Ah!,* thought Gabriel, *now it made sense.*

"Good to meet you, Councilwoman Campbell," said Gabriel. "My name is Gabriel Lang and I'm the pastor at All Saints Community Church." He removed his gardening gloves and shook her hand.

"Please, Pastor Lang, call me Brenda."

"And please, Brenda, call me Gabriel," he said, smiling. Gabriel invited Brenda to take a seat in one of the deck chairs on his front porch.

"So, what brings you around the neighborhood?" asked Gabriel.

"Well, I'm running for re-election in a few months and wanted to spend some time meeting more of my neighbors and hearing about what was on their minds."

"Well, actually, Brenda, I did have a question for you, regarding the pending request of Acme Industries for a permit to expand its factory into the Franklin marshes. I realize that this is a sensitive issue in our town"—Gabriel saw Brenda nod—"and so I don't want to lobby you one way or the other." Brenda's eyebrows rose a little, in mild surprise and curiosity. "Rather, what I wanted to ask you was how you go about thinking about decisions like this. That is to say, I was wondering what kinds of questions you ask as you think through such an issue, rather than what your actual position is."

"Well," said Brenda, a little hesitantly, "that's a really interesting question. I can't say that many people ask me that. Usually, folks are interested in how I'm going to vote on an issue or want to share with me their views on an issue." Brenda put her elbow on the armrest, rested her chin on her thumb, and tapped her index finger on her lips. In the distance, Gabriel could hear some children playing tag, laughing and shouting, "Not it! Not it!"

"I guess," Brenda finally began, "I try to look at both sides of the issue and find the strongest arguments each side has. Then, I compare them to each other."

"But, how do you do the comparison? What criteria do you use?" asked Gabriel.

Brenda paused. "Well, I believe that while there are times government needs to be involved in regulating and directly supporting parts of the community, most of the time, things will be better if government lets the private sector take the lead. So, I guess when comparing the various sides, I ask whether those who want government to take the lead have really made their case."

"Thank you, Brenda," replied Gabriel. "But I was wondering, would you mind if I pressed you further?" Gabriel saw that Brenda's head tilted a bit. "Maybe I should explain," Gabriel continued. "The people in my church hold various views on the Acme permit issue. I sometimes feel this is partly due to people holding different views regarding politics and economics. I'm trying to figure out how to help the different sides talk to each other about politics and economics, especially as it pertains to Acme's permit application."

Brenda looked thoughtful. The warmth of the sun and the gentleness of the breeze had a calming, soothing effect. Neighbors sitting on a front porch, talking politics on a sunny day, thought Gabriel, isn't this the romance of democracy?

"Your question is a really good one," Brenda began, "and I don't know if I can give you a complete answer. But maybe a more limited but practical answer will help."

"As I'm sure you know," said Brenda, "my fellow council-members also hold very different beliefs regarding politics and economics. We get along with each other, but some of our differences run deep. What I've found is that even in some of the most difficult issues, where what separates us are different understandings of the nature of fundamentals—things like liberty and freedom—nonetheless, there are some aspects of the issue that are not linked to such non-negotiables. If I can work with my colleagues in those areas where we can compromise, I've found we can often make more headway than any of us thought was possible. It's not perfect, but it's progress."

Gabriel thanked Brenda for her time and thoughtfulness as Brenda rose to excuse herself in order to meet some more of Gabriel's neighbors. The two shook hands, Brenda turned to walk down the street, and again Gabriel donned his gardening gloves. Perhaps political and economic differences, thought Gabriel, weren't as intractable as he sometimes feared. It's a little like gardening. Sometimes the work is major, fundamental: planting, transplanting, uprooting. But much of the work is indirect: pruning, fertilizing, pulling weeds. Somehow, all that "small stuff" adds up, and the garden grows and thrives. Maybe Brenda's idea of attending to this "small stuff," he thought, could help us work through the impact of political and economic views on the content of creation care.

INTRODUCTION

Both politics and economics study community—the shared life—and how communities are organized and allocate power and responsibility (politics) and goods and money (economics). As such, both fields study what we as a political and economic society are (and should be) and where we are (and should be) going. Given the importance of community in our lives, it should not surprise us that both fields exert a crucial influence on how we think of environmental stewardship. Our view of the structure of society leads to differences on the proper instruments of societal understanding and change, including understanding and change related to caring for the environment. Sociological research suggests, for instance, a relationship between political affiliation and acceptance of the IPCC-view of climate change as well as a relationship between religious affiliation and the willingness to accept climate change policy recommendations from scientists.[1] Theologian Max L. Stackhouse, in an introduction to a debate between Thomas Sieger Derr, James A. Nash, and Richard John Neuhaus on environmental ethics, notes that the differing views regarding the environment represented in that debate exemplify a collision not only between each person's "general theory of the bio-physical world in relationship to humanity and to God" but also between each person's "implied theory of how society ought to be organized to be most responsible for the earth, under God."[2] Our view of the trajectory of society can also lead to social conflict. Author Robert W. Merry argues that many debates in Western politics can be summarized as a clash between those who trust in progress and those who do not:

> Throughout American politics, as indeed throughout Western politics, a large proportion of major controversies ultimately are battles between the ichthyophils and the Burkeans, between the sensibility of the French Revolution and the sensibility of American Revolution, between adherents of the idea of progress and those skeptical of that potent concept.[3]

The *pluribus* in our society includes radical diversity on the nature of the *unum*.

But can we say more about the role of politics and economics on environmental stewardship beyond that it matters and that we have stark and strident differences in core understandings of how society should be organized and where society is heading? Can we say something beyond some sit on the left and others on the right? Or, are we left merely with what Gilbert and Sullivan wrote in *Iolanthe:*

> I often think it's comical—Fal, lal, la!
> How Nature always does contrive—Fal, lal, la!
> That every boy and every gal
> That's born into the world alive
> Is either a little Liberal
> Or else a little Conservative!
> Fal, lal, la![4]

How can we break down how we think about the role of the two determinants in questions of creation care, and do so in a way that is tractable?

1. Evans and Feng, "Conservative Protestantism," 595–96.
2. Stackhouse, "Introduction," 16.
3. Merry, "Fallacy."
4. Gilbert and Sullivan, "The Complete Plays."

The history and literature of politics and economics is voluminous, to put it mildly. What can we add that might help us think through the role of these two determinants?

As Max Stackhouse alluded to, many arguments about politics and economics and the environment involve the question of how much should government be involved.[5] Politically, does government play a large and active role in caring for the environment (e.g., regulation, civil and criminal law, administering of public goods, etc.) or a small and circumscribed role, thus leaving the vast majority of political power regarding the environment to individuals and non-governmental organizations? Economically, does government play a large and active role (e.g., socialism where government owns the means of production) or a minimal role (e.g., capitalism where the private sector owns the means of production) in running the economy in such a way as to support creation care? Examples abound of debate and argument over the proper role of government when it comes to environmental issues. Garrett Hardin's famous work "Tragedy of the Commons," uses game theory to argue that some environmental problems are intractable to ordinary methods and can only be solved by recourse to governmental coercion.[6] Others, such as Robert Higgs and Carl P. Close, are more skeptical as to the ability of "environmental bureaucracy" to achieve the goals of environmental protection.[7] The Cornwall Declaration and Evangelical Declaration also have different emphases regarding the role of government in solving environmental problems.[8]

Thus, in this section, we first analyze the political and economic aspects of creation care through the lens of more or less governmental involvement. While we take the question of governmental involvement as our starting point, we need to keep in mind that politics and economics encompass much more than that question. Other questions include the role of the individual versus the collective and the role of intermediate or mediating institutions (including the church), to name a few. However, surveying reasons for or against government involvement in the political and economic aspects of creation care will clue us in on a framework we can use to analyze the role of politics and economics, more generally, in creation care.

---

5. Defining a spectrum between two poles regarding democratic government involvement has a storied history. Alexis de Tocqueville observed that all free societies can be divided into two camps, one which wishes "to restrain the power of the people" and the other which desires "to extend it without limit" (Tocqueville, *Democracy*, 199–200).

6. Hardin, "Tragedy."

7. Higgs and Close, "Introduction," 4–6.

8. Cornwall Alliance, "Cornwall Declaration" and EEN, "Evangelical Declaration."

When we examine the issue of how much should government be involved in the political and economic aspects of creation care, we find, as we might expect, reasons for more involvement and reasons for less involvement. One reason given in favor of more government involvement deals with the shared nature of many environmental goods. Under Western social contract theory, management of public goods is delegated to the government, and so it would be natural for government to manage the shared (and thus public) goods of the environment. Another reason in favor for more government involvement is that rational private entities, because they are focused on their own self-interest, lack the ability to coordinate action for the common good. In contrast, public entities, most prominently the government, are concerned with group interests, and thus can coordinate action that goes beyond individual interests. A third reason given in favor for more government is that bureaucracies enable long-term policies to be executed by providing a stable infrastructure of personnel, procedures, resources, etc. Private entities, whether individual or collective, are quite ephemeral, and as many environmental problems require long-term efforts at monitoring, remediation, and regulation, only public, governmental entities possess the resources needed to address those kinds of problems.

With regards to the argument for less government involvement, one reason given is that government involvement threatens Constitutional protections of property. Whether through regulations that all but eliminate the owner's ability to use their property or directly through application of eminent domain, governmental involvement can severely impact the latitude given property owners. A second reason against government involvement in environmental problems is that the coercive powers of government make government a tempting target for rent-seeking behavior. Rent-seeking behaviors are those that aim to profit through special favors, such as through regulations that artificially decrease competition.[9] For instance, manufacturers may support stricter air quality standards partly because of a grandfather clause that treats existing manufacturers more leniently than new manufacturers.[10] A third reason against government involvement is that bureaucracies can be inefficient and inflexible because of the intrinsic monopoly government possesses and because of the relative lack of the carrot-and-stick managerial levers available in the private sector.[11]

In this brief recounting of reasons for more or less government involvement in environmental issues, we find that some reasons seem value

9. Henderson, "Rent Seeking."

10. Marxsen, "Prophecy," 31.

11. Klein, "Management 101."

driven while others seem more pragmatic or value neutral. This suggests that politics and economics, as disciplines, have two related but distinct modes of activity: as "philosophy" and as "policy studies." In political and economic philosophy, we focus on the values "encapsulated" by a political or economic system. These values are the core justifications for a political or economic system. Examples include the status, nature, and identity of rights and the relationship between prudential and moral judgment. In political and economic policy study, we focus on the categorization and analysis of political and economic policies. Political science as a science, public policy studies, public choice studies,[12] and econometrics are examples of subdisciplines that exhibit this mode of activity.

Between these two modes of activity, the philosophical mode is more fundamental than the policy study mode. This is because the meaning of the results of policy studies are set by the values of the political or economic system we use to interpret those results. For example:, someone who values economic growth would find more compelling policy analysis that identifies free-market systems as better performing than socialist systems as compared to someone who prioritizes distributional justice. The philosophical mode itself, in turn, is both an expression of and dependent upon our worldviews and understanding of what it means to be human.[13]

At the same time, the philosophical mode is affected by the results of the policy study mode. Political and economic values are not formed solely by deduction from first-principles but also utilize induction and other forms of knowing. Many policy studies, after all, make use of the scientific methodology and mathematical and statistical tools, and the fruits of those studies form part of the evidential cloud that informs political and economic values. As such, the history and epistemology of science gives us insights as to how the policy study mode may affect the philosophical mode. Just as scientific paradigms are overthrown through the influence of anomalies coupled with a competing paradigm, so too the results of policy studies can alter political and economic philosophy paradigms.

Finally, an implication of this two-aspect nature of politics and economics is that we have to consider both a philosophical and policy study approach to understand the role of politics and economics in determining creation care. In a way similar to what we found with science, we seldom can understand or resolve political and economic debates by only a policy study

12. Higgs and Close, "Introduction," 2–3.

13. "By comparing these descriptions and theories [of public choice], it becomes obvious that differences in political economy really boil down to differences about *personal* economy—that is, what it means to be human" [emphasis in original] (Muller, *Redeeming Economics,* 127).

approach. Sometimes creation care debates will be value debates (e.g., over the priority of distributional justice) while other times they will be over specific policy analysis results (e.g., unintended effects of regulations). Sometimes two people will agree on policy choices (e.g., a particular amount of government involvement) but will disagree wildly as to the reasons for the political dimension of that choice. Additionally, because what is primary are the values encapsulated in politics and economics, and not necessarily the role of government per se (though under some political and economic systems the question of the role of government is primary), there may exist political and economic systems worth considering that do not neatly fit into the traditional left-right spectrum. These "alternative" political and economic systems may also give us resources to understand the political and economic determinants in a fresh way and point towards possible routes for compromise.

To recap, our consideration of the question of more or less government has yielded a two-aspect framework (philosophical and policy study) that we can use to analyze politics and economics and creation in general. With this framework, we specifically analyze how politics and economics impact the content of creation care. Our analysis will not be limited to left-right differences and will involve more than questions of the level of governmental involvement. We consider principles that undergird both traditional (left-right) and alternative political and economic frameworks and consider tools to adjudicate conflicts regarding creation care that are driven by politics and economics. (Some of these tools come from considering alternative political and economic systems besides the traditional ones.) For the rest of this chapter, we address the following: First, we examine how the philosophy mode of politics and economics impacts the criteria for obedience. Second, we examine how the policy study mode of politics and economics impacts the criteria for obedience. Lastly, we draw conclusions about politics and economics and creation care and identify possible areas of debate, discussion, and compromise regarding politics and economics and creation care.

POLITICS AND ECONOMICS AND IMPORTANCE, GOALS, AND PRACTICE: PHILOSOPHY

In this section, we examine how the philosophy mode of politics and economics affects the three criteria for obedience. We first examine the range of justifications that are given for political and economic systems. That is to say, what kinds of reasons do we give in favor of a political or economic system? For instance, when a capitalist or socialist argues for their school

of economics, what kinds of justifications are provided? Second, we identify how, more generally, these justifications connect with the three criteria
(importance, goals, practice) for obedience. Afterwards, we take each of the
criteria for obedience in turn and examine what about the criteria are determined by political and economic philosophy.

Justifications for Political and Economic Systems

There are many different justifications for political and economic systems.
We group those justifications into three loose categories. The first category
is rights or duty-based justifications. This is similar to deontological ethics
in philosophy. The second category is efficiency or pragmatism-based justifications. This is similar to consequentialist ethics in philosophy. The third
category is eudaemonic or teleological/purpose-based justifications. This is
similar to virtue ethics and natural law in philosophy. In this subsection, we
list the major reasons given under each category of justifications. While not
exhaustive, our listing covers a substantial fraction of the reasons in each
category.

The first category, rights or duty-based reasons for a particular political or economic system, define goods that are understood as categorical
imperatives or goods with the status of divine command. We identify seven
justifications. First, political and economic systems are justified on the basis
of whether they promote the preservation or growth of freedom and liberty.
Freedom and liberty can be defined negatively, as the absence of tyranny or
coercion. Freedom and liberty can also be defined positively, as the presence
of opportunity, resources, and mobility (physical, social, religious, economic, etc.). Some definitions of freedom and liberty contain multiple aspects.
A Christian understanding of freedom, for instance, equally emphasizes
rights and responsibilities.[14] There are also different kinds of freedom for
a Christian, and while some kinds of freedom are imperatives, others may
not necessarily be so.[15]

A second rights-based justification for a political or economic system is whether the system promotes and exemplifies fairness or justice.
That fairness or justice may be cast in terms of an absolute distribution of
resources, a relative distribution, or a distribution of opportunity. It also
may be defined in terms of outcomes or output, rather than resources or
input. While the case of justice-in-outcomes appears to be consequentialist in nature (ends versus means), the justification itself is grounded upon

14. Hay, *Economics Today*, 84–87, 209.
15. Ibid., 87.

a rights-based framework; maximization of justice-in-outcomes is not the goal but rather justice as a categorical imperative.

A third rights-based justification is that the system promotes democracy and represents the will of the people. As we saw in chapter 5, there are different conceptions of what democracy entails. Roger A. Pielke, Jr., for instance, contrasted a vision of democracy based on pure-interest group competition versus a vision where democracy acts on recommendations from a leadership elites as leaders.[16] Each conception may be justified on various grounds (e.g., duty-based, efficiency-based), but the value of the good itself—of democracy itself—is usually considered a categorical good—good in and of itself and without need for justification.

A fourth rights-based justification is that the political or economic system provides the most efficient or "optimal" allocation of scarce resources. Often, we consider this as a pragmatic reason. However, efficiency can also be considered an automatic good, and thus closer to a categorical imperative than a prudential imperative. Public policy scholar Robert H. Nelson notes that market efficiency attains this status if we hold a view of "economic religion," wherein economic growth is seen as the route to deliverance from the problems of this world.[17]

A fifth rights-based justification for political or economic systems is whether the system supports a community's spiritual, emotional, and societal health, cohesion, and well-being. Here too, each of these reasons can be understood in a prudential light. We may, for instance, argue that social cohesion is a prudential good we should maximize and include it as a factor in a calculus to decide on the best political system. Achieving these goods, however, can also be understood in terms of duties or imperatives. For instance, conservative economists sometimes argue for the morality of free enterprise because it has enabled people to rise out of abject poverty.[18]

A sixth rights-based justification is whether the system strengthens a "good" culture, that is, a culture that makes it easier to be a good person.[19] Because such a culture enables the categorical good of people being "good" (however conceived), we can think of the strengthening of such a "good" culture as also a categorical good. Again, this particular justification can also be considered prudential.

16. Pielke, *Honest Broker,* 11–14.

17. Nelson, *New Holy Wars,* 100.

18. For instance, see Brooks, "Why Free Enterprise."

19. I read this definition of a "good" culture somewhere but cannot remember its source. I like the formulation and wanted to make it clear that I owe someone else for the definition.

A seventh rights-based justification is whether the system fulfills a duty grounded in a "command" from God. Here, we put "command" in quotes because such a command does not have to be explicitly nor directly given in Scripture; it can, for instance, be given as principles to apply rather than as specific action to undertake, and the commands may have a provisional nature. For example, economist Donald Hay examines the Old and New Testaments and derives biblical principles for thinking through economic issues. Yet, though these principles are taken from Scripture, Hay notes that "The derivation of these principles is provisional: they are open to a process of criticism and refinement in the light of the biblical material. We reiterate that their scope is quite limited. Few economic issues can be settled by direct appeal to Scripture."[20] Still, despite their provisional nature, they are commands in the sense they are non-negotiable because they come from divine revelation. They may not be the Ten Commandments but neither are they mere suggestions.[21] They have a claim on those who live under the authority of Scripture.

This seventh rights-based justification can be seen in sociological research that shows connections between our view of how God works in history and our view of economics.[22] This connection, while present, is not as straightforward as we might assume. For instance, sociologist Paul Froese notes that in the United States:

> Americans who feel that "God has a plan" for them and their country are much more likely to think that "success is achieved by ability rather than luck" and that "able-bodied people who are out of work should not receive unemployment checks." And over half (54 percent) of Americans who think God controls the economy feel that "anything is possible for those who work hard"; in contrast, only one-quarter of Americans who rely on human resourcefulness, rather than God's plan, feel this way."[23]

Yet, at the same time, this view of an "Authoritative God," in other countries, does not necessarily predict economic conservatism, as the U.S. results seem to suggest, but rather socialism.[24] Thus, the pathway that connects

20. Hay, *Economics Today*, 71.

21. For Scriptural principles regarding politics and economics, in general, we can also use our tripartite taxonomy of criteria for obedience—importance, goals, practice—to analyze how to translate these commands into obedience. This secondary level of analysis is beyond the scope of the present work.

22. Froese, "How Your View."

23. Ibid.

24. Ibid. Regarding the seeming inconsistency, Paul Froese speculates that:

our worldview to our political and economic views, in this rights-based or divine command way, exists but is not simple and straightforward.

The second category of justifications for a political or economic system is efficiency or pragmatism-based reasons. The goods in this second category are pragmatic in nature; we do not necessarily have a right to these goods, but they are very useful for practical living. Examples of such include growth and wealth, physical health and life-expectancy, and the solution of a particular (very important) problem of interest (e.g., corruption, inefficient allocation of resources, environmental degradation, etc.). Of course, some of these goods might also be considered rights and thus may also carry deontological warrant. For instance, earlier we saw that under "economic religion," market efficiency provides not only a pragmatic warrant but also a deontological warrant.[25] In those instances, one particular good provides both rights-based and pragmatism-based justifications for a political or economic system. These two kinds of justifications, however, are entirely different.

One feature of this second category of justifications is that these goods, being pragmatic, are not ultimate. Thus, to the extent these goods do not tie into a rationale with a stronger warrant, these pragmatic reasons may be "trumped" by those we consider rights-based. At the same time, efficiency reasons find wide acceptance, particularly in American society, which has a wide diversity of understandings of what constitutes a right as well as a strong strain of pragmatism.[26] "A chicken for every pot" can still be a potent

Perhaps it is the fervent individualism of American Christianity which makes free market capitalism seem like a Divine mandate. Because evangelicals assert that you alone are responsible for your eternal salvation, it makes sense that the individual is also responsible for his or her economic salvation without government assistance, especially if God is the only assistance you really need. (Ibid.)

25. Nelson, *New Holy Wars*, 100.

26. Alexis de Tocqueville, for instance, in describing the rationale behind the American focus on practical applications of science, notes:

Most people in such [democratic] nations are quite intent on immediate material gratifications, and since they are always unhappy with the position they occupy and always free to abandon it, they think only of ways to change or improve their fortunes. To minds so disposed, any new method that shortens the road to wealth, any machine that saves labor, any instrument that reduces the costs of production, any discovery that facilitates or increases pleasures seems the most magnificent achievement of the human mind. It is primarily for these reasons that democratic peoples devote themselves to science, understand it, and honor it. In aristocratic centuries men turn to science particularly to political slogan; all political rationales do not have to go back to "life, liberty, and the pursuit of happiness."[27]

The third category of justifications for a political or economic system is eudaemonic or teleological/purpose-based reasons. These justifications argue that certain political or economic systems fulfill a purpose (or *telos*) of intrinsic good. Attainment of that *telos* is not a duty or right, and the *telos* goes beyond the considerations of practical living (though *telos* might include practical considerations), and in these ways, this third category defines reasons based on a different kind of good from the other two. We identify three kinds of justifications of this category: that the system promotes "true" happiness, that the system flows from the nature of being human, and that the system is the culmination of history.

The first kind of eudaemonic or teleological justification is that the political or economic system promotes "true" happiness, the *summum bonum* of human life. "True" happiness, as we might expect, goes beyond the ephemeral emotionality we associate with contemporary uses of the term "happiness." One view is that given by Aristotle, who argued that the exercise of reason and the life of contemplation forms our highest good: In *Nicomachean Ethics*, Aristotle writes, "In other words, a life guided by intelligence is the best and most pleasant for man, inasmuch as intelligence, above all else, is man. Consequently, this kind of life is the happiest."[28] If we accept Aristotle's argument, we might justify our choice of political system on the basis of whether that system supports such a life of contemplation and conclude that that conception of happiness argues for an aristocratic political system. Alexis de Tocqueville makes just such an observation in comparing the relative hospitality of aristocracy versus democracy in nurturing the non-practical aspects of science:

> Nothing is more necessary to the cultivation of the higher sciences, or of the loftier aspects of the sciences, than meditation, and nothing is less suited to meditation than the circumstances of democratic society. In such a society one does not find, as in aristocratic nations, a numerous class that enjoys repose because it finds everything to its liking, and another that does not stir because it has abandoned hope that things will ever improve. Everyone is restless: some want to attain power, others to achieve wealth. In the midst of this universal tumult, this

gratify the mind; in democratic centuries they do so to gratify the body. (Tocqueville, *Democracy,* 526)

27. "A Chicken" and the U.S. Declaration of Independence.

28. Aristotle, *Nicomachean Ethics,* 291 [X.7, 1178a6–9].

constant clash of conflicting interests, this unending quest for fortune, where is the calm necessary to the deeper strategies of the intellect to be found? How is one to ponder some specific point when everything is in flux and one is daily swept along and buffeted about by the impetuous current that carries all things before it?[29]

Thus, an Aristotelian understanding of human happiness may lead to arguments for aristocracy as opposed to democracy (though, Tocqueville himself may not make such a conclusion).

For a second example of a justification for a political or economic system based on whether the system promotes true happiness, we consider one critique of today's dominant economic systems from the perspective of distributism. Distributism argues that the separation of ownership and work leads to a host of human (and environmental) ills.[30] Broad ownership of the means of production, in contrast, offers a means of connecting workers with their work in a way that enhances "true" human well-being, rather than only material or financial well-being.[31] (Note that broad ownership here does not generally mean state ownership, as in socialism.) As scholar Thomas Storck describes:

> Distributism, the system of widely distributed productive property, reunites work with ownership, thus orienting the producer not just toward sales, but toward pride in craftsmanship, care of the community, a realization that his own future is bound up with that of his neighbors, is woven into the texture of life in that particular place.[32]

Widely distributed ownership accomplishes this by aligning worker interests with owner interests (since workers are now owners) and decreasing labor mobility (since ownership is indissolubly co-located with labor).[33]

But what anchors this distributist critique is a commitment to a particular vision of human well-being. This vision understands human life as consisting of activities embedded in a hierarchy of purposes.[34] Efficiency and consumerism are considered relatively peripheral (and sometimes

---

29. Tocqueville, *Democracy,* 523.
30. Storck, "Capitalism."
31. Ibid.
32. Ibid.
33. Ibid.
34. Ibid.

detrimental) compared to community relationships and one's relationship with God. Thus, Storck argues that:

> But however this [safeguards to prevent greed, etc.] is done, distributism's aim is a society in which we can make use of earthly goods in such a way that we can turn our attention to the things that really matter: our families, cultural and intellectual activity, and the worship of God. Insofar as the economy supports and contributes to those activites [sic] it is good, but insofar as it detracts and distracts us from them, it has become an evil, has turned upon those whom it is supposed to serve. I submit that our present economy has so turned upon us and become our enemy. It is one major factor pulling apart families and communities, filling our minds with nonsense. Distributism can be an important means of restoring an economy to its proper function and purpose.[35]

Under this line of reasoning, the justification for the distributist economic system is a specific, prior understanding of the true good of human life as being found in our relationships with others.

Finally, while we often think of divine commands as producing rights or duty-based justifications for a political or economic system, we can also think of divine commands as providing eudaemonic justifications. If God creates, sustains, and loves human beings, it goes to reason that obedience to His commands will ultimately result in our blessing:

> So be careful to do what the Lord your God has commanded you; do not turn aside to the right or to the left. Walk in obedience to all that the Lord your God has commanded you, so that you may live and prosper and prolong your days in the land that you will possess.[36]

This blessing, we further reason from our premises, are not merely material riches but riches of the deepest kind: joy that flows from communion with the *summum bonum* of God Himself.[37] In this sense, God's commands not

---

35. Ibid.

36. Deut 5:32–33.

37. Besides the witness found in the Bible, the theme of God as sufficient permeates millennia of writings on the Christian life. Here are three examples. Blaise Pascal likens the human condition as one characterized by an interior "abyss" of that only God can fill:

> What else does this craving, and this helplessness, proclaim but that there was once in man a true happiness, of which all that now remains is the empty print and trace? This he tries in vain to fill with everything

only are duties we are obliged to follow but also the way of true happiness. Thus, to the extent divine command speaks to political and economic systems, we may also find in those commands eudaemonic "true" happiness justifications for those systems.

The second kind of eudaemonic or teleological/purpose-based justification for a political or economic system is that the system flows from the nature of being human. This can be similar to the first kind of eudaemonic/teleological justification, in that many arguments for "true" happiness are grounded in a particular understanding of human nature. (Natural law is one prominent example of this argument.) Still, we can identify justifications for a political or economic system that directly arise from human nature. Thomas Storck, for instance, argues that the differences between the major views of political philosophy are actually differences in their conceptions of the nature of human beings and the state.[38] He categorizes the conservative-liberal distinction as being merely a difference of emphasis within a Lockean philosophy that understands the purpose of society is to distribute material goods and the state is merely the result of a "social contract."[39] In contrast, Storck argues that Aristotelian and Catholic philosophy understands both human beings and the state as natural entities while Marxism understands the state as a non-essential byproduct of class struggle.[40] As Storck summarizes:

> around him, seeking in things that are not there the help he cannot find in those that are, though none can help, since this infinite abyss can be filled only with an infinite and immutable object; in other words by God himself. (Pascal, *Pensées,* 45 [Fragment 148])

We are, as Saint Augustine, argues, made for God and to praise Him, and only there do we find our home: "The thought of you [God] stirs him [man] so deeply that he cannot be content unless he praises you, because you made us for yourself and our hearts find no peace until they rest in you." (Augustine, *Confessions,* 21 [Book I, Chapter 1]) Finally, in a possibly more prudential way, Saint Teresa of Avila expresses that because of God's sufficiency, we need not fear to live for God alone:

> . . . if I were a person who had to advise others, I would never recommend anyone, when a good inspiration comes to him again and again, to hesitate to put it into practice because of fear; for, if one lives a life of detachment for God's sake alone, there is no reason to be afraid that things will turn out amiss, since He is all-powerful. (Teresa of Avila, *Life of Teresa,* 78)

38. Storck, "Superficiality."
39. Ibid.
40. Ibid.

> It [Marxism] rejects the state as the necessary, [sic] means for
> the harmonious existence of civil society, supposing that per-
> fected men can live without the state, yet still in society. Thus
> it finds the natural place of man to be in society but without
> any political apparatus, whereas Locke considered man's natural
> home to be outside both society and politics, and the Catholic
> tradition sees that both society and the state are according to
> human nature.[41]

In this line of argument, human nature itself distinguishes (and, thus, forms
the justification) of different political philosophies.

The third kind of eudaemonic or teleological/purpose-based justification for a political or economic system is that the system is the culmination
of history or progress. One of the better known examples of this kind of
justification for a political or economic system, particularly for those who
lived in the twentieth century, is Karl Marx's view that communism is the
destination of political and economic history. As politics scholar Robert C.
Tucker describes:

> In Marxism, which has its foundation in what they [Karl Marx
> and Friedrich Engels] variously called the "materialist concep-
> tion of history" or "historical materialism," socialist thought
> had—they said—graduated from its earlier "utopian" stage and
> become "scientific." Whereas the "utopian" socialists had visual-
> ized a socialist reorganization of society as something that *ought*
> to be realized, the materialist conception of history had con-
> clusively demonstrated that the human historical process was
> moving toward a worldwide anticapitalist revolution that would
> usher in socialism or communism (Marx and Engels tended to
> use these two words interchangeably). [emphasis in original][42]

Thus, communism is not merely a moral imperative but the inevitable
course of history.

A second, more recent example of the "culmination of history" argument sets Marxism on its head,[43] concluding that liberal-democratic ideology represents the inevitable ending point of global or universal political
ideological development. This "end of history," described by political scientist Francis Fukuyama, is characterized by a "universal homogenous state"
and is devoid of ideologically-driven large-scale conflict.[44] This does not

41. Ibid.
42. Tucker, "Introduction," xx.
43. Fukuyama, "The End of History?," 6.
44. Ibid., 5.

mean there will be a single world government nor does it mean that every nation will possess a functioning representative democratic government and live under the rule of law. Rather, this end of history means that the development of and competition between universal political ideologies has ended, with liberal-democracy as the victor. Writes Fukuyama: "But at the end of history it is not necessary that all societies become successful liberal societies, merely that they end their ideological pretensions of representing different and higher forms of human society."[45] The result: "International life for the part of the world that has reached the end of history is far more preoccupied with economics than with politics or strategy."[46] Terrorism and local wars will continue, "But large-scale conflict must involve large states still caught in the grip of history, and they are what appear to be passing from the scene."[47]

In all the above examples of eudaemonic or teleological/purpose-based justifications for political and economic systems, the goods the justifications appeal to are not duties nor are they merely practical in nature, but have a nature somewhere in-between. What unites these justifications is an understanding of humanity as having a direction, goal, or purpose, either individually and/or communally, and support of or consistency with the aim or movement towards that goal is the justification for the political or economic system. In some of the justifications, such as the *summum bonum* arguments, the goal is the good life. In others, such as some of the "end of history" arguments, the justifications are teleological in the sense that the political or economic system is claimed to be or moving towards an "endpoint" of history, but is not necessarily teleological in the sense of being "purposeful"; the endpoint the political or economic system is moving towards may not have any ultimate meaning or definitive form.[48] Regardless, this third category of justifications for political and economic systems rests on some notion of a purpose or goal.

We note, however, that eudaemonic or teleological/purpose-based justifications for political and economic systems are ultimately convincing only insofar as we find the purpose or goals fulfilled through the political or economic system to be convincing. A particular *summum bonum* argument

45. Ibid., 13.

46. Ibid., 16.

47. Ibid., 18.

48. Karl Marx was not a fan of teleology in the natural sciences (Marx, "Marx To Ferdinand Lassalle"), and so a Marxist may, in particular, argue that historical materialism is not teleological. But the argument that a political system represents the "end of history" does not mean that history necessarily has a purpose. The reason may be "teleological" only in the sense that *telos* implies culmination.

holds little sway if one holds a different understanding of the good life. Similarly, end of history arguments are ultimately unconvincing if one disagrees with the goals that are fulfilled in that culmination of history. While the idea of inevitability itself can be persuasive, if one opposes the goals fulfilled in that inevitability (one of which may be the idea of "progress," which can be a very potent goal), the persuasiveness of the justification results (at best) in a fatalistic acceptance. This is, in a way, another manifestation of the "is-ought" dichotomy we discussed in chapter 2. A political or economic system may be inevitable but unwelcome. Francis Fukuyama, for instance, closes his end of history argument by questioning whether the inevitable triumph of liberal-democratic ideology, and the concomitant elimination of ideological conflict, but also heroism and creativity, is very attractive:

> The end of history will be a very sad time. . . . In the post-historical period there will be neither art nor philosophy, just the perpetual caretaking of the museum of human history. . . . Even though I recognize its inevitability, I have the most ambivalent feelings for the civilization that has been created in Europe since 1945, with its north Atlantic and Asian offshoots. Perhaps this very prospect of centuries of boredom at the end of history will serve to get history started once again.[49]

Whether Fukuyama is serious or writing partly tongue-in-cheek is immaterial to our point:[50] to someone who does not value the goals fulfilled in the triumph of liberal-democracy—say a Promethean—Fukuyama's end of history is a fate to be avoided, not accepted. Thus, in general, the effectiveness of eudaemonic or teleological/purpose-based justifications for political and economic systems rests on our prior beliefs regarding the desirability of the purpose and goals that said political and economic systems fulfill.

How these Justifications Determine the Importance, Goals, and Practice of Creation Care

Political and economic systems encapsulate the values of an individual or society. That encapsulation, however, is simultaneously derived from our values as well as partially prescriptive of our ethical system and what values we find important. Our values start from the framework given by our worldviews, since worldviews are fundamental.[51] Those values interact

49. Fukuyama, "The End of History?" 18.

50. We have seen no report or claim that Fukuyama is writing tongue-in-cheek.

51. However, recall that worldviews are not necessarily directly prescriptive of values.

heavily with our ethics (and other inputs)—as ethics governs how we weigh different goods—to become our understanding of politics and economics. For example, someone who holds an ethical system that deontologically (that is, as a duty) values freedom over cultural well-being would tend to support political and economic systems that value the former over the latter.

Once defined, however, our chosen political and economic systems can in turn affect the values that we hold. That is to say, our values not only affect our choice of political and economic systems, but political and economic systems can also act as lenses through which we see the world and, accordingly, can color our interpretation of value in the world. After all, political and economic systems define language and criteria with which we evaluate possible allocations of power and goods. That language and those categories cannot help but influence our understanding of value. For example, if we prefer political and economic systems that maximize individual freedom, this will tend to sharpen the priority we put on freedom, since our analysis of politics and economics will be cast in "rights" terms. Likewise, if we prefer political and economic systems that maximize efficiency, this can encourage us to analyze issues through the lens of efficiency, which tends to decrease the importance of other lenses with which we can analyze those issues (e.g., social justice criteria, individual rights justifications, etc.). There may be a variety of avenues by which the influence is effected—e.g., sociological praxis, the effect of spending more time on one way of thinking versus other ways of thinking—but the net result is that our choice of political and economic systems colors the values we hold dear.

Given how our values interact with our choice of political and economic systems, we find that politics and economics, in their "philosophy" mode, determine the importance, goals, and practice of creation care in one primary way: criteria for obedience related to values encapsulated by our chosen political or economic system are sharpened and bolstered while those unrelated to the political and economic system are minimized or ignored. The values of a political and economic system create a "paradigm" that we can use to analyze a situation, decide what questions to ask, and judge what answers are correct. For example, we may believe a left-of-center political system, which values the use of government to address many environmental problems, is the most justified because it can overcome problems of cooperation (e.g., the Tragedy of the Commons). If so, when evaluating what kind of policies should be adopted (practice of creation care), we may give preference to creation care practices that involve governmental action, even if the particular problem of interest does not have a major "Tragedy of the Commons" dimension. As another example, we may believe that a right-of-center political system, which is wary of government involvement in addressing many environmental problems, is the most justified because it better preserves liberty through creating a larger space where private interests can act. If so, when evaluating the importance of creation care, we might compare those reasons with the value of human liberty, even if the particular problem of interest does not have a major human liberty component.

The dynamic we have described may sound like mere bias: liberals are biased towards government and conservatives are biased against government; socialists are biased towards public ownership and planning and capitalists are biased towards an unencumbered free-market. Certainly, in some cases, the charge of bias fits. Hyper-partisanship can sometimes lead towards a myopic view of the criteria for obedience. But just because bias fits the dynamic we have described does not mean the dynamic describes only bias. Rather, the dynamic of a political or economic "paradigm" affecting our understanding of the criteria for obedience is often merely the expression of the fact that many issues in the real-world are underdetermined by specific data and theories. We do not and often *cannot* know enough to make a judgment without the use of generalization, categorization, subjectivity, and assumptions. Or, more positively, we cannot make heads-or-tails of many real-world issues without creativity, imagination, wisdom, and intuition. Thus, to say the values of our preferred political and economic system sharpen the criteria for obedience related to those values is a natural implication of living in a hopelessly complex world. This is not to say we cannot critique paradigms. They are not givens and thus must be argued for, and we can question their accuracy, applicability, appropriateness, importance, and completeness. But their use can be a legitimate form of reasoning regarding the criteria for obedience.

Thus, we see that our choice of political or economic philosophy exerts considerable influence on our understanding of the criteria for obedience, and in a rather fundamental way. It will not do to excuse the values encapsulated in our political and economic leanings as "personal views" or "mere bias" that should be easily discarded in light of scientific findings or other presumably determinate authority. In some sense, we cannot and thus should not discard our political and economic values when considering the content of environmental stewardship. In the rest of this section we move from this general analysis and turn our attention to each of the criteria for obedience—importance, goals, and practice—and identify specific ways political and economic philosophy impacts the criteria, with respect to the environmental stewardship command.

Political and Economic Philosophy and the Importance of the Creation Care Command (Why Follow the Command)

Political and economic philosophy affects the importance of the creation care command through a weighing of the values behind the justifications for political and economic systems versus those values associated with aspects of creation care. For example, in determining the importance of the creation care command, if we subscribe to a political or economic system that values individual freedom, we may explicitly ask whether the value of caring for creation is more or less important than the value of individual freedom. Or, as another example, if we subscribe to a political or economic system that values a particular eudaemonic, purpose-driven conception of human happiness, and that value encounters a form of creation care that defines environmental integrity in a way that frustrates the human *telos,* the importance of such a creation care command will look very different to us as opposed to someone else who holds a different political or economic philosophy.

Since this is an exercise in weighing values, the rules we use for weighing those values will play an important role. Perhaps the most important consideration is the ethical theories we use for weighing values (e.g., deontology, utilitarianism, etc.). For instance, if we believe individual freedom to be a categorical imperative and creation care a lesser imperative (for instance, not a categorical one), we will favor maximizing individual freedom if that value conflicts with a value associated with creation care. Or, if we believe in a utilitarian weighing of value, we will calculate the pleasure and pain that results from our political or economic philosophy and weigh against that the pleasure and pain that would result from environmental stewardship. The net result of this pleasure/pain calculus reveals the importance of creation care.

In some cases, in addition to the ethical theories we use to weigh competing values, political and economic models themselves may give rules on how to weigh the relative value of creation care. These rules are consistent with the justifications for the given political or economic system, but they also suggest ways the values behind those justifications might interact with other values. For example, consider the case of neo-Scholastic economics and its rule for final distribution. Both classical and neoclassical economics lack a theory of final distribution, that is, a theory that explains the end for which economic activity occurs.[52] Neo-scholastic economics, however, by providing a rule for final distribution, provides a method to weigh non-

---

52. Muller, *Redeeming Economics,* 20, 22, 57, 89.

instrumental goods with one another. Our economic choices, in this way, reveal a "scale of preferences" that provide a valuation of non-instrumental goods. As John D. Muller explains:

> A miser is said to love money as his highest good, noted Augustine—yet he still parts with it to buy bread to continue living, thus showing that his deepest motive is love of self, not money. But it is not the case that every human acts solely for him- or herself. That is precisely what each person is free to decide. Every economic choice is therefore a moral choice. In other words, each of us has not only a scale of preferences for instrumental goods as means but also a scale of preferences for persons as ends of our actions.[53]

Thus, neo-Scholastic economics has, as part of its system, a methodology of allocating the good of creation care relative to other goods. The economic values encapsulated in neo-Scholastic economics can be weighed against the value of creation care, using a tool defined by the neo-Scholastic system itself. (We discuss neo-Scholastic economics in more detail later on in this chapter.)

Political and Economic Philosophy and the Goals of Following the Creation Care Command (What Following the Command Will Result In)

We identify two ways that political and economic systems, through philosophy, influence the goals of creation care. First, political and economic systems influence goals of creation care through (partially or completely) appropriating the goals of the political and economic systems themselves as the goals of creation care. That is to say, the goals of the political and economic systems we prefer can also become (in part or *in toto*) our understanding of what following the creation care command will result in. For instance, if we support a political system that understands promoting justice to be a categorical imperative, we may also be encouraged to understand creation care as primarily concerned with promoting an ecologically "just" order. Or, to take another example, if we believe the goal of an economic system is to optimize growth, we may also believe the goal of creation care is to enable the environment to help optimize economic growth (e.g., through providing "ecosystem services," such as wetland filtration of storm runoff).

---

53. Muller, *Redeeming Economics*, 23.

A second way the philosophy of political and economic systems influences the goals of creation care is through admitting certain points of view (but not others) into the shaping of the goals of creation care. As we mentioned earlier, political and economic theories provide a paradigm or way of thinking that suggests questions to ask, accepted ways of analysis, and useful/accepted strategies for obtaining answers. (This is similar to how paradigms function in Thomas Kuhn's theory of scientific revolutions.) This paradigm can guide and constrain the ways we think about the goals of creation care. For example, economic theories that center on utility will tend to cast all creation care goals into utility equivalents. Under this paradigm, analysis without using utility equivalents is essentially impossible. Thus, because this paradigm results in the expression of creation care goals in terms of utility, preference will be given to goals that are most convincingly described that way (which often are instrumental goals) while deprecating goals that are not as convincingly described that way (which often are non-instrumental goals).

Political and Economic Philosophy and the Practice of the Creation Care Command (How to Put the Command into Action)

The goals and paradigm associated with our preferred political and economic systems influence what creation care practices we adopt. We describe two particular ways this occurs. First, political and economic philosophies, through the ways they organize and allocate power and wealth, give preference to some practices over others. For example, limited government political philosophies favor practices that require minimal governmental involvement, such as tax or incentive mechanisms, over those requiring more governmental involvement, such as regulatory and compliance mechanisms, and thus tend to favor the former when addressing environmental problems. Socialist economic philosophies, however, favor practices that involve government ownership and management of production and distribution; applied to environmental issues, these philosophies will favor governmental solutions versus private-sector or market solutions.

In these examples, the practices favored by the goals of the political or economic philosophy are directly consistent with each other. Sometimes, the individual practices favored by the political or economic philosophy the paradigm may counter the goal of the philosophy, but as a set, taken together, better achieve the goal of the philosophy. For instance, limited government political systems may sometimes favor regulatory approaches, even though regulation tends to require more government involvement, when the alternative would result in more governmental intrusion—such as an overly complex tax regime that would be needed to accomplish the same goals.

A second way political and economic philosophies influence creation care practices is by specifying the terms under which, and the analytical tools with which, practices are evaluated. Practices that most easily yield to such methods have a greater likelihood of being adopted. For example, economic theories that monetize all value and whose goals, thus, are cast entirely in monetary terms, will naturally favor practices that lend themselves to cost-benefit analysis and the maximization of monetary cost over benefit, because those practices can be properly evaluated under the economic theories being used. Practices that lend themselves to cost-benefit analysis include those whose effects are part of a well-defined market (e.g., commodities) and so can be reliably priced. Practices that do not lend themselves to such analysis include those whose effects cannot be reliably priced. We expect the latter kind of practices may be deprecated, because the economic theory cannot properly evaluate it. As another example, we expect adherents of Robert H. Nelson's "economic religion," because they view economic efficiency and growth as the means by which people are saved from poverty and other problems,[54] will evaluate creation care practices using the standards of market efficiency and growth, because those are the metrics by which their system conceptualizes progress towards the goals of the economic system.

54. Nelson, *New Holy Wars,* 100. Nelson also notes that if economic efficiency is not an automatic good (a categorical imperative), then you have to come up with a reasonable justification for market efficiency:

> To ignore the costs of losers in the pursuit of "progress" is a social decision. No divine command—no religion of progress—requires a market system as the means of organizing society. Herein lies a dilemma that current economists have scarcely even recognized. One solution might be to justify the market in terms of the preservation of individual freedom—that would be the libertarian solution. But mainstream members of the economics profession, by contrast, still assign today the highest ultimate value to economic efficiency. Economic progress—not the maximization of liberty, or the preservation of any other particular good or value—is for them still the legitimizing goal of economic activity. But if—the assumptions of economic religion to the contrary—rapid economic growth and development is a false path of salvation, it would be impossible to give efficiency such an exalted status. (Ibid., 100)

POLITICS AND ECONOMICS AND IMPORTANCE, GOALS, AND PRACTICE: POLICY STUDIES

In addition to operating in a "philosophy" mode, politics and economics can also operate in a "policy studies" mode. In this section, we examine how in that mode, politics and economics influence the criteria for obedience. The field of policy study is vast and highly interdisciplinary, combining political science, economics, sociology, psychology, behavioral economics, game theory, public policy, and public choice studies. Certainly, we cannot address even a fraction of the field, nor can we adequately survey the range of arguments and positions that result from policy studies. Instead, we content ourselves to first, provide an overview of the more prominent political and economic policy study topics related to environmental issues and second, describe how political and economic policy study connects to the importance, goals, and practice of the creation care command. In the latter point, we find that while our list of prominent topics, restricted as it is, is quite broad, when we apply political and economic policy studies to the criteria for obedience, we interpret the results of policy studies by the values of political and economic philosophy.

Political and Economic Policy Study Topics Related to Environmental Issues: An Overview

Political and economic policy studies address many aspects of creation care. In particular, policy studies look at the characteristics of environmental problems, the ways we analyze environmental problems, and what kinds of solutions are available. Some policy studies relate to the issue of more or less government in politics and economics, but political and economic policy studies are not restricted to only that issue. In this section, we discuss three general areas that environmental stewardship-related policy studies address: issues involving shared goods, how to cost environmental harms and benefits, and issues regarding government bureaucracy and public provision.

Issues Involving Shared Goods

Because a substantial part of the environment consists of or produces shared goods—air, water, aesthetics, etc.—environmental problems often involve issues dealing with shared ownership, benefits, and/or harms. We describe three policy studies topics that stem from the shared nature of the environment. First, policy studies consider the implications of shared goods often lacking clear ownership. Property and use rights, in many cases with shared goods, are unclear or conflicting, and it may be difficult to find parties to defend the shared goods and resources produced by the environment.[55] For example, the atmosphere is all around us, needed by all but owned by none. Because of its ubiquity, it receives exhaust from any and all terrestrial processes, whether they be biological processes such as animal respiration or plant transpiration, individual human life activities such as driving a car or a backyard barbeque, or industrial processes that generate and release gaseous and aerosol compounds or particulate matter. What is the status of each of these uses of the atmosphere relative to one another and how do we determine that status? That is to say, who gets to use the atmosphere and for what purpose, and how do we decide the priority of different uses? How effective are different policy strategies or prescriptions we may propose to clarify the use rights to the atmosphere?

A second policy study issue that stems from the shared nature of many environmental goods is the "free-rider" problem. Many environmental goods have beneficiaries who do not pay for the cost of the good, which can result in the good being under-produced.[56] For example, a landowner who sets aside a coastal wetland area from development produces a number of goods—preservation of habitat, aesthetic benefits, protection against storm surge, filtering of runoff into coastal waters—that all may enjoy but at no cost. Only the landowner pays the cost of the set-aside. If all the beneficiaries of the good could (or would), in some way, contribute to the cost of the set-aside, more resources would be available to set-aside more coastal wetland acreage.

Third, policy studies examine the nature and dynamics of the cooperative solutions often required for the preservation and protection of shared goods. Shared goods, almost by definition, involve multiple parties, who may be not only geographically, sociologically, and psychologically disparate, but also temporally removed from each other (e.g., when considering the actions and condition of future generations). The presence of multiple parties may require cooperative solutions; these parties may need to act in concert in order for the solution to be viable. Perhaps because environmental goods are often shared and may require cooperative management, arguments from game theory that critique the adequacy of egoism to ensure cooperative goods have historically had a strong influence in the field of environmental ethics. The Tragedy of the Commons—which argues that

---

55. Cordato, "Market-Based Environmentalism," 369, 370, 372.

56. Higgs and Close, "Introduction," 12.

individuals sharing a common natural resource, when acting rationally, will collectively overuse the resource, because no one individual has an incentive to *not* use "a little more" of the resource—is perhaps the most famous of the game theory arguments justifying cooperative solutions to environmental problems.[57]

A variety of approaches have been proposed to address the challenges that come from the shared nature of environmental goods. The first, and one of the most common, approaches is public ownership and provision of the good. Some argue, in principle, that the proper body of jurisdiction of any shared good (whether environmental, infrastructure, etc.) is the government, because the good itself is not privately owned. Others take a more instrumental position, arguing that if the shared good is not provided by the private sector—perhaps because no market exists for the good—the public sector should then provide the shared good as there is no other alternative. For instance, consider the example of the free-rider problem described earlier, where reliance on private provision for wetland set-asides would limit the number of acres place under protection. The dominant strategy in this and similar cases of addressing the free-rider problem is to provide the good through public provision.[58] Thus, instead of relying on private landowners to set aside the wetland acreage, the government acquires the property using taxpayer funds (and, perhaps, eminent domain), which presumably spreads the cost of the good to all members of the community, eliminating the free-rider problem. While a common strategy, a variety of critiques have been made of public provision. Later on in this section, we will examine these critiques when we consider policy studies regarding bureaucracy and public provision, in general.

A second approach in dealing with the challenges of shared goods is to create minimally coercive or indirect legal structures to rectify the problems that lack of ownership and markets can produce. Environmental regulation is perhaps the best known directly coercive legal structure or mechanism (which we consider in the following paragraph as a third approach). Minimally coercive legal structures differ from directly coercive ones in that the legal structure does not, by itself, dictate specific actions. Instead, these legal structures help local communities, private organizations, and individuals create or implement rules to overcome issues arising from the lack of owners and markets. This may be in the form of structures that facilitate the development and enforcement of property and other (possibly new) individual rights with regards to environmental goods. For instance, economist

57. See, for instance, Hardin, "Tragedy."
58. Stroup, "Free Riders," 209.

Peter J. Hill suggests that if the government "registered" potential pollutants to enable tracking of pollutants, it would enable non-regulatory legal mechanisms such as liability and nuisance to be employed in preventing environmental harm.[59] Hill speculates as to how this might work:

> In Canyonlands National Park in Utah, effective monitoring and tracing of the pollutants from a particular source have been carried out by the addition of tracer chemicals to a smokestack .... It would also be possible to require all users of an herbicide to "brand" the product by adding a small amount of an inert chemical or radioactive isotope. If the brands were placed in a central registry, then, if the herbicide appeared in groundwater, the responsible party could be identified. It might be unnecessary for government to do anything more, particularly if the common law of nuisance were embraced.[60]

By increasing the level of information available, registration enables us to apply property rights and liability mechanisms to environmental issues that otherwise would have no connection to those mechanisms.

The third approach of dealing with the challenges arising from shared goods is to use coercion. As we noted earlier, historically, game theory analysis of cooperative solutions has tended to drive environmentalists toward these kinds of solutions. This coercion can take a "positive" form, where government creates incentive structures that encourage some behaviors over others. Examples of such policies include tax credits for the purchase of electric vehicles and grants for research and development in renewable energy supplies. Or, the coercion can take a "negative" form, where certain practices are banned or controlled. Environmental regulation is perhaps the most prominent example of this kind of coercive solution. The regulations may include bans of certain practices (such as the use of pesticides that affect the ecosystem) or restrictions of others (such as limits on air pollutants emitted from factories and power plants). Regulatory enforcement may be direct (such as through fines) or make use of market mechanisms (such as through tradable permits). While coercive strategies are prevalent and have been argued as necessary to solve some problems related to shared goods, others have argued that such strategies are less necessary than commonly assumed.[61] And, as we saw earlier, arguments for less coercive legal regimes

59. Hill, "Market-Based Environmentalism," 390.

60. Ibid.

61. For instance, Garrett Hardin, argues strongly for coercive policies to control human population because he perceives other solutions as unviable and the consequences of inaction as calamitous:

suggest that means besides direct coercion may be enough to solve the free-rider problem and other challenges associated with shared environmental goods.

Costing Environmental Harms and Benefits

Besides issues involving shared goods, another important area explored by policy studies is how to appropriately price environmental harms and benefits. Many environmental issues involve benefits and harms that are difficult to cost. This is partly due to the lack of a market for the goods, which determines the price of most goods.[62] We know how much bread costs because the innumerable number of daily transactions between buyers and sellers sets a price range for the goods, but no such market exists for bald eagles. In some cases, irrespective of whether a market exists for the good, the good has characteristics that make it impossible for us to attach a price; for instance, the good may be intangible (e.g., beauty) or unique (e.g.,

---

The most important aspect of necessity that we must now recognize, [sic] is the necessity of abandoning the commons in breeding. No technical solution can rescue us from the misery of overpopulation. Freedom to breed will bring ruin to all. At the moment, to avoid hard decisions many of us are tempted to propagandize for conscience and responsible parenthood. The temptation must be resisted, because an appeal to independently acting consciences selects for the disappearance of all conscience in the long run, and an increase in anxiety in the short.

The only way we can preserve and nurture other and more precious freedoms is by relinquishing the freedom to breed, and that very soon. (Hardin, "Tragedy," 196)

In contrast, Timothy Noah argues Hardin's fear, while theoretically possible, is not an inevitable outcome in the real world:

But as [Jonathan] Rowe points out in *Our Common Wealth,* the construct put forth in "The Tragedy of the Commons" is "an extrapolation from assumptions rather than an investigation of reality." Had [Garrett] Hardin bothered to consult empirical evidence, he would have learned that back in the days when actual farmers really *did* share land for hunting, foraging, and grazing, they did *not* behave like the utility-maximizing clods in his theoretical model. They worked together, sharing tools and labor to maintain the precious plots of land so that successive generations could prosper in the same place. This "worked well for hundreds of years," Rowe writes. [emphases in original] (Noah, "The Glory")

62. Pearce et al., "Economic Valuation," 171.

the Grand Canyon).[63] And, in many cases, it is difficult to cost the benefit or harm because the value is subjective or dependent on the person being affected.[64] For instance, one person may find elevated ground-level ozone concentrations to be a mild nuisance while another may find it debilitating. The value of measures to decrease ground-level ozone will likely wildly differ from the first to the second person.

Yet, despite the difficulty in correctly pricing environmental benefits and harms, many have argued we need to provide some sort of valuation in order to help politicians and other policymakers incorporate environmental considerations into the decision-making process.[65] Thus, policy studies have sought creative ways of assigning prices. Methods include looking at "use value" (the value associated with the use of the environmental good), the "option value" (the value associated with possible future use), and "existence value" (the value associated merely with the existence of some environmental good).[66] Some of these values, particularly use values, may be obtained from the record of actual transactions (e.g., access fees for a park, sales from films about a wilderness area). For cases where such data are not available, "contingent valuation," where the price of the environmental good is set by what people say (e.g., through polling) they would pay for the good, may be useful.[67] Some have questioned, however, the ability of polling to properly measure existence value, arguing that it is nearly impossible to frame polling questions of this sort in an informative but neutral way.[68]

Issues Regarding Government Bureaucracy and Public Provision

As we saw earlier when we considered public provision as a way to rectify the challenges associated with environmental goods being shared goods, environmental problems often involve governmental solutions. Those solutions, in turn, often involve government bureaucracy, and so the third general topic policy studies address is the issue of bureaucracy and public

---

63. Though, as David Pearce, Anil Markandya, and Edward B. Barber note, "Many things *cannot* be valued in money terms. That is altogether different from saying they are 'priceless' in the sense of having infinite values." [emphasis in original] (Pearce et al., "Economic Valuation," 179)

64. Cordato, "Market-Based Environmentalism," 375.

65. Pearce, "A Reply," 182–83.

66. Pearce et al., "Economic Valuation," 175–76.

67. Ibid. 177.

68. Nelson, "Does 'Existence Value' Exist?," 410–11.

provision.[69] One area of study regarding this topic is the nature of the resource flows government can bring to bear to environmental problems. On
the one hand, government has substantial resources, including coercive
powers, which can be formidable when correctly applied to the implementation of policy. On the other hand, the information flows needed to
efficiently and correctly apply fiat power and other resources are more trou-
blesome to come by. As it is impossible for centralized bodies to ascertain
all the needed information to properly allocate resources, the bureaucratic
implementation of governmental solutions to environmental problems may
be inefficient and fail to achieve the policy's goals.[70] Ironically, government
is simultaneously resource rich and resource constrained; sometimes the
latter thwarts the promise of the former.

A second area of study is the nature of the mechanisms of government
and their impact on the ability of government to protect and conserve environmental goods. While representative democracies confer a legitimacy to
government that all will recognize,[71] this does not mean that government
necessarily functions with the effectiveness worthy of that legitimacy. Voters may not always be well-informed, and special interests can exert substantial influence in policymaking.[72] Sometimes, inadequate attention is
paid in the design phase of a governmental program as to how the program
will actually be implemented, and the result is a program that is, almost
literally, designed for failure.[73] In addition, certain modes of governmental
operation, such as the centralized, "command-and-control" nature of some

69. Regardless of the kind of policy solution proposed (e.g., regulatory, tort, etc.),
the governmental component will almost always be implemented through a governmental bureaucracy. Even if research is the proposed policy solution, that research and
the expertise it generates must be solicited and managed. Typically, the bureaucracies
of governmental funding agencies (e.g., the National Science Foundation), science-
advisory panels, and regulatory agency science staffs (e.g., the Environmental Protection Agency) manage this work. (There are some methods of managing science, such
as prize-driven research, that requires little bureaucratic management, but these apply
to limited situations.)

70. Cordato, "Market-Based Environmentalism," 376.

71. For a fascinating analysis of this point, see Langdon Gilkey's account of life in
a Japanese internment camp in World War II. In this camp of civilian internees, unlike
prisoner-of-war camps, the internees did not suffer from physical and psychological
torture but nonetheless lived in a condition of want. The camp's experience in self-
government, and Gilkey's musings on how such a government can obtain legitimacy,
are illuminating (Gilkey, *Shantung Compound*, 122–28).

72. Stroup, "Free Riders," 209.

73. Eggers and O'Leary, *If We Can*, 51–77. "Fewer than one-third of America's
senior federal executives [in surveys by Eggers and O'Leary] believed the federal government to be effective at designing public policy." (Eggers and O'Leary, *If We Can*, 66)

regulations, may not only be inefficient but also counter-productive; for instance, political scientist Randy T. Simmons argues that the Endangered Species Act has failed to protect endangered species and that a decentralized policy that includes positive incentives for increased involvement by private landowners will more effectively protect habitat.[74] Of course, governmental mechanisms and bureaucracies do contribute to environmental protection; the Clean Air Act and the Clean Water Act, and the regulatory structure related to those and other legislation, have helped decrease air and water pollution. Studies of both successful and unsuccessful government programs reveal practical and effective steps we can take to increase the probability of successful governmental involvement. For instance, researchers William D. Eggers and John O'Leary note that explicit and concerted attention to analyzing and managing the risk of failure can play a critical role in creating successful governmental programs.[75] Policy studies help us better understand when governmental mechanisms do and do not work and suggest possible alternatives, both alternatives to governmental provision as well as alternatives that facilitate successful governmental involvement.

Finally, in addition to studying the resource flows and implementation mechanisms available to government, policy studies also examine unintended consequences of governmental solutions. For instance, while public provision is often intended as a solution to the free-rider problem, some argue that public provision itself is prone to the free-rider problem: the decision-making and bureaucratic processes involved in public provision are themselves public goods whose costs are often paid by a few private (e.g., special-interest lobbying organizations) and public (e.g., special-interest bureaucrats) actors, rather than the public as a whole.[76] Others have noted that public provision, in other contexts, may crowd out private provision.[77] In the case of environmental stewardship, this may result in barriers preventing private resources from being brought to bear to decrease pollution, preserve habitat, etc.

---

74. Simmons, "Fixing," 130–31. See also Simmons, "Who's Saving," 111–12 for a more detailed critique of the effectiveness of the Endangered Species Act.

75. Eggers and O'Leary, *If We Can*, 64–65, 131–32.

76. Stroup, "Free Riders," 210–15.

77. Richard L. Stroup argues that the public displacement of private provision can be seen in the positive effects of removing public church subsidies in Connecticut and Massachusetts two centuries ago (Stroup, "Free Riders," 220–21). In a more contemporary example, Seth Lipsky argues that the presence of government-subsidized journalism (such as National Public Radio) makes it difficult to raise funds for similar kinds of private journalism (Lipsky, "The Real Case").

Political and Economic Policy Study and the Importance, Goals, and Practice of the Creation Care Command

Clearly, political and economic policy studies cover a wide range of topics and offer an important critique regarding how environmental policies are structured and implemented. Yet, because the values of political and economic philosophy are primary, the influence of policy studies on the importance, goals, and practice of the creation care command predominantly occur through the mechanisms we described as part of our analysis of political and economic philosophy. That is to say, we interpret the results of policy studies using the values of political and economic philosophy.

Policy studies provide "evidence" or the exploration of reasons, rationales, and outcomes of policies, and this evidence is used by political and economic philosophies to make arguments and draw conclusions. This dynamic is similar to how science, as we saw in chapter 5, tells us about the state of nature but not the meaning of that state. Since policy studies often use methodologies similar to those used in the natural sciences, as well as mathematical and statistical analysis, this is not surprising. Thus, when parties with different political and economic outlooks come in dialogue with one another, it is important to first discern how each group understands the results (and methodology) of policy studies, rather than assuming policy studies are self-interpreting or have an obvious meaning. If we neglect to do so, such dialogue will likely suffer from miscommunication and misunderstanding.

For an example of this dynamic, consider the meaning of policy studies regarding bureaucratic inefficiency and its impact on environmental stewardship. As we saw earlier, a number of policy studies have suggested that government bureaucracy can be inefficient when dealing with environmental problems, with numerous researchers providing evidence of inefficiency in the governmental management of regulatory and other means of environmental protection. But what does this evidence mean? For someone who values political and economic efficiency, such policy studies provide evidence that we should be wary of (at least some) governmental solutions to environmental problems. Other actors, such as private individuals or non-governmental community organizations, can provide more efficient solutions, and thus can achieve higher levels of environmental protection at less cost (where cost may include non-monetary costs). But, for someone who values distributional justice more than efficiency, these policy studies may merely quantify the cost one has to pay in order to fulfill the demands of justice. To the extent that public provision better meets the requirements of distributional justice, policy studies that document government efficiency are somewhat beside the point. Thus, the political and economic philosophies we hold determine, to a great extent, the meaning of policy studies. This does not mean that data from policy studies do not play a role in our decision for one political or economic philosophy or another. In science, data certainly plays a role in our decisions for or against one theory or paradigm versus another. But just as the meaning of the theory or paradigm in science does not spring automatically out of the data (at least according to some of the epistemologies of science we considered in chapter 5), so too the meanings of policy studies are often intimately tied with and understood in light of our political and economic philosophies.

CONCLUSIONS

In this chapter, we categorized and summarized the range of political and economic philosophy and policy study modes and considered how these modes impact the criteria for considered obedience. In this section, using our summary, we draw some general conclusions about the relation of politics and economics to determining the content of creation care and examine possible areas of debate, discussion, and compromise regarding the interaction between politics and economics and creation care. Specifically, we consider the implications of the primacy of the philosophy mode over the policy study mode, the finding that not all political and economic values are imperatives, and the limits of consequentialism with regards to politics and economics. While political and economic differences are substantial and real, the implications we consider reveal more ground for compromise and dialogue regarding environmental stewardship than conventional wisdom suggests.

In the last section, we argued that the philosophy mode has primacy over the policy study mode. This is our first general conclusion: that the meaning of political and economic policy studies comes primarily from political and economic philosophy, rather than vice versa. We can draw at least two implications from this conclusion. First, the primacy of values over policy studies means that debates over the content of creation care require comparing not only policy study results but also political and economic values. We must practice ethics and metaethics, and we can use the principles for weighing values discussed in chapter 4 to weigh political and economic values against one another. For example, liberty is one value that is often involved in political and economic discussions regarding environmental issues. Some argue environmental regulations negatively and unreasonably impact liberty while others argue restriction of liberty—even coercion—is necessary to prevent severe environmental degradation. These claims obviously conflict with one another, and that conflict can only be addressed by analyzing what is the value of liberty (e.g., is it absolute; why or why not?) and what standards should we use to decide when encroachments on political or economic liberty are reasonable in considering creation care options. These value questions—and the debate over them—are fundamentally philosophical in nature and cannot be answered by policy studies alone.

Second, again similar to what we found with science, we may find that humble uses of policy studies (similar to the humbler models of science-policy connections described in chapter 5) may produce new policy options or more successfully connect scientific knowledge with environmental problems in a way unavailable to "policy prescriptive" uses of policy studies. Policy studies, being a social science, share many of the methods and epistemologies of the natural sciences, and to that extent, our analysis in chapter 5 regarding the role of science in environmental policymaking may also apply to policy studies. At the same time, the way the social sciences interact with policymaking can differ from the way the natural sciences interact with policymaking. For instance, while both environmental controversies such as climate change and political/economic controversies such as the choice of medical insurance systems each utilize mathematical modeling, the former suffers from a "scientization" of the controversy while the latter does not.[78] Perhaps in the case of political/economic controversies, there is an unsaid recognition that science cannot settle the question—an implicit recognition of the limits of the scientific method when applied to the complexities of human behavior—which prevents the controversy from being "scientized."[79] Either way, we assert this recognition suggests that humbler uses of policy studies may lead to more productive policymaking.

Our finding that not all values coded in political and economic systems are imperatives leads us to a second general conclusion regarding the connection between politics and economics and the content of environmental stewardship. If not all political and economic values are imperatives, then there is an "irreducible indeterminacy" in formulating policy.[80] That is to say, policymaking is not a fully prescriptive exercise—whether that prescription comes from science, worldviews, ethics, or another authority—and the limits indeterminacy places on policymaking must be overcome by non-imperative approaches such as prudence.

78. Sarewitz, "Environmental Controversies," 398.

79. Ibid.

80. Much of this section comes from a personal conversation with Daniel Philpott, a political scientist at the University of Notre Dame, on December 16, 2010.

If honestly acknowledged and respected, such indeterminacy can lead to dialogue, compromise, and policy stability. Categorical imperatives, by definition, are not open for debate. They are absolute, required, divine commands that must be obeyed. But imperatives, while producing certainty and clarity, tend to shut down dialogue: if two people hold different and conflicting categorical imperatives, what is there to talk about? Identifying, speaking into, and using as a policy foundation the political and economic values that are not imperatives is a first step in finding ground on which compromise and agreement can be built. Compromise, fairly won, can lead to acceptance of a policy even amongst antagonistic stakeholders. In a democracy, such policies are the only ones that have staying power.

Catholic social teaching provides an example of how we might deal with this indeterminacy and incorporate imperative values with non-imperative values in policymaking. Catholic social teaching begins with looking at biblical principles to glean imperatives. The set of imperatives, however, is relatively small and general. The Bible, for instance, tells us to love our neighbor but does not specify every aspect of what that love looks like. To biblical imperatives, natural law provides additional principles. Two of the most prominent are solidarity (the responsibility of every person for everybody else) and subsidiarity (the responsibility to push responsibility to the lowest level possible and thus avoid overriding initiative and autonomy).[81] From biblical principles, solidarity and subsidiarity, and other principles, Catholic social teaching derives additional political and economic principles. For instance, solidarity helps motivate Catholic social teaching's "preferential option for the poor and vulnerable."[82] From subsidiarity and a Catholic anthropology, Catholic social teaching argues that the social nature of humans is not entirely fulfilled in the State but is also fulfilled in "intermediary groups," and that the primary responsibility for economics is found not the State but rather individuals and groups.[83] Yet even with bibli-

81. More precisely, subsidiarity says higher order groups should not interfere with lower order groups:

> Here again the principle of subsidiarity must be respected: a community of a higher order should not interfere in the internal life of a community of a lower order, depriving the latter of its functions, but rather should support it in case of need and help to coordinate its activity with the activities of the rest of society, always with a view to the common good. (John Paul II, *Centesimus Annus*, 48)

82. USCCB, *Forming Consciences*, 15.

83. For instance, John Paul II argues:

> In contrast [to the Socialist conception of human beings], from the Christian vision of the human person there necessarily follows a correct

cal imperatives coupled with natural law principles, there remains quite a bit of room for prudence, where we apply principles to specific situations while taking into account proximate issues. This "prudential window" is wider or narrower, depending on the degree of indeterminacy for any given act or policy option. Still, what Catholic social teaching defines is a hybrid approach to policymaking that incorporates imperatives, principles, and prudence. Each dimension in this approach has a unique role *vis a vis* the others, and policymaking requires the contribution of all three dimensions.

Finally, our analysis in this chapter leads us to a third general conclusion, that the range of values coded in political and economic systems goes beyond those that can be weighed by a utilitarian calculus and thus requires an alternative method of engaging political and economic values. Some believe politics and economics must ultimately devolve into a utilitarianism that is weighed by cost-benefit analysis. For some this is conclusion based on philosophical principle while others hold this as a pragmatic proposition, believing only cost-benefit analysis can provide common ground between radically different factions. To others, the utilitarian method of incorporating political and economic values into creation care policymaking is cold and inadequate. Utilitarianism either drains even the transcendentals of existence—truth, love, beauty—into bloodless counters or altogether ignores that which makes human existence human. And yet, alternative ways of understanding politics and economics exist that do not require utilitarian weighing (and, in some cases, are also non-imperative). Such alternative ways may provide a middle-ground that enables us to weigh political and

---

> picture of society. According to *Rerum novarum* and the whole social doctrine of the Church, the social nature of man is not completely fulfilled in the State, [sic] but is realized in various intermediary groups, beginning with the family and including economic, social, political and cultural groups which stem from human nature itself and have their own autonomy, always with a view to the common good. This is what I have called the "subjectivity" of society which, together with the subjectivity of the individual, was cancelled out by "Real Socialism." [emphasis in original] (John Paul II, *Centesimus Annus*, 13)

Specifically, John Paul II suggests that while State activity is important, there are limitations to what the State can do with respect to economic life:

> Another task of the State is that of overseeing and directing the exercise of human rights in the economic sector. However, primary responsibility in this area belongs not to the State but to individuals and to the various groups and associations which make up society. The State could not directly ensure the right to work for all its citizens unless it controlled every aspect of economic life and restricted the free initiative of individuals. (John Paul II, *Centesimus Annus*, 48)

economic values without solely depending on cost-benefit analysis. Virtue ethics, Catholic social teaching, and distributism are examples of non-utilitarian methods of conceiving and weighing political and economic value.

What might such a non-utilitarian politics or economics look like? In the remainder of our discussion of this third general conclusion, we provide an extended description of one non-utilitarian alternative, neo-Scholastic economics. Neo-scholastic economics is a particularly apt counterpoint to utilitarianism. Conventional wisdom considers modern economics and cost-benefit analysis as joined at the hip. An alternative, yet comprehensive, approach to economics, by force of its existence, questions the necessity of such a connection. In doing so, it encourages us to consider whether our preconceived categories and assumptions regarding the nature of politics and economics are really as complete as we might believe.

In describing neo-Scholastic economics, we need to first examine the nature of economics and the history of economics. After establishing that context, we describe neo-Scholastic economics and how this school of economics claims to provide a theoretical foundation for describing the economic value of a broader range of economic activity. In particular, economic activity that generates value that is not reducible to utility is better treated by neo-Scholastic economics. We finish with possible implications of neo-Scholastic economics on how we determine the content of environmental stewardship. This section's description of the nature and history of economics, neo-Scholastic economics, and the importance of a theory of final distribution comes from John Mueller's work *Redeeming Economics*.[84]

To many, economics is synonymous with accounting. Yet, as important as "following the money" is to any economic analysis, it is the reasons and dynamics behind the flow of money (and goods, resources, services, labor, property, etc.) that forms the field of economics. As Muller says, understanding all human economic activity requires us to ask three questions: "Every human economic action raises three basic questions: First, *for whom* shall I provide? Second, *what* shall I provide? And third, *how* shall I provide it?" [emphases in original].[85] These three questions lead to the following four components of economic theory:[86]

1. A theory of final distribution: The question "for whom to provide" always has a person or persons as its ultimate answer. Those persons are also ends in and of themselves and are not a means to something (or someone) else. The theory explaining how this occurs, whether

84. Muller, *Redeeming Economics*.

85. Ibid., 18.

86. Ibid., 20.

personally by gift or crime or societally by distributive justice (the principles by which we allocate common goods), is a theory of final distribution.[87]

2. A theory of utility (or consumption): The question "what to provide" depends on the relative value of the goods (nonhuman or humans as means) we will use for others or provide to others.[88]

3. A theory of production: The question "how to provide" addresses the labor and property needed to produce a good, of how many and what is made.[89]

4. A theory of justice in exchange (equilibrium): The answer to the question of "how to provide" also includes an account of how producers (labor and property) are compensated for what they provide.[90]

One way of understanding the history of economics and the various schools of economics that have existed during its history is through the kinds of theories of final distribution, utility, production, and equilibrium that make up each school of economics. Muller breaks down the history of economics into four periods, with each period corresponding to the school of economics that was practiced during that period.[91]

1. Scholastic economics (c. 1250–1776):[92] Scholastic economics owes its formulation to St. Thomas Aquinas who, working off of and integrating Aristotle and St. Augustine, defined a school of economics with all four theories of economics: distribution, utility, production, and exchange.

2. Classical economics (1776–1871):[93] Adam Smith created the initial formulation of classical economics by simplifying the structure defined by Scholastic economics. In particular, Smith eliminated a theory of final distribution, assuming instead everyone never shares their wealth,[94] eliminated a theory of utility, assuming instead there is no value of use but only value in exchange,[95] and altered the theory of

87. Ibid., 20, 22.
88. Ibid., 20.
89. Ibid., 20, 50.
90. Ibid., 20.
91. The dates of these four periods are from ibid., ix.
92. Ibid., chapter 2.
93. Ibid., chapter 3.
94. Ibid., 57.
95. Ibid., 58–59.

production with the "labor theory of value,"[96] which reduces all production value to the value of labor, ignoring property.[97]

3. Neoclassical economics (1871–c. 2000):[98] In this school of economics, the theory of utility was restored by including value of use through the concept of marginal utility (i.e., the difference in value of an incremental change in the good).[99] In addition, neoclassical economics restored factors besides labor to production.[100] However, neoclassical economics did not reinstitute a theory of final distribution, instead sometimes assuming we can derive final distribution from utility.[101]

4. Neo-Scholastic economics (c. 2000–):[102] This recovery and extension of Scholastic economics integrates a theory of final distribution with modern neoclassical economics and the modern mathematical tools and concepts found in modern neoclassical economics.[103]

From this brief sketch of the history of economics, we see that what sets neo-Scholastic economics apart from its modern neoclassical (and classical) counterpart is the explicit inclusion of a theory of final distribution. But why is the lack of a theory of final distribution in economics problematic? Simply, without a theory of final distribution, economics inadequately describes gifts and any other non-exchange value. When we do not have a theory of final distribution, the only way to include ultimate value is through utility (as in neoclassical economics). In such a case, the value of all economic activity is reduced to its value in exchange, i.e., only as a means, never as an end. But, we know this is not true: In addition to valuing things as means, we also value things as ends in and of themselves. For instance, a husband values his wife for who she is (as an end in and of herself), not just for her companionship (a means to the end of having company). And the valuing of people as ends in and of themselves has an economic expression, for we give gifts to them. A gift is something we give without expectation of something in return (i.e., an exchange). Gifts are, in fact, the economic meaning of love, as love is a gift, not an exchange: "Rather than an exchange, love is best described in economic theory as a gift or voluntary 'transfer

96. Ibid., 61.
97. Ibid., 61–62.
98. Ibid., chapter 4.
99. Ibid., 80–81.
100. Ibid., 82–85.
101. Ibid., 89.
102. Ibid., chapter 5.
103. Ibid., 107.

payment'—that is, as a voluntary distribution out of one's resources not made in compensation for useful services rendered."[104] Put another way, gifts are the economic expression of a "weighing of persons" as ends:

> Our love for ourselves is expressed by allowing ourselves to use the things we own, while our love for others is expressed by allowing them to use the things we own. In economic theory, therefore, human love is essentially neither an emotion nor a weighing of utilities (though either or both may also be present) but rather a weighing of persons.[105]

In the end, this means that an economics based on utility inadequately describes the ends of economic activity. Indeed, the lack of a framework to describe the ends of economic activity outside of utility means modern economics cannot explain even very simple economic activities, such as how a mother decides what groceries to buy.[106]

But such an economics has an additional weakness: it lacks the most important categories needed to interface with ethics. Concerning this weakness, it is worth quoting Muller's extended response to the suggestion that ethics can be reconstructed on the basis of economics:

> First, as a matter of pure economic theory, not all human action can be reduced to utility, or else utility itself would be unexplained. All human economic action involves a weighing of persons as well as objects, of ends as well as means. This must be expressed in economic theory by recognizing that exchanges and gifts differ in kind. Gifts cannot be reduced to implicit exchanges, or else they are no longer gifts. Second, economic theory has nothing to say about the appropriate weights to be attached to persons and things, other than to point out that scarcity must be taken into account. Moral philosophy has a great deal to say about the appropriate ranking of persons and things. What kinds of things ought to be exchanged, what it means to love one's neighbor in a given situation, and what exactly constitutes distributive justice in a given society are questions that economist qua economist cannot answer. Far from being a vast new empire, economic theory always has been, and will always remain, a colony of moral philosophy.[107]

---

104. Ibid., 143.
105. Ibid., 143.
106. Ibid., 133–73.
107. Ibid., 128.

We began our discussion of neo-Scholastic economics by noting that the values coded in political and economic systems go beyond those amenable to a utilitarian treatment and that an alternative weighing needed to be found. In neo-Scholastic economics, we find not only an alternative method of engaging political and economic values but also one with the categories and theories needed to bring economics into a direct and explicit dialogue with ethics.

Finally, in the outline of neo-Scholastic economics, we also see a possible way of incorporating more kinds of environmental value into decision-making. We have seen that one criticism of modern economic theory when considering environmental issues is the lack of a mechanism to include value outside of utility. This results in an inability not only of expressing human gifts and crimes in economic terms but also the economic value of any goods with intrinsic value (i.e., value as ends instead of means). Thus, cost-benefit analysis of environmental goods has to reduce those goods in terms of their utility (e.g., recreational use, source of raw materials, etc.) in order to include their value into environmental decision-making (if at all).[108] Many find this state of affairs to be unacceptable. For those who ascribe independent moral status to the environment, this means modern economics provides essentially no way of incorporating that status into an economic description, as ends are not describable by modern economics. For those who would not go so far as to ascribe independent moral status to the environment, but would still ascribe some kind of non-instrumental value to nature, modern economics does not provide adequate ways of incorporating non-instrumental valuing. Neo-Scholastic economics, however, may provide an avenue of doing so, of capturing in economic analysis something of these alternate forms of the value of nature.

In sum, while the contribution of politics and economics to the content of creation care often appears polarizing, our analysis in this chapter offers rays of hope. Our taxonomy of different kinds of political and economic philosophies suggests that philosophical disagreements between different parties may not always be as absolute as the disagreements may seem; identifying the philosophical positions involved can help us identify possible grounds for compromise and agreement. The role of policy studies is also less categorical than often portrayed. Thus, while many conceive of the roles of politics and economics in determining the content of creation care in zero-sum terms, where one side's categorical imperatives triumph over the other side's categorical imperatives, or in desacralized utilitarian

---

108. Mark Sagoff argues, along the lines of classical economics, that nature has little to no economic value (Sagoff, "Locke Was Right").

terms, where environmental value is accounted for in strictly instrumental terms, alternatives exist that offer additional resources for bringing politics and economics to bear on the content of creation care, and thus offer additional grounds for compromise and agreement. Catholic social teaching and neo-Scholastic economics are two examples of such alternatives. In these examples, and our outline of the relationship between the political and economic philosophical and policy studies modes and the criteria for obedience, we find hooks for dialogue that may lead us past the deadlock of the traditional left-right debates.

DISCUSSION QUESTIONS

1. The author breaks down the influence of politics and economics on the content of creation care into two categories: a philosophical mode and a policy studies mode. Is such a categorization complete, or at least complete enough to help us think through the effects of politics and economics on environmental issues? Why or why not? In particular, does this taxonomy do justice to the role of human passion in politics and economics? Why or why not?

2. The author argues that some of the values encoded under the philosophical mode are moral imperatives while others are not and implies that a careful accounting of which values are and are not can help us better understand in what ways politics and economics should influence the content of creation care. What kinds of political and economic values do you hold? Are they imperatives or not? In what ways do you believe they should be part of discussions on the content of creation care? Why?

3. The author discusses three areas policy studies address: issues involving shared goods, the costing environmental harms and benefits, and those regarding government bureaucracy and public provision. What positions do you hold regarding these issues? How do you respond to policy studies that appear to argue against your values? How do your policy positions interact with the political and economic values you hold?

4. In this chapter, Catholic social teaching and neo-Scholastic economics are offered as examples of alternative frameworks that may help us better connect different kinds of political and economic values to the other values involved in environmental stewardship, and in ways that go beyond the traditional left and right spectrum. Do you agree or

disagree? Why? What additional reasons for or against this argument has the author missed?

5. In the conclusion, the author appears to be sanguine about the possibility of dialogue and compromise with regards to the influence of politics and economics in determining the content of creation care. What do you think? What grounds do we have for optimism? What grounds do we have for pessimism? What forces has the author ignored that might facilitate or prevent dialogue and compromise?

7

Not Just Hearers But Doers

THE PRACTICES OF STEWARDSHIP

A PARABLE, CONTINUED

Gabriel was out running errands when he happened to drive by the offices of Acme Industries. Outside the building were two small groups of protestors, holding up signs. In one group, the signs read "Save the Franklin marshes" and "No to corporate greed" while the other group held up signings saying "Save our jobs" and "Landowners rights." Passions on both sides were high, but both groups were civil: a little bit of "Minnesota nice," outside of Minnesota.

Gabriel continued driving and parked at the Food City supermarket. He was hosting a potluck at his home tonight, but hadn't figured out what he would contribute. Potlucks, mused Gabriel, are curious things. If you do some planning—say, have some families bring a meat dish, some a salad, and some a dessert—there's not a whole lot of "luck" in such a potluck, is there? But, if you let the dice roll and everyone brings whatever they want, you can end up with what happened a year ago when they had a table full of desserts. Well, at least the kids loved it, chuckled Gabriel to himself.

Gabriel was deep in thought about a fruit salad when he heard a woman calling his name: "Pastor Gabriel!" He turned around and saw Becky Maczek and her two daughters, Laura and Lily. Gabriel waved and walked towards them. "Shopping for the potluck?" he asked.

"Yep, we were thinking of bringing a casserole and were out of mushrooms and pasta," replied Becky. Becky and her family had been coming to All Saints for the past five years. When Gabriel had first met Becky, she had just moved recently to be closer to her parents, after the death of her husband Kallistos from cancer. Five years later, he could still see the sorrow of her loss in her eyes, but tempered with the love and support God and the All Saints family had shown her and her children.

In those five years, Becky had also found an unexpected outlet for her grief: car repair. While she had worked on cars since she was old enough to hold a socket wrench—her mother and father had, after all, met over an intake manifold in their voc-tech high school's engine performance lab—she had never thought of being a mechanic full-time. After the death of Kallistos, however, she found the time she spent working on her car after the kids were asleep to be some of the most personally restful and fulfilling hours of her day. She started out doing jobs for friends and then took the plunge and opened her own small repair shop.

Becky continued, "I had just returned home from the shop to meet the sitter when I realized we needed a few items. So, we all came out to the store." She looked at Gabriel's fruit-filled cart. "Fruit salad?" she said.

Gabriel nodded. "How'd the week go?" he asked.

"Pretty well, Pastor Gabriel," Becky said. "This week I had a minivan that ended up being a particularly difficult fix. The problem wasn't hard to pin down, but coming up with a solution was a bit of a challenge. Some mechanics would have thrown in the towel and opted for a complete engine rebuild, but I thought there might be something less drastic. It took a lot of thinking and tinkering with a bunch of different solutions before I settled on a suite of things to do. But it was worth it in the end."

Gabriel smiled. Years of seminary had only heightened the joy he took in a good engineering fix. "Very cool," he replied. "Particularly with the tough cases, it often does seem like the best solution isn't a single thing." Becky nodded back.

Gabriel and Becky exchanged a little more small talk and then parted to finish up their shopping and cooking in time for the potluck. As he made his way to the checkout line, Gabriel thought about his brief talk with Becky and the protest he had passed on the way to the supermarket. It struck him that in the debate over Acme Industries' expansion plans, one thing both sides shared was a conviction that there was only one response to the situation: either approve the permit or deny it. It made sense, he thought; after all, what other option was there besides approve or deny? But, he couldn't shake the feeling that maybe creation care often was, in this way, more like Becky's fix for that broken minivan than the impassioned nature of the debates seemed to admit.

INTRODUCTION

In the previous chapters, we have seen how the determinants contribute to the criteria for obedience—importance, goals, and practice—as well as how the criteria interact with one another. Needless to say, the interconnections between and amongst determinants and criteria are clearly complex. How then do we take this web of interconnections and turn it into a set of policies and practices we live out? In our final chapter, we take the first steps towards such a synthesis. In this penultimate chapter, we set up that discussion by examining the nature of creation care practices themselves. That is to say, while we have already asked how worldviews, ethical theories, science epistemology, science-policy connections, politics, and economics all affect practices, here we describe the kinds of choices of practices that are available for the determinants to act on. First, we examine what is the range of responses available for environmental problems and what is the process by which we choose which response(s) to take. With regards to the range of responses, we find that, contrary to conventional wisdom, the possible range of responses is quite broad. With regards to the process of choosing between responses, we take the description we have given throughout the book of how the determinants inform practice and apply it to the taxonomy of responses. In doing so, we find that one major way the determinants affect the task of choosing between practices is through the values the determinants specify; we thus unpack in more detail the ways these values impact the evaluation of different responses. Lastly, we consider strategies for handling the uncertainty inherent whenever we consider environmental problems and their responses. The management of uncertainty and risk is a part of all real-world policymaking, which occurs given imperfect knowledge and significantly impacts the practice criterion. Through this chapter's analysis, we will find additional reason to question the degree to which science can prescribe policy choice, further identify the values that come from the determinants of the criteria for obedience, and set the stage for our synthesis discussion in the final chapter.

THE RANGE OF RESPONSES AND CHOOSING BETWEEN RESPONSES

All problems can be thought of as having the following form: $A \rightarrow B$, where A is some action or activity, B is some consequence with undesirable traits, and "$\rightarrow$" is the causal connection between A and B. Thus, the four possible responses to any problem are to do nothing different,[1] eliminate or remove A, eliminate or remove the connection between A and B, or isolate B so none of the undesirable features of B can affect others. Symbolically and in an abbreviated way, we can write these four possible responses as:

1. Do nothing different
2. Eliminate A: $\cancel{A} \rightarrow B$
3. Eliminate the connection: $A \not\rightarrow B$
4. Isolate the harmful effects: $A \rightarrow \textcircled{B}$

This schema applies for all kinds of problems, not just environmental ones.[2] Consider one common problem: the flu. If A is the flu virus and B is fever, sneezing, etc., eliminating A may include removing the virus from where you are (e.g., through not going to work, wearing a face mask, etc.), eliminating the connection would include a drug that prevents the flu virus from causing the flu symptoms (e.g., through disruption of the flu virus' behavior), and isolating the harmful effects would include medications that treat the symptoms (e.g., acetaminophen, anti-histamines, etc.)

For the case of global warming, A might be anthropogenic emissions of carbon dioxide, B might be increased global mean surface temperature, and "$\rightarrow$" the greenhouse effect. Response 1 would be "business as usual." Examples of response 2 would be measures to decrease emissions of carbon dioxide, such as by decreasing fossil fuel use, capturing and sequestering carbon dioxide at the point of power generation, improved energy conservation

---

1. "Doing nothing different" is not necessarily the same as "doing nothing" nor is it necessarily the same as neutrality. "Doing nothing," strictly speaking, is an impossibility: even the lack of a response represents an action. Neutrality implies a non-committal position. We can, however, be quite convinced and certain that the "do nothing different" option is better than all other options; in such an instance, there is nothing neutral about the "do nothing different" position. (Thanks to David Barr at the University of Chicago for this line of reasoning.) Response 1, fundamentally, is the choice to continue with the *status quo*.

2. In many environmental problems, a non-trivial level of uncertainty exists as to whether A causes B. In those cases, the aim of the possible responses might be to decrease the risk of the problem rather than a complete solution. Our schema of possible responses then needs to be augmented with different ways of handling uncertainty, which we discuss later in this chapter.

measures, etc. We call these responses "mitigation." An example of response 3 is a proposal to place gigantic parasols in space to shade the Earth from part of the incoming solar radiation, to counteract the increase in temperature due to the increase in carbon dioxide.[3] Lastly, examples of response 4 include moving houses out of areas vulnerable to increased storm activity (such as floodplains), building sea walls to combat sea-level rise, etc. These activities are known as "adaptation."

Besides providing a taxonomy for describing the range of responses, this schema makes clear that if the policy goal is to prevent or remove undesirable traits of B, there is, in principle, more than one solution to the problem: *any* of responses 2–4 will suffice. Thus, the policy goal, in and of itself, does not determine which response is preferable, as any of the three "do something" responses can, in theory, achieve the policy goal. Of course, this does not mean that all possible responses are equally warranted; it does mean that something besides the policy goal is needed to justify one response over another. Questions we can ask to evaluate the various responses include:

1. Is it possible to eliminate A? At what cost?

2. Will eliminating A result in side-effects? Are they desirable or undesirable side-effects?

3. Is it possible to eliminate the connection between A and B? At what cost?

4. Does the connection between A and B have other effects that will also be eliminated if you eliminate the connection between the two? How desirable or undesirable are these other effects?

5. Will putting a "hedge" around B result in other side-effects? How desirable or undesirable are they?

6. Are the undesirable effects of B undesirable *enough* to justify action? If so, what kind of action?

7. Do I find a particular type of response more preferable, in principle?

In earlier chapters, we saw how worldviews and ethical theories contribute to the relative value of costs and benefits of different practices (their desirability and undesirability may be monetary in nature but may also

---

3. Some (but not all) of these "eliminate the connection" responses are called "geoengineering" solutions. "Geoengineering" refers to any solution to the global warming problem that involves large-scale alterations to the climate system. Some geoengineering solutions are also mitigation solutions (e.g., suggestions to add iron fertilizer into the ocean to increase plankton production and thus biologically absorb and sequester carbon dioxide).

be spiritual, moral, cultural, mental, etc.). We also saw that science might not prescribe either the goals or practices of environmental stewardship. Instead, both goals and practices also depend on the non-scientific determinants. Thus, the evaluation between possible responses will also involve a mix of determinants.

THE IMPORTANCE OF VALUES IN CHOOSING RESPONSES

In the mix of determinants we use to evaluate different responses, those that pertain to values play an important role. We can see this more clearly if we consider a non-environmental problem that is narrower and has fewer solutions to choose from. Consider the following fact: motor vehicle accidents kill people.[4] Based on our schema, A is motor vehicle accidents, B is the death of people, and the "$\rightarrow$" is the action of killing. Thus, the four possible responses to this problem are:

1. Do nothing different

2. Decrease and/or eliminate motor vehicle accidents

3. Prevent motor vehicle accidents from killing people

4. Make death less undesirable

What might be some specific policy options for each possible response, and how do we evaluate those responses? We generally reject the first and fourth options (or at least many examples of those options) out of hand.[5] But, why? Mainly, because we have a moral imperative to prevent accidents and deaths. Thus, we eliminate these two responses based on value reasons rather than scientific reasons.

There are a variety of ways we can enact responses 2 and 3, to decrease motor vehicle accidents and prevent accidents from killing people. We can criminalise behavior that increases the likelihood of accidents, such as driving while under the influence (DUI). We can design vehicles (such as

4. In 2009, for instance, in the U.S. there were 35.9 thousand deaths within one year of the accident (U.S. Census Bureau, *Statistical Abstract*, 693).

5. We do not always reject response 4 solutions out of hand. Nearly everyone does reject some examples of response 4, such as creating a culture that values death to mitigate the undesirability of death, but we commonly accept other examples, such as mandating liability insurance for all drivers; one purpose of insurance is to mitigate the negative effects of death and injury. Still, the larger point is that decisions for and against policy options usually include a value component. Here too, in the case of insurance, we see that a decision to require liability insurance inevitably requires balancing civil liberties and public health considerations, which is fundamentally a value proposition.

self-driving cars) that can avoid accidents.[6] We can require high-risk drivers (e.g., teens) to take steps to decrease their risk (e.g., take a driver's education class). And, we can build cars with airbags, seat belts, and pass laws requiring passengers to wear seat belts.

The choice for or amongst these (and other response 2 and 3 policies) may appear to be strictly determined by science or economics, through feasibility studies or cost-benefit analysis studies. Here too, however, values play an important role in determining how we consider responses. We legislate against DUI but do not legislate against other behaviors that would decrease motor vehicle accidents (e.g., just ban the production and driving of cars) because we believe DUI is morally wrong but not car ownership and use per se (in addition to civil liberties reasons). We may build safer cars but are wary about relinquishing human control of our cars to a computer and have to carefully think through issues of liability.[7] We may require teens to take driver's education classes, but in choosing to do so instead of prohibiting teens from driving entirely, we implicitly have decided the value of permitting teen driving, risks and all, is greater than the decrease in motor vehicle accidents that would result from such a prohibition. And while the development of safety technology like airbags and seat belts is a scientific issue, adoption of such technology (whether required or not) is not a scientific issue: civil liberties, economic values, ethics, etc. all play a major role. As we have seen earlier in the book, determining practice requires more than studies. As seen repeatedly in the car accidents example, the scope of responses is limited by values. In a number of cases, the science is really immaterial to the evaluation of a response: our moral sense of the appropriateness of the response settles whether it is an option.

Looking more generally, we can identify three major ways values enter into the evaluation of possible responses. First, our appraisal of possible responses depends on our understanding of the nature and value of what the responses act on, namely, on A, B, and/or their connection: Does A, B, or their connection have positive or negative value? What kind of value and what status does it have relative to other values? For instance, a person who considers A to have high positive value would be less willing to consider the "eliminate A" response, even given the harmful effects of B. In the climate change issue, an example of a person holding this view might be one who considers carbon dioxide emissions as necessary and beneficial because the energy use that results in such emissions generates economic growth. Such a person may thus be hesitant to adopt mitigation solutions if economic

6. Bilger, "Auto Correct."

7. Ibid.

growth were negatively impacted. On the other hand, someone who believes A to have, a priori, high negative value would be more apt to support an "eliminate A" response; in the climate change case, a Deep Ecologist who holds human non-intervention in the environment as a high value may thus have a preference for mitigation responses on the grounds that it reverses anthropogenic alteration of the atmosphere. In a similar (though different) way, the preference for simplicity and minimalism can also lead to a preference for the "eliminate A" response.

Because, for many environmental problems, there may be a number of consequences B, this may result in more ways for values to influence the evaluation of responses. A person may consider one negative consequence $B1$ to be of great importance but, because of their worldview or ethical views, disagree with someone else that a different consequence $B2$ is important or even harmful. In such a case, the two people may disagree in the evaluation of a response that isolates the harmful effects of $B1$ but not $B2$, or vice versa. For instance, a Leopoldian Land Ethicist who believes habitat has intrinsic value may feel the consequence of habitat alteration that results from the actions that cause global warming is unacceptable. Someone with a Romantic worldview, however, might not consider habitat as having intrinsic value and may, accordingly, be more willing to accept some forms of habitat alteration. The person with a Romantic worldview, however, might consider preserving the aesthetic value of wilderness to be a moral imperative and would be motivated by responses that address that goal. Of course, there is a great deal of overlap between the goals motivated by the values of different consequences B, so having differing values does not necessarily mean disagreement in terms of evaluating responses. Nonetheless, the rationales do differ, and that difference can influence how one evaluates responses.

The second way values enter into the evaluation of responses is in whether the responses themselves (outside of what those responses act on) have positive or negative value. For instance, a neo-Luddite who is skeptical of technology in general might object to responses that require substantial amounts of technology. In the case of climate change, most geoengineering proposals that sever the connection between A and B would likely require the use of substantial amounts of technology and thus would not be supported by those who strongly hold neo-Luddite values. Philosophical political progressives who believe in the need for a governmental response (perhaps, to overcome the problem of cooperation illustrated in the "Tragedy of the Commons") might be more supportive of comprehensive solutions versus local and limited responses. And policy study "conservatives"—who conclude from policy studies that incremental solutions are more effective at addressing complex environmental problems—may argue for modest and non-comprehensive responses.[8]

Finally, values enter into the evaluation of responses in terms of how we weigh and compare actions and their effects. An anthropocentric consequentialist, for instance, might weigh the positive and negative effects of B and the different kinds of responses by looking at their consequences upon some metric of human flourishing, e.g., monetary cost/benefit, maximizing pleasure, etc. A Romantic deontologist, on the other hand, might consider it an absolute duty to preserve wilderness and find that duty as all important in evaluating different responses; responses that do not adequately preserve wilderness will rank lower.

HANDLING UNCERTAINTY

In our analysis of the range of responses and the role of values in selecting between responses, we assumed that the certainty of our knowledge regarding the parts of $A \rightarrow B$ is inconsequential to our choice between responses. Yet, we know nearly all forms of knowledge have uncertainty (and thus risk)[9] associated with them, including science.[10] Thus, while we naturally seek to decrease uncertainties, often through further research, some amount of uncertainty is inherent to any environmental problem. This uncertainty is not only empirical and cognitive in nature—due to limitations in what we can measure, lack of historical data, immature theories, lacuna in understanding, etc.—but also psychological, a reflection of the diversity of disciplinary

8. For instance, Richard E. Benedick, who served as the chief U.S. negotiator for the Montreal Protocol that banned chlorofluorocarbons, argues that climate change should be addressed in smaller, more limited "parallel" negotiations between fewer participants, rather than in a comprehensive, "190 nations" negotiation as part of the Kyoto Protocol process, because the comprehensive approach has resulted in gridlock (Benedick, "Avoiding Gridlock"). Daniel Sarewitz also argues for an incrementalist approach: "'Sustainability,' write Rayner and Malone 'is about being nimble, not being right.' And being nimble is about taking small steps and keeping one's eyes open." [parenthetical citation removed] (Sarewitz, "Environmental Controversies," 400)

9. In many ways, handling uncertainty is about handling risk. If an uncertainty does not expose us to any risk—of a loss or other harm or of an opportunity cost or other forgone benefit—it would not matter much whether we felt certain or not about our knowledge regarding an environmental issue. (Again, we use cost, harm, and benefit in the broadest sense possible. These terms include not only economic costs and benefits but also spiritual, religious, social, political, psychological, intellectual, moral, etc. "costs" and "benefits.") Thus, in our discussion, we can use "handling uncertainty" and "handling risk" more or less interchangeably.

10. Although some logical positivists and rationalists would argue some forms of science or empirical study are completely certain.

perspectives in science, and dependent on political realities.[11] Thus, in order to understand how the determinants affect the practice criterion, we have to consider how to handle the uncertainty in the knowledge (scientific and otherwise) we possess. In this section, we consider two aspects of the issue of uncertainty: what ways do we have of handling uncertainty and how does handling uncertainty affect the practice criterion.

We can describe three different categories of ways to handle uncertainty. (These categories are not mutually exclusive.) In the first category are strategies that seek to prevent *any* harms from occurring, in spite of (or perhaps because of) the uncertainty. One of the better known in this category of strategies is the "precautionary principle." While there are a number of different formulations of the principle, we can describe the precautionary principle as a method where uncertainty becomes a reason to enact environmental regulations or to prevent activities that might cause harm—"*in dubio pro natura.*"[12] Procedurally, the precautionary principle can be expressed as a shifting of the burden of proof onto those who propose a course of action that may injure the environment, even if the risk of injury is small; such a precautionary stance is particularly warranted if the possible injury is potentially catastrophic.[13] In a criminal trial, the presumption that the defendant is "innocent until proven guilty" creates a high burden of proof for the prosecution to meet, which presumably decreases the likelihood of a wrongful conviction. With the precautionary principle, the requirement that a course of action is in some sense presumed "guilty until proven innocent" creates a barrier to the adoption of possibly environmentally harmful practices in the first place.

Does the precautionary principle work to prevent the environmental harms that possibly could occur? Critics have argued that the precautionary principle seems to presuppose precautionary measures are themselves risk-free; because there is no such thing as a zero-risk policy (outside of policies

11. See Sarewitz, "Environmental Controversies," 396 for a discussion of uncertainty and multiple disciplinary perspectives and how "political stakes" also determine the level of "acceptable" and achievable certainty.

12. Ambrus, "Precautionary Principle," 261. Precaution, of course, is not limited to environmental policy. In product safety, a 1960 version of the Delaney clause regulating color additives required the FDA to prohibit the commercial use of any additives that caused cancer in either people or animals, even if risk assessments showed negligible increase in cancer risk to people (Jasanoff, *The Fifth Branch*, 172–77). Presumably, the strictness of the regulation expresses the idea that even the possibility of an increased cancer risk from color additive use outweighs the arguments in favor for their use. We can understand the environmental precautionary principle as an environmental analogue of such reasoning.

13. Ambrus, "Precautionary Principle," 261.

and problems of a trivial nature), the principle seems unable to provide useful policy guidance.[14] The precautionary mindset, carried too far, may also lead to economic and technological paralysis. Numerous advances in public health and safety (e.g., the polio vaccine) would presumably never have seen the light of day if they had been required to meet the burden of proof required by a strong form of the precautionary principle,[15] and it may be difficult to properly weight low probability and high uncertainty events to avoid such paralysis. In addition, practically speaking it is difficult to see how to implement the precautionary principle; as Naomi Oreskes has pointed out, different people love different things to different extents and thus are willing to accept or reject different risks.[16] In response to some of these criticisms, some have argued that the precautionary principle does not have to be used as a blunt prohibition of any action but rather can be implemented through milder responses (such as pre-market risk assessment) and may consider all potential risks, including the risk of precaution.[17] Some formulations of the precautionary principle consider it not so much as a decision-rule but a reminder to decision-makers that policies must reflect "equitable attitudes."[18] These "softer" forms of the precautionary principle might be more justifiable and workable, but it is unclear the degree to which such forms motivate environmental policies that successfully deal with risk by eliminating the *need* to consider that risk. If not, the precautionary principle may be better implemented as part of a broader strategy at handling uncertainty rather than a singular attempt to make risk a non-issue.

In the second category, we find strategies that address uncertainty by limiting the *extent* of the harms that may result. These strategies differ from the first category in that they accept harms are likely to occur and, in response, seek only to minimize those harms. One example of this second category of strategies is to adopt incremental and reversible policies. In this strategy, we focus on enacting policies that take small, incremental steps and that are as reversible as possible, as opposed to large, comprehensive policies which may be difficult to change or undo. In this way, we hope to limit the possible harms of our actions as well as flexibly adapt to new information and changes in risk and uncertainty levels.[19] Under this strategy,

14. Ahteensuu , "Defending," 373–74 summarizes this position. Ahteensuu himself defends the precautionary principle.

15. Ibid. gives a summary of this argument. Ahteensuu himself defends the precautionary principle. See also Bailey, "Precautionary Tale."

16. Oreskes, "Proof," 379.

17. Ahteensuu , "Defending," 378.

18. John, "In Defence," 14.

19. Hallegatte, *Investment Decision Making*, 16. Daniel Sarewitz also defends

we accept the risk that our policies may be "too little" while hoping (because small steps more easily allow mid-course corrections) that the policies will not be "too late" or "too wrong." In return, we hope to avoid the possible (but unknown) harms associated with large, complex, and often expensive policy responses.

A second example of this class of strategies is the use of generous safety margins.[20] Engineering calculations—whether for the design load for a building, the level of coastal inundation from a storm surge, or the failure rate of the control systems of a vehicle—typically incorporate a "margin of safety" to guard against catastrophic events of low but uncertain probability. Thus, the critical systems of an aircraft usually have more than one backup. In terms of environmental policies, the use of safety margins might take the form of using a larger design storm event than justified by historical records, when designing a runoff routing system, in order to accommodate the possible but uncertain increase in extreme precipitation events under global warming,[21] or it might take the form of building codes that require stronger materials for home construction that would decrease the likelihood of catastrophic failure in high wind events. In these and other examples, the level of the added margin of safety is informed but imprecise and thus somewhat arbitrary. The margin attempts, however, to account for possible but uncertain risks at a tolerable cost.[22]

A third example of this category of strategies is to choose policies that reduce decision-making horizons.[23] Like incremental and reversible policies, policies that reduce decision-making horizons are more flexible, but this flexibility exists because of the short time-horizon of the policy, not because of any intrinsic reversibility of the policy. Economist Stéphane Hallegatte gives the example of choosing cheaper housing materials as an

---

incrementalism (Sarewitz, "Environmental Controversies," 400).

20. Hallegatte, *Investment Decision Making*, 16–17.

21. Ibid., 17.

22. In discussing the example of adding a safety margin in the design of a runoff drainage system, to account for possibly larger precipitation events under climate change, economist Stéphane Hallegatte notes:

> This move [using larger runoff figures in the design of the system] is justified by the fact that, in the design phase, it is inexpensive to implement a drainage system able to cope with increased precipitation. On the other hand, modifying the system after it has been built is difficult and expensive. It is wise, therefore, to be over-pessimistic in the design phase. (Ibid., 17)

23. Ibid.

example of a policy that utilizes reduced decision-making horizons.[24] Because the cheaper materials will wear out more quickly, the decision to build a home is no longer a hundred- or two-hundred-year decision but a thirty- or fifty-year decision. At the end of the house's lifespan, we can make a new decision regarding what materials to use in rebuilding/renovating the home; presumably, in the intervening years, the uncertainty that existed earlier has decreased and we can make this future decision with greater certainty and less risk. This strategy to deal with uncertainty, however, may lead to some waste and inefficiencies (e.g., more frequent demolition and rebuilding costs in the case of the house) than otherwise would have occurred.

A final example of the second category of strategies is to pursue "no regrets" responses.[25] "No regrets" policies are those that can be justified on the basis of motivations other than the environmental issue whose uncertainty is in question. Thus, if we adopt a preventative measure and it turns out the predicted (but uncertain) problem never occurs, our earlier policy choice is still justified. For example, while the possibility of catastrophic global warming might motivate a reduction in the use of fossil fuels, a "no regrets" strategy would justify the reduction of fossil fuel use on other considerations such as national security (since a large percentage of fossil fuel production occurs in politically volatile areas) or near-surface air pollution (electric vehicles, for instance, do not generate tailpipe exhaust). In that way, even if it turns out the possibility of catastrophic global warming was wrongly calculated, the policy choice of reducing fossil fuel use would still be justified. "No regrets" strategies offer the opportunity of broadening the support base for a given policy action. At the same time, if the policy was already fully justified by reasons unrelated to the uncertain environmental reason, why bring in the environmental reason in the first place?

In the third category are strategies that accept that intrinsic uncertainty means very severe harms may (or even will) occur and seek to mitigate the effects of those harms or compensate for those harms (as opposed to minimizing the extent of the harms or preventing the occurrence of the harms). Insurance may be the best known example of this category of strategies. In the insurance strategy, the (often catastrophic) loss covered by the insurance is (nearly) certain to occur to a pool of individuals, but it is impossible to determine whether any given individual will experience the loss. Thus, the individuals pool resources together to guarantee compensation for the loss to the individuals who experience the loss. This pooling of resources also ensures that the cost of compensation is divided amongst a large group

24. Ibid., 17.

25. For instance, see ibid., 16.

of individuals, and thus each individual's certain cost (i.e., the cost of the premium) is a tiny fraction of the cost of the benefit. For instance, we buy fire insurance because while we know that, statistically speaking, a certain number of houses burn down each year, we cannot predict whether ours will. Yet, if our house does burn down, the cost of replacement is almost surely out of reach for us to bear as an individual.[26] Fire insurance ensures an individual can replace the loss of a house at a fraction of the actual loss.

In order for insurance to work, however, a number of conditions need to be true. First, to figure out a proper premium, we need to have reasonable certainty of the average rate of loss. If the loss rate is unpredictable, it is not possible to correctly price the premium. In the case of some environmental problems, such as global warming, the statistics of loss (e.g., frequency of storms) are themselves uncertain. Second, the risk pool needs to be large enough to adequately spread the risk around. If 90 percent of all the homes in a fire insurance risk pool burned down every year, there would be little benefit to purchasing fire insurance, as the cost of the premiums would be nearly the same as the benefit. For some possible (but uncertain) environmental problems, the severity and extent of the problem makes it difficult to find an adequate risk pool, as the risk pool (those at risk of experiencing the loss) and the loss pool (those who actually experience the loss) are nearly one and the same. Third, the loss needs to have a well-defined replacement or "mitigation" price. If it is impossible to tolerate the loss or mitigate the damages in any way, insurance cannot work. Thus, while a human being is unique and irreplaceable, some damages associated with a death (e.g., lost future earnings, etc.) can be mitigated, and life insurance does exactly that. Life insurance, however, cannot (and does not claim to) mitigate the unmonetizable damages associated with a death (e.g., the intrinsic worth of a person). For environmental problems, there may be inherent limits to what can be compensated for.

How does handling uncertainty affect the practice criterion? First, the need to handle uncertainty introduces another area in which values play a critical role in determining the practice criterion. Each of these methods of handling (or tolerating) risk, as we have seen, has costs (including opportunity costs) and benefits, financial and otherwise. The value and meaning of these costs and benefits, similar to other environmental and human values, are dependent on our worldviews, ethical theories, and the other determinants of the criteria for obedience. Thus, not only is the evaluation

---

26. Of course, if we are extremely wealthy, we can afford to replace our home on our own. Such a choice is called self-insurance and is equivalent to the *caveat emptor* or "buyer beware" strategy. In that strategy, we accept whatever risks we face and live with the losses (if any) we actually encounter.

of possible responses a value-laden proposition, so too is the evaluation of possible ways of handling uncertainty. Our appraisal of different ways of handling uncertainty depends on our understanding of the nature and value of the risks associated with the uncertainty, the value associated with the risk-handling response itself, and the metrics and methods we use to weigh different risk-handling strategies.

Second, the presence of deep uncertainty will tend to emphasize responses derived using robustness analysis or experimentation rather than optimal analysis.[27] In optimal analysis, the costs and benefits are calculated for a variety of responses in a suite of scenarios, and the response is chosen whose benefits most exceed costs for the most likely scenario.[28] In situations characterized by deep uncertainty, we cannot determine which scenario is most likely.[29] An alternate approach, robustness analysis, adds the criteria of robustness to the factors being considered. We can think of robustness as the degree to which a policy can accommodate a range of possible (though uncertain) scenarios. Policy responses that cannot do so may be eliminated from consideration or adjusted to address vulnerabilities present in some of the scenarios, using the strategies described earlier for handling uncertainty. Another alternate approach, experimentation, is based on letting patterns emerge from small trial responses, since optimal analysis cannot tell us the right answer.[30] In experimentation, we accept that we do not know the right answer and instead look for positive alternatives to develop from a process characterized by open and creative testing and patience that tolerates failure.[31] Regardless of which alternative methods we use, uncertainty makes the strategy of "find the best solution" less fruitful while making other management strategies—such as "avoid problems," "be nimble," "add a safety margin," and "experiment"—more attractive as ways of determining the "best" solution.

Lastly, the need to handle uncertainty may—or perhaps should—lead us to a greater sense of humility that in turn can lead to better creation care

27. Hallegatte, *Investment Decision Making*, 13–15.

28. Ibid., 14. While our description of optimal analysis uses the language of cost-benefit analysis (CBA), we do not restrict "costs" and "benefits" to either economic value or utility, nor does "exceed" necessarily mean "greater numerically." Costs and benefits might be non-instrumental, moral, spiritual, or any of a number of other kinds. Weighing between costs and benefits might use a deontological mindset, a virtue ethic, or any of a number of other ways of weighing values.

29. Ibid., 14.

30. Snowden and Boone, "A Leader's Framework," 73–74. The experimentation approach is useful for complex contexts in general (Snowden and Boone, "A Leader's Framework," 73–74).

31. Snowden and Boone, "A Leader's Framework," 73–75.

practices. Such a sense of humility may, in the case of the precautionary principle, lead to a level of risk aversion that may or may not be entirely healthy. Such a sense of humility may lead to a desire to "hedge our bets" by choosing incremental responses or building in generous safety margins. But humility can also affect practice by setting the stage for dialogue. A common recognition of not only what we know but also what we do not know might form the grounds on which to build a compromise between disparate stakeholders. When we emphasize what we know over and above what we do not (sometimes to the point of ignoring uncertainty altogether), we can raise the stakes to being right, make disagreement and compromise into a personal and policy threat (for it may mean we are wrong), and harden policy positions to the point where power politics remains the only method of resolution. In contrast, the virtue of humility that uncertainty forces upon us holds the promise of dialogue that leads to more creative, stable, and effective creation care policies.

CONCLUSIONS

Our analysis of the range of responses as well as ways of handling uncertainty has led us to the following conclusions. First, for a given set of environmental stewardship goals, there exists a broad range of possible solutions that might not be mutually exclusive. Second, the evaluation and selection amongst these possible solutions is irreducibly a value proposition, whether one includes the issue of uncertainty or not. The help science provides in the selection process cannot replace the value judgments we make using the determinants. Indeed, the value assumptions we bring to the evaluation process can predispose us for or against entire classes and combinations of solutions. Third, our analysis has yielded the beginnings of a taxonomy of questions to use in analyzing solutions as well as a taxonomy of questions to use in analyzing how the values we hold affect our evaluation of the different solutions.

From these conclusions we can draw implications for the broader question of how we achieve excellent environmental stewardship. While we will address the preconditions for achieving excellent stewardship in more detail in the final chapter, here we enumerate a few implications that will set up that discussion. First, we need to take care not to prematurely restrict the range of responses we are willing to consider. If there is a broad range of policies that all equally fulfill the policy goals we hold, this provides an opportunity for us to consider creative and non-obvious solutions that may be fruitful grounds for compromise. Prematurely restricting the range of responses may result in this lost opportunity.

Second, because there is a breadth of responses that equally fulfill a given policy goal, this suggests that people who advocate policies we disagree with may actually still hold some of the same core goals. This is not to suggest that the policy disagreement is not real; indeed, the centrality of values in evaluating responses suggests that the policy disagreement has at least some grounding on real value differences. Nonetheless, it may be that people with different value positions hold the same core goals and values. A focus on identifying and building trust and agreement around those core goals may strengthen the common ground on which to resolve the differences.

Third, the centrality of values to policy evaluation suggests that a substantial amount of the disagreement over solutions (e.g., one person says only solution X is possible while another says only solutions Y and Z will work) comes from the value frameworks each person is using. Efforts to understand the frameworks being used and formulate compromises and define common ground by appealing to those frameworks may help resolve the disagreements.

Finally, our analysis suggests that understanding the trade-offs inherent in any proposed solution is not merely a policy analysis exercise but is fundamentally a *personal* endeavor. In saying so, this does not mean that policy analysis is merely subjective or that all policies are on equal footing. It does mean that the "costs" and "benefits"[32] of any policy are not only monetary or monetizable but may also be spiritual, cultural, mental, emotional, moral, physical, and environmental. That is to say, policymaking is an irreducibly *human* enterprise and must be engaged in those terms. Attempts to short-circuit the personal nature of policymaking through appeals to authority, whether that of science, Scripture, or some other source, can stunt the policymaking process and lead to the adoption of less stable and effective policies.

DISCUSSION QUESTIONS

1. The author argues there is a range of possible responses. Do you agree or disagree? Why? Does the idea of a range of possible responses imply the choice between responses does not matter? Why or why not?

---

32. Again, I am not using "costs" and "benefits" in a utilitarian sense but in a more general sense of positives and negatives.

2. What would you add or remove from the taxonomy of possible responses that the author gives? Why?

3. Of the possible responses in the range the author provides, which response do you find yourself gravitating towards? Why do you find some responses more compelling than others?

4. Of the general ways of handling uncertainty, which ones do you find more helpful? Least helpful? Why? Would you consider yourself risk-averse or comfortable with risk? Why? What contribution, if any, do you think your comfort level with risk has in determining what policies you prefer in handling uncertainty?

5. In choosing between different possible responses and ways of handling uncertainty, which values do you find yourself most prone to use? What effect do you think the use of those values has on which responses and ways of handling uncertainty most appeal to you?

8

It Isn't Easy Being Green

PUTTING IT ALL TOGETHER AND FINDING A "THIRD WAY"

A PARABLE, TO BE CONTINUED

The Sun was setting as Gabriel left his office and walked to the church conference room. *How does one tell if the Sun is rising or setting?* mused Gabriel. *It seems the only way is whether you feel awake or tired.* Gabriel definitely felt tired. Tonight the church's creation care committee would meet *redux*. Gabriel had spent the intervening time since the last meeting talking with various members in the committee but was still unsure what would transpire in this meeting. Ralph and Ramona both felt hurt and angry from their argument the previous meeting, and other members of the committee displayed varying shades of awkwardness and hostility.

When Gabriel arrived at the conference room, he found nearly everyone in the committee already seated. *When everyone arrives before the pastor,* thought Gabriel, *it's either a very good thing or a very bad thing.* Gabriel said hi to everyone and took his place at the table. Before he could start the meeting, Ralph Lee stood up.

"Pastor Gabriel, I was wondering if I could say a few words before we begin," said Ralph. Gabriel nodded. "When we were

last here, I said and did some very harsh things to Ramona"—
and here Ralph gestured to Ramona who, Gabriel realized with
a little surprise, was sitting next to Ralph—"and to others who
share many of the views Ramona holds."

Ralph continued. "For a long time after the meeting, I was
angry and hurt too. I felt misunderstood and unfairly judged.
But then, one morning while wallowing in my self-righteousness, my daily Bible reading led me to Matthew 5." Here, Ralph
opened his Bible and read Matthew 5:21–22:

> You have heard that it was said to the people long ago, "You shall
> not murder, and anyone who murders will be subject to judg-
> ment." But I tell you that anyone who is angry with a brother or
> sister will be subject to judgment. Again, anyone who says to a
> brother or sister, "Raca," is answerable to the court. And anyone
> who says, "You fool!" will be in danger of the fire of hell.

"I quickly shut my Bible and went pacing around the house,"
said Ralph. "When I had calmed down, telling myself I was
justifiably angry, not angry in the way Jesus was talking about,
I came back and continued reading. Then I read Matthew 5:23–
24: 'Therefore, if you are offering your gift at the altar and there
remember that your brother or sister has something against you,
leave your gift there in front of the altar. First go and be reconciled to them; then come and offer your gift.'" Ralph closed his
Bible. His hands were shaking a little.

"My immediate response," said Ralph, "was to scoff and condemn those who I felt were judging me—'Well, they sure haven't
come to be reconciled to me,' I said to myself. But then, I noticed
Jesus wasn't saying I should go talk to the other person only if I
was in the wrong but merely if the other person had something
against me."

The room was silent as Ralph paused. "I tried to ignore this
passage for a long time, but finally this week I asked Ramona if I
could come by and talk to her about the meeting," Ralph continued. "We talked for hours, and while at times our tempers would
flare up, I finally have a better understanding of her viewpoint."

"More importantly, I now understand that regardless of our
different views, she is a fellow human being and my sister in
Christ and deserves my respect. I asked for her forgiveness and
she graciously granted it to me," said Ralph, "but I wanted also
to ask all of you here for your forgiveness. My offense to her
was public and so should be my apology. But I also was disrespectful to all of you in the way I condemned Ramona's position,

particularly to those like Arnold who share her views"—here Ralph looked at Arnold Banks with sorrow. "Please forgive me."

Ralph sat down. Before someone could respond, Ramona patted her hand on Ralph's shoulder and stood up.

"Ralph, if there's anyone here who should be asking for forgiveness it should be me," began Ramona. "Everyone here I'm sure remembers the condemning words I said about businesses. And, I am sure, everyone remembers the personal attacks I leveled at Ralph and other business owners. They were inexcusable. Ralph," and here Ramona turned to face her neighbor, "thank you for your humility, and please forgive me for my unfair and harsh judgments of you. And to Lourdes and everyone else"—here Ramona looked at Lourdes Garcia and around the room—"please forgive me for my self-righteousness and harshness to you too." Ramona sat down with a tear in her eye, and Ralph put his hand on her shoulder.

Then, before Gabriel could say a word, something strange happened. First Arnold, then Lourdes, then several members of the committee stood up and apologized to the group. Some apologized for being judgmental, some for assuming ill will about others regarding creation care issues, some for being dismissive and unwilling to really listen to opposing positions, and still some for stereotyping the views of others. By the end of the sharing, people were discussing ways of clearing up misconceptions about one another's positions and how to explicitly address conflicts and disagreements, instead of allowing them to fester unspoken. The meeting's ending time came and went, and by the time the last member of the committee had left an hour later, the group had laid out a schedule of meetings to discuss one another's assumptions regarding creation care and to discuss the range of responses possible given those assumptions. By himself, Gabriel walked through the church building, turning off the remaining lights and adjusting the thermostats. It had been a long day, but it seemed to him that though he still felt tired, the Son was rising.[1]

INTRODUCTION

We have covered a lot of ground. We have described each of the determinants and have delineated ways these determinants affect the criteria for

---

1. This fictional story was inspired by a true story (unrelated to creation care) that Ken Sande tells (Sande, *Peacemaker*, 75–78).

obedience. Using the criteria, we can articulate what excellent environmental stewardship looks like. We now have a full deck: it's time to deal out the cards and play.[2] But if only environmental stewardship were as simple as a card game! If nothing else, the preceding chapters in this book have painted an exceedingly complex picture of environmental stewardship: worldview, ethical theories, science, and society are all interconnected in a web of many strands. We have a concept map of how the different areas of our taxonomy interact with one another, but concept maps are highly non-linear: they do not yield a neat, step-by-step flow chart that tells us what to do. Is there anything else we can do to help put this all together?

While we cannot produce an environmental stewardship "recipe," we can enumerate principles to guide us in the task of synthesis. That is, while the task of comprehensively specifying a robust synthesis of the criteria for obedience is beyond the scope of this book and remains as future work, we can specify constraints on any process of synthesis. Laying out these constraints is the task of this chapter. First, we articulate the goals and principles of synthesizing the determinants of the criteria for obedience. Second, we examine examples of what we call "predispositions" in determining the content of creation care. These are assumptions we make about the nature of environmental stewardship that need to be explicitly justified or altered. Third, given that environmental issues can involve controversy, we examine the nature of conflict and dialogue. Fourth, we tentatively suggest alternative ways forward that may result, eventually, in more excellent creation care. Lastly, we summarize the main points of this book and draw final conclusions.

GOALS AND PRINCIPLES OF SYNTHESIS

While the task of synthesis of the determinants of the criteria for obedience is non-linear, still we can define goals and principles to use in conducting synthesis. In this section, we describe five such goals and principles. We do not claim these goals and principles are incontrovertibly justified—say, from first-principles. Instead we propose them as useful guidelines for the activity of synthesis and assert that syntheses meeting these guidelines will be more useful, robust, and truthful.

The first goal for a synthesis is that it be logically consistent between the different parts of the synthesis. Thus, a conclusion based on worldview considerations should not contradict one based on ethical considerations,

---

2. Griffiths, *Electrodynamics,* 343. I love the card metaphor Griffiths uses and have adapted it for this introduction.

nor should a conclusion derived from political philosophy contradict one reached from science-policy studies. This is a difficult goal to achieve, because of the wide range of determinants and possible positions within each determinant. Nonetheless, the alternative—maximal logical *inconsistency* between the different parts of the synthesis—will almost surely result in a contradicting, contradictory, and useless synthesis.

A second goal for a synthesis is that it be properly weighted between components. While worldviews, ethical theories, science, and society form a tetrad, this does not necessarily imply that we should equally weight the contributions from each of the four determinants. What constitutes proper weighting is beyond the scope of this book, but as a starting point, we assert that a weighting that focuses on one or two of the determinants to the exclusion of the rest will probably not result in a robust synthesis. In such a skewed weighting, it is likely that at least one of the three criteria for obedience (importance, goals, practice) will be incompletely described.

In addition, we assert that a proper weighting has to address the issue of what it means to be human in a holistic way. That is to say, a proper weighting should take seriously all the dimensions of being human: spiritual, intellectual, emotional, ethical, individual, social, etc. This argument for holism implies that reductive models of being human—as calculating machines, as matter in motion, as pleasure-seeking hedonists—are unlikely to be useful in the task of synthesis. Holism also implies that the process of arriving at a synthesis of the determinants of the criteria for obedience is not merely an exercise in logic and analysis. The process must also provide room for passion, feeling, and worship. The synthesis process should avoid an overreliance on reason as well as the belief that sincere passion is enough. We argue that while much of our discussion of the determinants and criteria for obedience has been analytical, the taxonomy itself leaves room for such holism, through the categories of meaning, purpose, value, and the different kinds of knowledge associated with the various dimensions of being human. Reason and other ways of knowing (e.g., intuition, love) are all welcome in the taxonomy, and all forms of knowing, including reason, must justify themselves. In some parts of the synthesis, some aspects of being human and the forms of knowledge associated with those aspects will be more important than others, and will affect the weighting between the determinants accordingly.

A third goal for a synthesis is that it fails correctly. All frameworks will, at some point, fail to give useful or truthful guidance or will be self-contradictory (or at the very least paradoxical). There will be some environmental issue where our synthesis will give an incorrect answer. This often happens when we take a line of reasoning to an extreme. For instance, some suggest that the belief in anthropocentrism necessarily justifies wanton human destruction of nature and that the belief in independent moral status for nature necessarily leads to the denigration of human beings. A synthesis that includes anthropocentrism might, at some point, give advice that justifies wanton human destruction of nature. If so, this would indicate the synthesis has failed in some way, as this conclusion does not seem correct. Similarly, a synthesis that includes a belief in independent moral status for nature and then suggests human beings are of little worth would also be deemed to have failed in some way. The fact that all frameworks fail implies that in the task of synthesis, we should not be unduly concerned if our synthesis does not cover all edge cases. If someone else claims our synthesis has holes in it, this is not necessarily problematic. The failures may be welcome.

But, if all frameworks have limitations, what distinguishes a good synthesis from a poor synthesis? A good synthesis will fail "well" while a poor synthesis will not. For a good synthesis, the failure will give insight on how to improve the synthesis but will not shipwreck the synthesis. The portions of a synthesis that appear self-contradictory or paradoxical are the "right" contradictions: they are contradictions that yield a more fruitful understanding of the nature of creation care, of the nature of being human, and of a life of true meaning. (We will say more about "good" paradox later on in this chapter when we consider alternative ways forward.) For a poor synthesis, the failure will reveal that the synthesis itself is fatally flawed. The self-contradictions in the synthesis not only call the structure of the synthesis into question, they actually describe an understanding of being human that is more impoverished.

A fourth goal for a synthesis relates to the third goal; a good synthesis should provide "guardrails" that prevent logical conclusions that are destructive. For instance, left-of-center positions regarding creation care tend to include some form of non-anthropocentric understanding of the value of nature. Some have critiqued that position as being tantamount to worshipping nature or as justifying misanthropy, and while many of those critiques are inaccurate, some non-anthropocentric understandings of nature do have a logic that can lead to such extreme conclusions. Similarly, right-of-center positions regarding creation care tend to include some form of anthropocentric understanding of the value of nature. Some have critiqued that position as justifying the pillaging of natural resources, and while many of those critiques are inaccurate, some anthropocentric understandings of nature do have a logic that can lead to such extreme conclusions. A good left-of-center or right-of-center synthesis would provide robust principles or mechanisms preventing such destructive logical conclusions while also being consistent with the synthesis' understanding of the value of nature.

A fifth and final goal for a synthesis is that it should produce more than the "sum of its parts." By this, we mean that it gives useful guidance not only regarding well-known environmental issues but also lesser-known issues and issues that have yet to be discovered. Such a synthesis should give helpful guidance to the most thorny, contentious, and large-scale environmental issues while at the same time provide guidance to simple, amicable, and local environmental issues. We are interested in excellence in creation care whether the environmental issue is controversial or not, and a good synthesis should apply to both. A synthesis that produces more than the sum of its parts will also produce guidance that is *truly* useful. By that, we mean guidance on which we would be willing to stake our lives, reputation, and fortune. Such a synthesis is not merely an intellectual exercise but is instead a gift to be received with gratitude and used to the glory of God.

PREDISPOSITIONS IN DETERMINING CREATION CARE

The goals and principles of synthesis we have described provide positive guidance in our efforts to synthesize the determinants of the criteria for obedience. That is to say, the goals and principles provide a target for us to aim for as we work on a synthesis. In this section, we consider "predispositions" that are sometimes encountered during efforts to determine practices of creation care. Such predispositions can, unknowingly, impede our efforts at synthesizing the determinants of the criteria for obedience. In this section, we define what predispositions are, list a number of common predispositions, and comment on the importance of identifying our predispositions if we are to successfully arrive at a solid synthesis.

Predispositions are ways of understanding or approaching creation care that we reflexively and uncritically use. They affect our reasoning about the determinants of the criteria for obedience much like an offset in an electronic transistor circuit. An offset is a steady baseline voltage that enables a transistor to function with certain characteristics in order to correctly process an electrical input signal that is superimposed on top of the offset. If the offset is removed, the transistor will process the input signal in an entirely different way. So too with a predisposition: the presence and absence of a predisposition alters how we process or understand the meaning of the determinants of the criteria for obedience.

Predispositions, however, differ from electronic circuit offsets in that we are unaware we hold these predispositions and thus are unaware of the impact they have on our understanding of creation care. To have a predisposition is not necessarily evidence of a character flaw or moral failing. Many, if not most, of our beliefs and understandings in life are assumed and latent. Furthermore, predispositions are not projections we make onto others—that is, they are not the ways we misunderstand those we disagree with—but rather, they are characterizations of our own thinking patterns that we do not realize we are engaged in. In the case of a complex and passionate topic like environmental stewardship, however, an inordinate presence of predispositions of which we are unaware can make it difficult for us to achieve an honest synthesis of the determinants of the criteria for creation care, because the predispositions will exert a substantial yet unacknowledged influence on our synthesis effort.

In the following sections, we list a number of these predispositions. The list is arranged in the following categories: worldview predispositions, ethical theories predispositions, and processing dispositions. The first two predispositions, as their names suggest, relate to the worldview and ethical theories determinants. The third and last category relates to the way we process the determinants, either by ourselves or in a community. While we believe this list highlights a number of the major predispositions, it is not exhaustive. Indeed, any of the positions regarding the determinants that we described in the previous chapters can be a predisposition: if the position affects our understanding of creation care and we are unaware we hold the position, it is a predisposition. Instead, the items on the list illustrate how positions we have described in our examination of the determinants, as well as those related to our processing of those positions, can unknowingly take hold of our imaginations and become an assumed way of understanding environmental stewardship.

Worldview Predispositions

The first worldview predisposition is the assumption that "is" automatically dictates "ought," or that what something is (its ontology) directly dictates how we should treat it (our ethics). We argued in chapter 2 that in many, if not most, environmental issues, the two are not automatically connected: we need to provide additional principles in order to connect the nature of something with how we should treat it. However, this is a commonly held understanding and one we seldom question. Coupled with a belief that science provides an authoritative description of what something is, the assumption that "is" dictates "ought" makes it natural to conclude that the fact science shows nature behaves a certain way means that nature *should* behave the way science describes. This line of reasoning strongly supports a policy prescriptive view of the connection between science and policy, as well as a static ecocentrism or theocentrism (described in more detail below). This web of mutually reinforcing ideas, in and of itself, is not wrong, but when one or more are unacknowledged predispositions, it becomes substantially more difficult to achieve an honest synthesis of the determinants of the criteria for obedience, because core beliefs are hidden and cannot participate in dialogue.

A second worldview predisposition is the "positive pristine wilderness" predisposition. In this predisposition, we assume that "wilderness" means untrammeled or unaffected by human beings, and that this condition is to be categorically preferred. This assumption, when paired with an ethic of simplicity and minimizing human impact, strongly supports policies focused around the removal of land and ocean areas from any kind of human use. The positive pristine wilderness predisposition finds much support in arguments that connect with the aesthetic and non-instrumental value of nature. We have already seen, however, in chapter 3 that the idea of "wilderness" has changed dramatically over the course of human history and that the positive pristine wilderness view is of relatively recent origin, having developed in the last few centuries. Paleoclimatologist William Ruddiman has also argued that anthropogenic contributions to climate extend back to something on the order of 5,000–8,000 years before the present, implying that even the pre-industrial environment was significantly affected by human beings;[3] if so, the pristine aspect of wilderness lies not in the absolute absence of human impact as much as in either a relative degree of human impact or in a qualitatively different kind of human involvement with nature.

A third, related worldview predisposition is the implicit Romantic predisposition. In this predisposition, our reaction to environmental issues follows the paths described by the Romantic worldview, regardless of the worldview we consciously profess. Thus, while we may, for instance, consciously hold a materialist, Enlightenment worldview, an implicit Romantic predisposition may lead us to a strong sympathy for the aesthetic dimensions of nature (e.g., beauty, awe, etc.), regardless of the tenets of our conscious worldview. As a result, this predisposition, in general, leads towards goals of preserving the aesthetic aspects of the environment.

A fourth worldview predisposition, the static nature predisposition, understands the goal of environmental stewardship as preserving nature in its current form. (By "current" we do not mean necessarily "this very moment" but more "as we have experienced.") In a theocentric context, this predisposition says that the state of nature God values is the state that

3. Ruddiman, "Early Anthropogenic," 33–34.

nature is currently in. In an ecocentric context, this predisposition says the intrinsic value of nature is bound to the state that nature is currently in. This predisposition can complement any number of worldviews and supports goals of preserving the current dynamics and structure of ecosystems (e.g., prevention and removal of invasive species). This predisposition, however, may make it difficult to understand how environmental stewardship goals and practices ought to fit in with geological changes. Such changes can be relatively short-term (e.g., streambed changes that impact ecology) or long-term (e.g., changes in the Earth's orbital patterns).

The biological predisposition is a fifth worldview predisposition. This predisposition prompts us to understand environmental issues primarily through the lens of biology. In its simplest form, this may mean relying primarily on biological descriptions of environmental problems as the most pertinent descriptions. Thus, while physics and chemistry are important components of natural systems, biological dimensions (e.g., species diversity, ecosystem balance, etc.) play the dominant role in discussions over stewardship practice. In another form, a biological predisposition may mean applying biological principles and categories to environmental ethics. Philosopher James A. Nash, for instance, proposes an idea of "following nature" in the sense of "ecosystemic compatibility."[4] The good and right, in this understanding, can be found in "limits," "fittingness," sustainability, balance, and flexibility, principles found (though not necessarily exclusively) in ecological and biological study.[5] In this, Nash is hardly alone; indeed, Nash's use of the work of others (e.g., Rosemary Radford Ruether and Paul Hawken's) in his description of ecosystemic compatibility indicates the depth to which biological metaphors and principles pervade environmental ethics.[6] A third form a biological predisposition may take is in the metaphors that are used to discuss environmental issues. In both literary and cultural as well as scientific discussions about environmental issues, the metaphors we often use are biological. As we might expect, the biological predisposition can strongly support an understanding that the goal of nature—what the state of nature should be—is to support life or certain kinds of life. Such a view connects well with goals of preserving ecosystems, enhancing the health of specific species of plants or animals, or preserving or increasing biodiversity.

We have seen, however, that as valuable as biology is as a discipline to understanding environmental issues, other disciplines (both scientific

4. Nash, "Moral Norms in Nature," 244.

5. Ibid., 245.

6. Ibid., 244–45.

and non-scientific) provide valuable insights. But, as Daniel Sarewitz points out, different disciplines have different values.[7] A biological predisposition may thus lead to an understanding of environmental issues based upon the values of biology, rather than those of physics, chemistry, economics, sociology, etc. The contributions from non-biological fields may also have to be translated into a biological framework in order to be accepted and understood. All this may or may not be desirable, but, again, to the extent the biological predisposition is an unacknowledged assumption, it is difficult to analyze the role and desirability of the assumption.

Ethical Theories Predispositions

The first ethical theory predisposition is naturally found in evangelical churches but may also be prominent in Western culture in general. We term this predisposition the "sin model." In the sin model, we categorize all human actions, individual and corporate, as sinful or not sinful. We reject activities that participate in or enable sin, provisionally accept those that do not, and analyze situations using the mindset "how do I avoid sin." This model has no small amount of Scriptural backing, as God clearly loves righteousness and hates unrighteousness. Applied to personal acts defined as sinful in the Bible, this model yields some of the most important negative guidance found in Christian ethics. Stealing is sinful so do not steal. Coveting is sinful so do not covet. Adultery is sinful so do not commit adultery. Applied to the environment, this mindset implies certain ways of treating the environment are also sinful. Littering is sinful so do not litter. Polluting streams is sinful so do not pollute. Emitting carbon dioxide is sinful so do not emit carbon dioxide. Because we evangelicals habitually use the sin model in evaluating our behavior, this predilection to think in terms of avoiding doing wrong contributes to a preference for solutions that eliminate causes of environmental problems.

7. In a discussion of the controversy over genetically modified organisms (GMOs), Sarewitz notes:

> This alignment of disciplinary perspective and worldly interests is critically important in understanding environmental controversies, because it shows that stripping out conflicts of interest and ideological commitments to look at "what the science is really telling us" can be a meaningless exercise. Even the most apparently apolitical, disinterested scientist may, by virtue of disciplinary orientation, view the world in a way that is more amenable to some value systems than others. That is, disciplinary perspective itself can be viewed as a sort of conflict of interest that can never be evaded. (Sarewitz, "Environmental Controversies," 392)

As we have seen in chapter 4, a variety of different methods exist to weigh the various values associated with environmental issues; it is not clear that the sin model form of deontology is the best method to use in all environmental issues.[8] Additionally, as we have seen in chapter 7, a variety of different kinds of solutions (potentially) exist for environmental problems. The sin model predisposition may act to make alternate solutions (besides eliminating the cause) less likely to be considered.

A second ethical theory predisposition is to consider all issues involving environmental problems as answerable by appeal to a categorical imperative. As we have argued throughout the book, while categorical imperatives are part of creation care—God's command to care for the environment is non-negotiable—this does not mean that we can apply categorical imperatives to many (if not most) of the questions regarding the content of creation care. Much of the criteria for obedience are determined through a variety of factors and ways of weighing values against one another, not through the identification and application of a duty or imperative. Duties are more important than practical considerations, but there are substantially fewer duties in creation care practice than commonly believed. A predisposition towards categorical imperatives provides a powerful motivation to persevere in caring for the environment, even when doing so is difficult and unpopular. This predisposition, however, also discourages compromise. When the parties to a conflict all consider the position they hold to be a required and non-negotiable duty, relatively few means exist to resolve the conflict besides the exercise of power.

A third ethical theory predisposition is to assume that we should decide all issues regarding environmental stewardship through a utilitarian or consequentialist calculus. Particularly since many proposed responses to environmental problems make heavy use of public policy instruments, and public policy justifications often involve cost-benefit analysis and obtaining

8. Consider, for instance, scholar Robert Royal's criticism of considering carbon emissions as sins:

> Carbon emissions are not intrinsically wrong. All animals that inhale oxygen and exhale carbon dioxide do so by natural design all the time. Even cars, electricity generating plants, and mechanical appliances—though artificial devices—do much good in addition to adding to atmospheric greenhouse gases. Deciding when and how to use them is not like deciding to cheat on your wife, an intrinsic wrong that requires confession and penance. It's more like deciding how much of the family income to allot for a better gas-mileage car, and how much for food, housing, healthcare, or education for the children. In other words, it's always a choice among competing goods—not between good and evil—within limited resources. (Royal, "Expiating")

"the greatest good for the greatest number," it is natural to default to using consequentialism to weigh the different policy options. Yet, as we saw in chapter 4, many goods—both environmental goods as well as goods associated with human flourishing—resist consequentialist computation. Many goods cannot be meaningfully converted into monetary equivalents, and thus, consequentialism skews decision-making away from policies that address or protect those goods. Still, the disposition towards consequentialism can encourage some forms of compromise, as it provides a kind of meeting ground on which different interests can negotiate with one another. The consequentialist mindset also can encourage pragmatic and inclusive approaches to environmental stewardship.

Processing Predispositions

Processing predispositions are predispositions related to the way we process—analyze, understand, consider, and integrate—the determinants of the criteria for obedience. The first processing predisposition is the predisposition to hold unexamined assumptions regarding the knowledge-policy connection. The two main areas of knowledge in which we often hold unexamined assumptions are in the nature of science and the nature of biblical revelation, and how each of these connects to policy. As we already have seen in chapters 3 and 5, there are a range of understandings we may have about the natures of biblical revelation and science—how they work as ways of knowing, the authority of their knowledge, etc.—and a range of understandings of the ways we can connect that knowledge to inform policy. Yet, for many, the unexamined assumption is that either or both forms of knowledge always directly dictates policy. Such an assumption may be true in certain cases, but in other cases, such an assumption may not be warranted. It is also often unclear how the directness shows itself. The assumption itself is powerful, however, and heavily impacts which policies are supported and the ways we advocate for those policies (e.g., relying on scientific experts to justify the policy).

A second processing predisposition is the predisposition to dialogue for the purpose of convincing versus to dialogue for the purpose of understanding. That is to say, oftentimes in environmental issues, we begin our conversations with others assuming we already know what needs to be done (perhaps justified by a policy prescriptive view of science or Scripture). Especially when we are advocates for a particular policy, we enter dialogue with the belief that the other side is wrong—possibly dangerously so. We may tolerate another perspective, but only if that perspective supports the policy goals we advocate. Thus, an advocate for policies to decarbonize the global economy may find common cause with both a renewable energy supplier driven by business goals as well as an activist for decreased consumption who is driven by a love for simplicity. Dialogue between these parties is focused not on understanding their differences but on achieving what all parties already believe needs to be done.

Such a predisposition can lead to the building of a broad coalition in support of a given goal. The policy goal becomes a common denominator that welcomes (at least temporarily) a variety of motivations and practices. At the same, if we instead approach dialogue with an attitude of openness—focused on understanding the other party and learning from them—we may have greater hope of identifying broader areas of agreement and compromise through clearing away mutual misunderstandings. Additionally, from the standpoint of synthesizing the determinants of the criteria for obedience, a predisposition to dialogue to convince versus understand can short-circuit our own internal dialogue. Instead of bringing the full range of the determinants into conversation with one another, we may settle for a partial synthesis or simplify our decision-making by assuming one of the determinants trumps all the others. Instead of accepting the tension of uncertainty that a complete synthesis may require, we may opt for the certainty of a premature and incomplete synthesis.

A third processing disposition is the "sum-of-the-parts" predisposition. In this predisposition, we assume that our understanding of the whole is determined by our understanding of the individual constituents that make up the whole. We can find this predisposition present in any number of ways with respect to how we process the determinants of the criteria for obedience. One place is in the approach we take to the synthesis process. If we hold a sum-of-the-parts predisposition, we may consider the determinants "constituents" of the "whole" of the criteria for obedience and accordingly may try to "add up" the determinants like an arithmetic problem, without considering that the elements of various determinants differ in kind, not merely in quantity. In this manner, a sum-of-the-parts approach treats the weighing of different values and evidence much as utilitarianism treats the weighing of different goods.

Another place we can find the sum-of-the-parts predisposition is in the manner we handle evidence and knowledge. Such a predisposition suggests that the way we come to know something is by aggregating all pertinent facts about a topic. Put another way, truth comes from a straightforward counting of the evidence for and against. In environmental issues, we may find this predisposition involved when we use a count of the number of studies or experts who support a position as establishing the truth of that position. A belief in the incrementalness of knowledge—that another study will incrementally increase our certainty in a given conclusion—may also be related to a sum-of-the-parts predisposition.

A final example of where we find the sum-of-the-parts predisposition is in the way we process societal versus individual responsibilities. The sum-of-the-parts predisposition implies that a society is merely the aggregation of its members, and thus, any collective obligation is merely the aggregation of individual obligations. If a society ought to exhibit some kind of behavior, it means that each individual in that society ought to exhibit that kind of behavior. For example, if we conclude that society as a whole needs to decrease emissions of carbon dioxide, the sum-of-the-parts predisposition assumes that such an obligation also falls on each individual person *in the same way and to the same degree.* If it is a categorical imperative for society then it is a categorical imperative for the individual. Similarly, if we conclude that society must protect individual liberties, the sum-of-the-parts predisposition assumes that such an obligation also falls on each individual person. When applied to the relation between the individual and society, the sum-of-the-parts predisposition may encourage policies that address the behavior of all individuals (rather than targeted policies) in order to achieve societal goals.

The sum-of-the-parts predisposition finds substantial support in its naturalness and intuitiveness. Whether in the physics principle of superposition (which says the total force on an object is the vector sum of all component forces on the object), democracy (where each person has one vote and majority rules), or the arithmetic of everyday life (one apple plus one apple is two apples), we encounter the sum-of-the-parts idea practically everywhere. At the same time, many problems do not yield to an arithmetic accounting (e.g., as we noted in our appraisal of utilitarianism in chapter 4). Societal imperatives also do not necessarily directly translate into individual imperatives. For instance, the pro-life imperatives of Catholic social teaching, while certainly encouraging an individual pro-natal stance, do not require such a stance, as can be seen in the high value Catholic teaching also places on celibate vocations like the priesthood. Of course, in the logic of Catholic teaching, these positions are complementary, not contradictory. Our point in this and similar examples is merely that the connection between a societal and individual imperative can be deeper and less straightforward than the sum-of-the-parts-predisposition expects. The sum-of-the-parts predisposition, like all predispositions, may be correct in some cases and incorrect in others, but in either case, the predisposition needs to be explicitly justified.

The Importance of Identifying Predispositions

In our above discussion of worldview, ethical theory, and processing predispositions, we have seen that predispositions may be quite consequential because they are often part of a mutually reinforcing web of convictions regarding the determinants of the criteria for obedience. As a result, a predisposition does not exist in isolation. One predisposition may beget another predisposition; a predisposition may affect our understanding of one or another of the determinants. In turn, these predispositions and determinants affect our view of still other predispositions and determinants.

Second, we have seen that predispositions are no different from any other truth claim. Indeed, in the case of the first two categories of predispositions, they are merely positions we hold regarding the determinants of the criteria for obedience. Predispositions are not, generally, categorically problematic, but as with all truth claims, predispositions need to be justified and may be unjustified. As we have seen, while there are reasons for each predisposition, there are also serious arguments against each predisposition, and if those criticisms are valid, the predispositions may harm efforts to care for nature. The predispositions may result in a synthesis that in turn generates sub-standard stewardship practices. We suggest that we have made a *prima facie* case that predispositions cannot be assumed but must be demonstrated as valid.

Yet, by their very nature, predispositions are hidden and assumed. They cannot be challenged or supported, nor can predispositions engage in full dialogue with the other determinants, because we are often unaware of the predispositions we hold. Indeed, the above predispositions may have struck you as obvious, but it is precisely the obviousness of predispositions that suggests we may have unconsciously assumed their validity. Fundamentally, synthesis requires the explicit and deliberate dialogue between the various determinants of the criteria, in order to make conclusions regarding the importance, goals, and practice of environmental stewardship. Predispositions impede such efforts at dialogue because they are unacknowledged and thus unexamined. More tragically, though predispositions can exert substantial influence in the shape, contours, and warp and weft of the synthesis we arrive at, the unexamined and habitual nature of predispositions hinders us from describing their influence on our understandings of the content of creation care. In order to create a synthesis that honestly wrestles with the full range of determinants of the criteria for obedience, we need to take accurate stock of our predispositions.

THE NATURE OF CONFLICT AND DIALOGUE

While the two topics we have considered thus far in this chapter—the goals and principles we should use in synthesizing the determinants of the criteria for obedience and predispositions in determining the content of creation care—are vital to understand if we are to achieve a synthesis regarding the content of creation care, both topics are primarily reflective regarding the cognitive and affective dimensions of environmental stewardship. We know, however, that nearly all environmental issues are issues concerning a community, and in most communities whose populations are greater than one, there is a range of different understandings regarding the criteria for obedience concerning environmental issues. Thus, we need to consider not only how to reflect on environmental stewardship but also how to do so in a community where others disagree with our conclusions. In this section, we consider the nature of conflict and dialogue and the factors related to getting to an agreement over the content of creation care.

As with many of the topics discussed in this book, the literature on conflict and dialogue is vast. In this section, we confine ourselves to summarizing the topic through two lenses. First, we take a social psychology view of what factors influence the resolution of conflict and present a summary from social psychologist Morton Deutsch's classic work on the subject, *The Resolution of Conflict.*[9] Second, we take a specifically biblical approach to "peacemaking" and present a summary of the process from *The Peacemaker,* by professional conciliator Ken Sande.[10] The two approaches complement each other in many ways, though they differ from one another in some of their foundational assumptions, aspects of the epistemology each uses, and some of their conclusions. Through taking these two approaches together, we draw lessons for the task of synthesizing a more robust understanding of the content of creation care.

In his typology, Deutsch draws a distinction between destructive versus constructive conflict.[11] In the former, the tendency is for the conflict to grow while the latter is characterized by traits similar to those found in creative thinking.[12] Deutsch also finds that destructive conflicts are more likely when the relationship between the parties are competitive, while constructive or productive conflicts are more likely when the parties relate in a

---

9. Deutsch, *Resolution.* I am grateful to Catherine Marsh, Professor of Management and Leadership in the School of Business and Nonprofit Management at North Park University, for pointing me to Deutsch's work.

10. Sande, *Peacemaker.*

11. Deutsch, *Resolution,* 351.

12. Ibid. 351, 360.

cooperative manner.[13] In addition, Deutsch finds that the consequences of cooperation tend to result in more cooperation, while the consequences of competition tend to result in more competition.[14] As a result, we expect it to be easier to achieve agreement over the content of creation care when we behave cooperatively rather than competitively.

What might this look like? Deutsch defines and describes six factors that affect conflict resolution: "process," "prior relationship," "the nature of the conflict," "characteristics of the parties," "estimations of success," and "third parties."[15] We briefly summarize each in turn and offer comments regarding their applicability to resolving environmental conflicts.

"Process" refers to the practices or activities that the parties of the conflict engage in: Do the parties behave in a friendly manner or antagonistically? Do they display an interest in one another or suspicion or hostility? Do they view the conflict as a mutual problem to be solved or as a zero-sum contest?[16] The processes of a conflict can be affective or driven by an attitude or spirit of mutual benefit. Processes of a conflict can also be structural, such as the rules that will be followed during the course of the conflict. An example of the latter could be rules governing a public debate between parties in a conflict: a cooperative process might be a rule in the debate where each side shares their introductory speech with the other side weeks before the debate takes place, thus decreasing the sense of antagonism in the debate. While cooperative processes do not necessarily lead to resolution of the conflict, they will tend to produce more cooperative behavior, which further increases the likelihood that the conflict will be constructive.[17]

"Prior relationship" refers to the history and kinds of connections between the parties to the conflict.[18] History that generates trust, such as a track record of successful cooperation, will generate more trust, while the reverse occurs with a history of distrust.[19] Likewise, shared community supports patient and open communication while the lack of common community can encourage an "us-them" mentality.

"The nature of the conflict" is itself characterized by six dimensions: "conflict size," "issue rigidity," "centrality of the issues," "number and interdependence of the issues," "consensus on the importance of different issues,"

13. Ibid., 351.
14. Ibid., 367.
15. Ibid., 368–76.
16. Ibid., 368.
17. Ibid., 368.
18. Ibid., 368.
19. Ibid., 368.

and "consciousness of the issues."[20] Conflict size refers, naturally, to how large the conflict is. In Deutsch's understanding, however, the size is not merely a function of the disagreement between the parties but also the size of the impact to yourself if your side wins versus if the other side wins.[21] Thus, as Deutsch notes:

> A conflict may be big because the participants perceive themselves to have important interests that are in opposition to one another, or it may be large, despite the congruence of their interests, because they have opposing views of how to pursue their important mutual interests—each thinking that his own proposed course would be favorable and the other's would be disastrous to their common interests.[22]

In this latter situation, closely knit parties (such as families) may experience larger conflict size not in spite of their shared interests but because of the intensity of those interests: if you believe your brother or sister's actions will be injurious to the well-being of the entire family, you will invest the conflict with more significance than would be the case in the absence of sibling affection.

The second and third dimensions of the nature of the conflict, issue rigidity and centrality of the issues, refer to whether alternatives exist to resolve the issue and whether the issue is a core issue, respectively.[23] In the former case, if a conflict has low issue rigidity—if a number of alternatives exist to address the issue at stake—the conflict has greater chance of being resolved. In the latter case, the less central or pivotal the issues, the greater the likelihood of resolving the conflict. In contrast, issues of survival, for instance, have high issue centrality.[24]

The fourth and fifth dimensions of the nature of the conflict—the number and interdependence of the issues and the level of consensus on the importance of different issues, respectively—describe whether a conflict can be broken down into sub-conflicts and whether the parties have a similar view of the centrality of the different issues in the conflict, respectively.[25] In the former case, a conflict with many, interdependent issues is less likely to be resolved than a conflict with few issues that can each be addressed

20. Ibid., 369–73.
21. Ibid., 369.
22. Ibid.
23. Ibid., 370–71.
24. Ibid., 371.
25. Ibid., 372.

in isolation from the others.[26] In the latter case, disagreement between the parties on the importance of an issue can improve the chances of resolving a conflict over that issue.[27] The final dimension of the nature of the conflict, consciousness of the issues, refers to whether the parties in the conflict acknowledge the existence of and reasons for the conflict.[28] It is difficult to resolve a conflict if we do not believe we are in one.

"Characteristics of the parties" is the fourth factor that affects conflict resolution. These attributes include the beliefs, ideals, personality traits, etc. of the parties involved, and as we may expect, the kind of person we are and the way we think can greatly influence the trajectory of a conflict.[29] For example, if both the parties in a conflict have personalities that are more inclined towards cooperation—for instance, if both have a "win-win" outlook—this may increase the likelihood that the conflict will be resolved, as each party will gravitate towards cooperative actions that can fuel a productive outcome. In contrast, if both parties have antagonistic personalities, this may help escalate the conflict. Note that as the name suggests, the characteristics of the parties are attributes of the people or groups involved in the conflict, not attributes of the conflict itself or of issues related to the conflict.

"Estimations of success" is the fifth factor that affects conflict resolution. This factor describes the various ways parties can conceive of whether the conflict will conclude favorably or not, and whether those conceptions support a competitive or cooperative stance.[30] For instance, a party that believes a favorable outcome for the conflict is one that permits the parties involved to work together in the long-term will tend towards cooperative behaviors and processes.[31] In contrast, a party that understands success in adversarial, legal terms may tend towards competitive processes.

The sixth and final factor affecting conflict resolution is the presence and activity of third parties. Deutsch notes that while sometimes a third party can worsen a conflict, often the mere presence of a third party can help move a conflict towards resolution.[32] The widespread use of third parties as mediators, arbiters, and judges—whether in the form of a jury in a

---

26. Ibid., 372.
27. Ibid.
28. Ibid.
29. Ibid., 373–75.
30. Ibid., 375–76.
31. Ibid., 376.
32. Ibid.

courtroom or a referee in a soccer game—attests to the usefulness of third parties in resolving conflicts.

What aspects of these six factors affecting conflict resolution do environmental controversies exhibit? It probably comes as little surprise that while some environmental conflicts (particularly local ones) exhibit characteristics that lead to constructive resolution of the conflict, many environmental controversies exhibit the characteristics Deutsch associates with competitive factors that lead to destructive conflicts. Consider, for instance, the conflict over global warming. First, the process of this conflict is often characterized by a zero-sum mentality. Second, since many of the proposed solutions involve decarbonization of the global economy, nearly every possible interest group is impacted, and the breadth of kinds of parties involved in the conflict decreases the likelihood of a prior relationship or shared community between them. Each side comes from a different world. Third, because the conflict is often framed as a choice between two catastrophes (destruction from extreme weather events and inundation from sea-level rise on the one hand and destruction of the global economy on the other), discussions of solutions focus on the "eliminate the cause" option, the controversy is heavily scientized, and the nature of the conflict is marked by large conflict size, high issue rigidity, high centrality of the issues, large number and interdependence of the issues, unhelpful consensus on the importance of the different issues, and low consciousness of the issues involved in the conflict (outside of the science). Fourth, again because global warming touches such a wide range of interest groups, the characteristics of the parties involved cover the spectrum of ideologies, beliefs, and personalities, and the estimations of success of these parties cover the gamut of those that encourage cooperation and those that encourage competition. Finally, in the global warming debate, few neutral third parties exist. Even those that have putatively played a mediating role, such as the Intergovernmental Panel on Climate Change, have at times found themselves embroiled in controversy or accused of being a party to the conflict. Taken together, the global warming conflict possesses many of the factors Deutsch identifies as hindering constructive resolution. The case of global warming, admittedly, is somewhat unique; few contemporary environmental issues or their proposed solutions have, for instance, a similar level of potential impact on people and ecosystems. Nonetheless, a number of the factors related to the resolution of conflict that we find in the global warming conflict are also shared by other environmental controversies. As we have seen in the preceding chapters of this book, differing worldview, ethical theories, and understandings of science and society determine our estimations of the importance, goals, and practice of creation care. These determinants and criteria also influence Deutsch's factors related to the resolution of conflict.

Deutsch's social psychology taxonomy helps us identify factors that make successful conflict resolution more or less probable and as such provide a framework of behaviors and attitudes to encourage or discourage. Sande's biblical peacemaking approach, in many places, supports Deutsch's taxonomy. Sande's approach, however, provides additional guidance and resources for conflict resolution. For example, Sande's process provides context-independent rationales and encouragement for choosing cooperative behaviors and attitudes even when a chorus of pressures tells us to do otherwise. A biblical framework also addresses not only what we can do to make conflict resolution more probable but also the root causes—causes connected not merely to the nature of the conflict or even the nature of the parties of the conflict but to the nature of being human—of destructive conflicts. Most importantly, Sande's process centers conflict resolution on living in the power and example of Jesus Christ whose own sacrificial death for us reconciles us to God the Father. Emulation of Jesus—being a "little Christ"—and empowered to do so by the Holy Spirit, is central to life.

Sande identifies four principles to Christian peacemaking, which he calls the "Four G's": "glorify God," "get the log out of your own eye," "gently restore," and "go and be reconciled."[33] The first principle, "glorify God," tells us to ask, "How can I please and honor God in this situation?"[34] The first impulse for many of us, when we find ourselves in a conflict, is to focus on the conflict itself and our interests in the conflict. The Bible, however, asks us to instead focus on obeying and honoring God. This is a holistic activity. It occurs not only in the decisions we make and actions we take in the conflict, but also in the attitudes we have as we decide and act. We trust that God is in control, that He gives us the strength to obey Him, and that we can rely on Him for what is best.[35] Honoring God may also involve sacrifice: it may mean voluntarily yielding our rights in love to others, choosing to forgive in the midst of hurt or anger, or working to understand the other party in the conflict even when they seem unreasonable. And, the first "G" recognizes that achieving peace—an honest, true, lasting peace—itself brings glory to God because He is the original Peacemaker.

The second "G," "get the log out of your own eye," tells us to ask, "How can I show Jesus' work in me by taking responsibility for my contribution to

33. Sande, *Peacemaker*, 38.

34. Ibid., 17.

35. Ibid., 31.

this conflict?"[36] Again, this is in contrast to our natural tendency to justify ourselves or take umbrage at the way we believe the other party is treating us. The Bible instead tells us to ask in what ways I have contributed to the conflict and to confess our sins and ask for forgiveness from those we have wronged. We tend to see our own faults as small and those of others as large. The reverse, Jesus tells us, is what often is true, and the only way we will be able to help someone with their faults is to first deal with our own.[37]

The third "G," "gently restore," tells us to ask, "How can I lovingly serve others by helping them take responsibility for their contribution to this conflict?"[38] At first glance, this may seem contradictory to the first two principles: it sounds as if we are being told to be self-righteous and judgmental, preoccupied with correcting the other party's faults. Nothing could be further from the truth. The third "G" recognizes that in many conflicts, most if not all of the parties to the conflict have contributed something negative to the conflict. In a Christian community, we are called to be patient, humble, sacrificial, and non-judgmental, but we are also called to love others and help them leave sin, which harms both others and themselves.[39] To the extent that the other party in the conflict has committed a major offense, Christian peacemaking calls us to walk alongside and restore our brother or sister from that offense. This is to be done with the utmost humility, respect, gentleness, and wisdom.[40] Even so, such efforts at restoration are sometimes misunderstood. Yet, biblical peacemaking would not be complete without the restoration principle since biblical peace is not merely the absence of war between two separate parties but the presence of *shalom* between us and God and with one another. The goal is not only to stop fighting but for all parties in the conflict to become more like Jesus Christ.

The fourth and final "G," "go and be reconciled," tells us to ask, "How can I demonstrate the forgiveness of God and encourage a reasonable

---

36. Ibid., 75.

37. Matt 7:3-5 [Jesus speaking]:

> "Why do you look at the speck of sawdust in your brother's eye and pay no attention to the plank in your own eye? How can you say to your brother, 'Let me take the speck out of your eye,' when all the time there is a plank in your own eye? You hypocrite, first take the plank out of your own eye, and then you will see clearly to remove the speck from your brother's eye.

38. Sande, *Peacemaker*, 139.

39. Gal 6:1.

40. See Sande, *Peacemaker*, chapter 8 for specific suggestions on how to gently restore another.

solution to this conflict?"[41] In this principle, we see again that the goal of biblical conflict resolution is not the mere cessation of hostilities but the restoration of relationship. The *shalom* between God and us is to permeate into all of our relationships with one another, especially into those relationships that have been marked with enmity. But how is this to be achieved? Particularly in conflicts where we have been grievously wronged, how do we ever achieve reconciliation? The key and first step is God-empowered forgiveness, the voluntary yielding of our right to hold the wrong against the offender. Sande describes forgiveness as an act of the will where we make four promises to the offender:

> "I will not dwell on this incident."
> "I will not bring up this incident again and use it against you."
> "I will not talk to others about this incident."
> "I will not let this incident stand between us or hinder our personal relationship."[42]

Forgiving is not easy, nor is it a one-time act; we often need to forgive one another day after day. Only through first forgiving, however, can we achieve reconciliation. Sande describes the process this way:

> Making the four promises of forgiveness is an event that knocks down a wall that stands between you and a person who has wronged you. Then a process begins. After you demolish an obstruction, you usually have to clear away debris and do repair work. The Bible calls this "reconciliation," a process involving a change of attitude that leads to a change in the relationship. More specifically, to be reconciled means to replace hostility and separation with peace and friendship. This is what Jesus had in mind when he said, "Go and be reconciled to your brother" (Matt. 5:24; cf. 1 Cor. 7:11; 2 Cor. 5:18–20).[43]

The process of reconciliation is slow and difficult and involves not only the repair of the personal issues impacted by the conflict but also the resolution of the material ones related to the conflict.[44] When the resolution of the latter requires negotiation, Sande recommends cooperative versus competitive negotiation.[45] He notes biblical passages that counsel us to look

---

41. Sande, *Peacemaker*, 201.
42. Ibid., 209.
43. Ibid., 219.
44. Ibid., 225.
45. Ibid., 226–27.

"to the interests of the others"[46] and concludes that Scripture encourages us to practice cooperative negotiation.[47] Sande then lays out five tasks of cooperative negotiation, summarized in the acronym PAUSE: "prepare," "affirm relationships," "understand interests," "search for creative solutions," and "evaluate options objectively and reasonably."[48] By paying attention to these tasks as we negotiate, we can improve our chances of a positive outcome.

What might the Four G's tell us about navigating an environmental controversy? Perhaps first and foremost, these principles challenge us to redefine what a successful resolution to a conflict looks like. Our natural inclination is to consider "success" as when our policy position prevails over the alternatives. We may also hope for an outcome where hard-feelings are minimized and the least amount of legal and political pressure is used to accomplish our victory, but these are secondary to achieving the "main" objective. The Four G's ask us to re-evaluate whether such a bar for success is too low or the wrong bar to begin with. This biblical framework challenges us to both attend to the process we use to achieve our outcomes as well as to our choice of outcomes. For instance, the Four G's may ask us to consider whether our approach to solving every environmental issue should be the application of all the levers of power politics; perhaps not every such lever, in every instance, glorifies God. Or, the Four G's may ask us to consider more closely the needs and considerations of our opponents. Is it really true that our own policy preference is the only one worth adopting? Are there ways we might alter our policy goals to enable us to honorably achieve both our core goals as well as those of our opponents?

Second, Sande's framework challenges us to walk in humility rather than self-righteousness. Particularly in environmental controversies that have been thoroughly scientized, there is little room to acknowledge weaknesses or lacunae in the scientific evidence backing one's position on the issue. An attitude of humility seems tantamount to surrender in the policy debate. The Four G's, with their emphasis on acknowledging and dealing with our own shortcomings, prior to helping correct the shortcomings of others, challenges us to do otherwise, to choose humility even in the midst of conflict. We are encouraged towards patience with others and a spirit of compromise and away from over-claiming the evidence for our own position or vilifying our opponents.

Finally, the Four G's challenge us to remember the conflict is not merely one over ideas but is a conflict between people. In a conflict, we need to

46. Phil 2:3–4.

47. Sande, *Peacemaker*, 227.

48. Ibid., 227–28.

attend not only to the truth and persuasiveness of our arguments but also to the love and care we show our neighbor who stands on the other side from us in the conflict. Environmental controversies often exhibit traits that make it difficult for us to meet this challenge. Because of the role of science in environmental issues, it is easy to consider environmental conflicts as bloodless, mere analytical battles over policy. At the same time, because our stance on an environmental issue draws heavily from our worldview, ethical, political, and economic understandings, we cannot help but experience a passionate connection to that stance. We care, and it is important that we care. However, "objective-passion" is a mix that can easily result in competitive attitudes and behaviors that escalate the conflict and damage relationships and people. The Four G's ask us, instead, to include reconciliation outcomes as part of our goals for solving an environmental conflict. (Pragmatically, such reconciliation may increase the chances of policy stability, but we are also challenged to consider reconciliation as an end in itself.)

Environmental issues are often contentious, but conflicts do not have to be destructive. Instead, conflicts present an opportunity for creativity, dialogue, and reconciliation. Deutsch and Sande's frameworks outline the steps needed to minimize the likelihood of environmental controversies becoming intractable and harmful while maximizing the likelihood of resolving the conflict in a healthy and productive manner. In the next section, as we consider alternative ways forward with regards to environmental stewardship, we also attend to examining how these alternative ways may help or hinder the resolution of environmental controversies.

ALTERNATIVE WAYS FORWARD

We began this chapter by setting out goals and principles we should use in synthesizing the determinants of the criteria for obedience. Then, we examined predispositions in determining the content of creation care, enumerating some pitfalls to avoid as we engage in synthesis. In the previous section, we considered the nature of conflict and dialogue and factors to consider in resolving conflict over the content of creation care. In this section, building off of the ground we have covered in this book, we propose alternative approaches to use in creating a synthesis regarding environmental stewardship. These approaches are not, in and of themselves, a synthesis of the determinants of the criteria for obedience. Neither are they goals of synthesis nor predispositions to be careful of, which we discussed earlier. Rather, our list of "ways forward" provides advice regarding how we might achieve a synthesis that is more fruitful and results in more creative, cooperative, and politically stable creation care practices than current approaches built around power and dominance. They are not prescriptions of moral command but rather propose a path to take. To expand the analogy further, if a proper synthesis of the determinants of the criteria for obedience—a synthesis that leads to excellent creation care—is the "destination" of a journey, the goals and principles of synthesis (that we presented earlier in this chapter) are a travel guide description of the destination. The predispositions we described earlier in this chapter are forks that lead us down side trails. Some side trails may lead us far away from our destination. Other side trails may end up being rabbit trails, ending nowhere and circling in on themselves. Still other side trails may, eventually, lead us to our desired destination, but not without a lot of bushwhacking along the way. The alternative ways forward that we propose are a solid, well-hewn trail to our destination. It is not a freeway. The trail is still a trail. It is uneven and is not easy to walk. Roots stick out of the ground here and there. We may stumble and fall while hiking on it and never reach our destination. Still, the trail does work. It is a fruitful path to walk and a good first choice for taking us to our destination. The path of alternative ways that we propose has six elements: consider a multiplicity of solutions, utilize multiple understandings of environmental value, recognize multiple forms of knowledge, avoid zero-sum thinking, acknowledge inherent paradoxes and legitimate differences, and realize people and relationships matter.

The first element in our alternative approach towards a synthesis concerning environmental stewardship is to consider a multiplicity of solutions. We saw in chapter 7 that, in principle, there is a broad range of possible solutions for any problem. Not all the options in that range are necessarily good options in every situation, and for some environmental problems, only a few options may be reasonable to entertain. Many environmental problems, however, do not fall under such a category: these problems have many reasonable solutions and the best solutions (from a policy stability standpoint) are obtained through dialogue and compromise. Yet, particularly when we utilize the "sin model" in thinking through the solutions to problems, we often default to just one class of possible options—eliminating the cause—and do so unnecessarily. In doing so, in forgetting that many environmental problems are different from other problems (such as personal sin) and may have many valid solutions, we limit our ability to engage in excellent creation care. In contrast, when we seek to consider a broader range of possible solutions, either in principle or with regards to a particular environmental issue, we create opportunities: more possible ways to balance competing values and decreased issue rigidity that enables more opportunities for dialogue between stakeholders.

The second element in our alternative approach is similar to the first: we suggest that the process of synthesis is more likely to be successful when we utilize multiple understandings of environmental value and how to weigh values related to environmental issues. In chapter 4, we surveyed many of the major theories regarding what has value in the environment and how do we weigh differing values against one another. In considering the former, we found that in many cases the various theories of value in the environment are complementary or supplementary to one another, rather than necessarily mutually exclusive with each other. In considering the latter, we argued that different paradigms for weighing values (deontology, consequentialism, virtue ethics, etc.) not only have different strengths and weaknesses but also differing levels of applicability depending on the context. Environmental issues, which often operate under multiple contexts, may thus benefit from the use of multiple ways of weighing values.

Arguing for the use of multiple ways of valuing and weighing values is not, as some might fear, a brief for relativism. In suggesting the use of multiple ways of valuing, we are not saying that all ways are valid because none are "true." We are not saying all that matters regarding the value of the environment is personal preference. Instead, because the different ways of valuing are not, in general, mutually exclusive, the use of multiple ways of valuing has little to no impact on the truth claims of each kind of value. In terms of the weighing of values, the use of multiple paradigms also creates no argument for relativism, if we use the paradigms in different contexts. One way of valuing can be true in one circumstance while another can be true in a different circumstance.

Debates over environmental ethics, however, do often sound as if they are winner-take-all contests between two competing versions of the true and the right. One side claims the other views nature as a vending machine for raw materials while the other side replies that at least they are not worshipping microbes. Each side claims right is on their side and that if we do not fight for what is right, nothing will change. And, each side seems concerned that admitting the other side's ways of valuing will not only undercut their own position but also lead to a cascade of harms: encouraging the greedy exploitation of nature, legitimizing the denigration and dehumanizing of people, etc. We fear that tolerance of another way of valuing (let alone selective use of multiple ways of valuing in a synthesis of the determinants of the criteria for obedience) is tantamount to calling a falsehood, truth, a wrong, right.

Perhaps these fears are legitimate. And yet, our reluctance to consider multiple ways of valuing comes with its own costs. As we have seen in earlier chapters, many environmental issues are complex and do not easily fit into neat categories. Environmental issues, particularly controversial ones, involve many different kinds of values under many different contexts, can be riddled with uncertainties, often defy prescriptive ways of creating successful policy responses, and frequently spill out of the control of the individual into the realm of the community. An insistence on there being only one way of understanding and weighing values makes it that much harder to arrive at prudent and stable solutions. Regarding these missed opportunities, it is worth quoting at length arguments by theologian Cristina L. H. Traina (in discussing the advantages of a natural law approach to environmental ethics):

> Second, environmental ethics has frequently been hamstrung by debates over which moral standpoint should anchor the conversation (animal rights, species preservation, ecosystematic balance for its own sake, or ecosystematic balance for the sake of human flourishing) and over what degree of commitment is necessary (conservation within an existing life-style versus radical social and economic transformation). Just as problematic as these impasses are authors and activists who either combine these rhetorics without acknowledging tensions among them or falsely treat them as mutually exclusive. As Drew Christiansen has pointed out, natural law thought has something to teach us here: the prudent, self-conscious, and appropriate use of multiple strategies.
>
> For instance, there may need to be a distinction between the minimal precepts of ecological justice that everyone must fulfill and the ecological counsels of perfection embraced by deep ecology. The latter keep an inspiring, prophetic ideal before everyone but demand a level of commitment not to be expected of people for whom the goal of living as lightly as possible on the earth may need to give way slightly to other ends like basic survival or a vocation of service to others. Similarly, all must adhere to public standards of justice, but there is also the order of charity in which I and those closest to me deserve my special consideration; global thinking must never preclude social action. Likewise, self-sacrifice, even martyrdom, commands a high value, but self-preservation is a basic and appropriate human inclination. Each of these rational impulses contains an invaluable insight, but none is, in practice, adequate in itself. It would thus be inappropriate either to reduce the natural law tradition to any one of these elements or to minimize the potential for conflict between them. Rather, the point is to use measures of justice and urgency to blend them in different proportions in

diverse situations, depending upon what is at stake, in light of the supreme criterion of charity.[49]

We suggest prudent openness to multiple ways of understanding value regarding the environment offers more hope of achieving a successful synthesis than the alternative.

The third element in our alternative approach towards a synthesis concerning environmental stewardship is to appreciate and incorporate multiple forms of knowledge into the task of determining the content of creation care. This can take place in a variety of dimensions: the rational with the non-rational (intuitive and subjective), empirical with the non-empirical, special revelation with general revelation, etc. Science, Scripture, philosophy, intuition, love, compassion, a sense of place, aesthetics, and other ways of knowing all have their place in the task of determining the content of environmental stewardship. As we have seen throughout this book, the different types of knowledge have strengths and weaknesses and their own proper domains of authority. We have also seen that we often utilize a small subset of the forms of knowledge to the exclusion of the others. For instance, we sometimes treat reason as if it were omnicompetent, but while reason is an extremely powerful and important way of knowing, it too has limits in what it can tell us, particularly regarding the value of things. Our reasons to use reason may not always be reasonable. When we use only a few ways of knowing, we may miss insights available through the other forms of knowledge, or we may end up at conclusions that are not quite so well-founded because we ignored correctives those other forms of knowledge would have provided. We have also seen that a proper and complete evaluation of the criteria for obedience, in all likelihood, requires multiple forms of knowledge. With many of the determinants, there is a complex interplay between philosophy or values and empirical investigations through the natural and social sciences, and the use of one form of knowing without considering the other forms of knowing can lead to major lacunae in our evaluation of the criteria for obedience. Explicitly incorporating multiple forms of knowledge (in their appropriate realms of applicability) can help prevent the creation of such blind spots.

The fourth element in our alternative approach is to avoid a zero-sum mentality. We can identify at least two ways a zero-sum mentality influences our determination of the content of creation care. First, on a practical level, a zero-sum mentality makes it more difficult to engage in productive dialogue, consider multiple viewpoints, compromise, and create a broad versus narrow synthesis. A zero-sum mentality, as the term suggests, means that

49. Traina, "Response," 253.

one side in an issue or conflict can win or succeed only at the cost of the other side: "This town ain't big enough for the both of us," as the steely-eyed Wild West sheriff might have said to the hardened outlaw. However, while we are supposed to root for the righteous lawman, a zero-sum mentality, as suggested in our earlier discussion of social psychology principles related to conflict resolution, can make destructive conflict more likely and a constructive resolution of a conflict less likely.

Zero-sum mentalities are perhaps most obvious in conflicts: If I win, you lose, or vice versa. But, a zero-sum mentality can also affect how we process an issue. For instance, if we understand the different forms of valuing nature—anthropocentric, ecocentric, etc.—as always mutually exclusive, we will process the determinants of creation care differently than if we admit that some of the different ways of valuing nature can be complementary to one another. This difference in understanding the nature of the value of nature can lead to real differences in the creation care practices (both which practices and their justifications) we advocate for. In general, when our positions regarding the determinants of the criteria for obedience tend towards exclusivity—that is, where our understanding of the correctness of our position automatically prevents us from considering how other positions might inform our appraisal of the determinants—our processing of the determinants will naturally be affected. In many cases, this will result in a use of a narrower range of forms of knowing, rather than a broader range.

A second way a zero-sum mentality can affect our analysis of environmental stewardship is also philosophical, but in this category, the effect is not through our adoption of a zero-sum position regarding a determinant (i.e., where our position excludes other positions) but rather through the intrinsic propensity of some positions regarding the determinants to cast reasoning about creation into zero-sum terms. For instance, many (though not all) advocates of a simpler lifestyle argue that human consumption, driven by a consumerist culture, leads to environmental destruction. This logic connects a material activity (consumption) to a material effect (environmental destruction). We have seen earlier that because of the is-ought distinction, such logic is incomplete if it is to undergird an ethical argument; we need to provide a value proposition in order to complete the argument as an ethical argument (e.g., environmental destruction is categorically wrong).

The incomplete logic of the argument has another effect. By leaving out the value proposition but claiming validity, the argument implicitly argues for a materialistic ontology and ethic, where the only form of being is material and material effects automatically result in ethical obligations. But matter is inherently zero-sum. In a Galilean-Newtonian sense (as expressed in the law of conservation of mass), the only way to increase the amount of matter in one place is to take matter away from another. In the context of the consumption issue, the implication is that because consumption and environmental well-being are entirely material, the benefit of one has to come at the expense of the other. The framing effect of the consumption-environmental destruction argument is thus to encourage a zero-sum understanding of the environmental issue, an understanding that can artificially narrow our analysis of the issue and impede the creation of novel and innovative solutions to the problem.

This framing effect is not only unfortunate but also—at least in our example of the consumption-environmental destruction argument—unnecessary. Traditionally, ethical arguments for a simple lifestyle or sacrificial giving have not been based on a materialistic ethic but rather on notions of love, community, and place as well as virtue and the good life. Even sacrificial giving—the kind of charity exemplified by the early Christians—has traditionally been justified using a non-zero-sum, non-materialist ethic; ethicist Daniel Kim notes that early Christian leaders, for instance, "conceived sacrificial charity as being beneficial to both the giver and the community."[50] These kinds of justifications would neither view consumption as inherently wrong (instead critiquing "excess" or "improper" consumption) nor feel compelled to do so. These kinds of justifications would view consumption as one human activity among many, prone to abuse to be sure, but not *necessarily* yoked to environmental degradation. An ethic based on a materialist ontology has greater difficulty in justifying such nuance.

In reply, we might argue that even if we try to avoid a zero-sum mentality, some situations have some zero-sum element to them. Are we then to assume a Pollyannaish attitude towards the zero-sum elements and ignore them? No. Sometimes, there are irreducible conflicts between different positions and compromise is not possible. But, as we have seen throughout this book, the range of compatible positions with regards to the determinants is substantial and suggests that many of the zero-sum choices we encounter in environmental issues are more apparently zero-sum than actually so. In those cases, we can work through the apparent zero-sum nature through clarifying assumptions and finding common ground as well as through choosing policies that build ground on which to counteract zero-sum thinking. We elaborate on the latter in the next few paragraphs as we address the fifth element in our alternative approach.

The fifth element in our alternative approach is to accept inherent paradoxes and legitimate differences and build policy solutions that are resilient to those paradoxes and differences. We have seen, throughout this

---

50. Kim, "Explaining," 16.

book, a nearly overwhelming range of positions regarding the determinants of the criteria for obedience and how those positions may interact with one another in determining the criteria for obedience. Even if this diversity of positions often does not demand a zero-sum mentality, as we argued above, clearly there are paradoxes and differences between the range of possible positions. In this fifth element of an alternative approach, we argue for room to accept and strategies to accommodate those paradoxes and differences.

In commending paradox and the tension it begets, we must first note that we are not arguing against logical consistency within an argument or a position. Earlier in this chapter in our description of the goals of synthesis, we argued that a proper synthesis of the determinants of the criteria for obedience should have logical consistency between the parts of the synthesis. Non-contradiction is a powerful characteristic of truth. Yet, we also noted earlier that all syntheses will fail; while truth cannot contradict itself, our limited and finite models of the truth may. The question for us, rather, is whether our synthesis will fail "well" or not. Our understanding of creation care will contain paradoxes: what we get to choose is the kind of paradoxes they have and how will we respond to those paradoxes.

One way of approaching the issue of paradoxes regarding the content of creation care is a pragmatic one. We acknowledge that environmental stewardship requires the juggling of a cornucopia of different values, some of which are contradictory to one another, and we decide the best way to do so is to do "what works." We learn to live with some baseline level of uncertainty and adopt an attitude characterized by openness, the reserving of judgment, and compromise. A pragmatic approach does not necessarily do away with principle and commitment, but prudential choices occupy a much more prominent place under such an approach of dealing with paradoxes. We saw some elements of this approach earlier this chapter in our extended quotation by Cristina L. H. Traina, who observed that the quest for a kind of value "purity" regarding environmental issues has been a dead-end; instead, the prioritization of multiple values expressed through prudence and the use of multiple approaches may be the more productive route.

Pragmatism, however, is not the only way to deal with the paradox inherent in any framework for determining the content of creation care. Taking a cue from virtue ethics, which views following exemplars as one of the primary ways of learning virtues, we find that perhaps the best illustrations of how to accept paradox positively are found in the lives of the virtuous and the ways they deal with paradox. One reason to look at a life, rather than a philosophy, to understand paradox is that a life naturally integrates discordant and contradictory elements in a synthesis that transcends the individual elements themselves. That is to say, there is something about human living itself that organically synthesizes ideas in a way that description, reason, and analysis cannot. The synthesis is not merely in the thoughts of a person or even their actions but rather in the entirety and integrity of the person. Preeminently, we see this in the integrity of the nature of who Jesus was, is, and will be: fully man and fully God. In a much smaller way, we see this in our own lives, in our nature as both material and spiritual beings, as well as in the lesser paradoxes that are part of who we are as persons.

Of course, such a synthesis is best apprehended through actually knowing and sharing in the life of a person, not merely through reading about a life. What is true about mentoring and discipleship—that more is caught than taught—is true about our efforts at learning from the lives of others, particularly when we want to learn about an aspect of living that is characterized by extreme subtlety and paradox. Still, perhaps there is something we can learn about what it means to accept paradox in environmental issues by pondering one particular exemplar: our parents. All of us, whether we knew them or not, have parents, and many of us have experienced being a parent. These experiences are obviously multi-faceted, but they are also suffused with paradox. One moment your child thinks you are the worst father or mother in the world for not letting them play with their friends while the next moment your child wants you to sing them a lullaby before they sleep. One moment your child treats their brother or sister with the most endearing and considerate tenderness while the next moment you are disciplining them for an angry tantrum directed at that same brother or sister. To be a parent is to be tired, frazzled, worried, willful, angry, hypocritical ("do what I say, not what I do"), overbearing, feeling guilty at being overbearing, harried, and poor. To be a parent is also to be proud, joyful, beloved, moved to tears, satisfied, purpose-filled, humbled, and rich. To be a parent is to experience in a microcosm the sacrificial love of God, our Heavenly Father, of whom the Bible says: "But God demonstrates his own love for us in this: While we were still sinners, Christ died for us."[51]

What does being a parent tell us about accepting paradox with regards to environmental issues? First, it tells us that paradox is not something to avoid—being neither possible to avoid nor desirable to avoid—as the "mass of hard prosaic reality"[52] of life lies in those paradoxes. Second, being a parent tells us that coherence can exist amidst contradiction. We try to be consistent in our teaching, discipline, and treatment of our children, but the lack of consistency does not automatically invalidate our parenting goals

51. Rom 5:8.

52. Hardy, *Far From*, 339. Hardy used this phrase in a different way than we are using it.

and actions. We sometimes have to tell our children, "Yes, I know I told you that, but . . . ," yet doing so does not mean our parenting has become a random free-for-all. Third, accepting paradox is partly analytical but is mostly relational. As parents, we weigh pros and cons of how to raise our children and try to figure out what is right and wrong. We read Scripture, books on parenting, talk with those who have gone before us in our child's stage of life, and pray—a lot. But, the core of parenting is the relationship we have with our children. That is to say, being a parent is not fundamentally a job but a relationship, one that is bound with sacrifice, trust, loyalty, communion, and love. It is a connection between two *persons* (indeed, the first natural connection of all human beings), not a connection between two roles or positions.[53] We accept paradox the way we accept children or friends, not the way we accept anything else: ideas, circumstances, etc. Fourth and finally, in the paradoxes of parenting, we see love really does cover a multitude of sins, both the sins of the parents and the sins of the children. So too, love covers a multitude of contradictions in a framework for understanding environmental stewardship. This does not mean sentimentality obviates reason. It does mean that just as love between parents and children cover many failures of both, so too love—of and by God and people—covers failures in our synthesis of the determinants of the criteria for obedience.

In addition to accepting inherent paradoxes, we suggest that an alternative way forward should also include the acceptance of legitimate differences between people regarding environmental issues. We contend that many of the differences between the various positions regarding environmental issues are legitimate rather than illegitimate differences. This is not to say that there cannot be sharp disagreements between the different positions or that all viewpoints are correct or truthful. Rather, legitimate differences are those that can be tolerated while illegitimate differences are those that cannot be tolerated. By "tolerance," we do not mean moral neutrality. Rather, following political ethicist J. Budziszewski, we understand that, "To tolerate something is to put up with it even though we might be tempted to suppress it."[54] Suppression of arguments often creates evils of its own, and so Budziszewski argues that we use the following test to decide when to tolerate: "When the evil that suppression engenders equals or exceeds the evil that it prevents, we ought to put up with the thing in question instead of suppressing it."[55]

---

53. The relational core of parenting is what enables parenting to survive the contradictions of life.

54. Budziszewski, "Illusion."

55. Ibid.

Thus, accepting legitimate differences means to tolerate them, which means not to suppress those who hold an opposing view. Argue and persuade, passionately even, but tolerate. Yet, so much of what passes today as dialogue regarding environmental issues skates awfully close to the line of suppression, and sometimes (perhaps often) crosses over. Environmental issues may be charged with the tone of a moral crusade where dialogue, let alone, compromise, is understood as "selling out." Those who disagree with our position are insulted, isolated, and demonized. The views they hold are ridiculed and labeled as unbiblical, anti-science, paranoid, ignorant, or beyond the pale of what "right and reasonable" people would hold. (To argue that a certain position does not follow from the clearest reading of Scripture is not the same as calling the position unbiblical. Likewise, to argue that a certain position is not justified by the current scientific evidence is not the same as calling the position anti-science. The key differentiation is that in the latter cases, the claim (unbiblical, anti-science) is geared to isolate the position rather than engage it.) While such tactics may, particularly by low-power groups, be effective in advancing an agenda,[56] they neither enhance dialogue nor build policy stability and are often disrespectful.

If we choose to accept inherent paradoxes and legitimate differences, how do we design policy solutions that are resilient to those paradoxes and differences? Accepting paradoxes and differences should not have to result in gridlock, inaction, avoidance, or capitulation. In a zero-sum environment, where conflict is adjudicated by power, those appear to be the consequences of tolerance. There are, however, alternative ways of designing policy solutions that can both support the acceptance of paradoxes and differences as well as nurture policies. We have seen a few of these methods in the earlier chapters of this book. For instance, moderate, iterative approaches, built from reversible steps, help limit the risk inherent in uncertainty and paradox (and help avoid zero-sum scenarios) while enabling policy movement.[57] Roger A. Pielke, Jr.'s honest broker model offers a framework for including science into the policymaking process that leaves more room for legitimate differences while also facilitating a richer dialogue regarding what science says about the problem and how value judgments might enter into the policymaking process.[58] Finally, Daniel Kemmis's collaboration method of resource management policymaking, that relies on local knowledge to bring together disparate stakeholders in creating a shared management plan, may

56. Deutsch, *Resolution,* 399.
57. Sarewitz, "Environmental Controversies," 400.
58. See chapter 5 for a description of Roger A. Pielke's honest broker model.

lead to new ways of listening and to policies that are more resilient to multiple viewpoints.[59]

The sixth and final element in our alternative approach towards a synthesis concerning environmental stewardship is to remember that people and relationships matter. Earlier in the chapter, in our survey of work regarding conflict resolution and interpersonal reconciliation, we were reminded that the task of achieving excellent creation care is not merely an intellectual exercise but a relational one, and that as a relational endeavor, we would be well-served to work on encouraging constructive conflict rather than destructive conflict, both for reasons of conscience as well as expedience. As we saw in our previous discussion regarding accepting paradoxes, people and relationships also matter in our choice of whether our dialogues will be marked by mutual respect or vilification. We have argued for the route characterized by tolerance and respect. But, people and relationships may matter not only in how we interact with one another but also more directly in the substance of our interactions. In chapter 6, we saw how neo-Scholastic economics offers a theory that can incorporate the economic impact of valuing of things as ends. That is to say, neo-Scholastic economics may give us a means of accounting for the economic form of love and other gifts. In that chapter, we suggested that an alternative way of understanding economics such as neo-Scholastic economics offers the possibility of bringing policy analysis and ethics into dialogue with one another. If so, an alternative way forward in creating a synthesis regarding creation care that consciously accounts for people and relationships, not just analysis and argument, may result not only in more peaceable and productive dialogue but also in a richer and more complete analysis and argument.

The alternative approach to environmental issues we have described—one that considers a multiplicity of solutions, utilizes multiple understandings of environmental value, recognizes multiple forms of knowledge, avoids a zero-sum mentality, accepts paradoxes and legitimate differences, and realizes people and relationships matter—is certainly no panacea to either environmental problems or the conflicts over the best solutions to those problems. We suggest, however, that such an approach offers the promise of a more fruitful synthesis of the determinants of the criteria for obedience. To the extent our efforts at creation care are hampered by premature and artificial narrowing of policy options, unrealistic expectations of policy prescription from Scripture and science, and the dynamics of destructive conflicts, the alternative approach we have sketched—the beginnings of a

---

59. See chapter 5, footnote 154 for a partial description of Daniel Kemmis's method.

possible "third way"—may help us achieve an excellence in creation care to match our hope for faithfulness.

CONCLUSIONS

We began this chapter lamenting the complexity of synthesizing a comprehensive and just understanding of environmental stewardship. As we argued in chapter 1, obtaining such a synthesis is an underdetermined problem. In chapters 2–7, we have seen just how underdetermined the problem is: the differences between the various ways of knowing and valuing that are pertinent to environmental issues (and pertinent to different aspects of the issue), the limits to what a worldview and ethical theory can provide to help us understand an environmental problem and its proposed solutions, the complexities of adjudicating different visions of society and navigating the relational nature of conflict, and the range of possible practices of environmental stewardship. The underdetermined nature of environmental stewardship is present throughout each of the determinants of the criteria for obedience (worldviews, ethical theories, science, and society) and so the criteria themselves (importance, goals, and practice) are also underdetermined. Thus, if we were to distill this book down to a single point, we would not greatly err with the following: the nature of environmental stewardship is exceedingly complex and reductionist efforts that aim to prescribe the importance, goals, and practice of creation care based on few determinants will inevitably fall short.

This book does, however, make at least one other main point, on par with the first: obedience to the creation care command can be reasonably understood through the use of a taxonomy that addresses the impact of worldviews, ethical theories, science, and society on the criteria for obedience. This taxonomy can clarify our thinking regarding the content of creation care, motivate and encourage creative thinking with regards to creation care practices, give us categories with which we can better understand those who hold positions contrary to our own, and propose possible avenues for dialogue and areas of compromise. We hope that you experienced this as we examined the determinants of the criteria for obedience: that you discovered both new ways of understanding environmental stewardship as well as new ways of understanding your own position. Thus, we have seen that the nature of environmental stewardship, while underdetermined and complex, does not compel us to respond with pessimism. Indeed, we have argued that rather than make the conclusion of the relativist—that with the complexity of environmental stewardship, all we have are different people holding different values with no one being right—our examination of the nature of environmental stewardship instead justifies an optimism regarding the future. For with the taxonomy that we have proposed, we are able to take value differences seriously and address them explicitly. Such an engagement with the differences between our core values is the prerequisite to true dialogue: a dialogue that admits the possibility of each party being affected by the truths contained in the other's positions and a dialogue that can result in principled compromise—the product of a clear-eyed examination of where dueling principles do and do not permit the application of prudence—rather than a mere pragmatic compromise driven by the practicalities of power politics. In the end, then, the nature of environmental stewardship contains the seeds of both difficulties that can lead to poor stewardship as well as complexities that can lead to excellent stewardship. The difficulties and complexities are, in fact, one and the same. How we respond to the challenges posed by the nature of environment stewardship is ours to make.

DISCUSSION QUESTIONS

1. What would be your synthesis of the various determinants of the criteria for obedience? Does your synthesis achieve the goals for a synthesis that the author presents or other goals? Share your synthesis with someone and ask for their judgment of how successful your synthesis is.

2. What might be the critique given by someone who disagrees with your synthesis of the various determinants of the criteria for obedience and the conclusions that your synthesis provides regarding the content of creation care? What areas of dialogue might you and your critic pursue, and how would you pursue that dialogue, so that the dialogue would result in constructive conflict rather than destructive conflict?

3. Does the picture laid out in this book of the nature of creation care help clarify your understanding of what constitutes excellent creation care content or does it obscure and confuse the issue? Why or why not?

4. The complexities of environmental stewardship may be understood as making that stewardship harder to fulfill because certainty is more difficult to attain, or it may be understood as making that stewardship

less demanding because it is more accommodating. Which critique (or neither or both) would you agree with? Why?[60]

5. The author concludes on both a pessimistic and optimistic note. Do you agree or disagree? What causes for optimism and pessimism do you see with regards to practicing excellence in creation care?

---

60. I am grateful to Wesley Lindahl, Dean of and Professor of Nonprofit Management in the School of Business and Nonprofit Management at North Park University, for the genesis of this question.

Glossary

Anthropogenic: Caused, made, generated, or produced by human beings.

Anthropocentrism: Anthropocentrism believes value is determined by the needs, desires, wishes, and/or morals of human beings.

Biocentrism: The belief that value applies not just to human beings, but to (all) other forms of life; value adheres to living things because they are alive.

Buddhist worldview: The belief that follows the teachings of Buddha and sees the world and all reality as sharing the same existence and thus as being interrelated.

Categorical imperative: A duty or obligation that all people, at all times, must fulfill, in order to be moral beings. The obligation impresses itself upon us merely because of what it is; it requires no other authority to justify it.

Classical economics: Initially formulated by Adam Smith, simplified the structure of Scholastic economics by eliminating theories of final distribution and utility and casting production entirely in terms of labor.

Confucian worldview: The belief that all the world is interrelated, with human beings having the responsibility of an elder brother to the rest of the universe.

Consequentialism: The view that an action is good or bad depending on the consequences that result from the action. This is the broader category of which utilitarianism is a specific example.

Considered obedience: Obedience to commands for which the criteria for obedience are not characterized by clarity and thus require analysis of the criteria for obedience.

Cosmology: The study of the origin, development, and destiny of the universe.

Cost-benefit analysis: A method of determining whether an action is desirable based on tallying up all the (usually monetary) costs and benefits of the action.

Christian worldview: The belief that the world is created by a personal God and is best known and cared for in reference to God's view of the world.

Criteria for obedience: The importance, goals, and practices of a command we are asked to obey.

Deep ecology: A view that understands the natural world (both living and non-living) as having independent moral status and sees human beings as being able to participate in identification with the natural world.

Deontology: The view that right and wrong is determined by laws/rules/duties, and morality is judged by one's intent to fulfill those laws/rules/duties.

Dependent moral status: An entity has dependent moral status if that status is conferred on it by another entity.

Determinants of the criteria for obedience: Non-mutually exclusive influences on the criteria for obedience.

Dominionism model: A model of Christian creation care that places relatively greater emphasis on human rule over nature. In that rulership, humans work to "tend" a garden.

Enlightenment worldview: The belief that the world is fundamentally "matter in motion" and is best understood through science and reason.

Epistemic: Dealing with knowledge or knowing; dealing with epistemology.

Epistemology: The philosophy of knowledge; "how do we know what we know."

Eudaemonic: Dealing with "true" human flourishing and happiness.

Fact-value distinction: The idea that just because you can describe what something is, this does not mean you can necessarily conclude how you should treat it. Also known as the "is-ought" distinction.

Fact-value dualism model: A model of understanding science-policy interactions that understands science as limited to discovering facts about a problem that are then presented to policymakers to use (in conjunction with values) to craft policies.

First-principles: The axioms or starting points for a line of reasoning. In philosophy, usually refers to the assumptions of a logical argument. In physics, usually refers to fundamental natural laws (e.g., the conservation of energy, momentum) using which we can derive other physical equations and relationships.

Four G's: Four biblical principles of peacemaking formulated by Ken Sande.[1]

Geocentrism: The idea that the Earth is at the center of the universe.

Heliocentrism: The idea that the Sun is at the center of the Solar System.

Hermeneutics: Principles of interpretation.

Honest Broker of Policy Alternatives model: Model of science-policy interactions where scientists work to increase, rather than decrease, the number of policy options under consideration.

Human exceptionalism: The belief that human beings are special in some unique way(s).

Hypothesis-testing model: Model that understands science as consisting of repeated cycles of hypothesis generation, experimental tests, and hypothesis evaluation.

Independent moral status: An entity has independent moral status if that status is conferred without reference to another entity.

Instrumental value: You value something instrumentally when you value it so that you can obtain something else; you value it because it is useful to you.

Intrinsic value: This is sometimes used synonymously with independent moral status while other times it is used synonymously with non-instrumental value. The specific meaning is usually understood based upon the context in which the term appears.

Is-ought distinction: See "fact-value distinction."

---

1. Sande, *Peacemaker*.

Kantian deontology: The school of deontology exemplified by the work of Immanuel Kant. More precisely, Kant sought to ground a duty-focused ethic on reason alone.

Leopoldian land ethic: The ecological philosophy of Aldo Leopold which sees the land, in some ways, as being an organism.[2]

Materialism: The belief that everything is mere matter.

Monetizable: Able to be adequately converted into monetary equivalents.

Moral considerability: Possessing moral status. Entities having moral considerability can be understood as being able to make moral claims on others. Even though dependent moral status is a kind of moral considerability, discussions regarding moral considerability in environmental ethics are usually discussions about whether an entity has independent moral status.

Moral status: An entity has moral status if it can make demands on other entities to treat it a certain way.

Neoclassical economics: Modern school of economic theory that builds upon classical economics, adding a theory of marginal utility.

Neo-Scholastic economics: Modern school of economic theory that builds upon the tools and theories of modern neoclassical economics, adding a theory of final distribution.

Non-anthropocentrism: Believes value is determined by something(s) besides human beings.

Non-instrumental value: You value something non-instrumentally when you value something for what it is, for its own sake.

Ontology: The philosophy of being, that is, the study of the nature and structure of existing.

Paradigm shift: In Thomas Kuhn's model of science, a paradigm shift is when there is a change in the "framework" that scientists use to conduct "normal" science.

Policy prescriptive model: A model of science-policy connection that says the findings of science directly dictate the contents of policy (public and private).

2. Leopold, "The Land Ethic."

Popperian falsification model: Model of science that believes hypotheses cannot be proved true, only proved false, and thus that science progresses not by establishing positive truths but by eliminating untruths.

Romantic worldview: The belief that the world is best understood aesthetically and through the fine arts and immediate experience.

Scholastic economics: School of economics formulated by St. Thomas Aquinas, building off of work by Aristotle and St. Augustine. Includes a theory of final distribution, utility, production, and exchange.

Scientize: To recast discussion of a topic in terms of what science says about the topic.

Simple obedience: Obedience to commands for which the criteria for obedience are characterized by clarity.

Status conferring characteristic: A feature such that if an entity possess it, that entity is given independent moral status.

Stewardship model: A model of Christian creation care that places relatively greater emphasis on a restrained care for nature in light of its natural rhythms.

Strong anthropocentrism: Strong anthropocentrism believes that the value of nature is based only on human desire and that this desire cannot be judged as wrong as long as someone has the desire (insofar as the value of nature is concerned).

Supporting Role-Science May Not Be Neutral: Model of science-policy interaction that understands science as one form of knowing amongst many. Science thus occupies the same playing field as ethics, politics, economics, etc.

Supporting Role-Science Neutral model: Model of science-policy interaction that understands science as playing a non-prescriptive supporting role to policymaking, though retaining some "epistemically neutral" characteristics.

Taoist worldview: The belief that the world is characterized by interrelatedness and is best engaged by cooperation with natural rhythms.

Teleological: Having to do with having a goal or purpose.

Telos: A goal, end, or purpose.

Theocentrism: The belief that things have value because God confers that value to them; God is the source of value.

Tragedy of the Commons: This refers to this scenario: You have a group of people, each of whom use a shared resource. The tragedy is that if each individual behaves rationally with respect to his/her own self-interest, the shared resource will be depleted.

Trinitarian: The Christian belief that the one God exists in three Persons: Father, Son, and Holy Spirit.

Utilitarianism: The view that the right action is that which maximizes the total amount of pleasure versus pain. This is a form of consequentialism.

Virtue: A characteristic that enables something to do its work well, especially a character trait that enables a human being to live well.[3]

Virtue ethics: Sees living the good life as becoming a certain kind of person, one characterized by virtues.

Weak anthropocentrism: Weak anthropocentrism believes human valuing is the source of value of nature, but it tempers strong anthropocentrism by saying you can use cultural, religious, etc., standards to judge whether a human desire is appropriate, when valuing nature.

Worldview: What we "see" when we view the world/universe; what we think the world/universe "is." In other contexts, worldview refers to one's understanding of the ultimate nature of reality.[4]

Wu-wei: The Taoist principle of "letting be," of cooperating with nature.

---

3. Benson, *Environmental Ethics*, 68–69.
4. Sire, *The Universe Next Door*, 17.

Bibliography

Agresti, James. "Bans on Plastic Bags Harm the Environment." *The Wall Street Journal* (June 15, 2012). No pages. Accessed August 23, 2014. Online: http://online.wsj.com/news/articles/SB10001424052702303822204577468790467880088.

Ahn, Ilsup. "Immanuel Kant." Lecture given at North Park University, Chicago, IL, February 8, 2008.

Ahteensuu, Marko. "Defending the Precautionary Principle against Three Criticisms." *TRAMES* 11 (2007) 366–81.

Ambrus, Monika. "The Precautionary Principle and a Fair Allocation of the Burden of Proof in International Environmental Law." *Review of European Community & International Environmental Law* 21 (2012) 259–70.

Aristotle. *Nicomachean Ethics*. Translated by Martin Ostwald. Indianapolis, IN: Liberal Arts, 1962.

Augustine, Saint. *Confessions*. Translated by R. S. Pine-Coffin. London: Penguin, 1985.

Bailey, Ronald. "Precautionary Tale." *Reason Magazine* (April 1999). No pages. Accessed April 15, 2008. Online: http://www.reason.com/news/show/30977.html.

Barr, Stephen M. *Modern Physics and Ancient Faith*. Notre Dame, IN: University of Notre Dame Press, 2006.

———. *A Student's Guide to Natural Science*. Wilmington, DE: ISI, 2006.

Beisner, E. Calvin. *Where Garden Meets Wilderness: Evangelical Entry into the Environmental Debate*. Grand Rapids: Acton Institute for the Study of Religion and Liberty, 1997.

Benedick, Richard E. "Perspectives: Avoiding Gridlock on Climate Change." *Issues in Science and Technology* 23 (Winter 2007). No pages. Accessed August 21, 2014. Online: http://issues.org/23–2/p_benedick/.

Benson, John. *Environmental Ethics: An Introduction with Readings*. New York: Routledge, 2000.

Bergant, Dianne. "Restoration as Re-creation in Hosea 2." In *The Ecological Challenge: Ethical, Liturgical, and Spiritual Responses*, edited by Richard N. Fragomeni et al., 3–15. Collegeville, MN: Liturgical, 1994.

Berry, Wendell. "An Argument for Diversity." In *What Are People For?* 109–22. Berkeley, CA: Counterpoint, 2010.

Bialik, Carl. "How to Be Sure You've Found a Higgs Boson." *The Wall Street Journal* (July 6, 2012). No pages. Accessed June 5, 2014. Online: http://online.wsj.com/news/articles/SB10001424052702303962304577509213491189098.

Bilger, Burkhard. "Auto Correct." *The New Yorker* (November 23, 2013). No pages. Accessed January 17, 2014. Online: http://www.newyorker.com/reporting/2013/11/25/131125fa_fact_bilger.

Bontrager, Krista. "God as the Source of Knowledge." No pages. Accessed March 18, 2015. Online: http://www.reasons.org/articles/god-as-the-source-of-knowledge.

Bouma-Prediger, Steven. *For the Beauty of the Earth: A Christian Vision for Creation Care*. Grand Rapids: Baker Academic, 2001.

Briggle, Adam. "Let Politics, Not Science, Decide the Fate of Fracking." *Slate* (March 12, 2013). No pages. Accessed August 13, 2014. Online: http://www.slate.com/blogs/future_tense/2013/03/12/fracking_bans_let_politics_not_science_decide.html.

Brooks, Arthur C. "Why Free Enterprise is about Morals, Not Materialism." *FoxNews.com*, June 19, 2012. No pages. Accessed June 19, 2012. Online: http://www.foxnews.com/opinion/2012/06/19/free-enterprise-is-about-morals-not-materialism/.

Budziszewski, J. "The Illusion of Moral Neutrality." *First Things* (August 1993). No pages. Accessed May 15, 2015. Online: http://www.firstthings.com/article/1993/08/003-the-illusion-of-moral-neutrality.

Calhoun, Nora. "Learning from Bodies." *First Things* (August 2014). No pages. Accessed July 23, 2014. Online: http://www.firstthings.com/article/2014/08/learning-from-bodies.

Carter, Joe. "Should Christians Discard the Term 'Supernatural?'" *First Things, First Thoughts*, July 15, 2009. No pages. Accessed February 13, 2015. Online: http://www.firstthings.com/blogs/firstthoughts/2009/07/should-christians-discard-the-term-supernatural/.

Castel, Boris, and Sergio Sismondo. *The Art of Science*. North York, ON: Higher Education University of Toronto Press, 2008.

"'A Chicken in Every Pot' Political Ad and Rebuttal Article in *New York Times*, 10/30/1928." U.S. National Archives and Records Administration. National Archives Identifier 187095. Collection HH-HOOVH: Herbert Hoover Papers, 1913–1964. Series: Herbert Hoover Papers: Clippings File, compiled 1920–1964. October 30, 1928. Accessed February 26, 2015. Online: http://research.archives.gov/description/187095.

Clark, Greg. "What Is the Good of Human Life?: Jesus/Christian Thought." Lecture given at North Park University, Chicago, IL, February 19, 2010.

Clifton-Soderstrom, Karl. "Becoming Native: Grounding Environmental Ethics in Our Local Places, Narratives, and Communities." *The Covenant Quarterly* 67 (2009) 39–55, 57–58.

———. *The Cardinal and the Deadly: Reimagining the Seven Virtues and Seven Vices*. Eugene, OR: Cascade, 2015.

———. "Discussion." Discussion at North Park University, Chicago, IL, February 16, 2009.

———. "Environmental Ethics." Lecture given at North Park University, Chicago, IL, January 25, 2008.

———. "Response: Karl Clifton-Soderstrom." *The Covenant Quarterly* 67 (2009) 16–17, 36–37.

———. "Summary Oversimplification of Worldview Differences." April 22, 2010.

———. "Virtues and the Human Good." Lecture given at North Park University, Chicago, IL, February 13, 2009.

Cordato, Roy E. "Market-Based Environmentalism and the Free Market: They're Not the Same." In *Re-Thinking Green: Alternatives to Environmental Bureaucracy*, edited by Robert Higgs, et al., 367–82. Oakland, CA: The Independent Institute, 2005.

Cornwall Alliance. "The Cornwall Declaration on Environmental Stewardship." 2005. Accessed February 13, 2015. Online: http: //www.cornwallalliance.org/docs/the-cornwall-declaration-on-environmental-stewardship.pdf.

Cosgrove, Charles H. *Appealing to Scripture in Moral Debate: Five Hermeneutical Rules*. Grand Rapids: Eerdmans, 2002.

Crichton, Michael. "Aliens Cause Global Warming." Lecture given at the California Institute of Technology, Pasadena, CA, January 17, 2003. No pages. Accessed June 5, 2014. Online: https://web.archive.org/web/20060106040600/http://www.crichton-official.com/speeches/speeches_quote04.html.

Cronon, William. "The Trouble with Wilderness; or, Getting Back to the Wrong Nature." In *Uncommon Ground: Rethinking the Human Place in Nature*, edited by William Cronon, 69–90. New York: Norton, 1995. Accessed March 6, 2015. Online: http://www.williamcronon.net/writing/Cronon_Trouble_with_Wilderness_1995.htm.

Curry, Janel. "Christians and Climate Change: A Social Framework of Analysis." *Perspectives on Science and Christian Faith* 60 (2008) 156–64.

Cushing, James T. *Philosophical Concepts in Physics: The Historical Relation between Philosophy and Scientific Theories*. Cambridge: Cambridge University Press, 1998.

Danielson, Dennis, and Christopher M. Graney. "The Case against Copernicus." *Scientific American* 310 (January 2014) 72–77.

Deutsch, Morton. *The Resolution of Conflict: Constructive and Destructive Processes*. New Haven, CN: Yale University Press, 1973.

DeWitt, Calvin B. "Ecology and Ethics: Relation of Religious Belief to Ecological Practice in the Biblical Tradition." *Biodiversity and Conservation* 4 (1995) 838–48.

Dilling, Lisa, and Maria Carmen Lemos. "Creating Usable Science: Opportunities and Constraints for Climate Knowledge Use and Their Implications for Science Policy." *Global Environmental Change* 21 (2011) 680–89.

Dyrness, William. "Stewardship of the Earth in the Old Testament." In *Tending the Garden: Essays on the Gospel and the Earth*, edited by Wesley Granberg-Michaelson, 50–65. Grand Rapids: Eerdmans, 1987.

Eggers, William D., and John O'Leary. *If We Can Put a Man on the Moon . . . : Getting Big Things Done in Government*. Boston, MA: Harvard Business Press, 2009.

Elshtain, Jean Bethke. "My Mother, the Expert." *First Things* (October 1991). No pages. Accessed October 8, 2012. Online: http://www.firstthings.com/article/2007/11/002-my-mother-the-expert-5.

Evangelical Environmental Network (EEN). "An Evangelical Declaration on the Care of Creation." 1994. No pages. Accessed February 13, 2015. Online: http://www.creationcare.org/blank.php?id=39.

Evans, John H., and Justin Feng. "Conservative Protestantism and Skepticism of Scientists Studying Climate Change." *Climatic Change* 121 (2013) 595–608. DOI: 10.1007/s10584-013-0946-6.

Foot, Philippa, and Rick Lewis. "Interview: Philippa Foot." *Philosophy Now* (April/May 2015). No pages. Accessed May 19, 2015. Online: https://philosophynow.org/issues/41/Philippa_Foot.

Fox, Warwick. "Transpersonal Ecology and the Varieties of Identification." In *Environmental Ethics: An Introduction with Readings*, by John Benson, 253–61. New York: Routledge, 2000.

Froese, Paul. "How Your View of God Shapes Your View of the Economy." *Religion and Politics* (June 13, 2012). No pages. Accessed June 18, 2012. Online: http://religionandpolitics.org/2012/06/13/how-your-view-of-god-shapes-your-view-of-the-economy/.

Fukuyama, Francis. "The End of History?" *The National Interest* (Summer 1989) 3–18.

Gilbert, William Schwenk, and Arthur Sullivan. "The Complete Plays of Gilbert and Sullivan: The 14 Gilbert and Sullivan Plays." Last updated February 4, 2013. No pages. Accessed May 21, 2015. Online: http://www.gutenberg.org/files/808/808-h/808-h.htm.

Gilkey, Langdon. *Shantung Compound.* New York: HarperCollins, 1975.

Griffiths, David J. *Introduction to Electrodynamics.* 3rd ed. New Jersey: Prentice-Hall, 1999.

Gross, Rita M. "Towards a Buddhist Environmental Ethic." *Journal of the American Academy of Religion* 65 (1997) 333–53.

Grossman, Lisa. "String Theory Finally Does Something Useful." *Wired* (2010). No pages. Accessed June 2014. Online: http://www.wired.com/2010/09/stringy-quantum/.

Grundmann, Reiner. "Ozone and Climate: Scientific Consensus and Leadership." *Science, Technology and Human Values* 31 (2006) 73–101. DOI: 10.1177/0162243905280024.

Gustafson, James M. "The Place of Scripture in Christian Ethics: A Methodological Study." *Interpretation* 24 (October 1970) 430–55. DOI: 10.1177/002096437002400402.

Haarsma, Deborah B., and Loren D. Haarsma. *Origins: Christian Perspectives on Creation, Evolution, and Intelligent Design.* Revised. Grand Rapids: Faith Alive Christian Resources, 2011.

Hallegatte, Stéphane, et al. *Investment Decision Making Under Deep Uncertainty: Application to Climate Change.* Policy Research Working Paper, No. WPS 6193. Washington, DC: World Bank Group, September 2012. Online: http://documents.worldbank.org/curated/en/2012/09/17158712/investment-decision-making-under-deep-uncertainty-application-climate-change.

Hardin, Garrett. "The Tragedy of the Commons." In *Environmental Ethics: An Introduction With Readings*, by John Benson, 185–96. New York: Routledge, 2000.

Hardy, Thomas. *Far From the Madding Crowd.* London: Pan, 1995.

Harvey, B. "The Democratization of Science." *First Things* 101 (March 2000) 17–20. Accessed June 11, 2014. Online: http://www.firstthings.com/article/2000/03/the-democratization-of-science.

Hay, Donald A. *Economics Today: A Christian Critique.* Grand Rapids: Eerdmans, 1989.

Henderson, David R. "Rent Seeking." In *The Concise Encyclopedia of Economics,* Library of Economics and Liberty, 2008. No pages. Accessed October 10, 2014. Online: http://www.econlib.org/library/Enc/RentSeeking.html.

Higgs, Robert, and Carl P. Close. "Introduction." In *Re-Thinking Green: Alternatives to Environmental Bureaucracy,* edited by Robert Higgs et al., 1–20. Oakland, CA: The Independent Institute, 2005.

Hill, Peter J. "Market-Based Environmentalism and the Free Market—Substitutes or Complements?" In *Re-Thinking Green: Alternatives to Environmental Bureaucracy,* edited by Robert Higgs, et al., 383–92. Oakland, CA: The Independent Institute, 2005.

Howarth, Jane. "'Neither Use Nor Ornament: A Consumers' Guide to Care.'" In *Environmental Ethics: An Introduction With Readings,* by John Benson, 161–70. New York: Routledge, 2000.

Hutchinson, Ian H. "Warfare and Wedlock: Redeeming the Faith-Science Relationship." *Perspectives on Science and Christian Faith* 59 (2007) 91–101.

Intergovernmental Panel on Climate Change (IPCC). "Working Groups / Task Force." No pages. Accessed June 14, 2014. Online: http://www.ipcc.ch/working_groups/working_groups.shtml.

Janis, Irving L. *Groupthink.* 2nd ed. Boston: Wadsworth, 1982.

Jasanoff, Sheila. *The Fifth Branch: Science Advisers as Policymakers.* Cambridge: Harvard University Press, 1990.

John, Stephen. "In Defence of Bad Science and Irrational Policies: An Alternative Account of the Precautionary Principle." *Ethical Theory Moral Practice* 13 (2010) 3–18. DOI: 10.1007/s10677-009-9169-3.

John Paul II. Encyclical Letter. *Centesimus Annus.* May 1, 1991. Online: http://www.vatican.va/holy_father/john_paul_ii/encyclicals/documents/hf_jp-ii_enc_01051991_centesimus-annus_en.html.

Johnson, R. Boaz. "A Biblical Theology of the Environment in the Creation Narrative." *The Covenant Quarterly* 67 (2009) 3–16.

———. "Crisis in World Religions and the Environment." Lecture given at North Park University, Chicago, IL, January 22, 2007.

Kemmis, Daniel. "Science's Role in Natural Resource Decisions." *Issues in Science and Technology* 18 (Summer 2002). No pages. Accessed August 12, 2014. Online: http://issues.org/18-4/p_kemmis/.

Kim, Daniel. "Explaining Early Christian Charity: A Psychosocial Theories Approach." *Interdisciplinary Journal of Research on Religion* 6 (2010) Article 8, 1–21. Online: http://www.religjournal.com/articles/article_view.php?id=47.

Kinsley, David. *Ecology and Religion: Ecological Spirituality in Cross-Cultural Perspective.* Englewood Cliffs, NJ: Prentice Hall, 1995.

Klein, Joe. "Management 101: What the Democrats Need to Learn." *Time Magazine* (May 6, 2010). No pages. Accessed April 4, 2013. Online: http://www.time.com/time/magazine/article/0,9171,1987607,00.html.

Koeller, David. "Newton, Matter and Motion." Lecture given at North Park University, Chicago, IL, February 5, 2007.

Kraynak, Robert P. "Justice without Foundations." *The New Atlantis* (Summer 2011) 103–20.

Kuhn, Thomas S. *The Structure of Scientific Revolutions.* 2nd ed. Chicago: University of Chicago Press, 1970.

Leopold, Aldo. "The Land Ethic." In *Environmental Ethics: An Anthology,* edited by Andrew Light et al., 38–46. Malden, MA: Blackwell, 2003.

Leshner, Alan I. "Science and Public Engagement." *The Chronicle of Higher Education* 53 (October 13, 2006) B20.

Lewis, C. S. "Is Theology Poetry?" In *The Weight of Glory and Other Addresses,* revised and expanded ed., edited by Walter Hooper, 74–92. New York: Collier, 1980.

———. "Meditation in a Toolshed." In *God in the Dock: Essays on Theology and Ethics,* edited by Walter Hooper, 212–15. Grand Rapids: Eerdmans, 1979.

———. *Mere Christianity.* New York: Collier, 1960.

———. *The Pilgrim's Regress.* Grand Rapids: Eerdmans, 1992.

———. *The Screwtape Letters.* Rev. ed. New York: Collier, 1982.

———. "The Weight of Glory." In *The Weight of Glory and Other Addresses,* revised and expanded ed., edited by Walter Hooper, 3–19. New York: Collier, 1980.

Lin, Johnny. "Little Things." *UCLA Graduate Science Journal* 1 (2000) 31–34. Accessed July 14, 2014. Online: http://www.johnny-lin.com/papers/gsj_stoch_idx.html.

Lin, Johnny Wei-Bing. "The Role of Science in Defining the Content of Creation Care." *The Covenant Quarterly* 67 (2009) 20–34, 37–38.

Lindzen, Richard S. "The Climate Science Isn't Settled." *The Wall Street Journal* (November 30, 2009). No pages. Accessed February 21, 2015. Online: http://www.wsj.com/articles/SB10001424052748703939404574567423917025400.

Lipsky, Seth. "The Real Case for Defunding NPR." *The Wall Street Journal* (October 23, 2010). No pages. Accessed February 27, 2015. Online: http://www.wsj.com/articles/SB10001424052702303738504575568222953428174.

Logan, T. J. "Johann Georg Hamann, Radical Enlightener." *First Things, On the Square,* March 15, 2013. No pages. Accessed March 15, 2013. Online: http://www.firstthings.com/onthesquare/2013/03/johann-georg-hamann-radical-enlightener.

Lomborg, Bjørn. *The Skeptical Environmentalist: Measuring the Real State of the World.* Cambridge: Cambridge University Press, 2001.

Marx, Karl. "Marx to Ferdinand Lassalle in Berlin." Letters: Marx-Engels Correspondence 1861. January 16, 1861. No pages. Accessed May 28, 2013. Online: http://www.marxists.org/archive/marx/works/1861/letters/61_01_16.htm.

Marxsen, Craig S. "Prophecy de Novo: The Nearly Self-Fulfilling Doomsday Forecast." In *Re-Thinking Green: Alternatives to Environmental Bureaucracy,* edited by Robert Higgs et al., 23–42. Oakland, CA: The Independent Institute, 2005.

McGrath, Alister. *The Reenchantment of Nature: The Denial of Religion and the Ecological Crisis.* New York: Doubleday, 2002.

McKim, Robert H. *Experiences in Visual Thinking.* 2nd ed. Boston: PWS Engineering, 1980.

McNie, Elizabeth C. "Reconciling the Supply of Scientific Information with User Demands: An Analysis of the Problem and Review of the Literature." *Environmental Science and Policy* 10 (2007) 17–38. DOI: 10.1016/j.envsci.2006.10.004.

Merry, Robert W. "The Fallacy of Human Freedom." *The National Interest* (July–August 2013). No pages. Accessed June 26, 2013. Online: http://www.nationalinterest.org/bookreview/the-fallacy-human-freedom-8652.

Mills, Thomas J., and Roger N. Clark. "Roles of Research Scientists in Natural Resource Decision-Making." *Forest Ecology and Management* 153 (2001) 189–98.

Morrison, Margaret. "Models, Measurement and Computer Simulation: The Changing Face of Experimentation." *Philosophical Studies* 143 (2009) 33–57. DOI: 10.1007/s11098-008-9317-y.

Muller, John D. *Redeeming Economics: Rediscovering the Missing Element.* Wilmington, DE: ISI, 2010.

Naess, Arne. "The Deep Ecological Movement: Some Philosophical Aspects." In *Environmental Ethics: An Anthology,* edited by Andrew Light, et al., 262–74. Malden, MA: Blackwell, 2003.

————. "Identification, Oneness, Wholeness and Self-Realization." In *Environmental Ethics: An Introduction with Readings*, by John Benson, 243–51. New York: Routledge, 2000.

Nash, James A. "In Flagrant Dissent: An Environmentalist's Contentions." In *Environmental Ethics and Christian Humanism*, 105–24. Nashville, TN: Abingdon, 1996.

————. "Seeking Moral Norms in Nature: Natural Law and Ecological Responsibility." In *Christianity and Ecology: Seeking the Well-Being of Earth and Humans*, edited by Dieter T. Hessel et al., 227–50. Cambridge: Harvard University Center for the Study of World Religions Publications and Harvard University Press, 2000.

National Research Council (NRC). *Using Science as Evidence in Public Policy*, edited by Kenneth Prewitt et al. Washington, DC: The National Academies Press, 2012.

National Science Board (NSB). *Science and Engineering Indicators 2008*. Volume 1, NSB 08-01. Arlington, VA: National Science Foundation, 2008.

Neidhardt, W. Jim. "Personal Knowledge: An Epistemology of Discovery." *Journal of the American Scientific Affiliation* 29 (September 1977) 118–23. No pages online. Accessed February 21, 2015. Online: http://www.asa3.org/ASA/PSCF/1977/JASA9-77Neidhardt.html.

Nelson, Robert H. "Does 'Existence Value' Exist?" In *Re-Thinking Green: Alternatives to Environmental Bureaucracy*, edited by Robert Higgs, et al., 395–416. Oakland, CA: The Independent Institute, 2005.

————. *The New Holy Wars: Economic Religion Versus Environmental Religion*. University Park, PA: The Pennsylvania State University Press, 2010.

Noah, Timothy. "The Glory of the Commons." *The Washington Monthly* (July/August 2013). No pages. Accessed July 13, 2013. Online: http://www.washingtonmonthly.com/magazine/july_august_2013/on_political_books/the_glory_of_the_commons045642.php?page=all.

Norton, Bryan G. "'The Cultural Approach to Conservation Biology." In *Environmental Ethics: An Introduction With Readings*, by John Benson, 144–51. New York: Routledge, 2000.

————. "Environmental Ethics and Weak Anthropocentrism." In *Environmental Ethics: An Anthology*, edited by Andrew Light et al., 163–74. Malden, MA: Blackwell, 2003.

Oakes, Edward T. "On Some Epistemic Pathologies, or Why the Human Mind is a Terrarium for So Many Lies." *First Things, On the Square*, April 6, 2009. No pages. Accessed April 6, 2009. Online: http://www.firstthings.com/onthesquare/?p=1354.

O'Brien, Matthew B., and Robert C. Koons. "Who's Afraid of Metaphysics?" *Public Discourse* (June 10, 2011). No pages. Accessed August 25, 2014. Online: http://www.thepublicdiscourse.com/2011/06/3356/.

Oreskes, Naomi. "Science and Public Policy: What's Proof Got to Do With It?" *Environmental Science & Policy* 7 (2004) 369–83.

Pascal, Blaise. *Pensées*. Rev. ed. Translated by A. J. Krailsheimer. London: Penguin, 1995.

Pearce, David. "A Reply to Some Criticisms." In *Environmental Ethics: An Introduction with Readings*, by John Benson, 181–83. New York: Routledge, 2000.

Pearce, David, et al. "Economic Valuation of Environmental Goods." In *Environmental Ethics: An Introduction with Readings*, by John Benson, 171–80. New York: Routledge, 2000.

Pielke, Roger A., Jr. *The Honest Broker: Making Sense of Science in Policy and Politics.* New York: Cambridge University Press, 2007.

Pielke, Roger A., Jr., and Michele M. Betsill. "Policy for Science for Policy: A Commentary on Lambright on Ozone Depletion and Acid Rain." *Research Policy* 26 (1997) 157–68.

Quigley, Thomas M., et al., tech. eds. *Integrated Scientific Assessment for Ecosystem Management in the Interior Columbia Basin and Portions of the Klamath and Great Basins.* Gen. Tech. Rep. PNW-GTR-382. Portland, OR: U.S. Department of Agriculture, Forest Service, Pacific Northwest Research Station, 1996.

Rasmussen, Larry L. "Creation, Church, and Christian Responsibility." In *Tending the Garden: Essays on the Gospel and the Earth,* edited by Wesley Granberg-Michaelson, 114–31. Grand Rapids: Eerdmans, 1987.

Rees, Matthew C. "*The Structure of Scientific Revolutions* at Fifty." *The New Atlantis* 37 (Fall 2012) 71–86. Online: http://www.thenewatlantis.com/docLib/20121116_TNA37Rees.pdf.

Rodin, R. Scott. *Stewards in the Kingdom: A Theology of Life in All Its Fullness.* Downers Grove, IL: IVP, 2000.

Royal, Robert. "Expiating Our Eco-Sins?" *First Things: Web Exclusives,* September 20, 2007. No pages. Accessed May 21, 2015. Online: http://www.firstthings.com/web-exclusives/2007/09/expiating-our-eco-sins.

The Royal Society. *Knowledge, Networks and Nations: Global Scientific Collaboration in the 21st Century.* RS Policy Document 03/11. London: The Royal Society, 2011.

Ruddiman, William F. "The Early Anthropogenic Hypothesis: Challenges and Responses." *Reviews of Geophysics* 45 (2007) RG4001. DOI: 10.1029/2006RG000207.

Sagoff, Mark. "Genetic Engineering and the Concept of the Natural," *Philosophy and Public Policy Quarterly* 21 (Spring/Summer 2001) 2–10.

———. "Locke Was Right: Nature Has Little Economic Value." *Philosophy and Public Policy Quarterly* 25 (Summer 2005) 2–11.

Sande, Ken. *The Peacemaker: A Biblical Guide to Resolving Personal Conflict.* 3rd ed. Grand Rapids: Baker, 2004.

Sandler, Ronald L. *Character and Environment: A Virtue-Oriented Approach to Environmental Ethics.* New York: Columbia University Press, 2007.

Sarewitz, Daniel. "How Science Makes Environmental Controversies Worse." *Environmental Science & Policy* 7 (2004) 385–403.

Schienke, Erich W., et al. "Intrinsic Ethics Regarding Integrated Assessment Models for Climate Management." *Science and Engineering Ethics* 17 (2011) 503–23. DOI: 10.1007/s11948-010-9209-3.

Simmons, Randy T. "The Endangered Species Act: Who's Saving What?" In *Re-Thinking Green: Alternatives to Environmental Bureaucracy,* edited by Robert Higgs et al., 109–27. Oakland, CA: The Independent Institute, 2005.

———. "Fixing the Endangered Species Act." In *Re-Thinking Green: Alternatives to Environmental Bureaucracy,* edited by Robert Higgs et al., 129–55. Oakland, CA: The Independent Institute, 2005.

Sire, James W. *The Universe Next Door: A Basic Worldview Catalog.* 4th ed. Downers Grove, IL: IVP, 2004.

Snell, R. J. "Utilitarianism." Lecture given at North Park University, Chicago, IL, February 15, 2008.

Snowden, David J., and Mary E. Boone. "A Leader's Framework for Decision Making." *Harvard Business Review* 85.11 (2007) 68–76.

Snyder, Samuel. "Chinese Traditions and Ecology: Survey Article." *Worldviews* 10 (2006) 100–134.

Solomon, S., et al. "Technical Summary." In *Climate Change 2007: The Physical Science Basis. Contribution of Working Group I to the Fourth Assessment Report of the Intergovernmental Panel on Climate Change,* edited by S. Solomon, et al., 19–92. Cambridge: Cambridge University Press, 2007. Accessed June 12, 2014. Online: http://www.ipcc.ch/pdf/assessment-report/ar4/wg1/ar4-wg1-ts.pdf.

Stackhouse, Max L. "Introduction." In *Environmental Ethics and Christian Humanism,* 11–16. Nashville, TN: Abingdon, 1996.

Storck, Thomas. "Capitalism, Distributism and the Hierarchy of Human Goods." *Anamnesis Journal* (December 2011). No pages. Accessed February 26, 2015. Online: http://anamnesisjournal.com/2011/12/thomas-storck-2/.

———. "The Superficiality of 'Left' and 'Right.'" *The Distributist Review* (October 19, 2010). No pages. Accessed May 25, 2013. Online: http://distributistreview.com/mag/2010/10/the-superficiality-of-left-right/.

Stroup, Richard L. "Free Riders and Collective Action Revisited." In *Re-Thinking Green: Alternatives to Environmental Bureaucracy,* edited by Robert Higgs et al., 209–25. Oakland, CA: The Independent Institute, 2005.

Swearer, Donald K. "Principles and Poetry, Places and Stories: The Resources of Buddhist Ecology." *Daedalus* 130 (Fall 2001) 225–41.

Taylor, Charles. "What Is Human Agency?" In *Human Agency and Language: Philosophical Papers I,* 15–44. Cambridge: Cambridge University Press, 1985.

Taylor, Daniel. *The Myth of Certainty: The Reflective Christian and the Risk of Commitment.* Waco, TX: Word, 1986.

Taylor, Paul W. "Respect for Nature." In *Environmental Ethics: An Introduction with Readings,* by John Benson, 215–22. New York: Routledge, 2000.

Teresa of Avila, Saint. *The Life of Teresa of Jesus: The Autobiography of St. Teresa of Avila.* Translated by E. Allison Peers. Garden City, NY: Image, 1960.

Tocqueville, Alexis de. *Democracy in America.* Translated by Arthur Goldhammer. New York: The Library of America, 2004.

Traina, Cristina L. H. "Response to James A. Nash." In *Christianity and Ecology: Seeking the Well-Being of Earth and Humans,* edited by Dieter T. Hessel et al., 251–60. Cambridge: Harvard University Center for the Study of World Religions Publications and Harvard University Press, 2000.

Tuana, Nancy. "Leading with Ethics, Aiming for Policy: New Opportunities for Philosophy of Science." *Synthese* 177 (2010) 471–92. DOI: 10.1007/s11229-010-9793-4.

Tucker, Robert C. "Introduction." In *The Marx-Engels Reader,* 2nd ed., edited by Robert C. Tucker, xix–xxxviii. New York: Norton, 1978.

Uebel, Thomas. "Vienna Circle." *The Stanford Encyclopedia of Philosophy* (Spring 2014 Edition), edited by Edward N. Zalta. No pages. Accessed July 17, 2014. Online: http://plato.stanford.edu/archives/spr2014/entries/vienna-circle/.

United States Conference of Catholic Bishops (USCCB). *Forming Consciences for Faithful Citizenship.* Publication No. 7-026. Washington, DC: USCCB, 2007.

U.S. Census Bureau, *Statistical Abstract of the United States: 2012.* 131st ed. Washington, DC: U.S. Census Bureau, 2011. Accessed February 27, 2015. Online: http://www.census.gov/compendia/statab/.

U.S. Department of Agriculture (USDA) Forest Service, Pacific Northwest Research Station (PNW), "ICBEMP." No pages. Accessed August 7, 2014. Online: http://www.icbemp.gov/.

Van Dyke, Fred, et al. *Redeeming Creation: The Biblical Basis for Environmental Stewardship.* Downers Grove, IL: IVP, 1996.

Warners, David, et al. "Reconciliation Ecology: A New Paradigm for Advancing Creation Care." *Perspectives on Science and Christian Faith* 66 (December 2014) 221–35.

"Westminster Shorter Catechism (1674)." No pages. Accessed March 18, 2015. Online: http://www.ccel.org/creeds/westminster-shorter-cat.html.

Wildman, Wesley J., and Charles Demm. "Bibliography in Ecological Ethics and Eco-Theology." No pages. Accessed March 18, 2015. Online: http://people.bu.edu/wwildman/WeirdWildWeb/proj_bibs_ecoethics_00.htm.

Wise, Steven M. "Animal Rights." *Encyclopædia Britannica Online.* Last updated June 12, 2014. Accessed May 21, 2015. Online: http://www.britannica.com/EBchecked/topic/25760/animal-rights.

Wolt, Peter. "Is String Theory Even Wrong?" *American Scientist* 90 (2002) 110. DOI: 10.1511/2002.2.110.

Wolterstorff, Nicholas, "Teaching for Shalom: On the Goal of Christian Collegiate Education." In *Educating for Shalom: Essays on Christian Higher Education,* edited by Clarence W. Joldersma, et al., 10–26. Grand Rapids: Eerdmans, 2004.

Young, Richard A. *Healing the Earth: A Theocentric Perspective on Environmental Problems and Their Solutions.* Nashville, TN: Broadman and Holman, 1994.

Index

Acoustic Thermometry of Ocean Climate (ATOC), 133–34, 157
Acts
  4:12, xii
  10:15, 58
adaptation, 133, 226
American Scientific Affiliation, xv
anomalies. *See* science: paradigms.
anthropocentrism. *See* ethical theories: anthropocentrism.
Aristarchus of Samos, 117
Aristotle, 94, 111, 115n19, 126n51, 189, 216
Augustine, Saint, 122n38, 191–92n37, 199, 216
authority, 15, 125. *See also* science: reason.

Barber, Edward B., 207n63
Barr, Stephen M., 119n33
Beisner, E. Calvin, 52n18, 54n29, 54n31, 55n32, 56, 73n68
beloved country, 69–70, 128
Benedick, Richard E., 230n8
Benson, John, xiv, 87
Bergant, Dianne, 59n42
Berry, Wendell, 69–70, 128–29
biocentrism. *See* ethical theories: biocentrism.
Bouma-Prediger, Steven, xiv, 51n16, 53, 88, 95, 106
Brand, Raymond, 66
Briggle, Adam, 147n117, 157n150
Buddhism. *See* worldviews: Buddhism.

Budziszewski, J., 274

Calhoun, Nora, 30–31n22
capitalism. *See* politics and economics.
Castel, Boris, 107n5, 109, 110, 121, 125, 127n58
categorical imperatives. *See* ethical theories: categorical imperatives. *See also* command.
Catholicism
  human beings, view of, 192, 213–14
  social teaching, 213–15, 254
  solidarity, 213–14
  state, view of, 192
  subsidiarity, 213–14
  tradition, 193
chlorofluorocarbons (CFCs), 75, 145, 161, 172, 230n8
Christian worldview, xiii, 23, 26, 32, 36, 40, 41–42, 138–40, 141, 170, 282. *See also* Catholicism.
  agrarian metaphors, 38, 39, 68–69
  biblical hermeneutics, 57–60, 74n72
  conflict between different models, 54–57
  contingency, 55, 63
  dominionism model, 52–57, 282
  fallenness of creation, 23, 50, 64, 65–66, 70–71, 74, 139
  goals criterion and, 64–71
  humility. *See* humility.
  human vocation relative to nature, 51–52

Christian worldview *(continued)*
  importance criterion and, 63–64
  interconnectedness, 53, 54
  interpreting biblical commands,
    57–64, 74, 187–88
  ontology of nature, 62–63, 69,
    70–71, 284
  ownership of nature, 54–55
  peace. *See* Christian worldview:
    shalom.
  personal Word, 57–60, 61–62
  practice criterion and, 71–75
  range of goals. *See* range of goals or
    practice.
  relationship with God, 60–62, 63,
    64–65n48, 66, 67–68
  role of nature for humanity, 51
  shalom, 67–68, 263
  source of value of nature, 54, 72–73
  stewardship model, 52–57, 285
  theocentrism. *See* theocentrism.
  view of how reality is known, 50–51
  view of reality, 49–50, 62–63, 69, 72
  worship of God, 66–67, 69, 138
  written Word, 57–60
Clark, Roger N., 152
Clifton-Soderstrom, Karl, 78, 81
climate, 70
  change of, 4, 17–18n22, 97, 136,
    172, 179–80, 248
  model of, 114, 139n91
  ozone depletion, stratospheric, 145,
    161, 172, 230n8
  responses to change, 225–26,
    228–29, 234, 235, 251n8, 260–61
  science, 116n22, 132–34, 151n127
Close, Carl P., 181
coercion. *See* government: coercion.
Colossians
  1:17, 38
command, 42, 187. *See also* ethical
    theories: categorical imperatives.
  clarity, 4–5, 9, 18
  direct, 36–37
  God. *See* God: command.
  indirect, 36–37

interpreting biblical commands. *See*
    Christian worldview: interpret-
    ing biblical commands.
  relative importance, 7, 64, 187
  sufficient conditions for obedience,
    4–6
  trajectory for history and, 64–65
conflict. *See* dialogue. *See also* policy:
    conflict. *See also* politics and
    economics: conflict.
consensus, 116–17, 134
consumption, 40–41, 87, 253, 270–71
Copernicus, Nicolaus, 117, 119n33,
    122
The Cornwall Declaration on Envi-
    ronmental Stewardship, 5–6, 52
Cosgrove, Charles H., 60n44
creation, xiii, 49–51
creation care, ix, xiii
creativity, 53–54
Crichton, Michael, 116–17
criteria for obedience, 7–13, 282
  considered, 9, 13, 15, 281
  importance, 7, 32–35, 63–64,
    98–99, 166–67, 198–99, 210–11
  goals, 7, 8, 35–41, 64–71, 99,
    167–69, 199–200, 210–11
  practice. *See* practice.
  simple, 9, 285
Cronon, William, 68–69
Cushing, James T., 131n69

Deep Ecology. *See* ethical theories:
    Deep Ecology.
democracy. *See* politics and econom-
    ics: democracy.
deontology. *See* ethical theories:
    deontology.
Descartes, René, 110
determinants, 10–13, 282
  worldview. *See* worldviews.
  ethical theories. *See* ethical
    theories.
  science. *See* science.
  society. *See* society.
  sources of knowledge, 12–13
Deuteronomy
  5:32–33, 191

22:6–7, 37, 59, 71
Deutsch, Morton, 256–61
DeWitt, Calvin B., 66
dialogue, 15–16, 174–75, 213,
    219–20, 236–37, 256–65, 275,
    277–78. *See also* predispositions:
    dialogue.
  characteristics of the parties, 259
  constructive and destructive con-
    flict, 256–57, 276
  estimation of success, 259
  forgiveness, 262–64
  gently restore, 262
  get the log out of your own eye,
    261–62
  glorify God, 261
  go and be reconciled, 262–64
  nature of the conflict, 257–59
  negotiation, 263–64
  prior relationship, 257
  process, 257
  reconciliation, 262–64
  third parties, 259–60
dichlorodiphenyltrichloroethane
    (DDT), 134–35n82
Dilling, Lisa, 151n127
discussion questions, 18, 44–45, 75,
    102, 175–76, 220–21, 238–39,
    278–79
disposable society, 168–69
Dyrness, William, 67–68
economics. *See* politics and
    economics.
ecosystem
  dynamics, model of, 106
  services, 199
ecosystemic compatibility, 89n22, 249
efficiency. *See* government: efficiency.
Eggers, William D., 208n73
Einsteinian mechanics, 16, 116,
    119–20, 126n51
Elshtain, Jean Bethke, 128
Endangered Species Act, 208–9
Enlightenment. *See* worldviews: En-
    lightenment. *See also* science.
Environmental Protection Agency
    (EPA), 150n123, 154–55n142,
    164–65

epistemology, 282. *See also* science.
  context dependence, 126
  falsification. *See* science:
    falsification.
  figuring something out, 107, 197
  general ways of knowing, 107
  humility. *See* science: humility.
  knowledge by authority, 107, 113
  lived experience, 128–29
  local knowledge, 128–29,
    158–59n154
  non-scientific, 10, 107, 127–29,
    130, 140, 197
  prescriptive knowledge, 15
  reason, 109–13, 124–26
  relativism. *See* relativism.
  revealed knowledge, 107
  sources of knowledge, 12–13
  ways of knowing, 10, 50–51, 61,
    140, 158–59n154, 183, 197
ethics. *See* ethical theories.
ethical theories, 11–12, 78–80
  anthropocentrism, 31, 86, 87, 230,
    245, 281, 284, 285, 286
  biocentrism, 33, 81n3, 86, 87, 88,
    100, 281
  categorical imperatives, 61–62, 92,
    198, 199, 212, 219–20, 281. *See
    also* predispositions: categorical
    imperatives, appeal to.
  consequentialism, 90–92, 167, 230,
    281. *See also* ethical theories:
    utilitarianism.
  cost-benefit analysis, 90–92, 167,
    201, 214, 236, 282
  Deep Ecology, 40, 86–87, 282
  deontology, 92–94, 198, 230, 251,
    282
  dependency chain, 85
  directly determined by worldviews,
    28–32
  ecocentrism, 31, 79, 248, 249, 270
  economics, and, 218
  human exceptionalism, 88, 283
  instrumental, 31, 51, 59n42, 72, 79,
    85–86, 88, 100, 199, 200, 283

ethical theories *(continued)*
  intrinsic value, 12, 83, 87, 219, 229,
    283
  is-ought dichotomy. *See* is-ought
    dichotomy.
  land ethic, 88, 229, 284
  moral considerability, 33, 284
  moral demands, 34, 42–43, 284
  moral status, dependent, 84–85,
    282
  moral status, independent, 31,
    83–84, 219, 245, 283
  moral value, 80–81, 100, 148
  moral voice, 96–97, 98
  natural law, 89–90n22, 192, 213,
    268–69
  non-instrumental, 72, 79, 85–86,
    88, 91n25, 97, 100, 142, 198–99,
    200, 219, 284
  non-moral value, 81–82
  predispositions. *See* predisposi-
    tions: ethical theories
  rights, 34, 73n68, 81n3, 83–84,
    92–94, 101, 147n117, 183,
    185–88, 191, 196, 203, 204–5,
    213–14n83, 261, 268–69
  rights conferring characteristic, 93
  sources of value, 85–88
  spectrum, 87–88
  status conferring characteristic, 84,
    86, 285
  utilitarianism, 90–92, 198, 214–15,
    219–20, 254, 286. *See also* ethical
    theories: consequentialism. *See
    also* ethical theories: cost-benefit
    analysis. *See also* politics and
    economics: utility. *See also* pre-
    dispositions: utilitarian.
  value of nature, 80–88
  value preferences, 34
  valuer, 85
  values. *See* values.
  vices, 94–95
  virtue ethics, 94–97, 215, 286
  virtues, 69, 94–95, 286
  weighing values, 89–98, 188, 198,
    217–19, 251n8
evaluations

strong, 7–8
weak, 7–8
excess of objectivity. *See* science:
  excess of objectivity.

fact-value distinction. *See* is-ought
  dichotomy.
falsification. *See* science: falsification.
falsification, Popperian. *See* science:
  falsification.
flu, 225
food, 51, 73–74, 97–98, 134–35n82,
  251n8
Food and Drug Administration
  (FDA), 152–54, 154–55n142,
  164–65, 231n12
forgiveness. *See* dialogue.
Fox, Warwick, 31
Froese, Paul, 187, 187–88n24
Fukuyama, Francis, 193–94, 195

Galatians
  6:1, 262
game theory, 204, 205
Genesis
  1, 74
  1:26, 53
  9:3, 51
genetically modified organisms
  (GMOs), 164, 250n7
geocentrism, 116, 283
geoengineering, 226n3
Gilbert, William Schwenk, 180
global warming, 132n72, 136, 172,
  179–80, 225–26, 228–29, 234,
  235, 251n8, 260–61. *See also*
  climate.
goals. *See* criteria for obedience: goals.
God, 138, 191–92, 273
  attributes, 49–51, 63, 111
  Authoritative, 187–88
  command, 64, 71, 191, 251
  communication from, 57–58, 71
Gödel, Kurt, 111
Gödel's Theorem, 111–12, 111n13
government. *See also* politics.
  bureaucracy, 182, 207–9
  centralization, 208–9

coercion, 82n4, 181, 205–6, 211–12
efficiency, 182, 186, 208, 210–11.
    See also politics and economics:
    efficiency.
incentives, 205, 209
information flows, 208
mechanisms, legal, 204–5
public goods, 182, 204
public provision, 204, 207–9
registration, 204–5
regulation, 184, 200–201, 204–5
rent-seeking, 182
unintended consequences to, 209
Gross, Rita, 40–41
groupthink, 97
Gustafson, James M., 59

Hallegatte, Stéphane, 233–34
Hardin, Garrett, 82, 181, 205–6n61
Hardy, Thomas, 273
Hay, Donald A., 59n42, 187
Hebrews
    1:3a, 50
heliocentrism, 116–18, 119n33, 122,
    283
Higgs, Robert, 181
Hill, Peter J., 204–5
Howarth, Jane, 91n26
human exceptionalism, 54
humility, 71–72, 126–27, 129, 236–37,
    264. *See also* science: humility.
husbandry, 69–70
Hutchinson, Ian, 128, 130–31

incremental solutions. *See* practice:
    incremental solutions.
instrumental. *See* ethical theories:
    instrumental.
insurance. *See* uncertainty: insurance.
intangibles, 206
Intergovernmental Panel on Climate
    Change (IPCC), 132–33, 179–80,
    260
Interior Columbia Basin Ecosystem
    Management Project (ICBEMP),
    151–52, 171. *See also* policy: sup-
    porting role (science is neutral)
    model.

intrinsic value. *See* ethical theories:
    intrinsic value.
is-ought dichotomy, 29–30, 30–31n22,
    36, 37n34, 65n49, 99–100,
    144–45, 247–48, 270, 283

Jasanoff, Sheila, 143–44n100,
    145n107, 146, 149n122, 150–51,
    152–54, 154–55n142, 158, 163,
    164–65
Jesus, 51, 138, 261, 273
John Paul II, 68n60, 213n81,
    213–14n83
John, Stephen, 232
Johnson, R. Boaz, 64–65n48
justice, 5, 7, 40n37, 168, 183, 184,
    185–86, 196, 199, 210–11.

Kekulé, 110
Kemmis, Daniel, 158, 158–59n154,
    275
Kim, Daniel, 271
Kinsley, David, 29n19
knowing. *See* epistemology.
knowledge. *See* epistemology.
Kuhn, Thomas, 118, 119, 121–22,
    126n51, 200. *See also* science:
    paradigms.

language, impact of, 38n36
Lemos, Maria Carmen, 151n127
Leshner, Alan, 148, 155
Lewis, C. S., xiii, 31n22, 35n27, 58,
    61n45, 125n49, 127
liability, 205
Lindzen, Richard S., 132n72
lived experience. *See* epistemology:
    lived experience.
local knowledge. *See* epistemology:
    local knowledge.
Lomborg, Bjørn, 106
love, 7, 9, 10, 12–13, 51, 59, 61, 63,
    68–70, 128–29, 199, 217–18,
    264–65. *See also* beloved country.

Mahan, David, 66
Markandya, Anil, 207n63

markets. *See* politics and economics: markets.

Matthew
 5:21–22, 241
 5:23–24, 241
 7:3–5, 262
 23:23, 7
 22:37–38, 7
 22:40, 7

Merry, Robert W., 180
Mills, Thomas J., 152
mitigation, 226, 235
Montreal Protocol, 145, 230n8
moral considerability. *See* ethical theories: moral considerability.
moral demands. *See* ethical theories: moral demands. *See also* ethical theories: value preferences.
moral status. *See* ethical theories: moral status, dependent. *See also* ethical theories: moral status, independent.
Morrison, Margaret, 114n18
motor vehicle accident deaths, 227–28
Muller, John D., 91n25, 183n13, 199, 215, 217–18

Naess, Arne, 87
Nash, James A., 81, 89n22, 249
nature
 as a created entity, 49–50
 as a resource, 51, 54
 as a witness to God, 51
natural, 21, 49
natural law. *See* ethical theories: natural law.
Nehemiah
 9:5b–6, 67
Neidhardt, W. Jim, 122n38, 124n44
Nelson, Robert H., 55–54n33, 186, 201
Newtonian mechanics, 16, 115, 116, 119–20, 126n51, 270
no regrets responses. *See* uncertainty: no regrets responses.
Noah, Timothy, 205–6n61
non-instrumental. *See* ethical theories: non-instrumental.

nuisance, 205

Oakes, Edward T., 110n10
obedience, 15. *See also* criteria for obedience.
objective-passion, 265
Office of Technology Assessment, 161
offset, electronic circuit, 246–47
O'Leary, John, 208n73
On the Care of Creation: An Evangelical Declaration on the Care of Creation, 5–6, 52
ontology. *See* worldviews. *See also* Christian worldviews: ontology of nature.
Oreskes, Naomi, 106, 133–34, 134–35n82, 232
ownership. *See* politics and economics.

paradigm shifts. *See* science: paradigms.
paradigms. *See* science: paradigms.
parallax, 117n26, 118
parameterizations, 114, 139n91
Pascal, Blaise, 17, 191–92n37
Pearce, David, 207n63
Philippians
 2:3–4, 264
philosophy, 126, 130
Pielke, Jr., Roger A., 4, 142, 143n98, 146, 147n118, 160–62, 165–66, 275
place, 69–70
policy. *See also* criteria for obedience: practice.
 adaptive, 172
 boundary institutions, 149n122, 154–55n142
 choosing between science-policy models, 163–66, 170–71
 collaboration, 158, 158–59n154, 275–76
 conflict, 147, 150, 157–58, 164, 172, 230n8
 epistemology of science and science and, 170

fact-value dualism model, 147–51, 283

gridlock. *See* policy: conflict.

Honest Broker of Policy Alternatives, 160–63, 275, 283

hybrid science-policy models, 164

incremental solutions. *See* practice: incremental solutions.

information policymakers need from science, 146n113, 151n127

iron triangle of shared interests, 146–47

limits of scientific model to prescribe, 145–46, 164–65, 168, 170

no-regrets strategies, 172

policy prescriptive model, 143–47, 212, 284

power, 173

science and, 141–66

scientific advisory boards, 150, 152–54, 158

scientization. *See* scientization.

spectrum of science-policy models, 173–74

stability, 154, 165, 171–73, 213, 238. *See also* policy: conflict.

stealth issue advocates, 162

supporting role (science may not be neutral) model, 156–60, 285

supporting role (science is neutral) model, 151–56, 285

worldviews and science and, 169–70

politics and economics. *See also* government. *See also* Catholicism.

aristocracy, 189–90

capitalism, 73n68, 181, 184, 187–88n24, 197

Classical economics, 216–17, 281

command fulfilling, 187, 191–92

communism. *See* politics and economics: Marxism.

community well-being, 186

comparing philosophy and policy studies, 183–84, 210–12

conflict, 194

conservatism, 187, 192, 197–98, 200–201, 229–30

contingent valuation, 207

cooperative solutions, 203–4

cost-benefit analysis. *See* ethical theories: cost-benefit analysis.

costing environmental goods, 206–7

culture, 186

democracy, 165–66, 186, 254

distributism, 190–91, 215

efficiency and pragmatism-based justifications, 188–89, 190–91, 201

equilibrium, 216

ethics and economics, 218–19

eudaemonic and teleological/purpose-based justifications, 189–95

existence value, 207

fairness, 185. *See also* justice. *See also* politics and economics: justice.

final distribution, 198–99, 215–17

free-rider problem, 203, 204, 209

freedom, 185

gifts, 217

growth, 199, 201, 228–29

happiness, 189–91

hierarchy of purposes, 190–91

history, trajectory of, 187–88, 193–95

human nature, 192–93

interpreting policy studies, 210–11

irreducible indeterminacy, 212–13

justice. *See* justice.

labor theory of value, 216–17

liberalism, 192

liberty, 185

Lockean philosophy, 192–93

marginal utility, 217

markets, 183, 186, 188, 197, 200, 201, 204, 205, 207

Marxism, 192–93

neoclassical economics, 217, 284

neo-Scholastic economics, 198–99, 215–20, 276, 284

option value, 207

ownership, 190, 203, 204–5

paradigm, as a, 196–97, 200, 211

politics and economics *(continued)*
  philosophy mode, 183, 184–201
  policy studies mode, 183, 202–12
  production, 216–17
  public goods, 182, 202–6
  religion, economics as, 186, 188,
    201
  rights and duty-based justifications,
    185–88
  scarcity, 218
  Scholastic economics, 216, 285
  scientization. *See* scientization.
  shared goods. *See* politics and eco-
    nomics: public goods.
  socialism, 183, 184, 187, 200
  taxes, 205
  use value, 207
  utility, 200, 216–18, 219
  values, affected by, 196–97
Polyani, Michael, 122n38
Popper, Karl, 116
positivism, logical, 130, 167
practice, 7, 8, 41–43, 71–74, 99–100,
    169–74, 200–201, 210–11. *See
    also* policy. *See also* uncertainty.
  do nothing different, 225
  eliminate *A*, 225
  eliminate the connection, 225
  evaluating responses, 226
  importance of values to, 227–30
  incremental solutions, 229–30,
    230n8, 232–33, 275
  isolate the harmful effects, 225
  range of responses, 225–27, 238
  uncertainty. *See* uncertainty.
pragmatism. *See* synthesis: prag-
    matism. *See also* politics and
    economics: efficiency and
    pragmatism-based justifications.
praxis, 10, 34–35, 43, 100, 196
precautionary principle. *See* uncer-
    tainty: precautionary principle.
predispositions, 243, 246–55
  assumptions, unexamined, 252
  biological, 249–50
  categorical imperatives, appeal to,
    251
  consequentialist, 251–52

dialogue, 252–53
ethical theories, 250–52
importance of, 255
is-ought dichotomy, 247–48. *See
  also* is-ought dichotomy.
nature, static, 248–49
processing, 252–54
romantic, implicit, 248
sin model, 250–51, 266
sum-of-the-parts, 253–54
utilitarian, 251–52
wilderness, positive pristine. *See*
  wilderness.
worldviews, 247–50
productivity, 54
progress, 180, 195, 201n54
property. *See* politics and economics.
Proverbs
  31:10, xv
prudence, 95, 212, 213–14, 268–69
Psalms
  19:1–4a, 139
puzzle-solving. *See* science: paradigms

range of goals or practice, 71–73
Rasmussen, Larry L., 53n27
reason. *See* science: reason. *See also*
  epistemology: reason. *See also*
  synthesis: reason.
reconciliation. *See* dialogue.
Rees, Matthew C., 122–23
registration. *See* government:
  registration.
regulation. *See* government:
  regulation.
relativism, 126n51, 267
risk, 230n9. *See also* uncertainty.
  assessment, 150
  management, 150
  value judgment, as a, 150
Romans
  5:8, 273
  8:21, 50
Royal, Robert, 251n8
Ruddiman, William, 248

Sande, Ken, 261–65

Sarewitz, Daniel, 134n80, 134–35n82, 135, 136, 137, 145, 155, 230n8, 231n11, 250
scarcity. *See* politics and economics: scarcity.
science, 12, 128, 188–89n26. *See also* worldviews: Enlightenment.
 bias, avoiding, 109, 126
 clarity, 130
 consensus. *See* consensus.
 creativity in, 109–11
 demarcation, 125–26n50, 131n68, 138
 ethics, 123n43
 excess of objectivity, 136, 147
 experiments, 114–15
 falsification, 115, 116–18, 285
 human endeavor, 127n58
 humility, 122–23, 126–28, 157, 160, 165. *See also* science: privilege, epistemic.
 hypothesis generating, 116n22
 hypothesis-testing model, 108, 113–15, 129, 138, 140, 144, 283
 incompleteness, 141–42, 148, 197
 judgment in, 109–11, 128–29
 kinds, multiple, 129–37
 logic, 109–13, 124–25, 128–29, 140
 mathematical-logical model, 130
 meaning and, 138–40, 166–67
 measurements, 118
 models, computer, 114
 monolithic, 129–37
 neutrality, 126, 151, 155, 160–61, 162–63
 non-comprehensive model, 130–31
 normal, 119, 123n43
 objectivity, 123–24, 130, 149
 paradigms, 118–22, 126n51, 138, 183, 200, 211, 284
 policy and. *See* policy: science and.
 pre-science, 116n22
 privilege, epistemic, 114n18, 125–26, 156, 159, 164, 165, 170, 247–48. *See also* science: humility.
 public support, 143
 puzzle-solving. *See* science: paradigms.
 qualitative, 122
 quantitative, 122
 reason, 109–13, 125n49, 126, 128–29, 140
 relativism. *See* relativism.
 reproducibility, 117, 130
 revolution, 119n33, 200
 Scientific Method, 108
 scientization. *See* scientization.
 social constructionism, 120–23, 125–26, 130
 spectrum of kinds, 129–37
 testability, 115–16
 tests, appropriate, 113–15
 truth, 120, 125, 126n51, 135, 139–40
 uncertainty, 118, 125, 134, 158–59n154
 what can it say about nature, 137–40, 167–69
science-policy. *See* policy. *See also* science.
scientization, 135, 137, 149, 155, 156, 212, 264, 285
sentience, 84, 93
Sheldon, Joseph, 66
shopping bags, 168–69
simplicity, 168, 270–71
sin model. *See* predispositions: sin model
Sismondo, Sergio, 107n5, 109, 110, 121, 125, 127n58
socialism. *See* politics and economics.
society, 12. *See also* politics and economics.
solidarity. *See* Catholicism: solidarity.
Stackhouse, Max L., 180
status conferring characteristic. *See* ethical theories: status conferring characteristic.
stewardship, Christian, 51–52. *See also* Christian worldview: stewardship model.
Storck, Thomas, 190–91, 192–93
string theory, 115, 116n22, 139n90

subsidiarity. *See* Catholicism: subsidiarity.
sulfites, 152–54
Sullivan, Arthur, 180
summum bonum, 189, 191, 194
superstring theory. *See* string theory.
synthesis, 14–16, 240–79
 contradictions, 245
 goals and principles, 243–46
 consistency, logical, 243–44
 failure, 244–45
 guardrails, 245
 holism, 244
 human, being, 244
 knowing, 244, 269
 living, human, 272–73
 paradox, 245, 271–74
 parenting, 273–74
 pragmatism, 272
 predispositions. *See* predispositions.
 reason, 244
 relationships, 276
 science with worldview, 137–40
 social framework of analysis, 17–18n22
 solutions, multiplicity of, 266
 sum of its parts, more than, 246
 value, multiplicity of understandings, 267–69
 ways forward, 265–77
 weighting, proper, 244
 zero-sum mentality, avoiding, 269–70

Taylor, Charles, 7–8, 91n26
Taylor, Paul W., 33
telos, 31, 33, 95, 96, 120, 189, 194n48, 198, 286
teleology, 81, 285
Teresa of Avila, Saint, 191–92n37
theocentrism, 55, 71–72, 85–86, 248–49, 286
2 Timothy
 3:16, 58n37
Tocqueville, Alexis de, 181, 188–89n26, 189–90
tolerance, 267, 273–75

Tragedy of the Commons, 82, 82n4, 181, 196, 203–4, 205–6n61, 229, 286
Traina, Cristina L. H., 89–90n22, 268–69, 272
transcendental qualities, 168, 214. *See also* ethical theories: virtues. *See also* worldviews: Romantic.
Tuana, Nancy, 123n43, 157n150
Tucker, Robert C., 193

uncertainty, 230–37. *See also* risk.
 buyer beware strategy, 235n26
 decision-making horizons, 233–34
 empirical, 230–31
 experimentation, 236
 incremental solutions. *See* practice: incremental solutions.
 insurance, 234–35
 no regrets responses, 234
 optimal analysis, 236
 precautionary principle, 231–32
 psychological, 230–31
 robustness analysis, 236
 safety margins, 233
 values and, 235–36
underdeterminedness, 16–17, 197, 277. *See also* politics and economics: irreducible indeterminancy.

value preferences. *See* ethical theories: value preferences. *See also* ethical theories: moral demands.
values, 34, 137n89, 148, 154, 157, 188, 196, 198, 207, 217–18, 227, 238, 267–69. *See also* ethical theories: weighing values.
Van Dyke, Fred, 66
virtues. *See* ethical theories: virtues

wilderness, 34, 42, 68–69, 80, 96, 167, 207, 229, 230, 248.
Wolt, Peter, 115
Wolterstorff, Nicholas, 67n57
worldviews, 11, 21, 98–99, 286
 action prescribing component, 42
 basic questions addressed by, 21–22

Buddhism, 23–24, 32, 40–41, 106, 141, 170, 281

Christianity. *See* Christian worldview.

Confucian, 24, 26, 28, 281

differences between, 26

directly determining ethics and, 28–32

Enlightenment, 25, 27, 30–31, 106, 125n49, 127n56, 130n65, 141, 167, 170, 248, 282. *See also* science.

foundational context, as, 32

goals criterion and, 35–41

history and trajectory and the goals criterion, 37–38, 64–65

holism, 23–26

importance criterion and, 32–35

intuitive consistency and the goals criterion, 38–40

is-ought dichotomy. *See* is-ought dichotomy.

lens, as a, 32

limits to what they provide, 26–32, 35–36

material, 23n5, 25, 31, 34, 43

moral considerability and, 33

naturalism and the naturalistic assumption, 31

non-material, 23n5

non-religious, 26

practice criterion and, 41–43

predispositions. *See* predispositions: worldviews.

prescribing actions and, 26–28, 55–57

range of, 22–26

reductionism, 27–28, 43, 131n69

religious, 26

Romantic, 25, 42, 170, 229, 230, 248, 285

similarities between, 26

substrate for reflection and action, as, 32, 40–41

Taoist, 24–25, 27, 285

what they provide, 32, 36–41

wu-wei, 25, 286

worship of God. *See* Christian worldview: worship of God.

Young, Richard A., 51n13